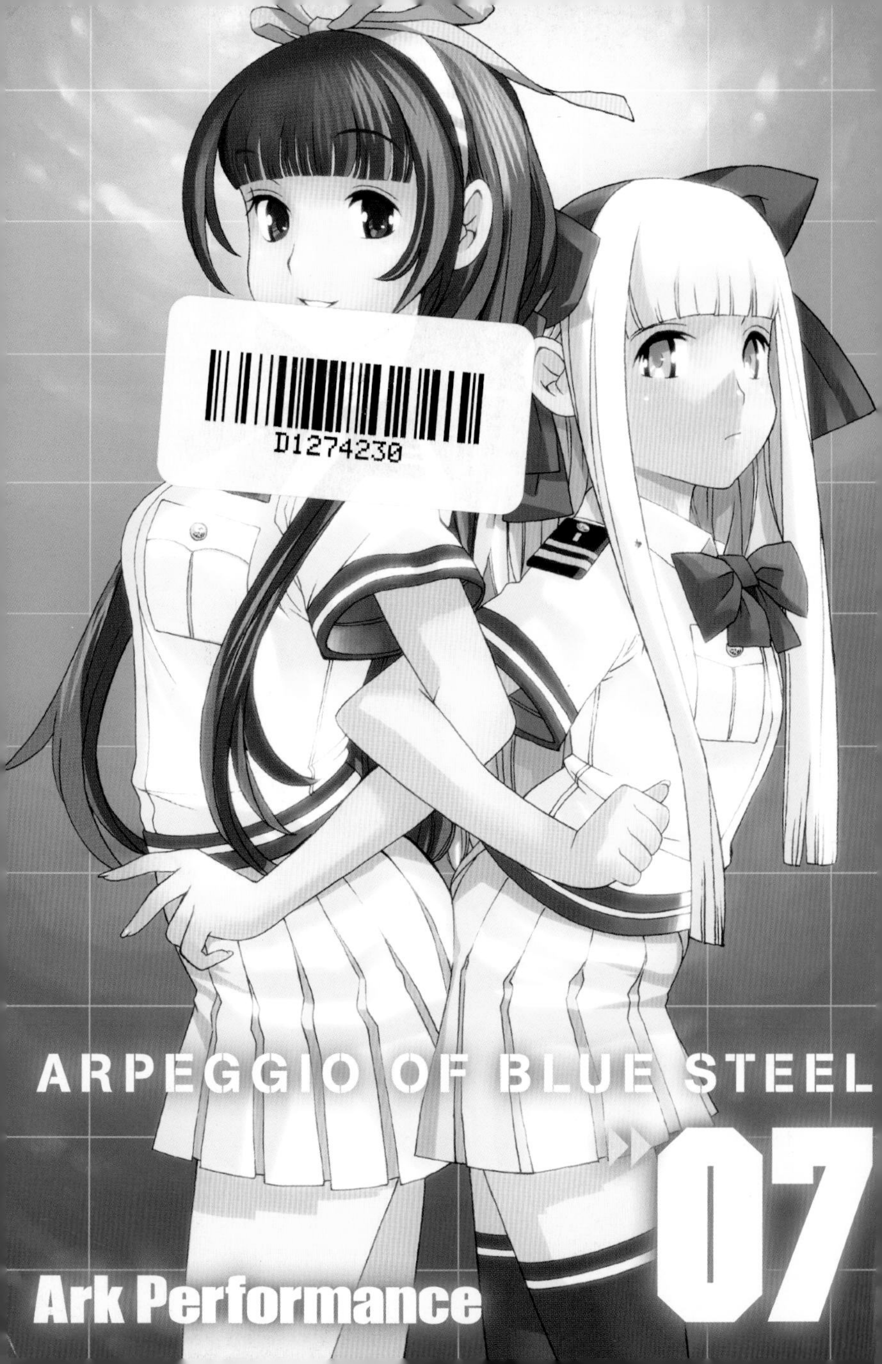
ARPEGGIO OF BLUE STEEL
07
Ark Performance

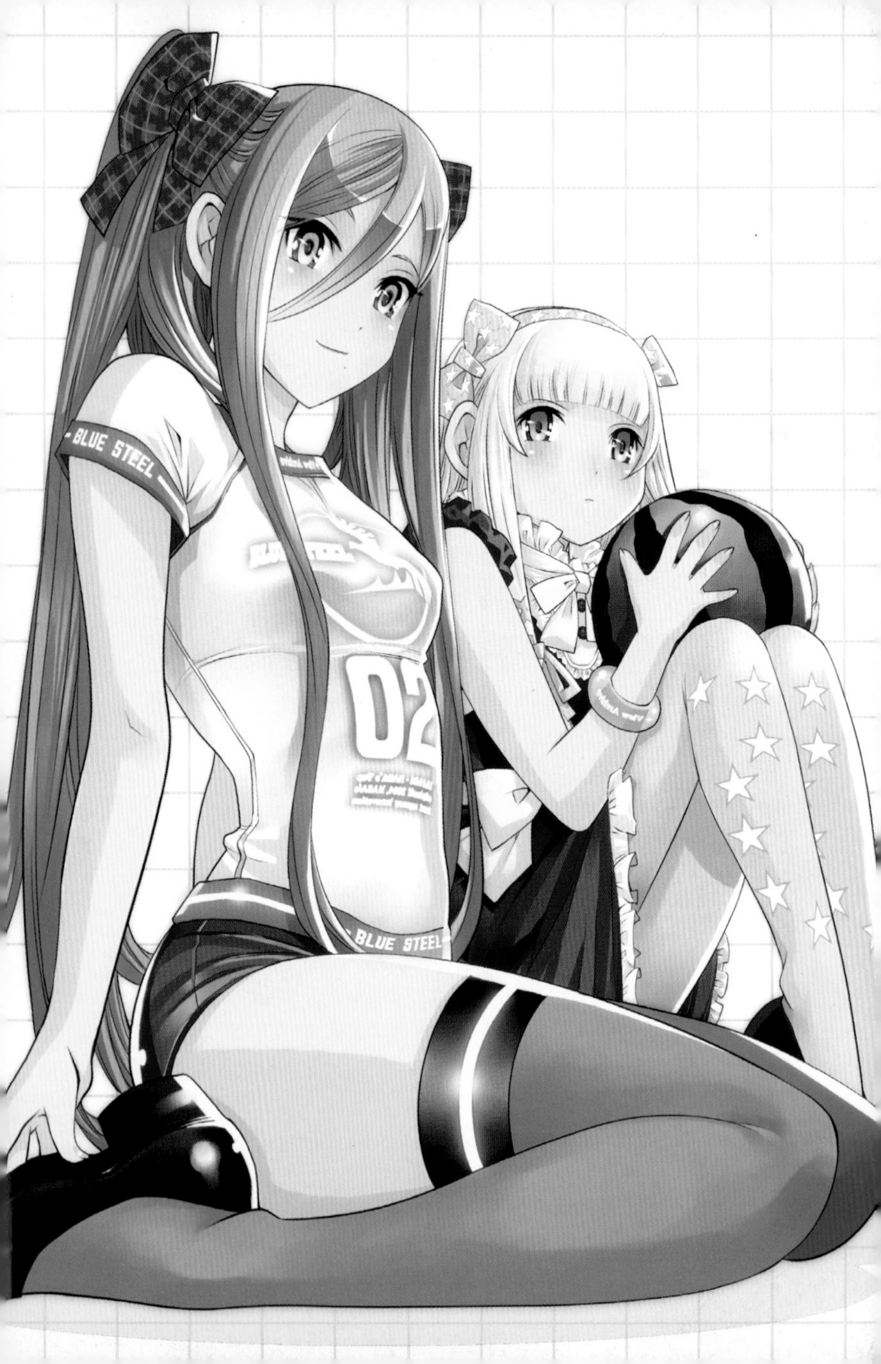
BLUE STEEL
02
BLUE STEEL

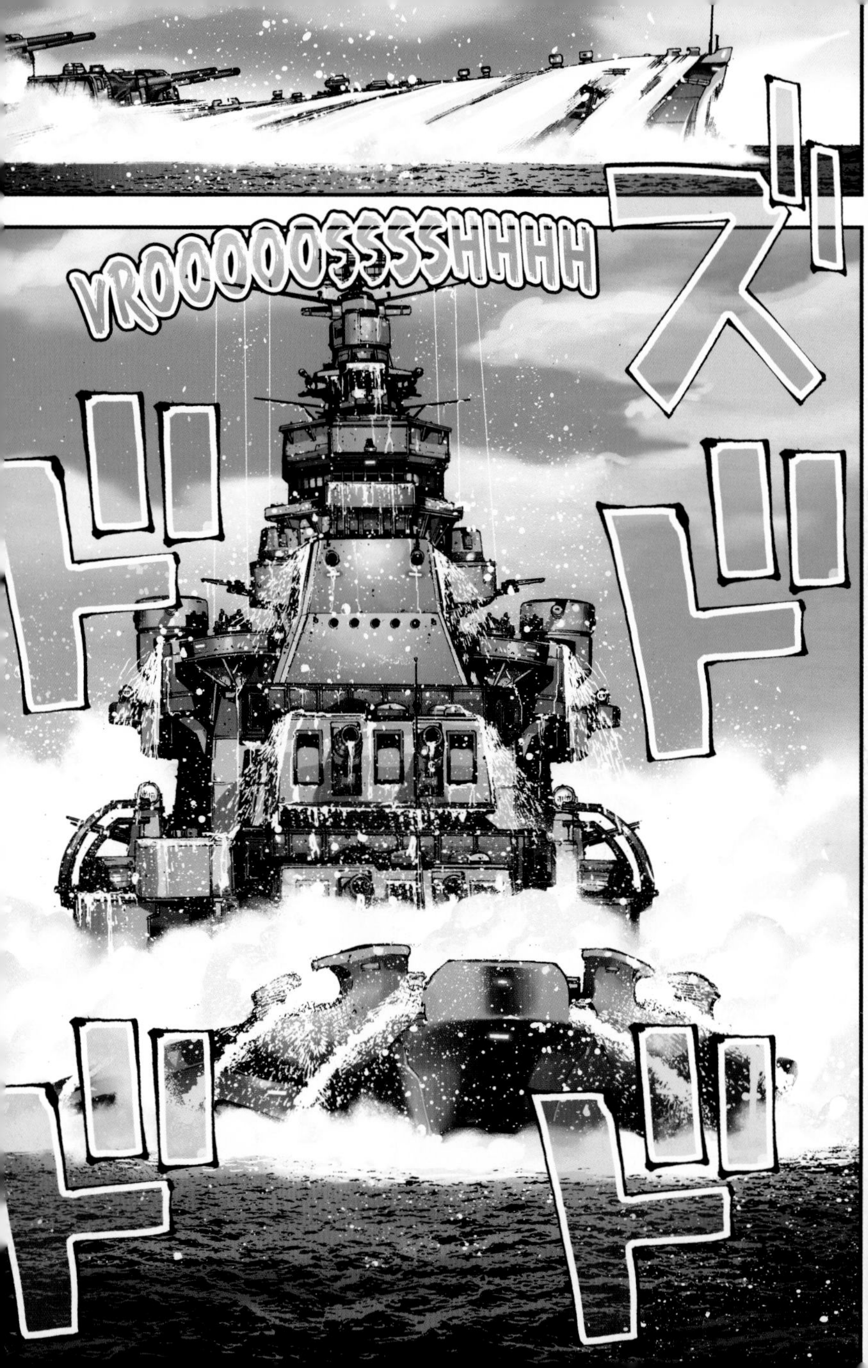
ズ
VROOOOOSSSSHHHH
ドド
ドド
ドド

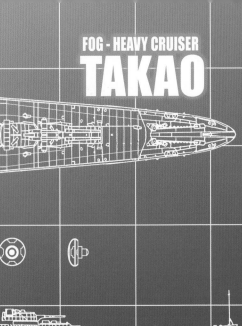

FOG - HEAVY CRUISER

TAKAO

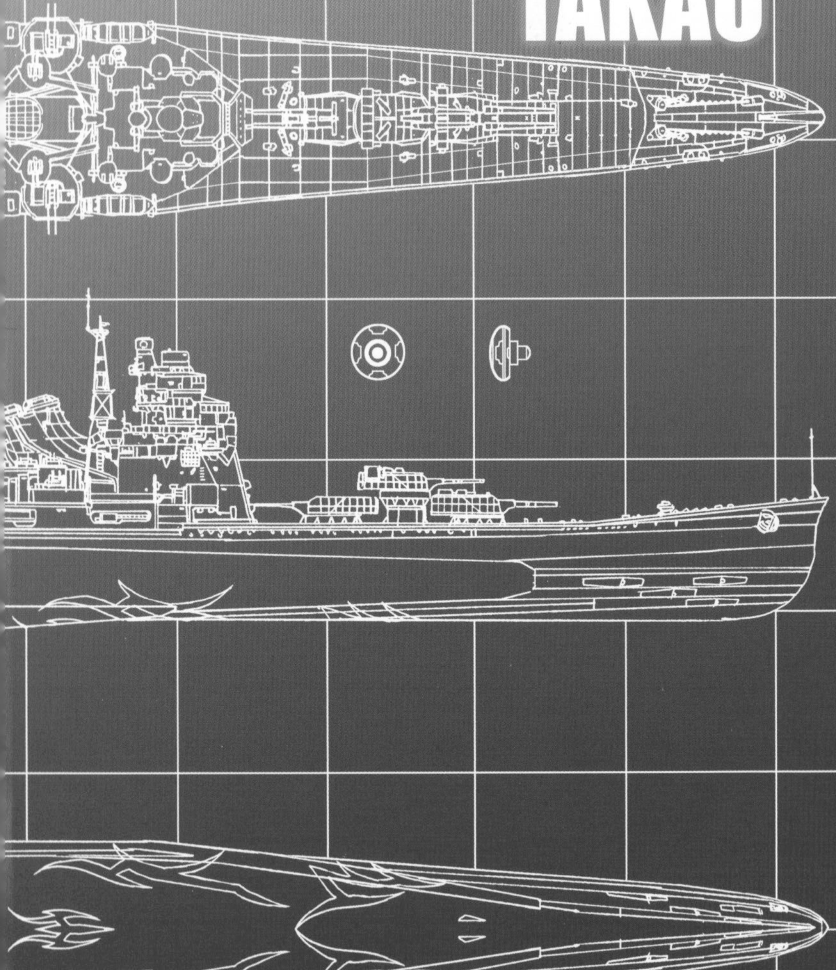

Depth:037

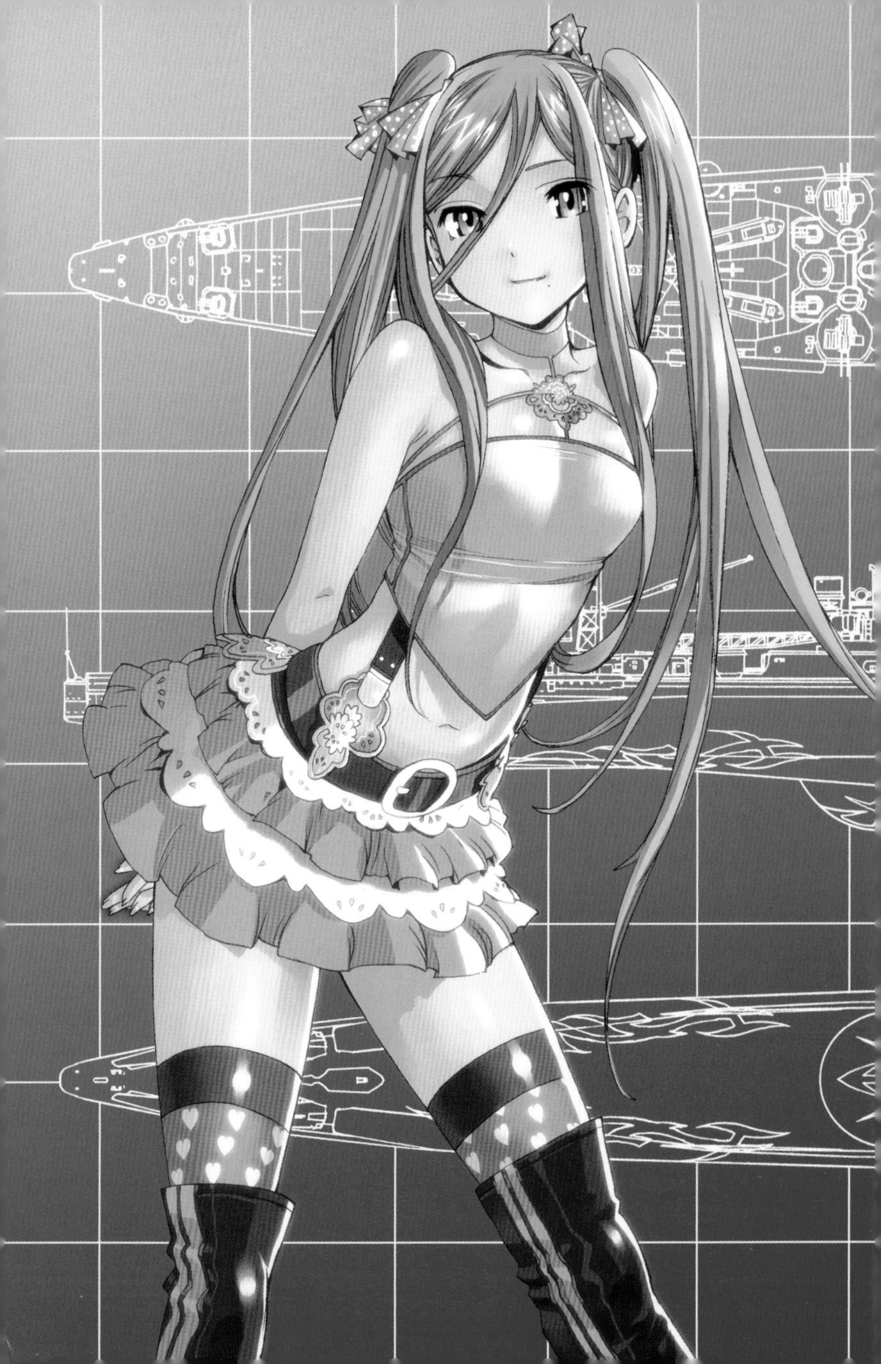

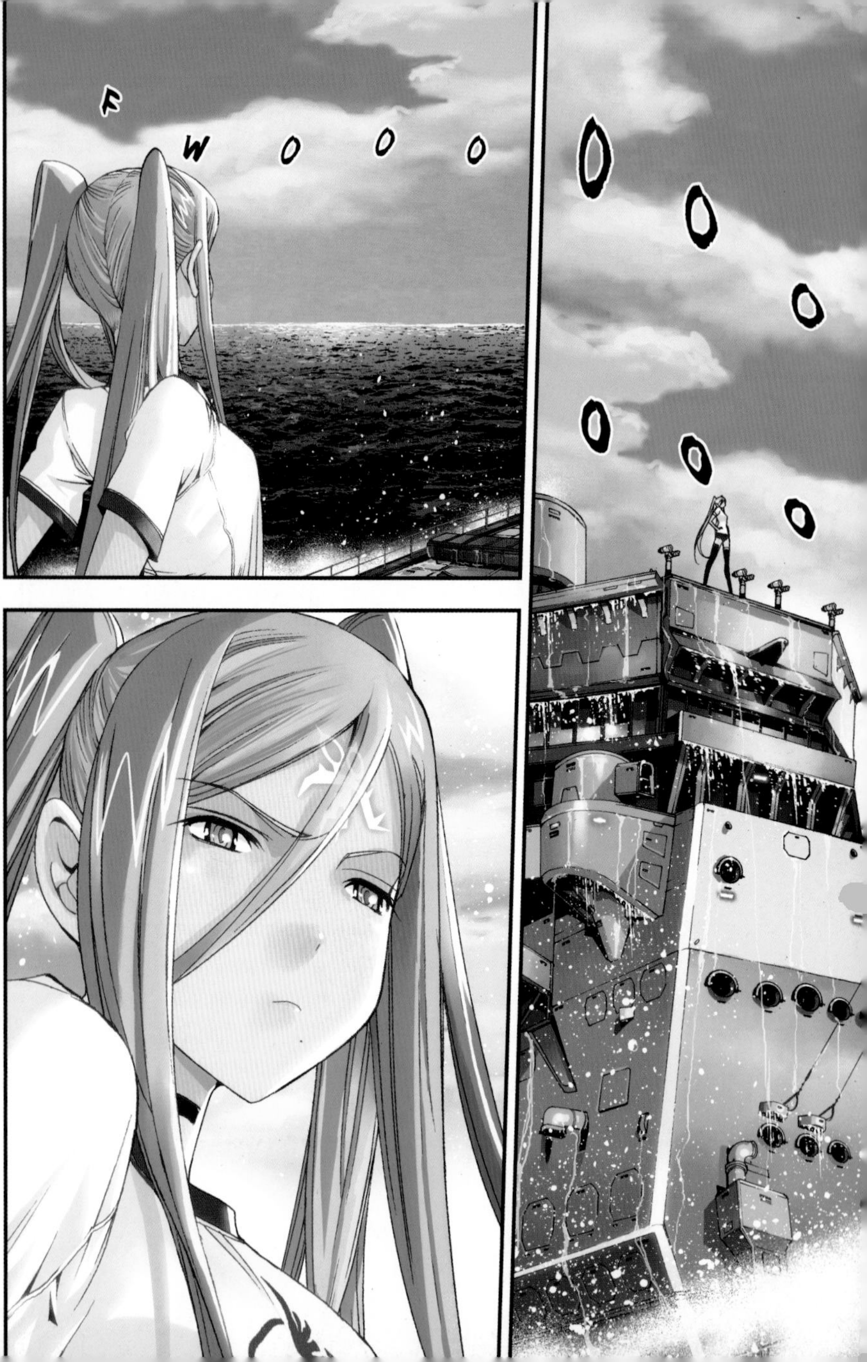
FWOOOOOOOOO

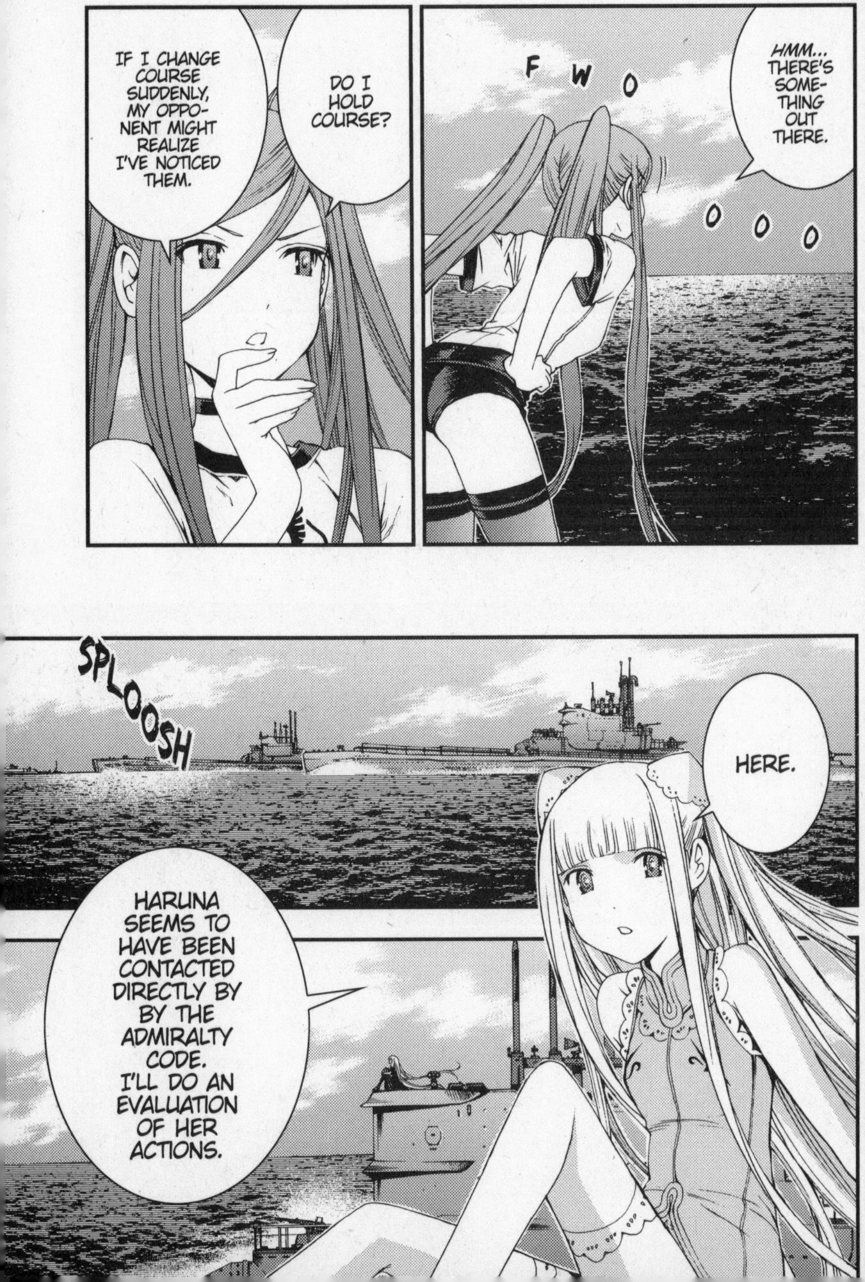
HMM... THERE'S SOME-THING OUT THERE.
FWOOOOO
DO I HOLD COURSE?
IF I CHANGE COURSE SUDDENLY, MY OPPO-NENT MIGHT REALIZE I'VE NOTICED THEM.
SPLOOSH
HERE.
HARUNA SEEMS TO HAVE BEEN CONTACTED DIRECTLY BY BY THE ADMIRALTY CODE. I'LL DO AN EVALUATION OF HER ACTIONS.

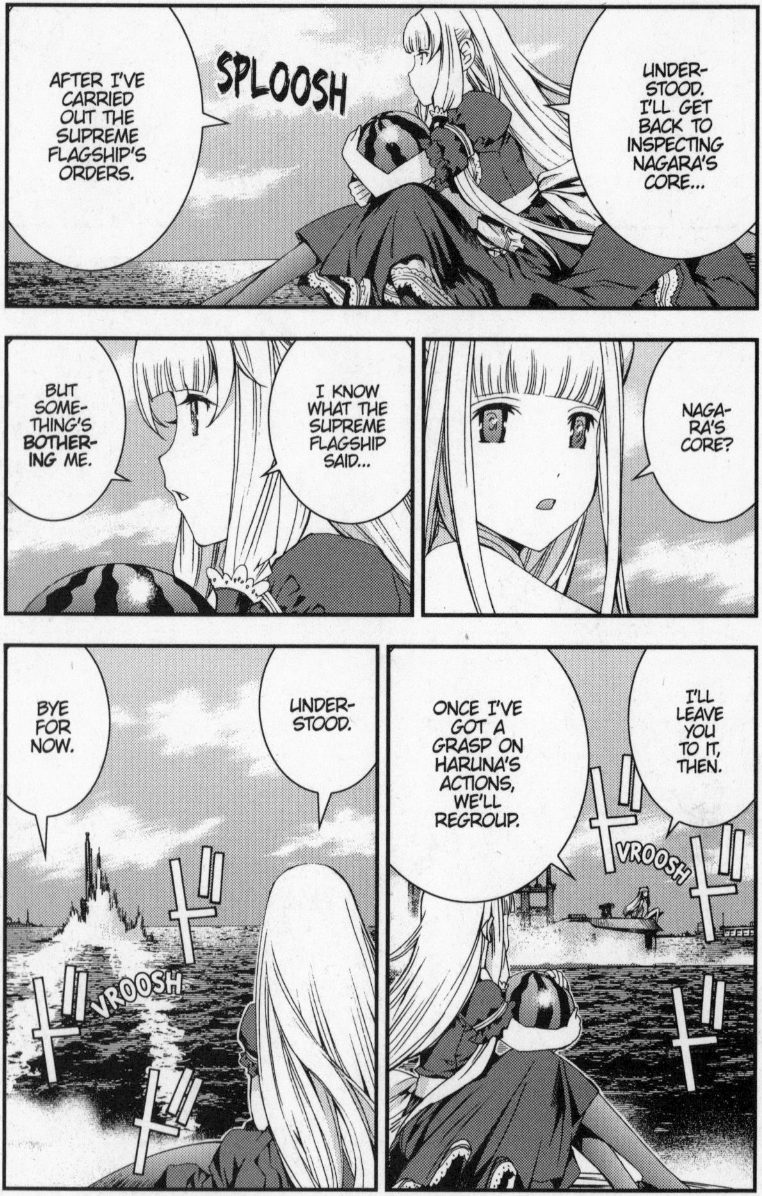
UNDER-STOOD. I'LL GET BACK TO INSPECTING NAGARA'S CORE...
SPLOOSH
AFTER I'VE CARRIED OUT THE SUPREME FLAGSHIP'S ORDERS.
NAGARA'S CORE?
I KNOW WHAT THE SUPREME FLAGSHIP SAID...
BUT SOMETHING'S BOTHERING ME.
I'LL LEAVE YOU TO IT, THEN.
ONCE I'VE GOT A GRASP ON HARUNA'S ACTIONS, WE'LL REGROUP.
VROOSH
UNDER-STOOD.
BYE FOR NOW.
VROOSH

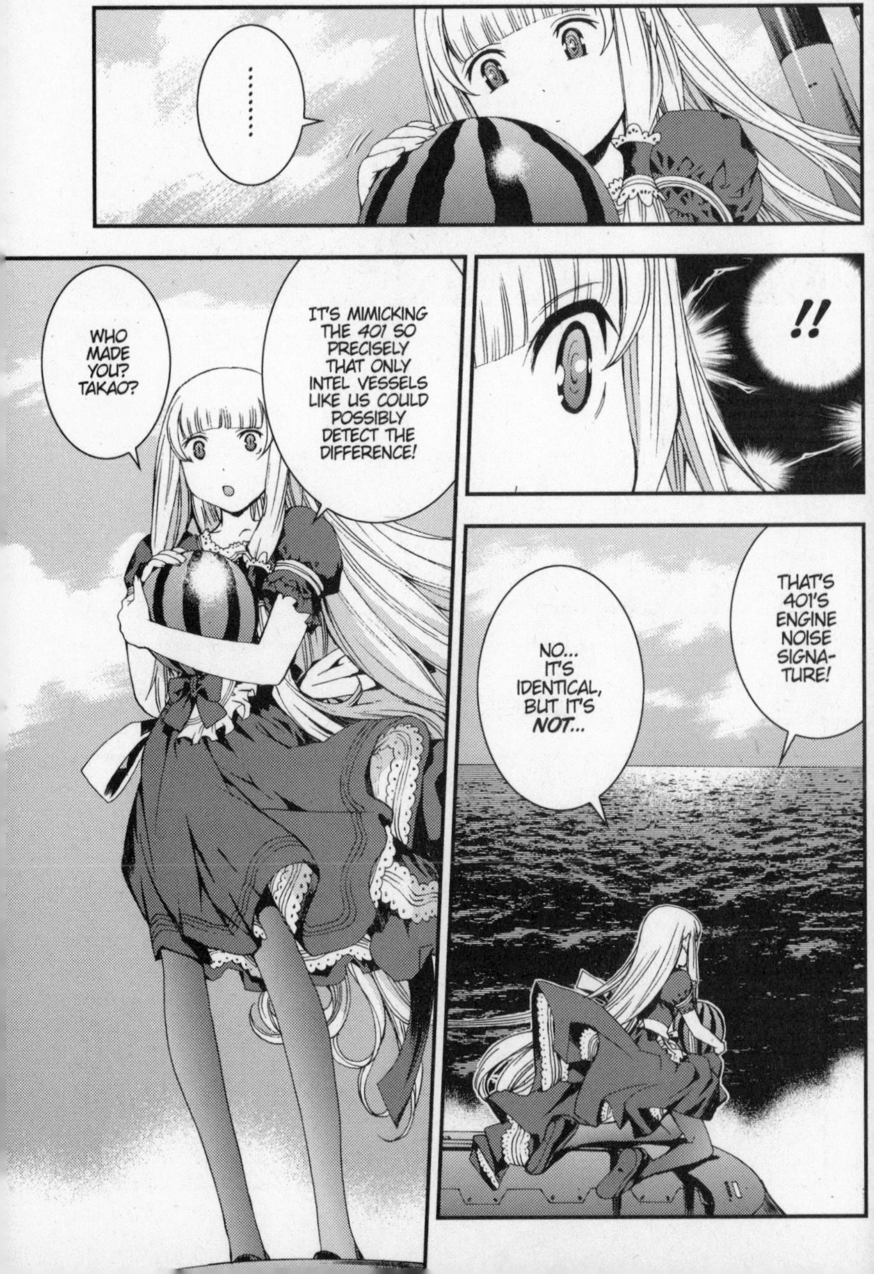
......
!!
THAT'S 401'S ENGINE NOISE SIGNA-TURE!
NO... IT'S IDENTICAL, BUT IT'S *NOT*...
IT'S MIMICKING THE 401 SO PRECISELY THAT ONLY INTEL VESSELS LIKE US COULD POSSIBLY DETECT THE DIFFERENCE!
WHO MADE YOU? TAKAO?

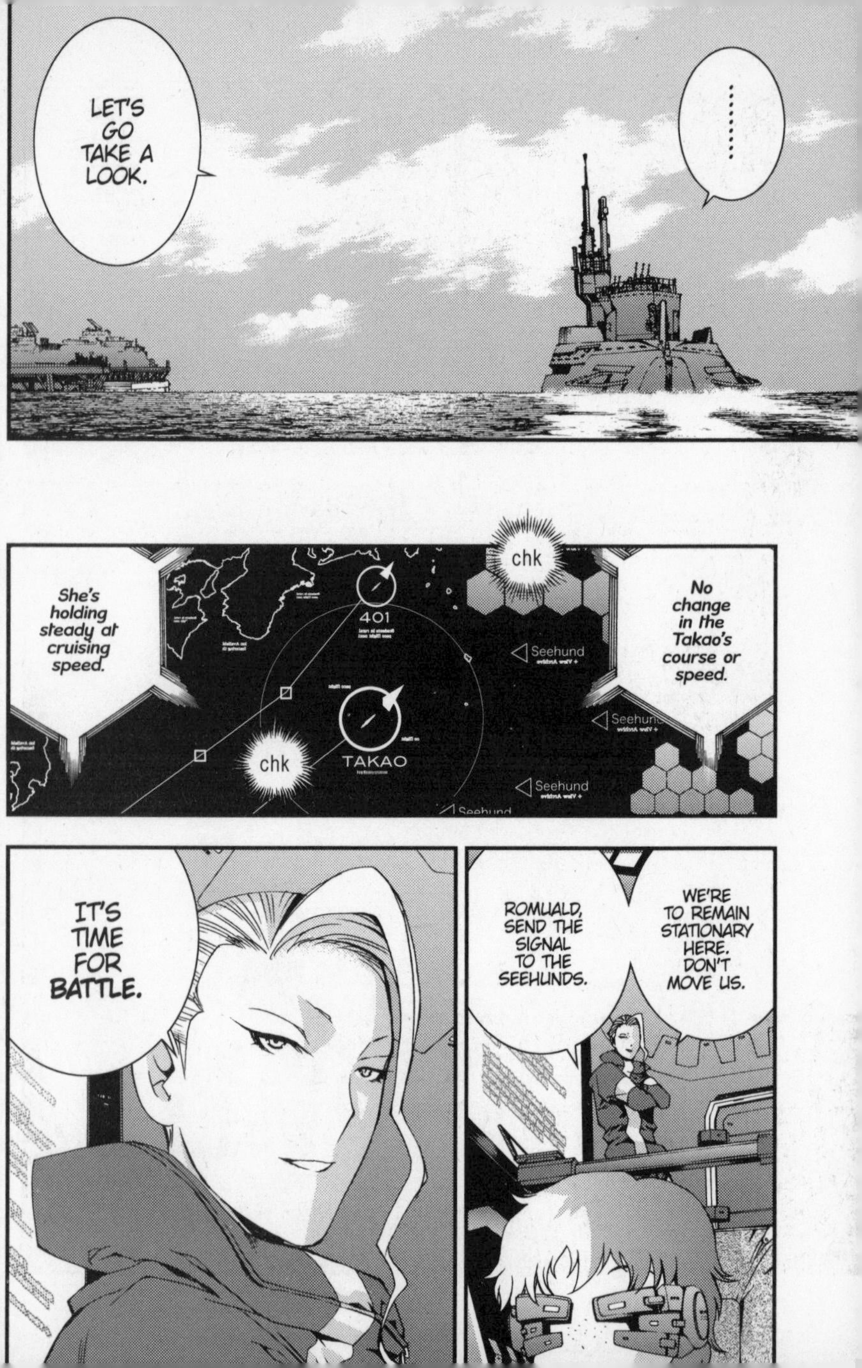
……
LET'S GO TAKE A LOOK.
chk
No change in the Takao's course or speed.
Seehund
Seehund
Seehund
401
TAKAO
chk
She's holding steady at cruising speed.
WE'RE TO REMAIN STATIONARY HERE. DON'T MOVE US.
ROMUALD, SEND THE SIGNAL TO THE SEEHUNDS.
IT'S TIME FOR BATTLE.

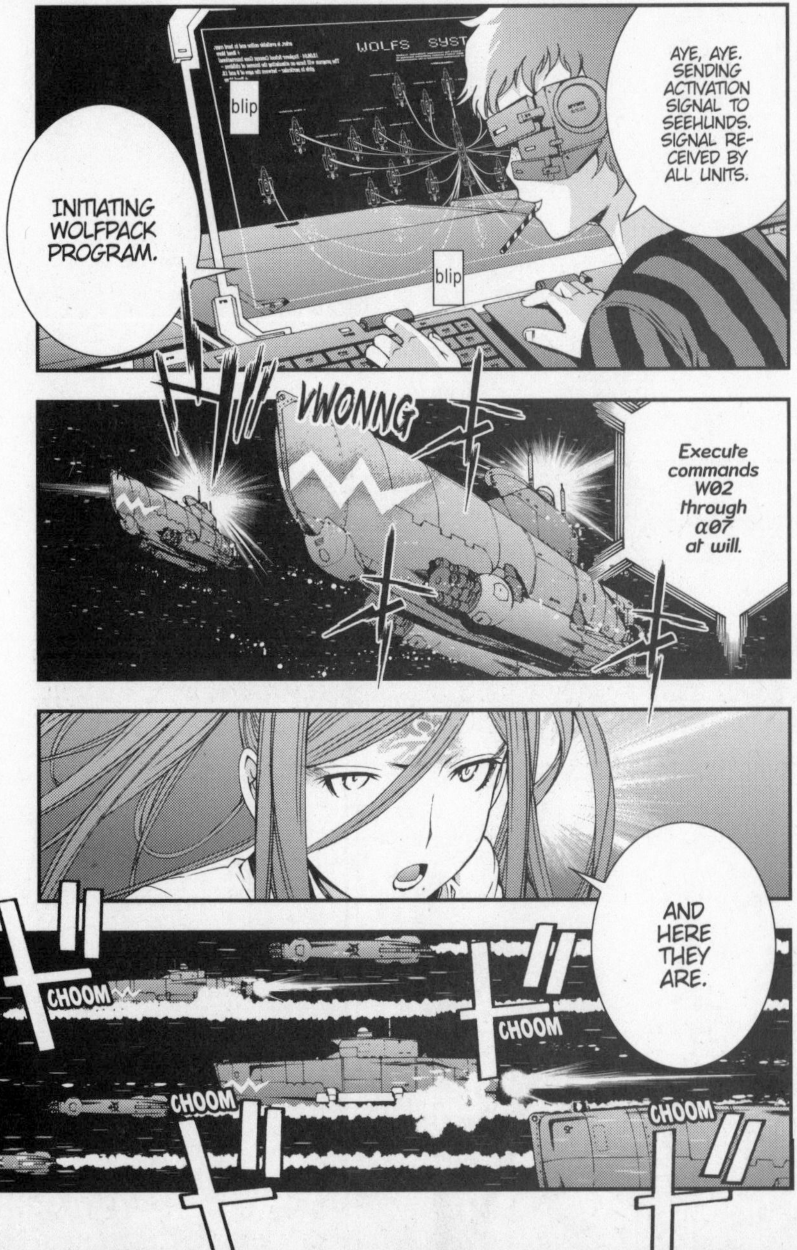
AYE, AYE. SENDING ACTIVATION SIGNAL TO SEEHUNDS. SIGNAL RE-CEIVED BY ALL UNITS.
WOLFS SYST
blip
INITIATING WOLFPACK PROGRAM.
blip
Execute commands W02 through α07 at will.
VWONNG
AND HERE THEY ARE.
CHOOM
CHOOM
CHOOM
CHOOM

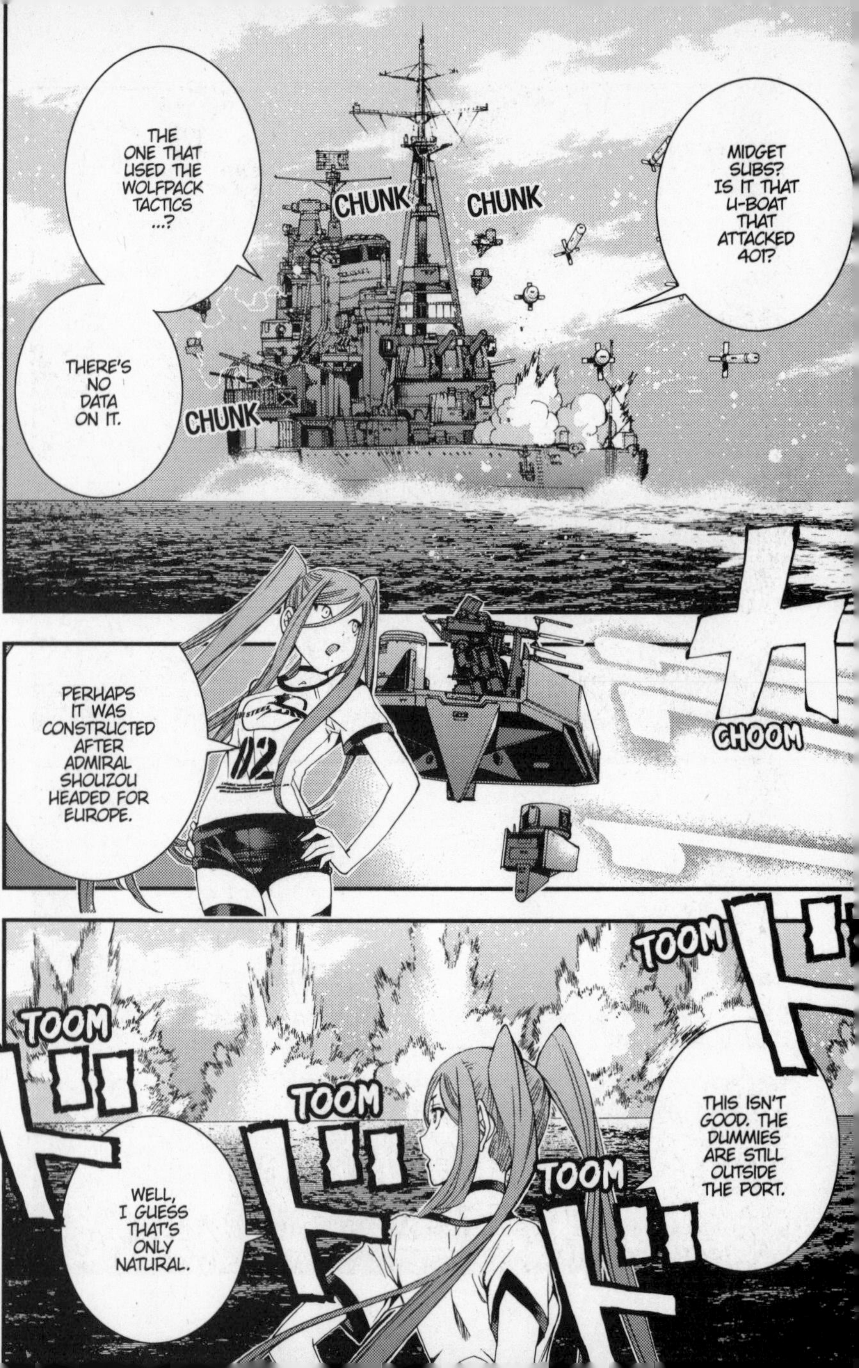
MIDGET SUBS? IS IT THAT U-BOAT THAT ATTACKED 401?
CHUNK
CHUNK
THE ONE THAT USED THE WOLFPACK TACTICS ...?
THERE'S NO DATA ON IT.
CHUNK
CHOOM
PERHAPS IT WAS CONSTRUCTED AFTER ADMIRAL SHOUZOU HEADED FOR EUROPE.
TOOM
THIS ISN'T GOOD. THE DUMMIES ARE STILL OUTSIDE THE PORT.
TOOM
TOOM
TOOM
WELL, I GUESS THAT'S ONLY NATURAL.

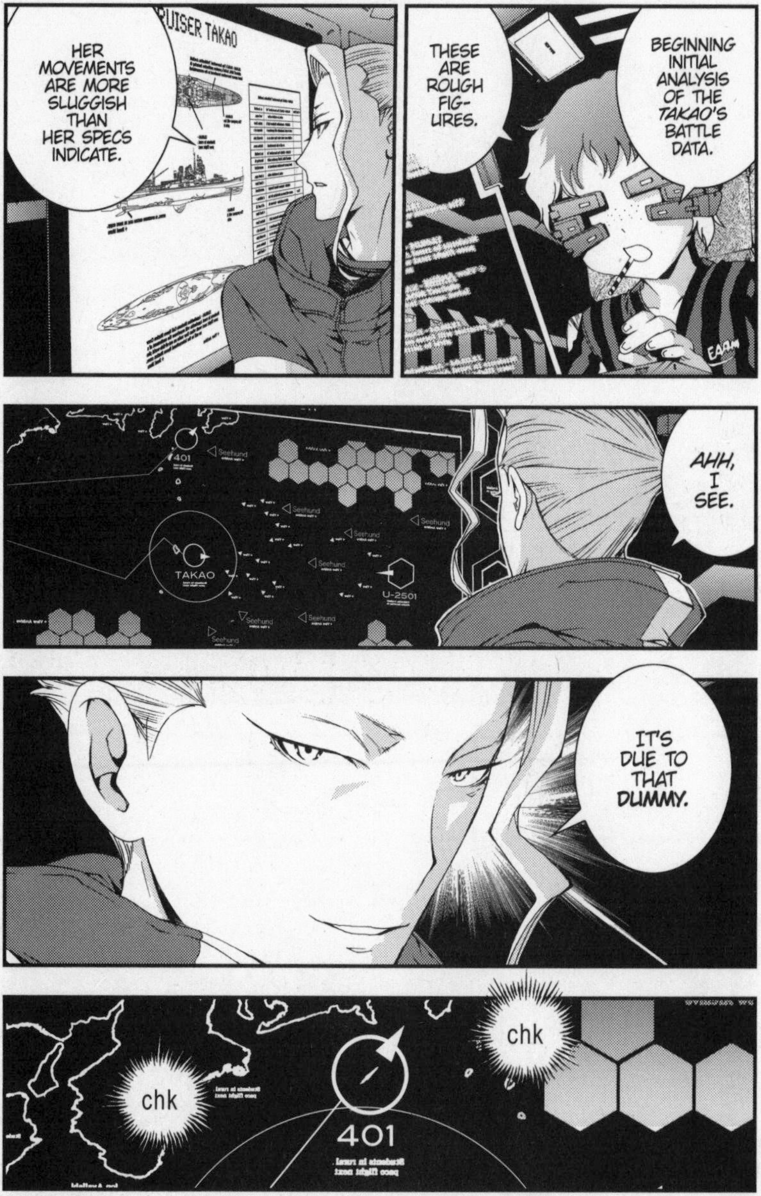
BEGINNING INITIAL ANALYSIS OF THE *TAKAO'S* BATTLE DATA.
THESE ARE ROUGH FIG-URES.
RUISER TAKAO
HER MOVEMENTS ARE MORE SLUGGISH THAN HER SPECS INDICATE.
AHH, I SEE.
401
Seehund
TAKAO
U-2501
IT'S DUE TO THAT DUMMY.
chk
chk
401

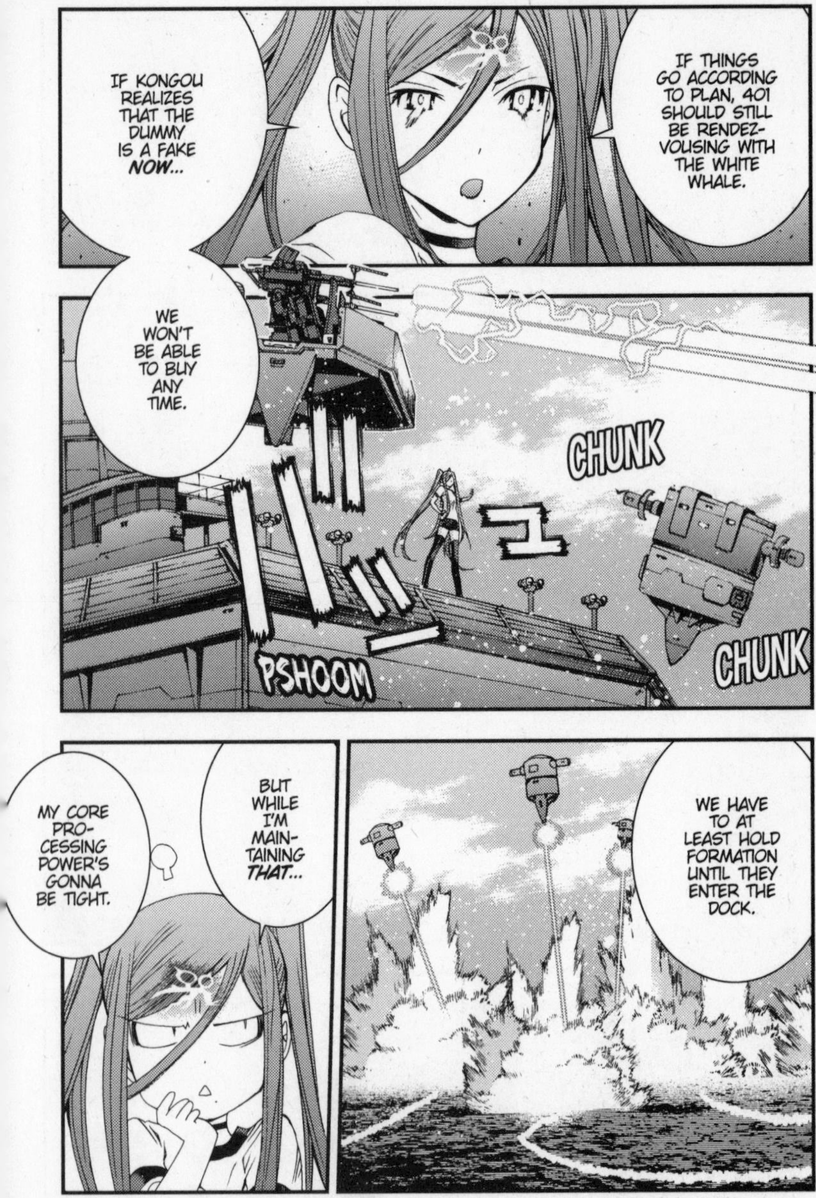
IF THINGS GO ACCORDING TO PLAN, 401 SHOULD STILL BE RENDEZ-VOUSING WITH THE WHITE WHALE.
IF KONGOU REALIZES THAT THE DUMMY IS A FAKE *NOW*...
WE WON'T BE ABLE TO BUY ANY TIME.
CHUNK
CHUNK
PSHOOM
WE HAVE TO AT LEAST HOLD FORMATION UNTIL THEY ENTER THE DOCK.
BUT WHILE I'M MAIN-TAINING *THAT*...
MY CORE PRO-CESSING POWER'S GONNA BE TIGHT.

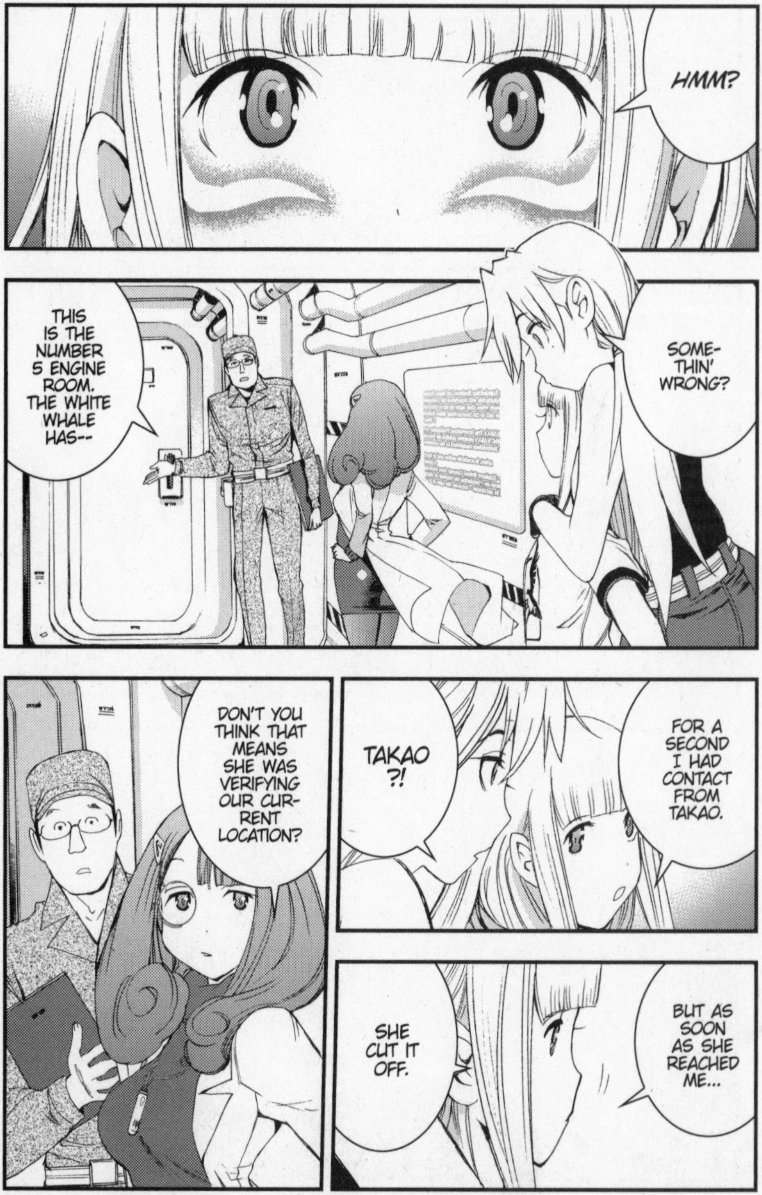
HMM?
SOME-THIN' WRONG?
THIS IS THE NUMBER 5 ENGINE ROOM. THE WHITE WHALE HAS--
FOR A SECOND I HAD CONTACT FROM TAKAO.
TAKAO ?!
BUT AS SOON AS SHE REACHED ME...
SHE CUT IT OFF.
DON'T YOU THINK THAT MEANS SHE WAS VERIFYING OUR CUR-RENT LOCATION?

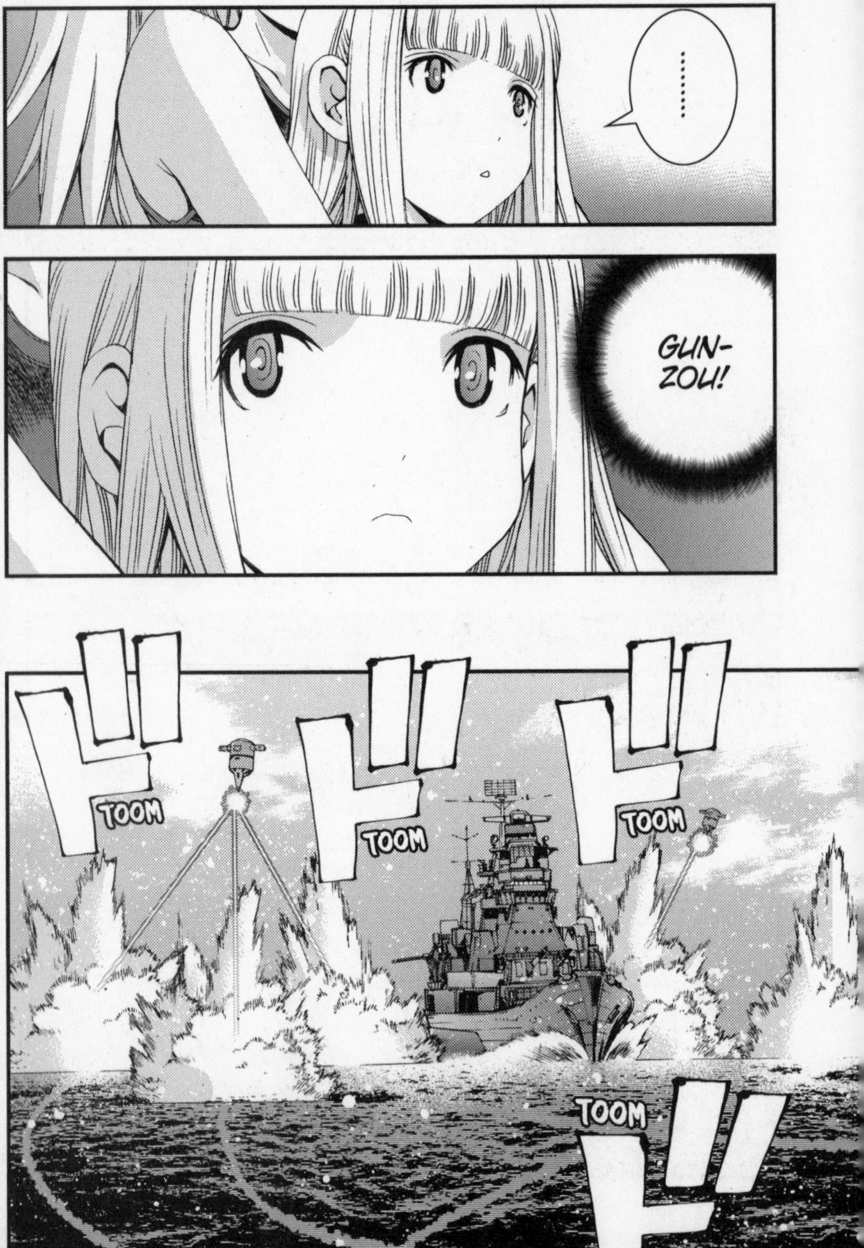
......
GUN-
ZOU!
TOOM
TOOM
TOOM
TOOM

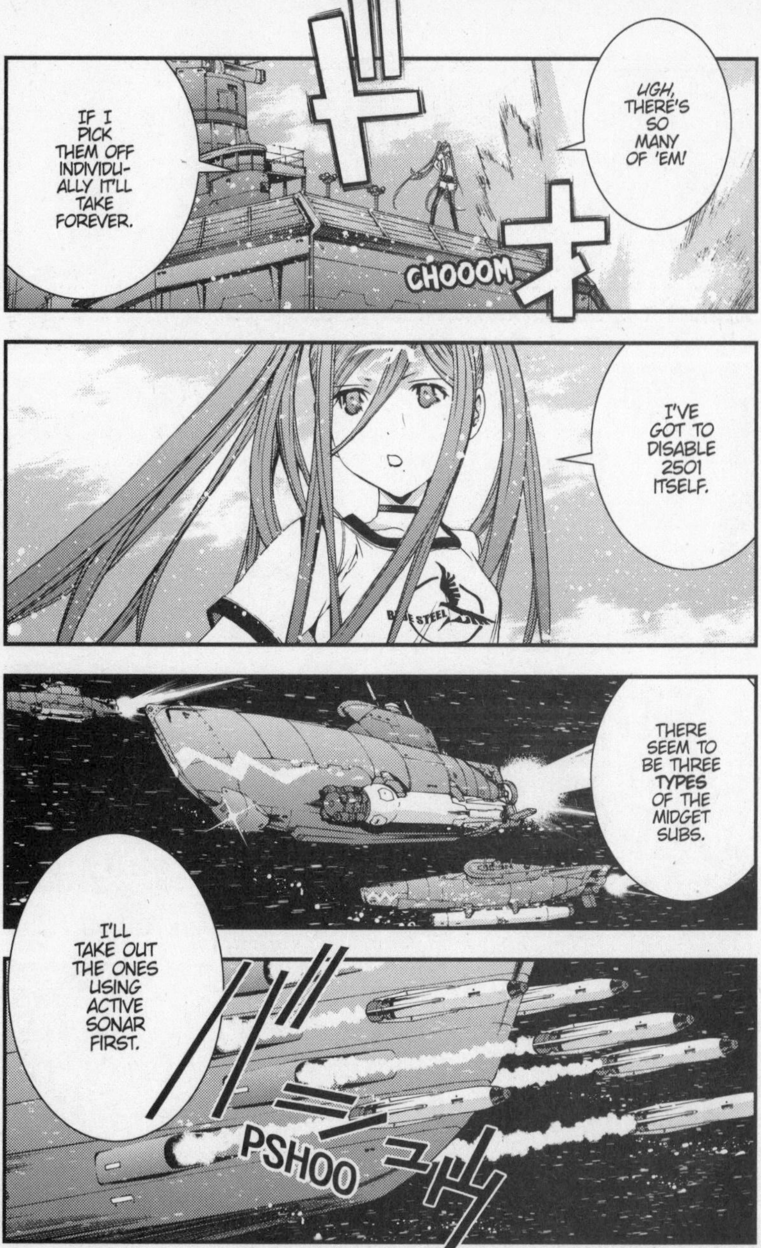
UGH, THERE'S SO MANY OF 'EM!
IF I PICK THEM OFF INDIVIDU-ALLY IT'LL TAKE FOREVER.
CHOOOM
I'VE GOT TO DISABLE 2501 ITSELF.
THERE SEEM TO BE THREE TYPES OF THE MIDGET SUBS.
I'LL TAKE OUT THE ONES USING ACTIVE SONAR FIRST.
PSHOO

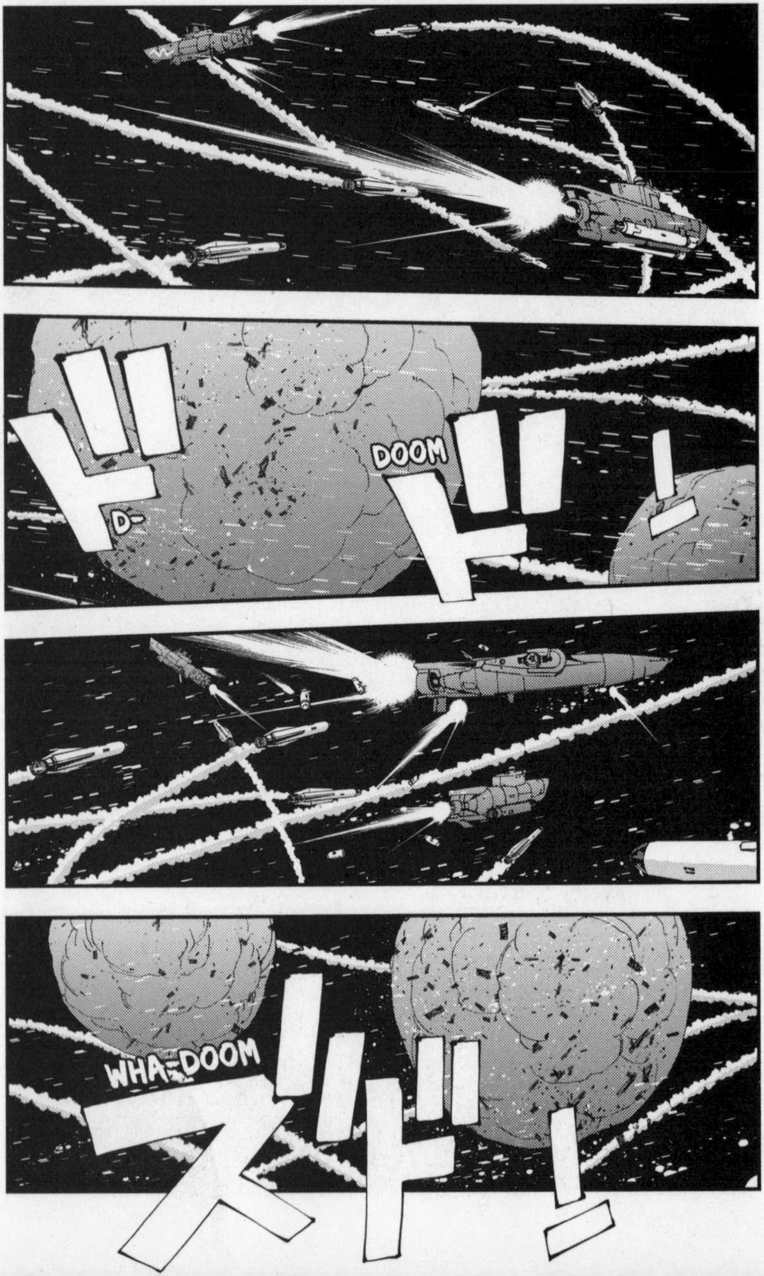
ドー
DOOM
ド
D-
ズドー
WHA-DOOM

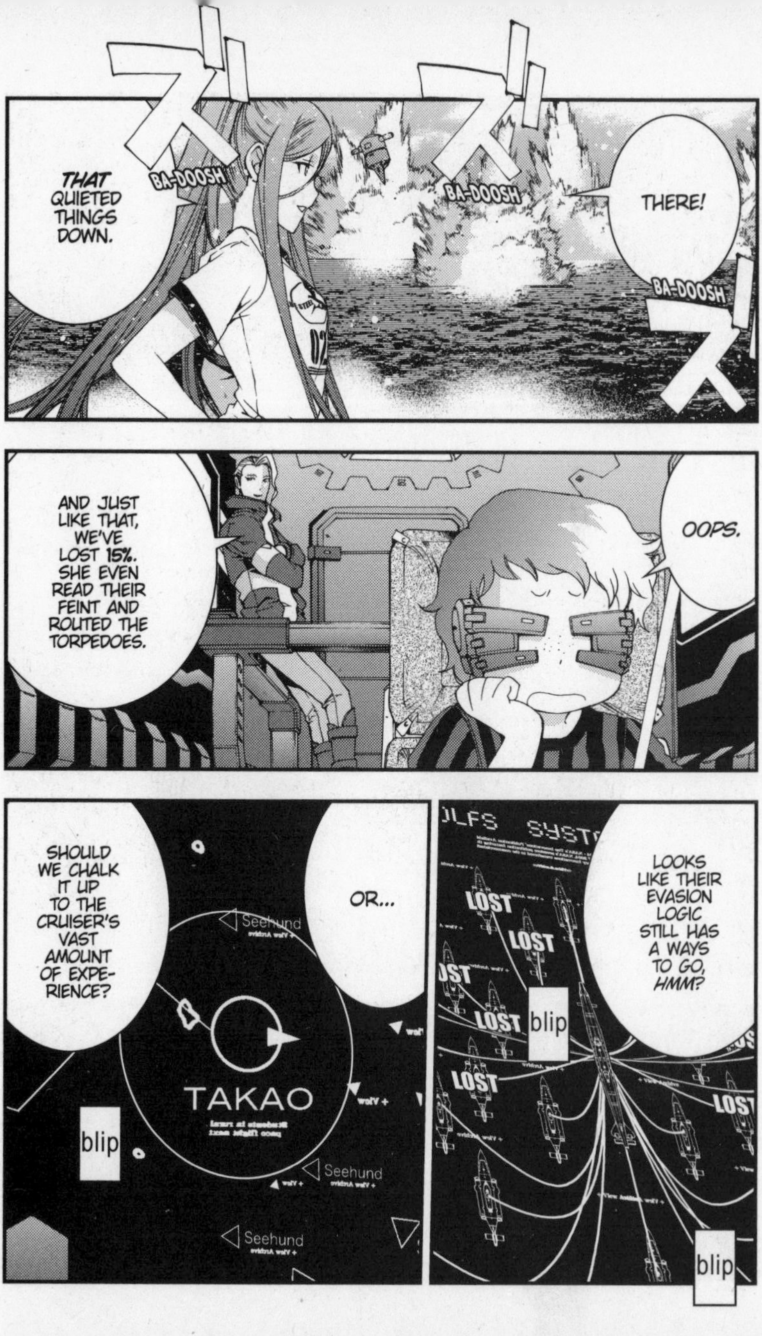
THERE!
BA-DOOSH
BA-DOOSH
THAT QUIETED THINGS DOWN.
BA-DOOSH
OOPS.
AND JUST LIKE THAT, WE'VE LOST 15%. SHE EVEN READ THEIR FEINT AND ROUTED THE TORPEDOES.
LOOKS LIKE THEIR EVASION LOGIC STILL HAS A WAYS TO GO, *HMM?*
LOST
LOST
LOST
LOST
blip
blip
OR...
SHOULD WE CHALK IT UP TO THE CRUISER'S VAST AMOUNT OF EXPE-RIENCE?
Seehund
TAKAO
Seehund
Seehund
blip

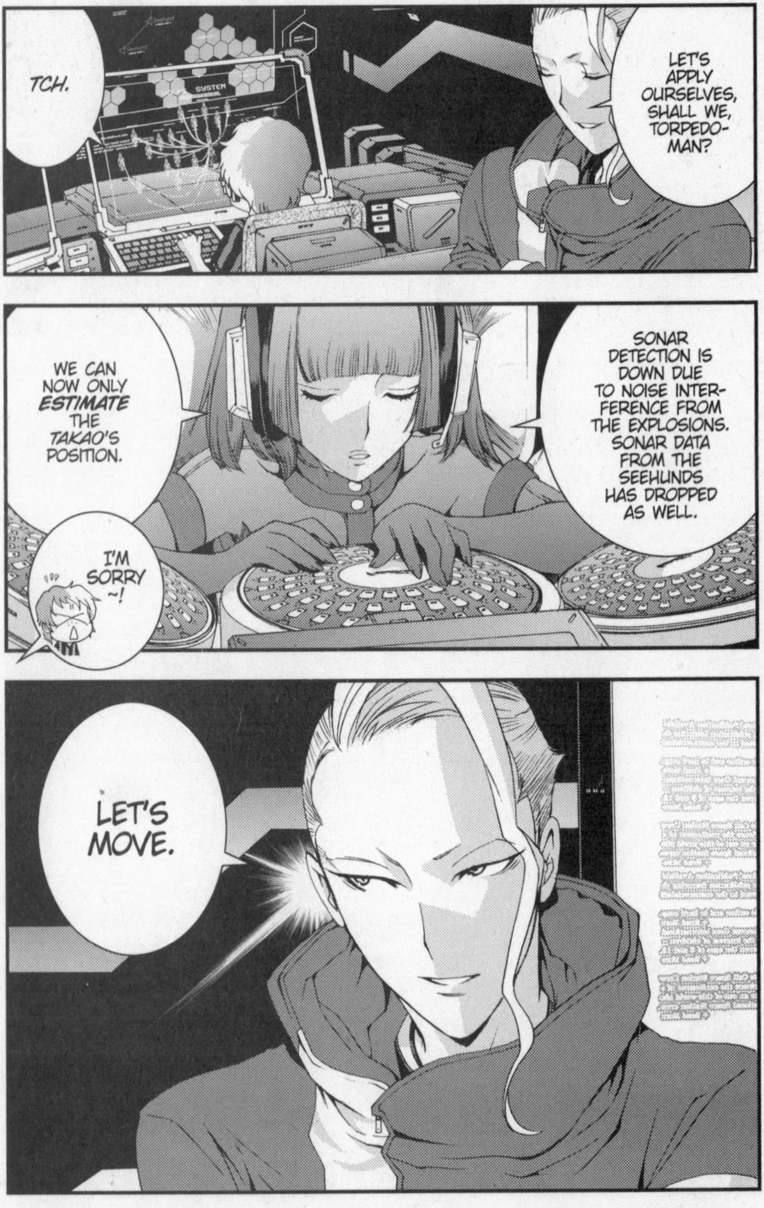
LET'S APPLY OURSELVES, SHALL WE, TORPEDO-MAN?
TCH.
SONAR DETECTION IS DOWN DUE TO NOISE INTER-FERENCE FROM THE EXPLOSIONS. SONAR DATA FROM THE SEEHUNDS HAS DROPPED AS WELL.
WE CAN NOW ONLY ESTIMATE THE TAKAO'S POSITION.
I'M SORRY ~!
LET'S MOVE.

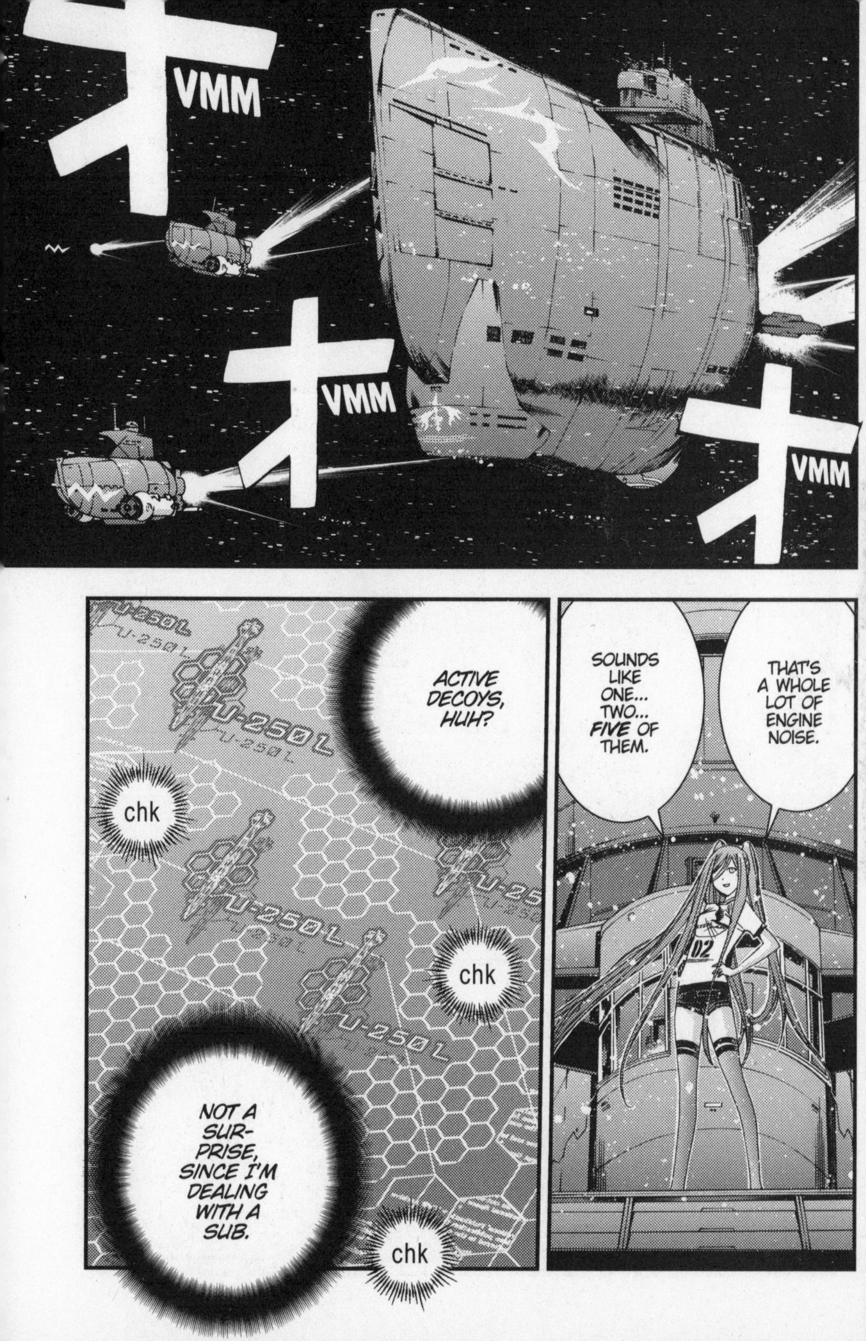
オ
VMM
オ
VMM
オ
VMM
THAT'S A WHOLE LOT OF ENGINE NOISE.
SOUNDS LIKE ONE... TWO... *FIVE* OF THEM.
ACTIVE DECOYS, HUH?
U-250L
chk
chk
NOT A SUR-PRISE, SINCE I'M DEALING WITH A SUB.
chk

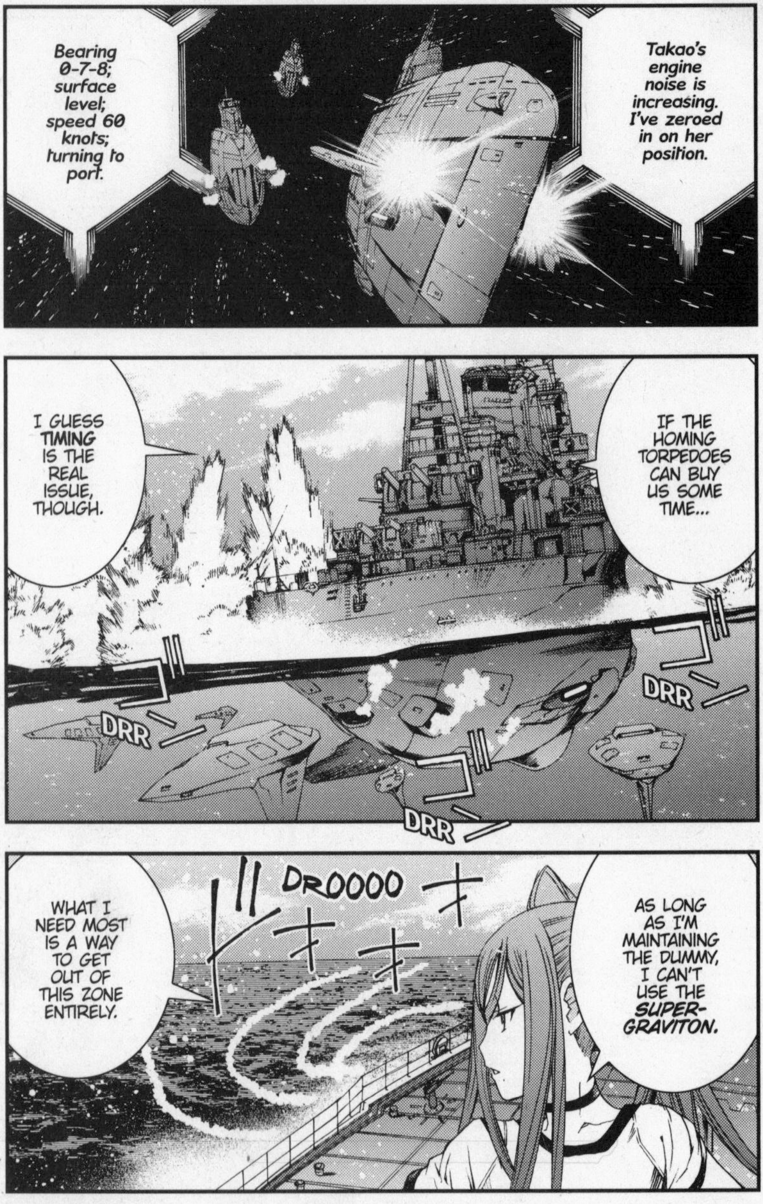

Takao's engine noise is increasing. I've zeroed in on her position.
Bearing 0-7-8; surface level; speed 60 knots; turning to port.
IF THE HOMING TORPEDOES CAN BUY US SOME TIME...
I GUESS TIMING IS THE REAL ISSUE, THOUGH.
DRR
DRR
DRR
AS LONG AS I'M MAINTAINING THE DUMMY, I CAN'T USE THE SUPER-GRAVITON.
DROOOO
WHAT I NEED MOST IS A WAY TO GET OUT OF THIS ZONE ENTIRELY.

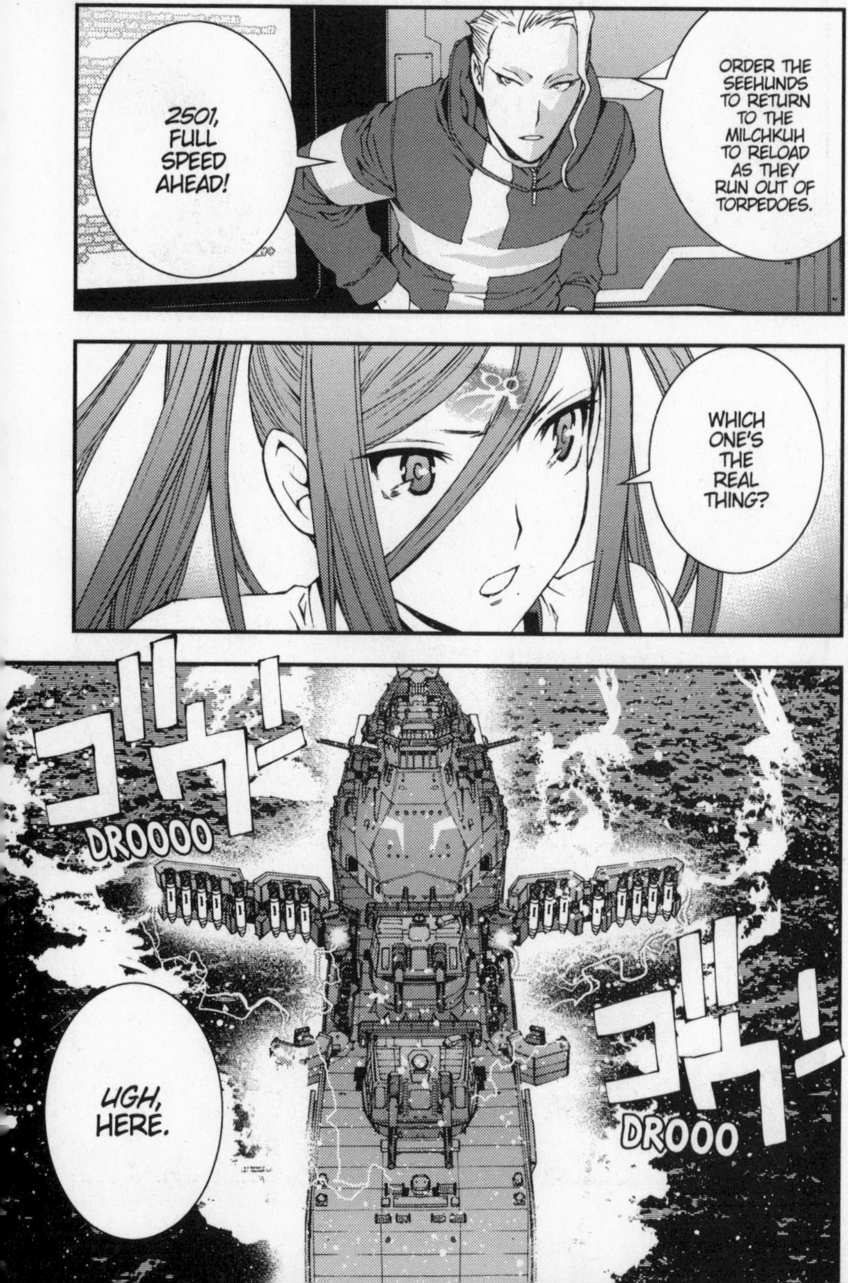
ORDER THE SEEHUNDS TO RETURN TO THE MILCHKUH TO RELOAD AS THEY RUN OUT OF TORPEDOES.
2501, FULL SPEED AHEAD!
WHICH ONE'S THE REAL THING?
DROOOO
DROOO
UGH, HERE.

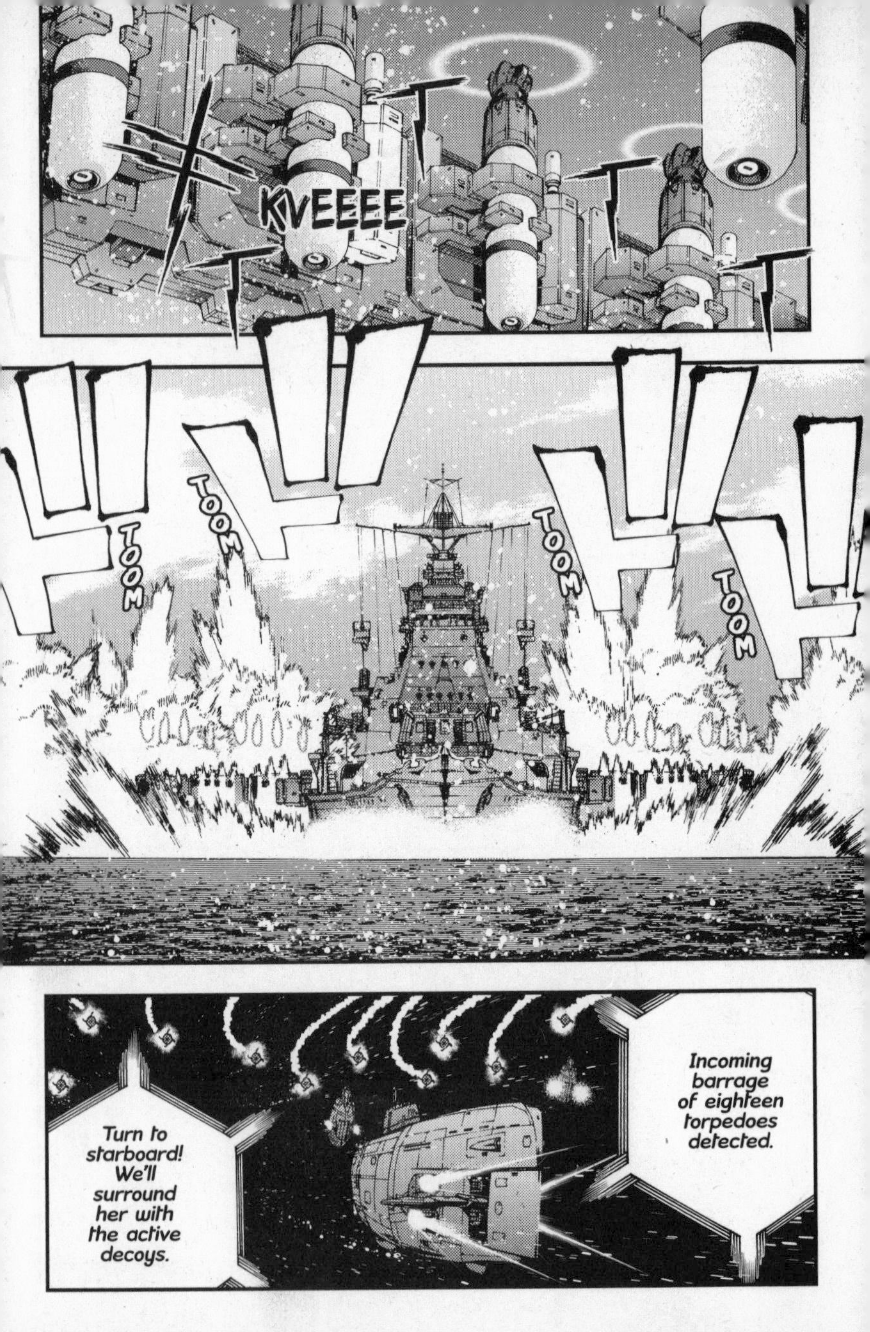
KVEEEE
TOOM
TOOM
TOOM
TOOM
Incoming barrage of eighteen torpedoes detected.
Turn to starboard! We'll surround her with the active decoys.

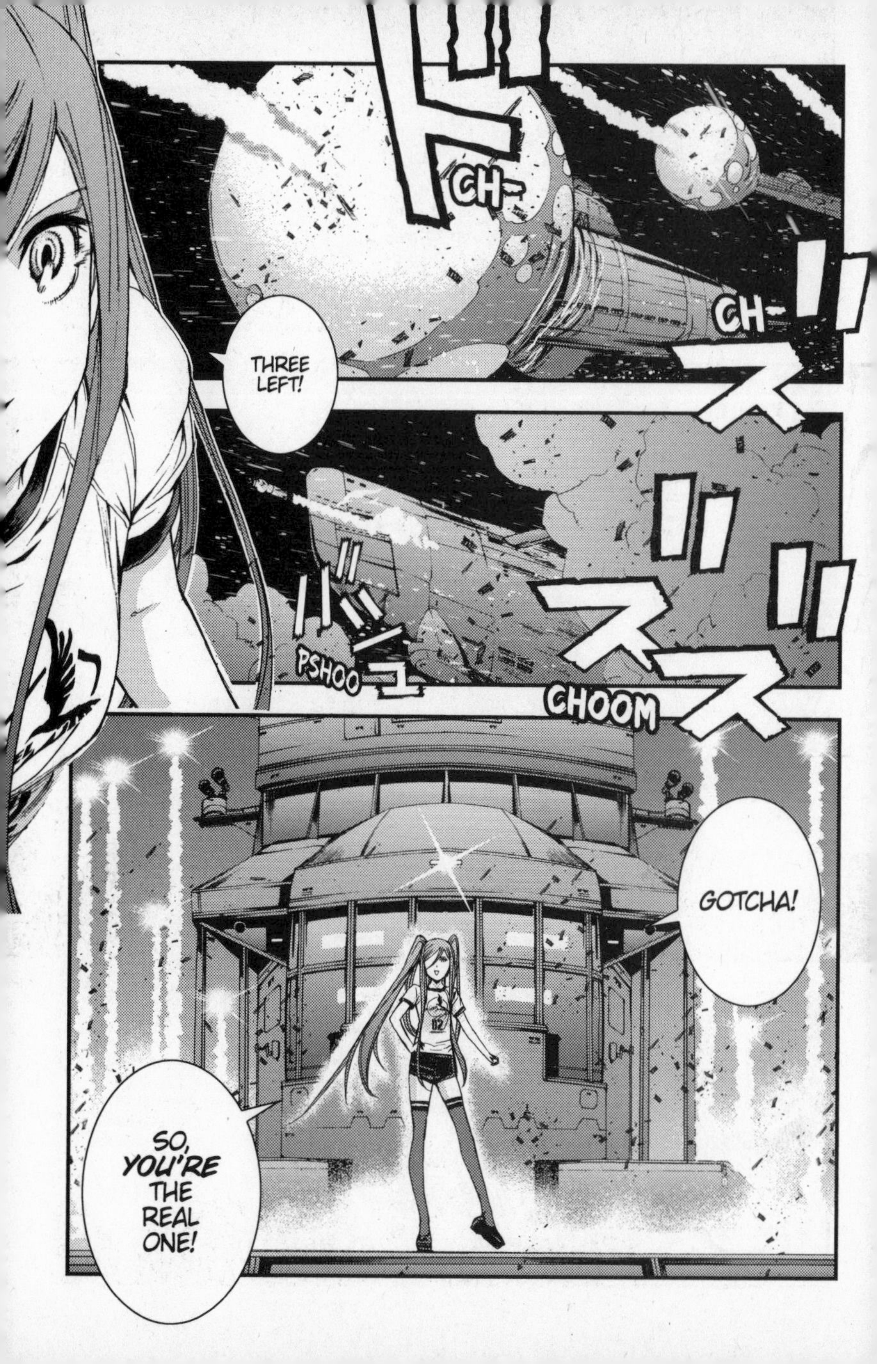
CH-
CH-
CHOOM
PSHOO
THREE LEFT!
GOTCHA!
SO, *YOU'RE* THE REAL ONE!

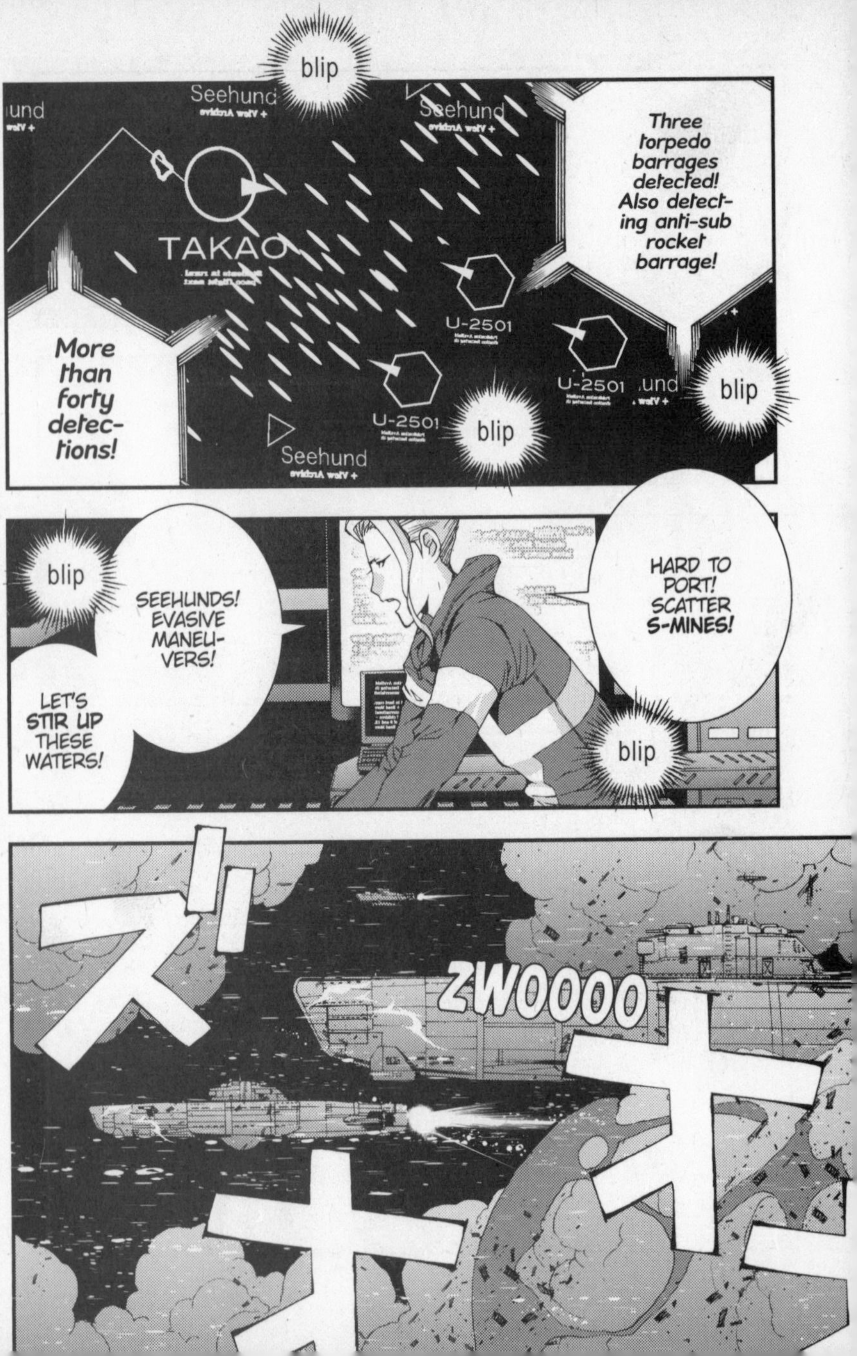
blip
Seehund
Seehund
und
TAKAO
Three torpedo barrages detected! Also detecting anti-sub rocket barrage!
More than forty detections!
U-2501
U-2501
U-2501
blip
blip
Seehund
HARD TO PORT! SCATTER S-MINES!
blip
SEEHUNDS! EVASIVE MANEUVERS!
LET'S STIR UP THESE WATERS!
blip
ZWOOOO
ズオオ

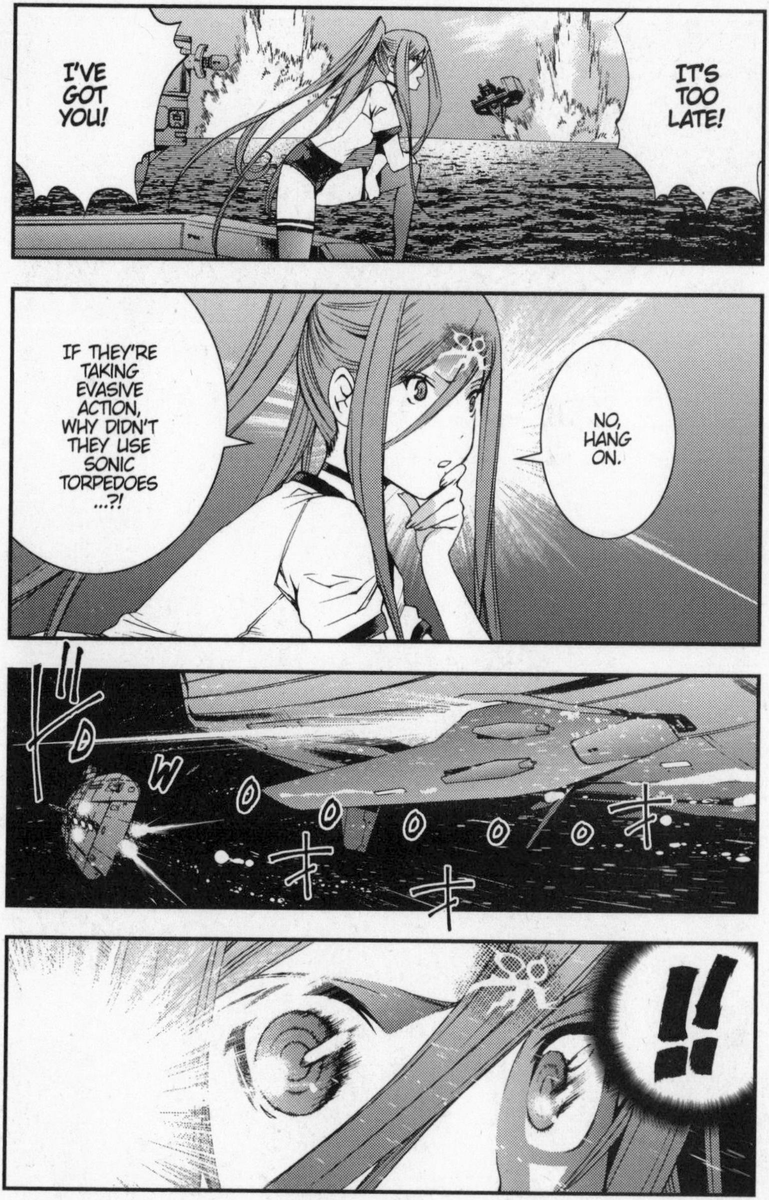
IT'S TOO LATE!
I'VE GOT YOU!
NO, HANG ON.
IF THEY'RE TAKING EVASIVE ACTION, WHY DIDN'T THEY USE SONIC TORPEDOES ...?!
DWOOOOO
!!

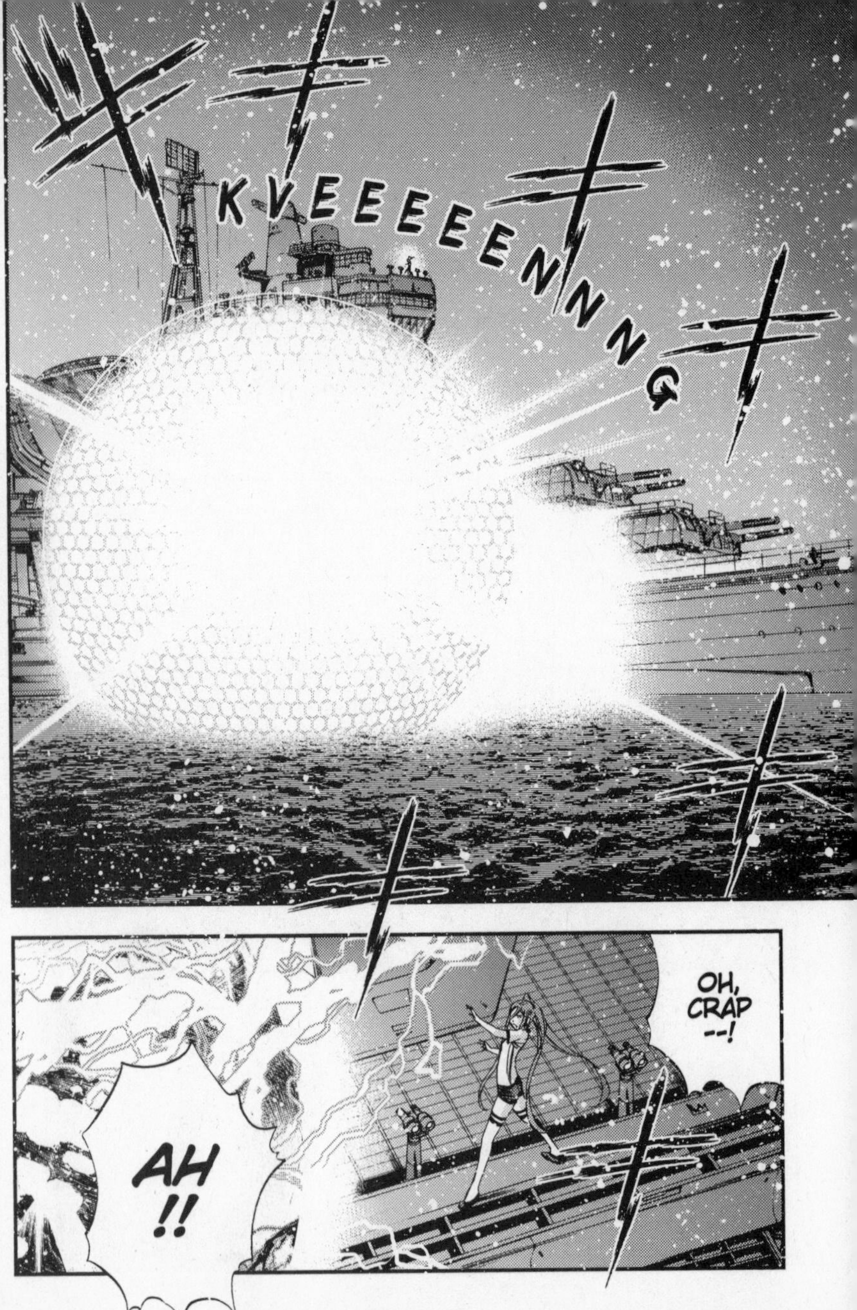
KVEEEEENNNG
OH, CRAP --!
AH !!

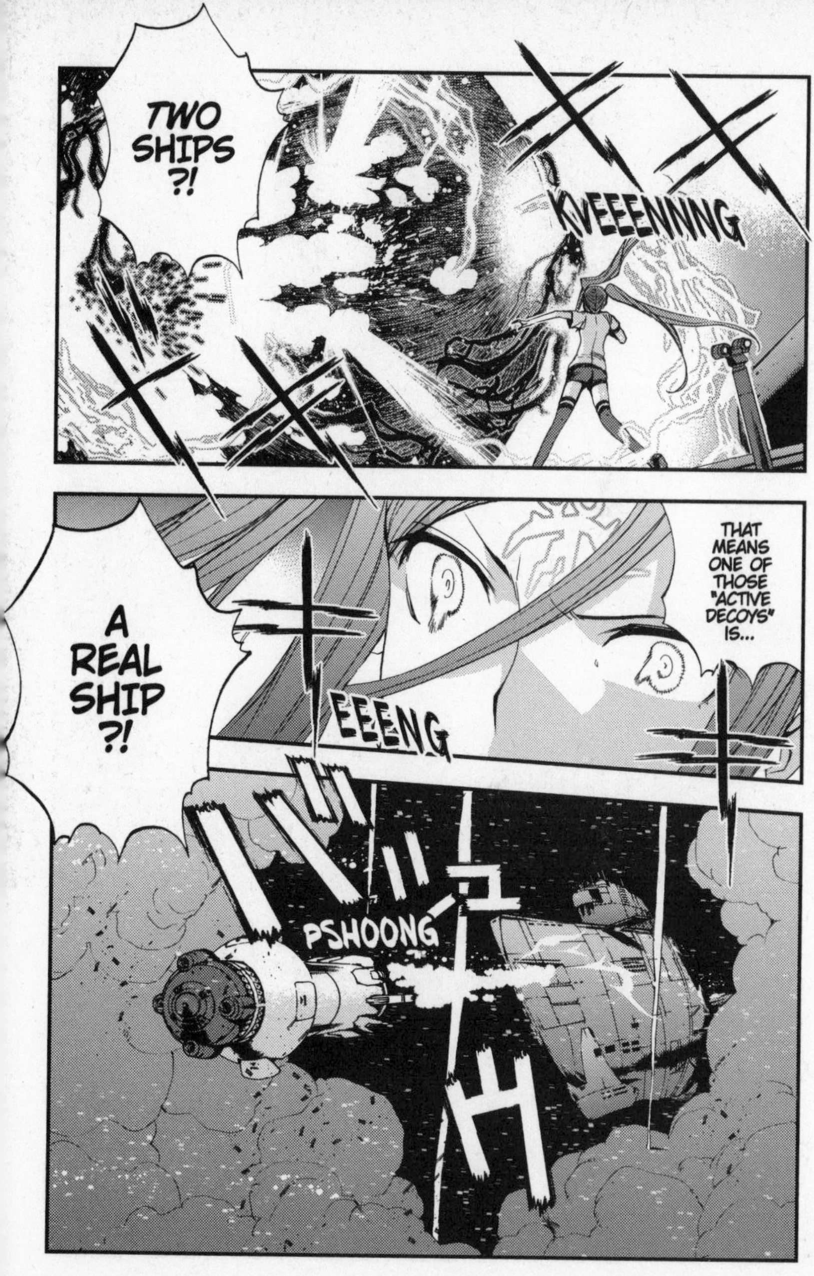
TWO SHIPS ?!
KVEEENNNG
THAT MEANS ONE OF THOSE "ACTIVE DECOYS" IS...
A REAL SHIP ?!
EEENG
PSHOONG

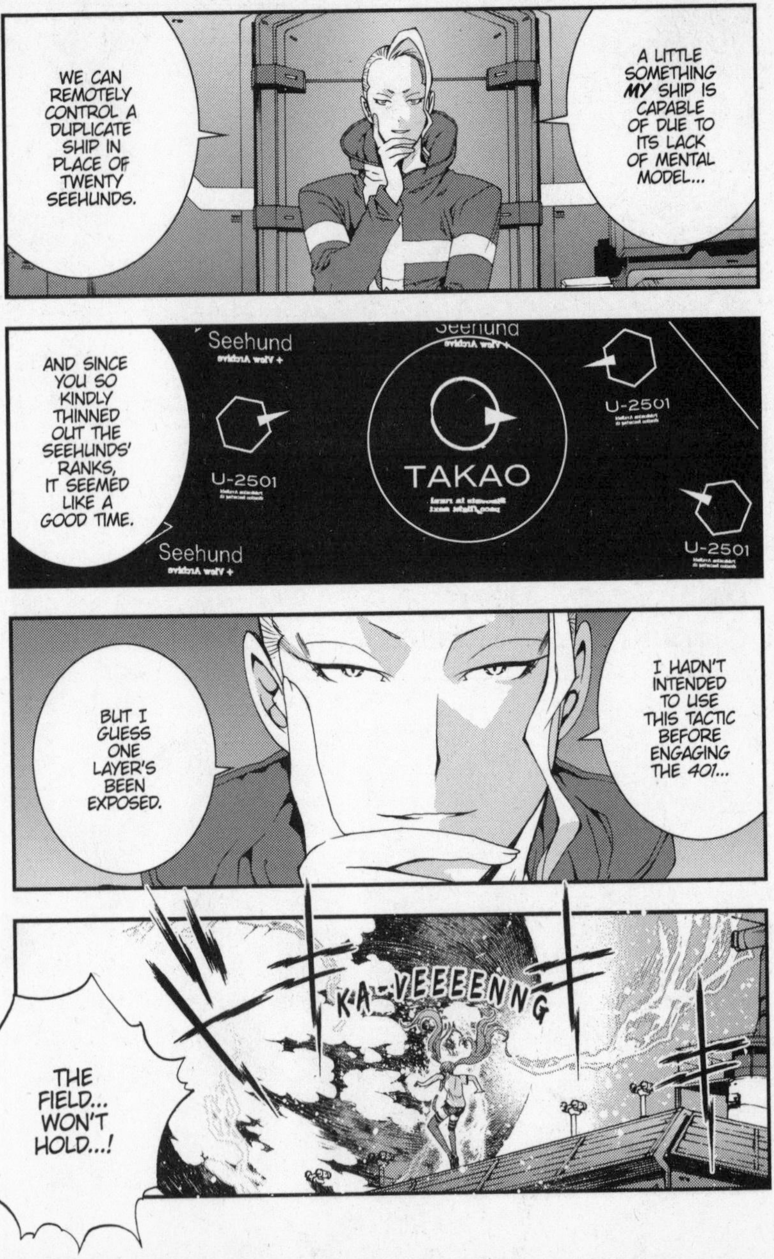
A LITTLE SOMETHING *MY* SHIP IS CAPABLE OF DUE TO ITS LACK OF MENTAL MODEL...
WE CAN REMOTELY CONTROL A DUPLICATE SHIP IN PLACE OF TWENTY SEEHUNDS.
U-2501
Seehund
TAKAO
U-2501
U-2501
Seehund
Seehund
AND SINCE YOU SO KINDLY THINNED OUT THE SEEHUNDS' RANKS, IT SEEMED LIKE A GOOD TIME.
I HADN'T INTENDED TO USE THIS TACTIC BEFORE ENGAGING THE 401...
BUT I GUESS ONE LAYER'S BEEN EXPOSED.
KA-VEEEENNG
THE FIELD... WON'T HOLD...!

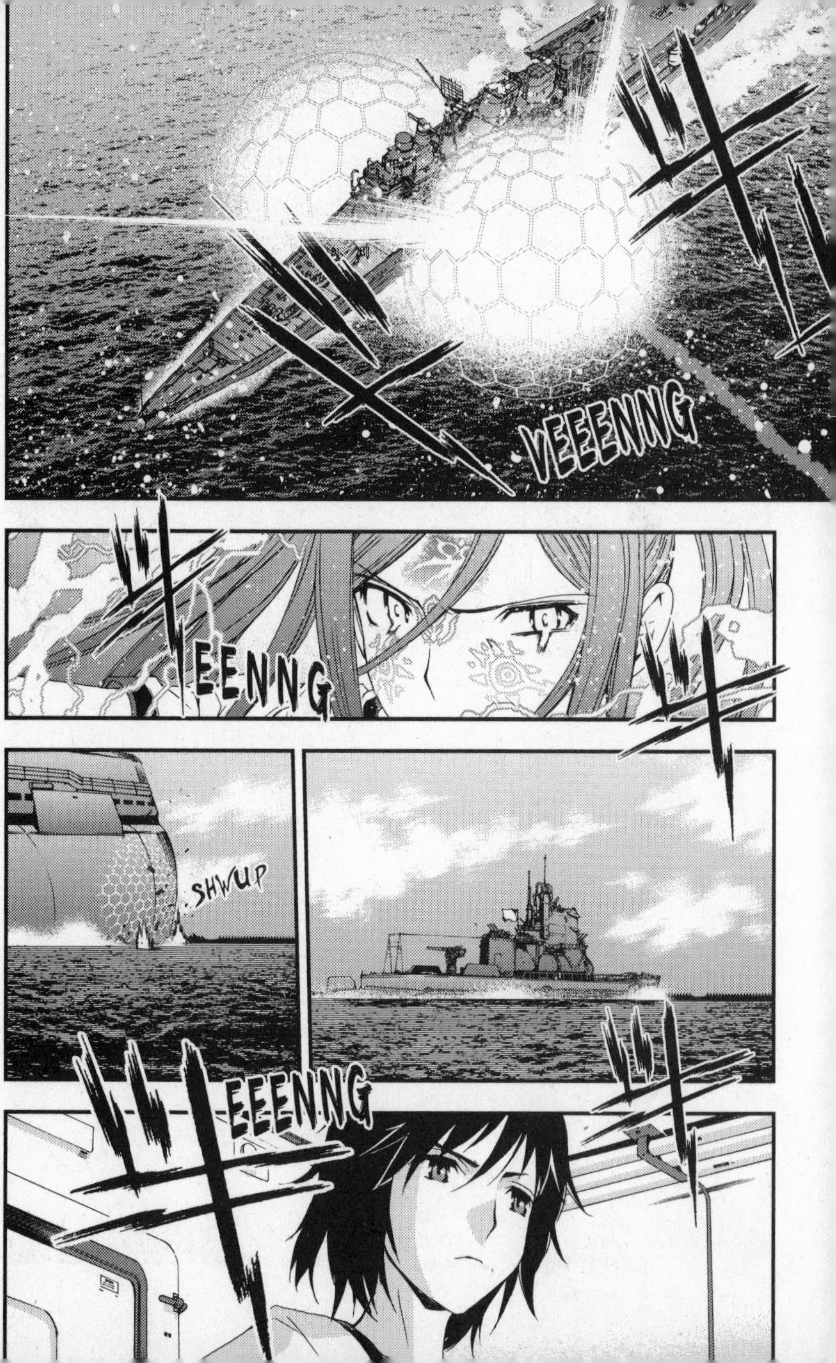
VEEENNG
EENNG
SHWUP
EEENNG

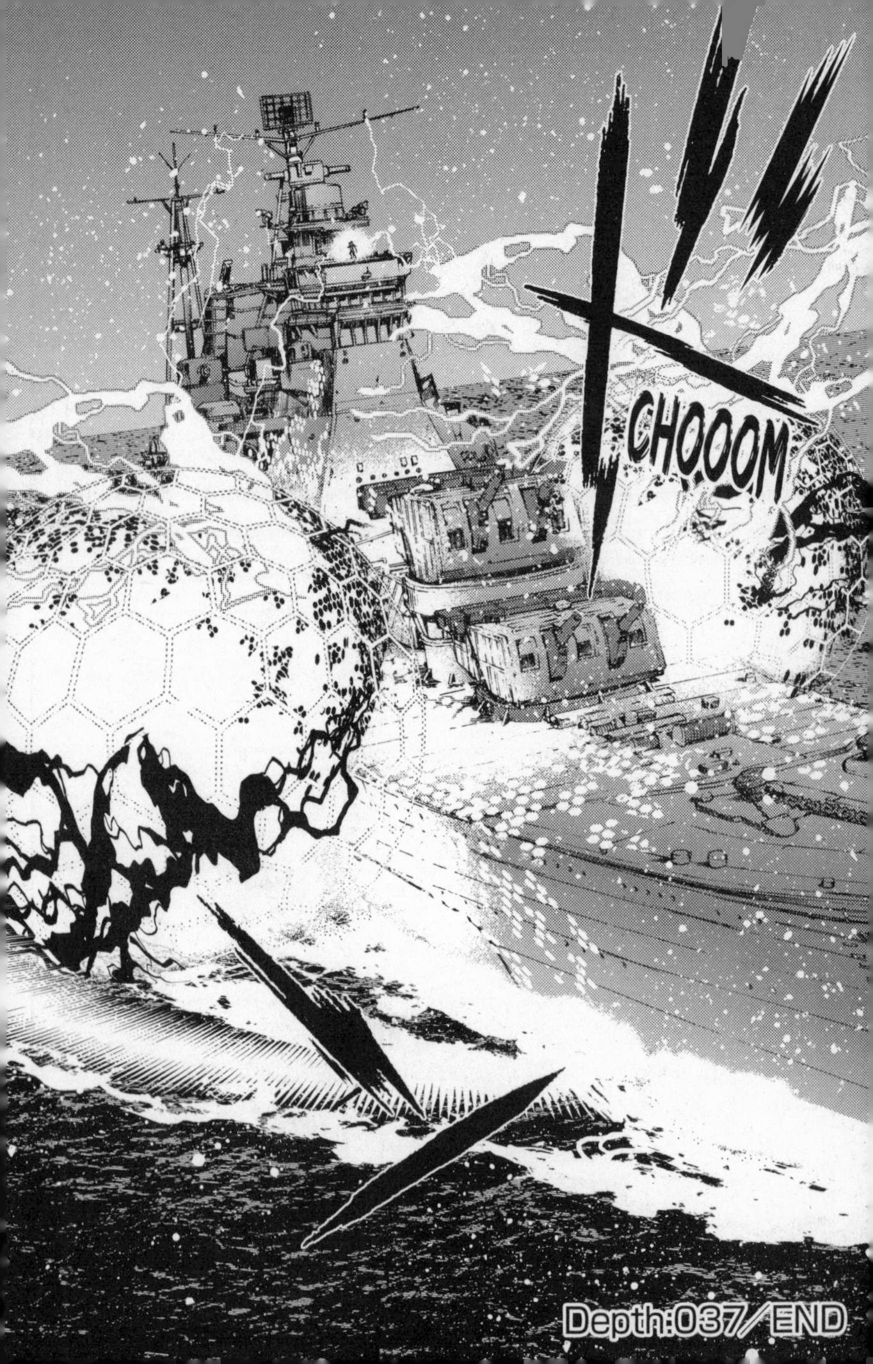
CHOOOM
Depth:037/END

Depth:038

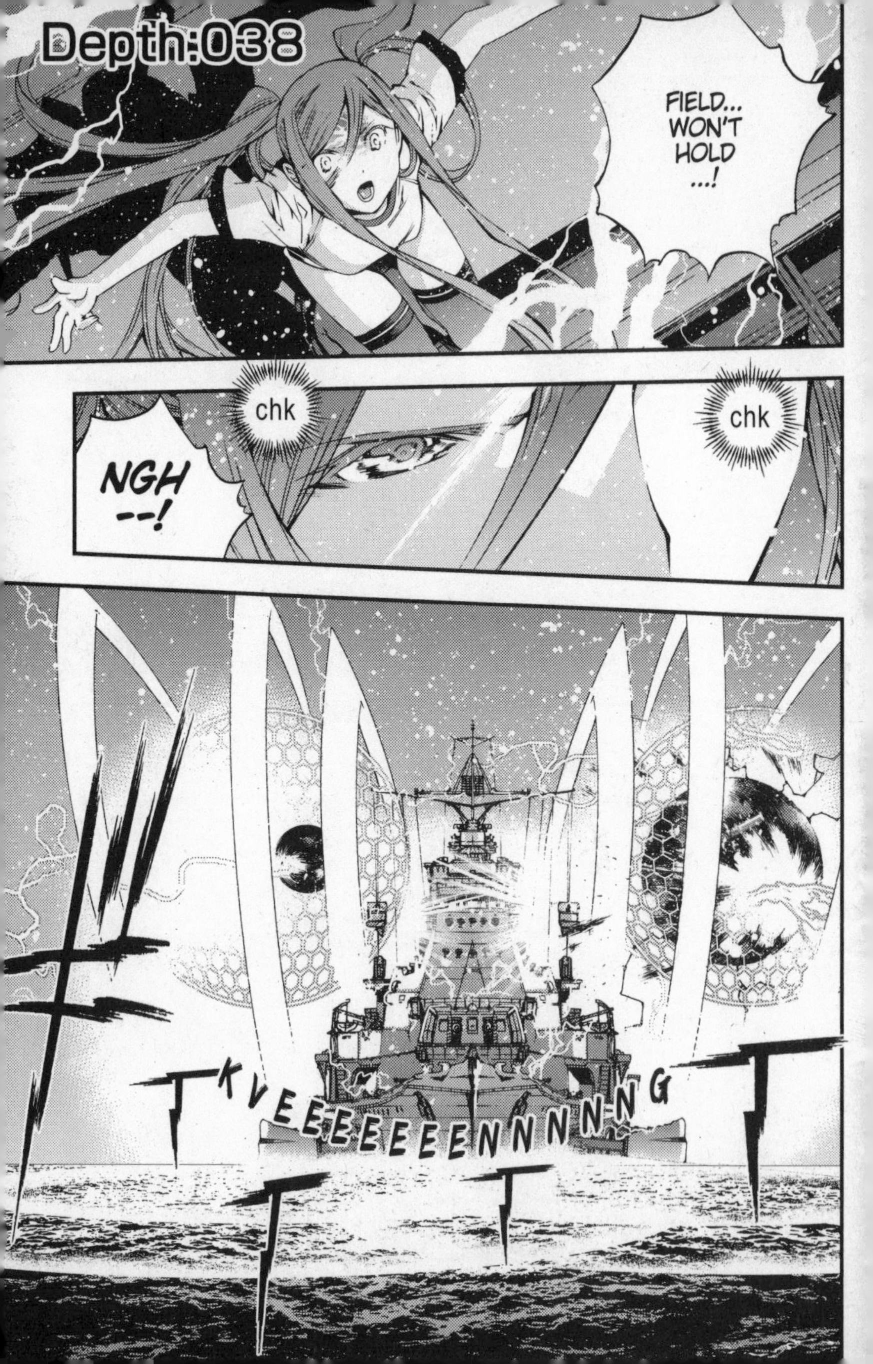
FIELD... WON'T HOLD ...!
chk
chk
NGH --!
TKVEEEEEEEENNNNNG

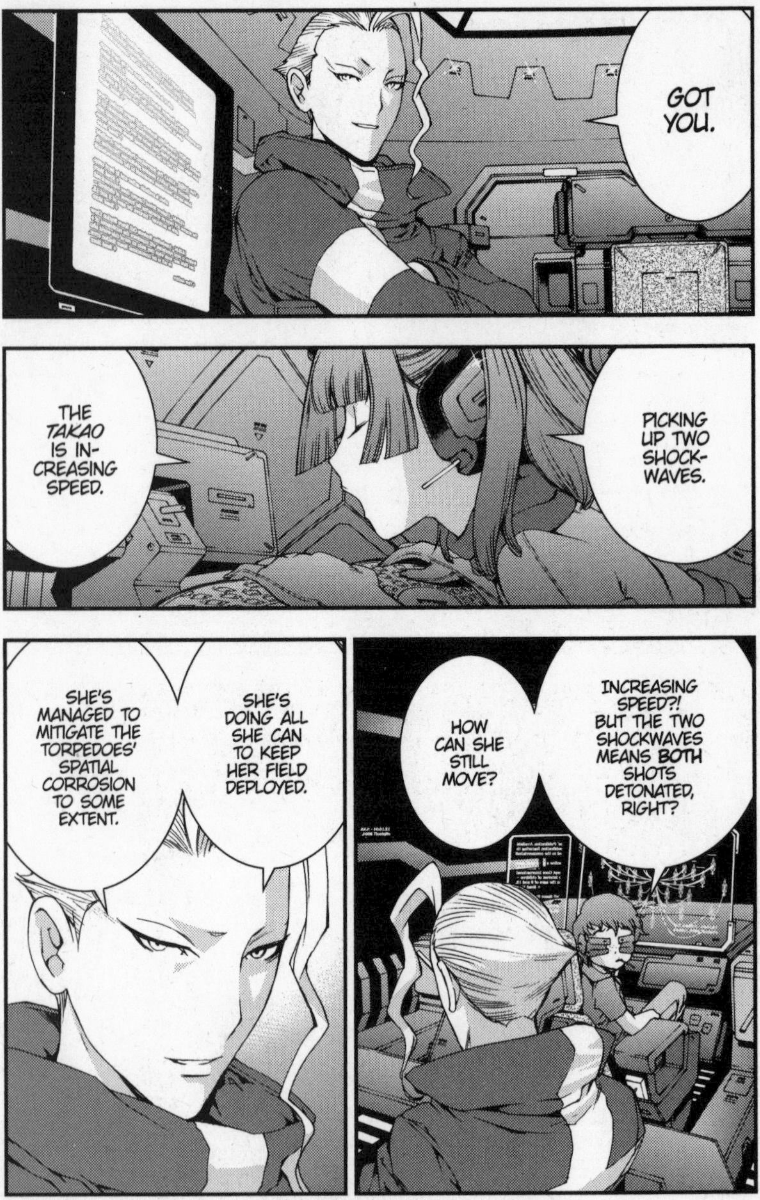
GOT YOU.
PICKING UP TWO SHOCK-WAVES.
THE *TAKAO* IS IN-CREASING SPEED.
INCREASING SPEED?! BUT THE TWO SHOCKWAVES MEANS **BOTH** SHOTS DETONATED, RIGHT?
HOW CAN SHE STILL MOVE?
SHE'S DOING ALL SHE CAN TO KEEP HER FIELD DEPLOYED.
SHE'S MANAGED TO MITIGATE THE TORPEDOES' SPATIAL CORROSION TO SOME EXTENT.

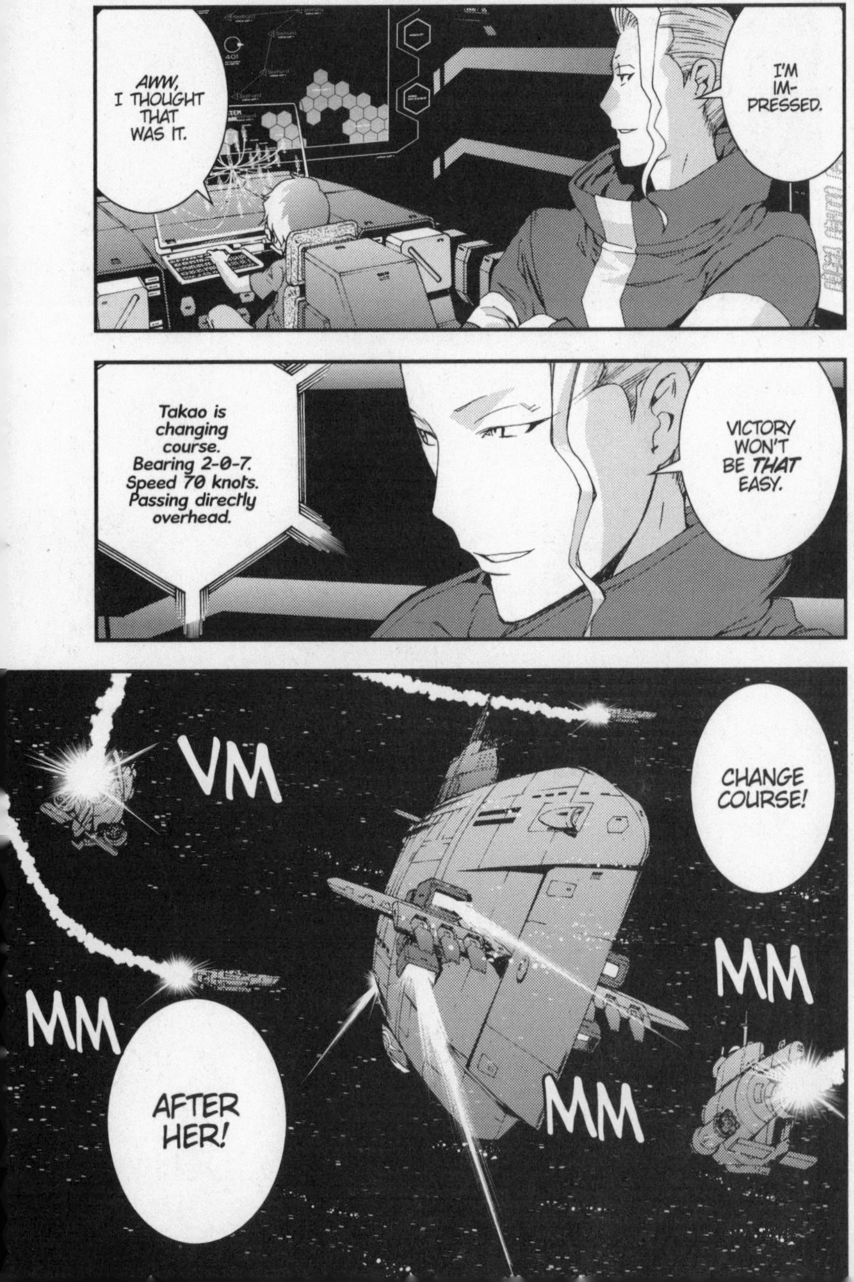
I'M IM-PRESSED.
AWW, I THOUGHT THAT WAS IT.
VICTORY WON'T BE THAT EASY.
Takao is changing course. Bearing 2-0-7. Speed 70 knots. Passing directly overhead.
CHANGE COURSE!
VM
MM
MM
MM
AFTER HER!

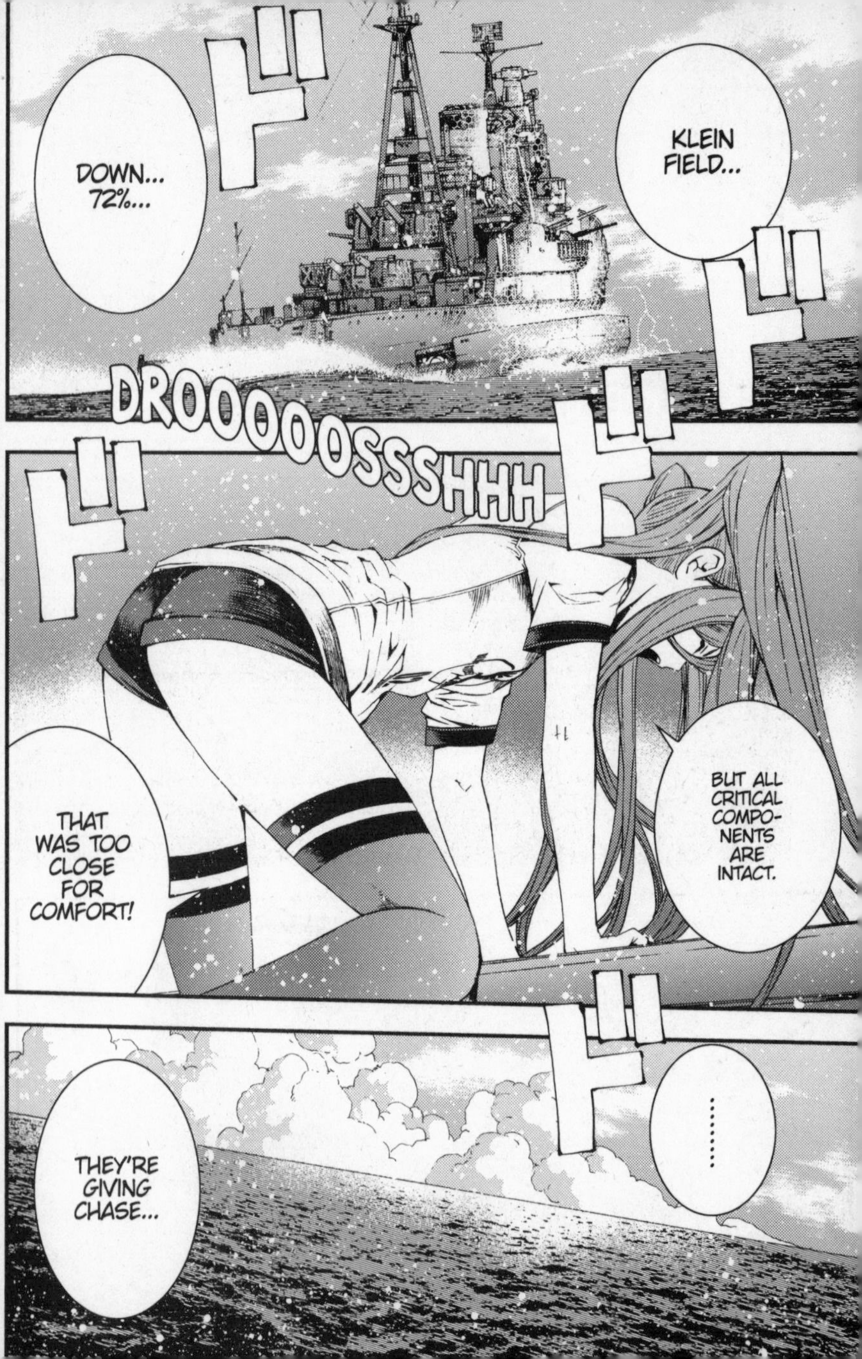
KLEIN FIELD...
DOWN... 72%...
ドド
DROOOOOSSSHHH
BUT ALL CRITICAL COMPO-NENTS ARE INTACT.
THAT WAS TOO CLOSE FOR COMFORT!
......
THEY'RE GIVING CHASE...

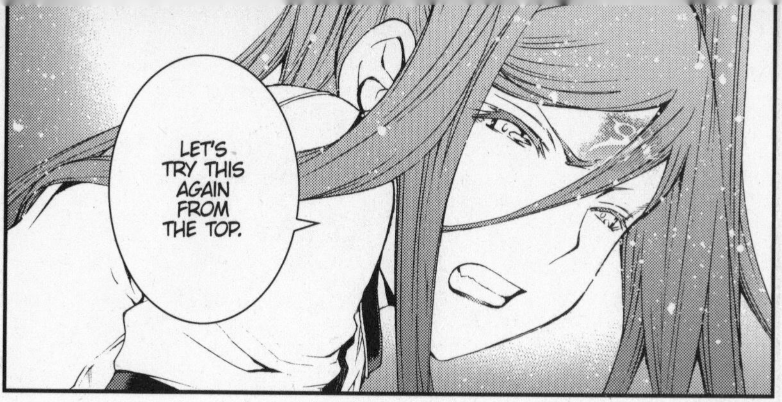
LET'S TRY THIS AGAIN FROM THE TOP.

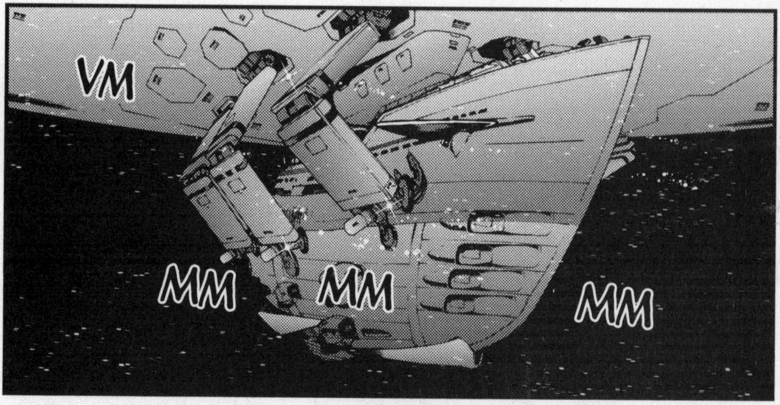
VM
MM
MM
MM

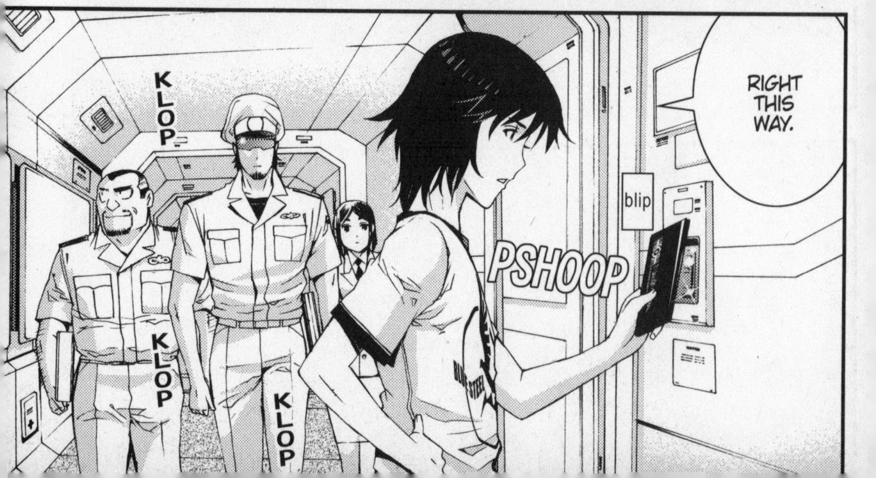
RIGHT THIS WAY.
blip
PSHOOP
KLOP
KLOP
KLOP
KLOP

PLEASE COME IN.

THANK YOU.

KLOP

KLOP

KLOP

KLOP

HAVEN'T BEEN ON THE 401 SINCE YOUR FATHER'S SENDOFF.

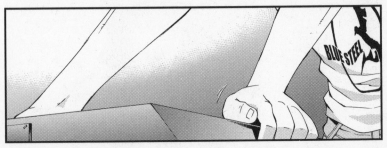

BLUE STEEL

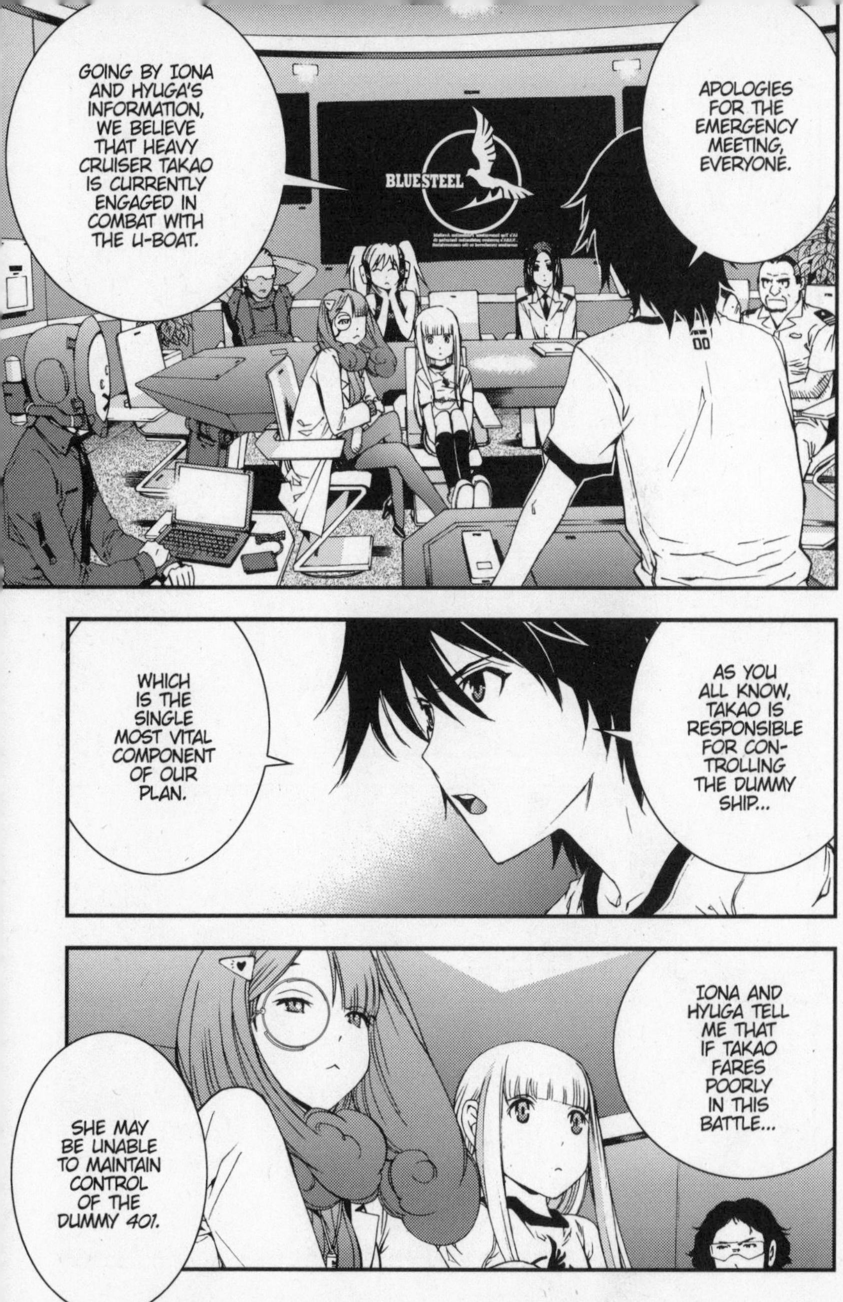
APOLOGIES FOR THE EMERGENCY MEETING, EVERYONE.
BLUESTEEL
GOING BY IONA AND HYUGA'S INFORMATION, WE BELIEVE THAT HEAVY CRUISER TAKAO IS CURRENTLY ENGAGED IN COMBAT WITH THE U-BOAT.
AS YOU ALL KNOW, TAKAO IS RESPONSIBLE FOR CON-TROLLING THE DUMMY SHIP...
WHICH IS THE SINGLE MOST VITAL COMPONENT OF OUR PLAN.
IONA AND HYUGA TELL ME THAT IF TAKAO FARES POORLY IN THIS BATTLE...
SHE MAY BE UNABLE TO MAINTAIN CONTROL OF THE DUMMY 401.

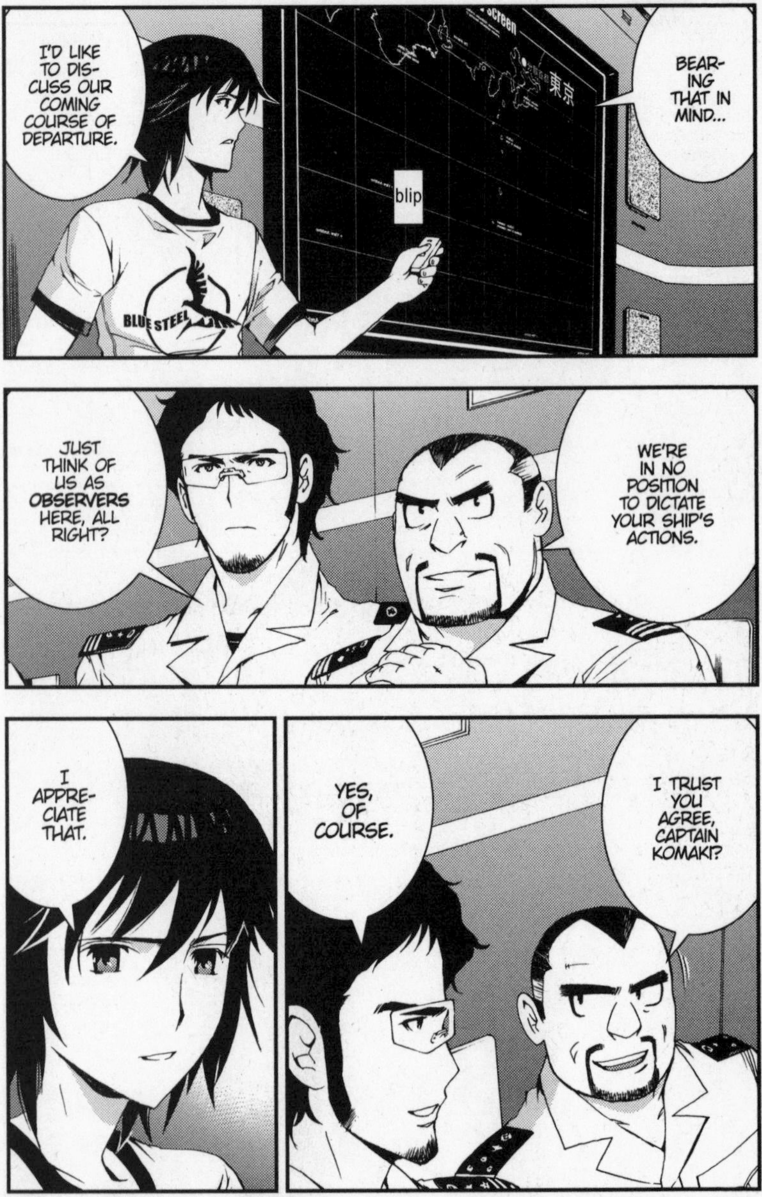
BEARING THAT IN MIND...
I'D LIKE TO DISCUSS OUR COMING COURSE OF DEPARTURE.
blip
BLUE STEEL
東京
WE'RE IN NO POSITION TO DICTATE YOUR SHIP'S ACTIONS.
JUST THINK OF US AS OBSERVERS HERE, ALL RIGHT?
I TRUST YOU AGREE, CAPTAIN KOMAKI?
YES, OF COURSE.
I APPRECIATE THAT.

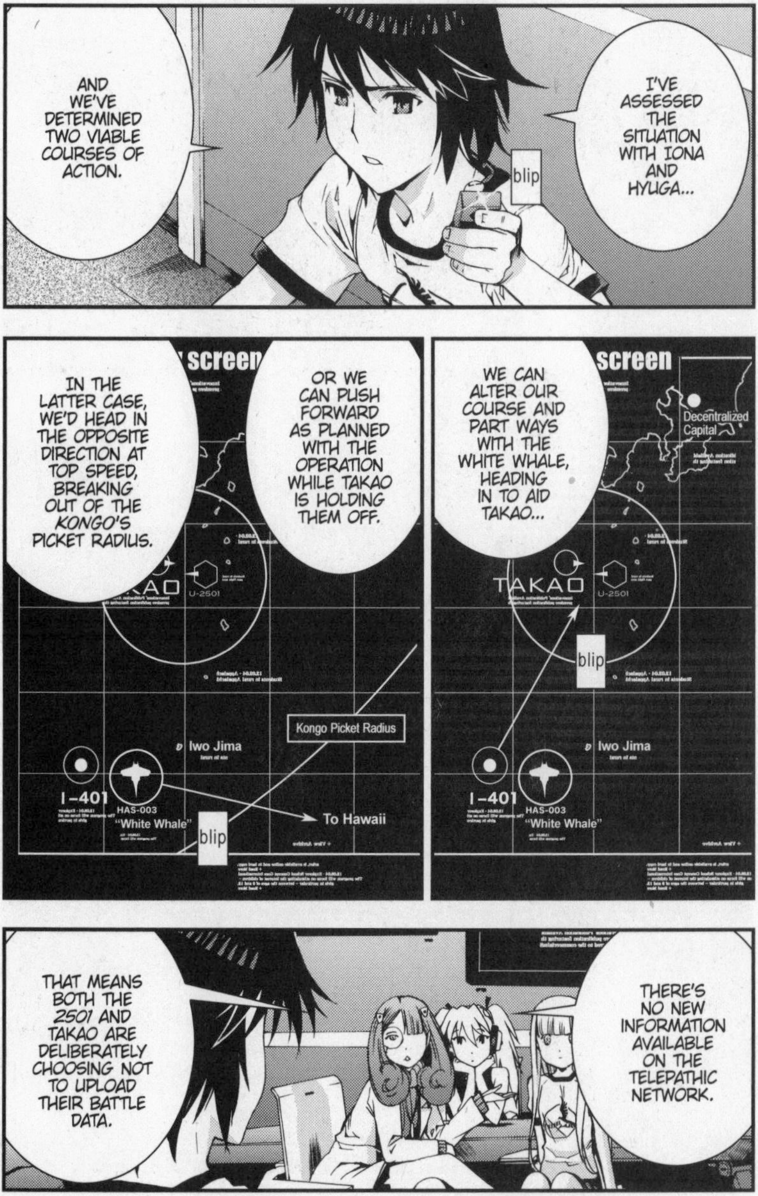
I'VE ASSESSED THE SITUATION WITH IONA AND HYUGA...
blip
AND WE'VE DETERMINED TWO VIABLE COURSES OF ACTION.
screen
Decentralized Capital
WE CAN ALTER OUR COURSE AND PART WAYS WITH THE WHITE WHALE, HEADING IN TO AID TAKAO...
TAKAO
U-2501
blip
Iwo Jima
I-401
HAS-003
"White Whale"
OR WE CAN PUSH FORWARD AS PLANNED WITH THE OPERATION WHILE TAKAO IS HOLDING THEM OFF.
IN THE LATTER CASE, WE'D HEAD IN THE OPPOSITE DIRECTION AT TOP SPEED, BREAKING OUT OF THE *KONGO'S* PICKET RADIUS.
screen
U-2501
Kongo Picket Radius
Iwo Jima
I-401
HAS-003
"White Whale"
To Hawaii
blip
THERE'S NO NEW INFORMATION AVAILABLE ON THE TELEPATHIC NETWORK.
THAT MEANS BOTH THE *2501* AND TAKAO ARE DELIBERATELY CHOOSING NOT TO UPLOAD THEIR BATTLE DATA.

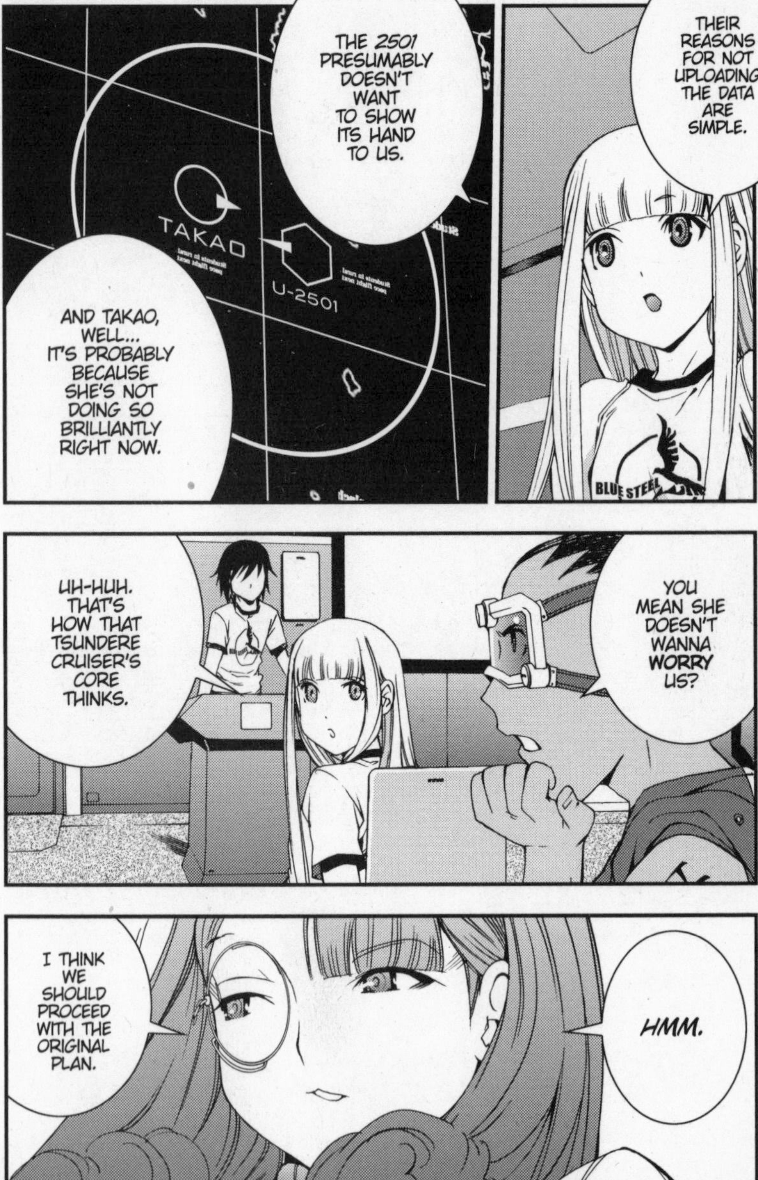
THEIR REASONS FOR NOT UPLOADING THE DATA ARE SIMPLE.
BLUE STEEL
THE 2501 PRESUMABLY DOESN'T WANT TO SHOW ITS HAND TO US.
TAKAO
U-2501
AND TAKAO, WELL... IT'S PROBABLY BECAUSE SHE'S NOT DOING SO BRILLIANTLY RIGHT NOW.
YOU MEAN SHE DOESN'T WANNA **WORRY** US?
UH-HUH. THAT'S HOW THAT TSUNDERE CRUISER'S CORE THINKS.
HMM.
I THINK WE SHOULD PROCEED WITH THE ORIGINAL PLAN.

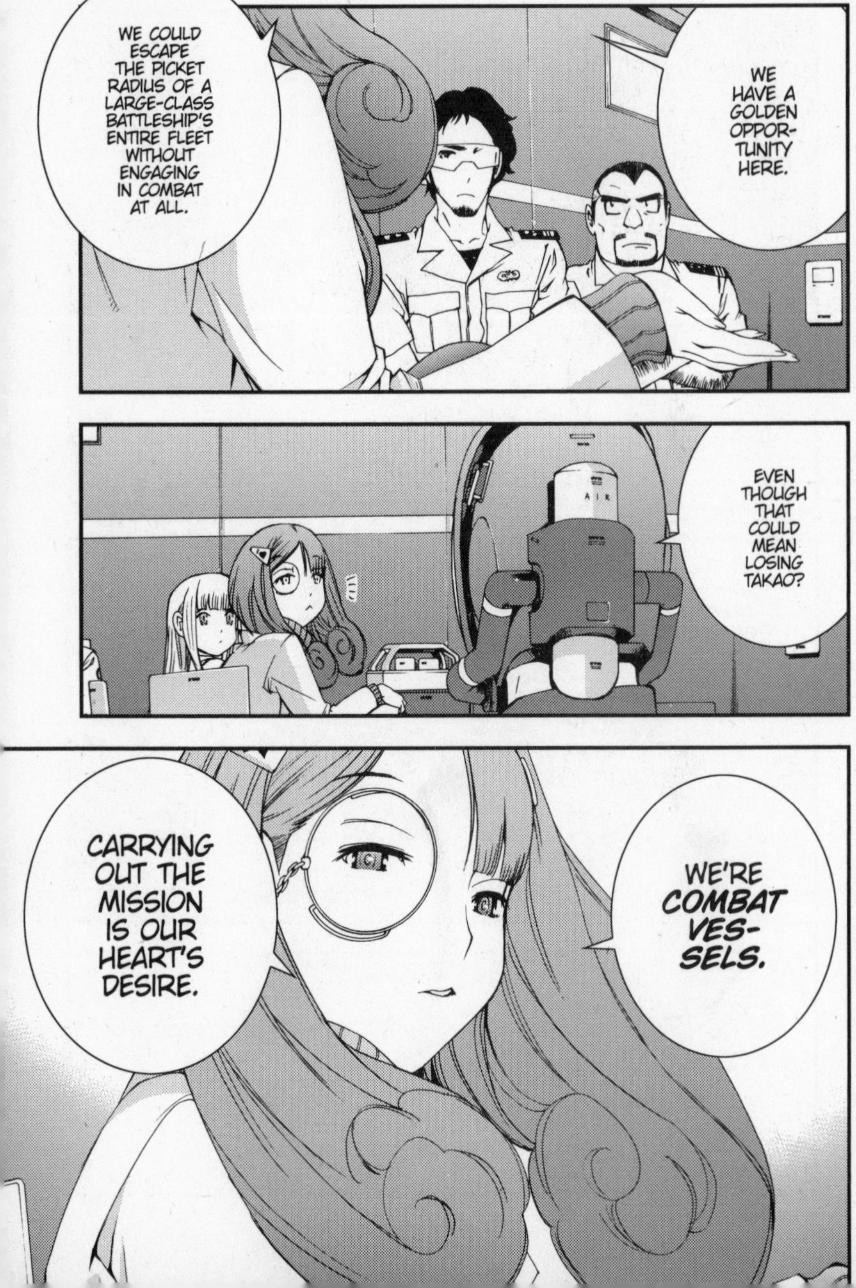
WE HAVE A GOLDEN OPPORTUNITY HERE.
WE COULD ESCAPE THE PICKET RADIUS OF A LARGE-CLASS BATTLESHIP'S ENTIRE FLEET WITHOUT ENGAGING IN COMBAT AT ALL.
EVEN THOUGH THAT COULD MEAN LOSING TAKAO?
WE'RE **COMBAT VESSELS.**
CARRYING OUT THE MISSION IS OUR HEART'S DESIRE.

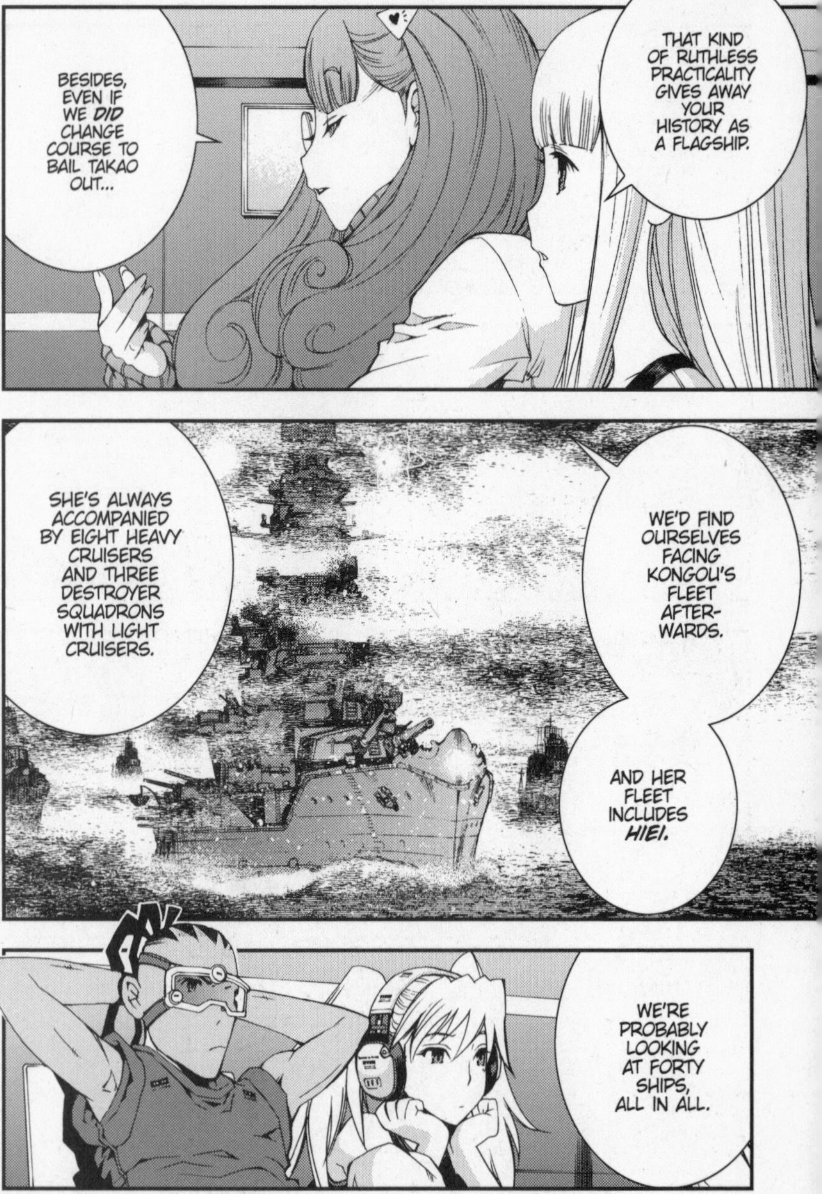
THAT KIND OF RUTHLESS PRACTICALITY GIVES AWAY YOUR HISTORY AS A FLAGSHIP.
BESIDES, EVEN IF WE *DID* CHANGE COURSE TO BAIL TAKAO OUT...
WE'D FIND OURSELVES FACING KONGOU'S FLEET AFTER-WARDS.
SHE'S ALWAYS ACCOMPANIED BY EIGHT HEAVY CRUISERS AND THREE DESTROYER SQUADRONS WITH LIGHT CRUISERS.
AND HER FLEET INCLUDES ***HIEI.***
WE'RE PROBABLY LOOKING AT FORTY SHIPS, ALL IN ALL.

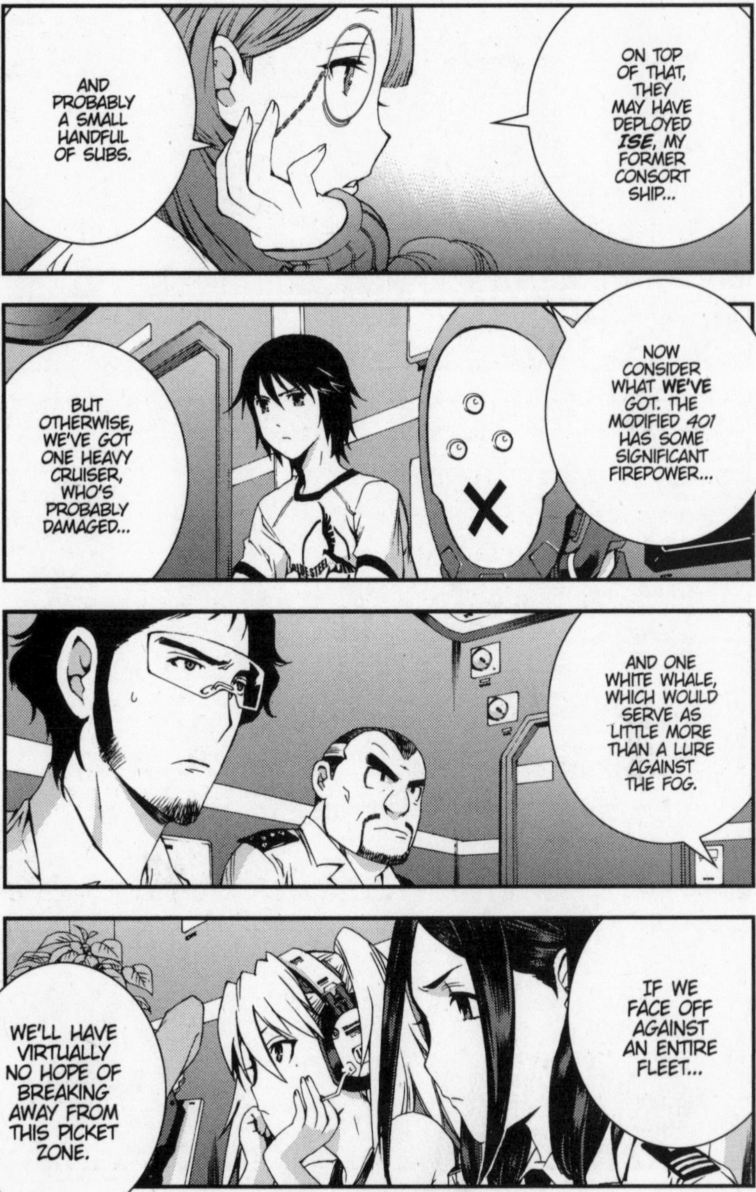
ON TOP OF THAT, THEY MAY HAVE DEPLOYED ISE, MY FORMER CONSORT SHIP...
AND PROBABLY A SMALL HANDFUL OF SUBS.
NOW CONSIDER WHAT WE'VE GOT. THE MODIFIED 401 HAS SOME SIGNIFICANT FIREPOWER...
BUT OTHERWISE, WE'VE GOT ONE HEAVY CRUISER, WHO'S PROBABLY DAMAGED...
AND ONE WHITE WHALE, WHICH WOULD SERVE AS LITTLE MORE THAN A LURE AGAINST THE FOG.
IF WE FACE OFF AGAINST AN ENTIRE FLEET...
WE'LL HAVE VIRTUALLY NO HOPE OF BREAKING AWAY FROM THIS PICKET ZONE.

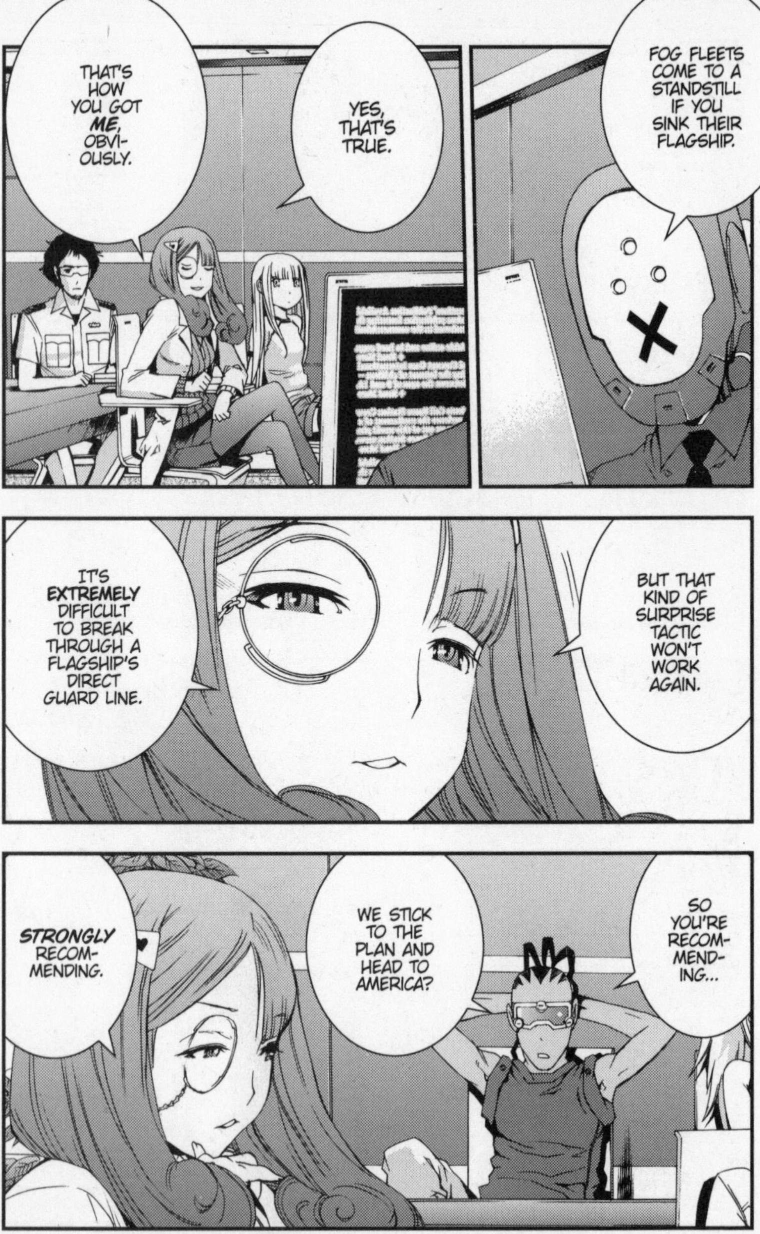
FOG FLEETS COME TO A STANDSTILL IF YOU SINK THEIR FLAGSHIP.
YES, THAT'S TRUE.
THAT'S HOW YOU GOT *ME*, OBVI-OUSLY.
BUT THAT KIND OF SURPRISE TACTIC WON'T WORK AGAIN.
IT'S **EXTREMELY** DIFFICULT TO BREAK THROUGH A FLAGSHIP'S DIRECT GUARD LINE.
SO YOU'RE RECOM-MEND-ING...
WE STICK TO THE PLAN AND HEAD TO AMERICA?
STRONGLY RECOM-MENDING.

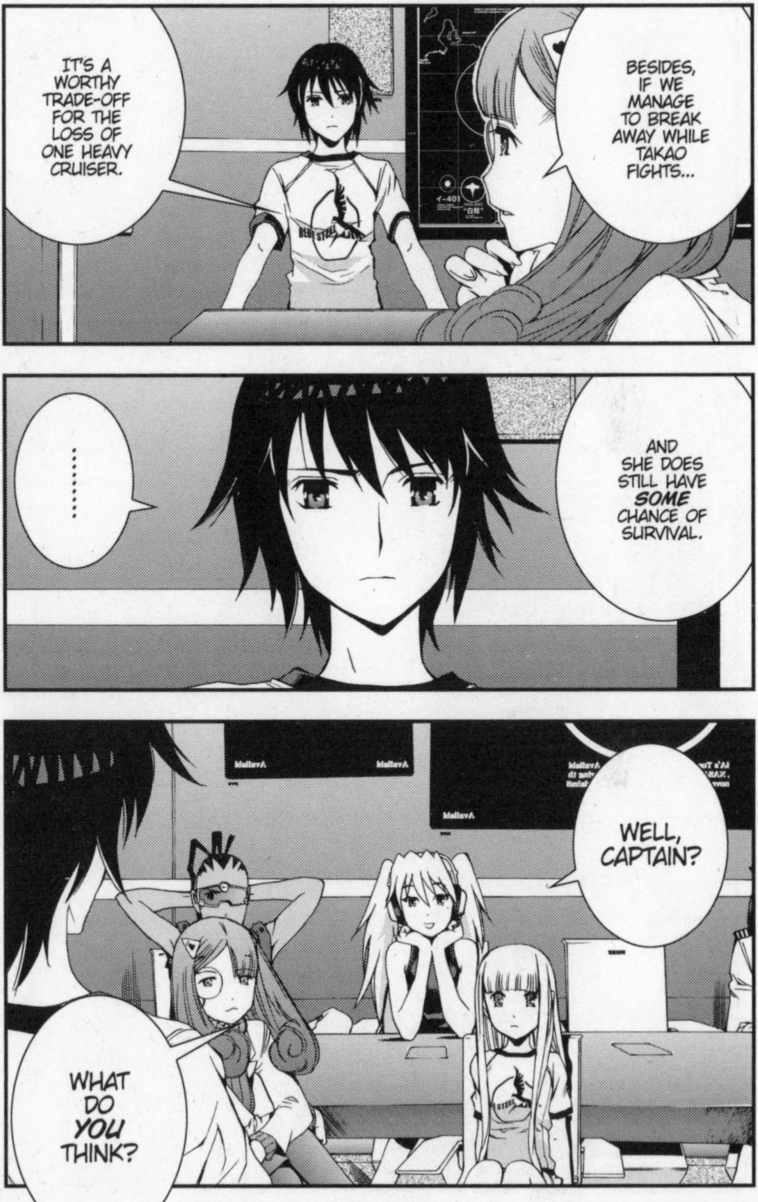
BESIDES, IF WE MANAGE TO BREAK AWAY WHILE TAKAO FIGHTS...
IT'S A WORTHY TRADE-OFF FOR THE LOSS OF ONE HEAVY CRUISER.
AND SHE DOES STILL HAVE SOME CHANCE OF SURVIVAL.
......
WELL, CAPTAIN?
WHAT DO YOU THINK?

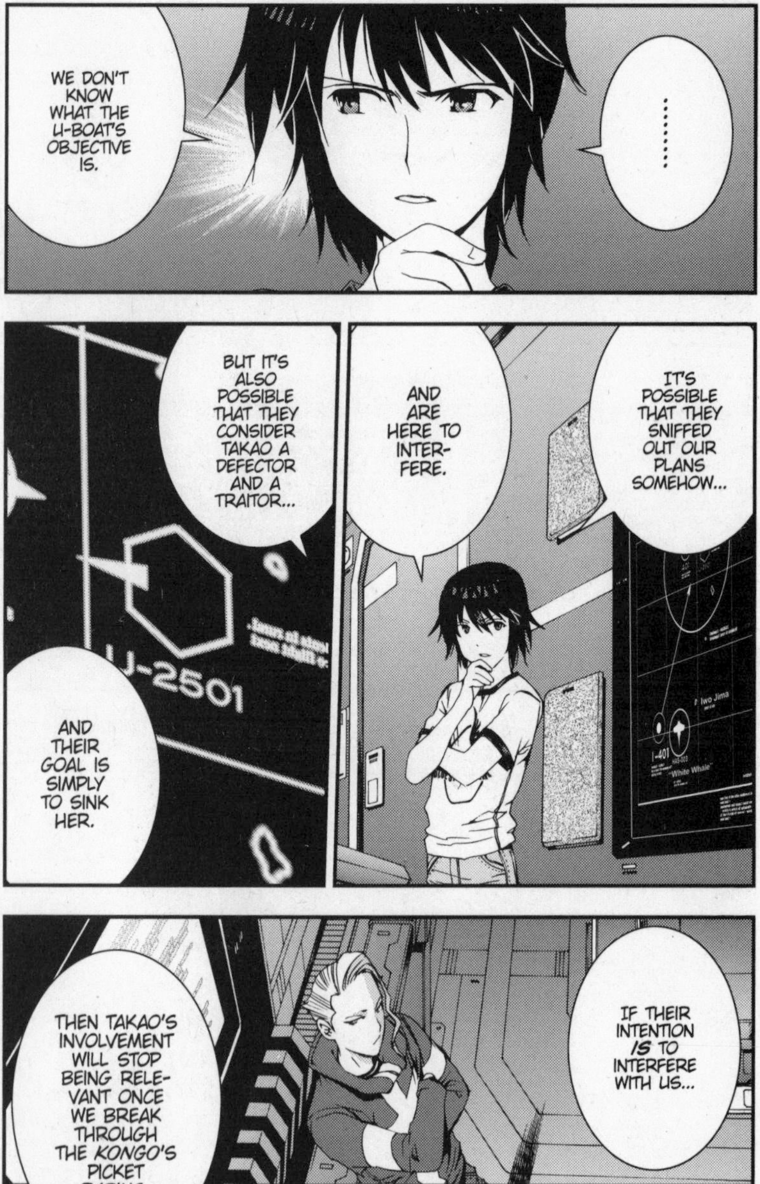
……
WE DON'T KNOW WHAT THE U-BOAT'S OBJECTIVE IS.
IT'S POSSIBLE THAT THEY SNIFFED OUT OUR PLANS SOMEHOW...
AND ARE HERE TO INTER-FERE.
Iwo Jima
I-401
"White Whale"
BUT IT'S ALSO POSSIBLE THAT THEY CONSIDER TAKAO A DEFECTOR AND A TRAITOR...
U-2501
AND THEIR GOAL IS SIMPLY TO SINK HER.
IF THEIR INTENTION *IS* TO INTERFERE WITH US...
THEN TAKAO'S INVOLVEMENT WILL STOP BEING RELE-VANT ONCE WE BREAK THROUGH THE *KONGO*'S PICKET RADIUS.

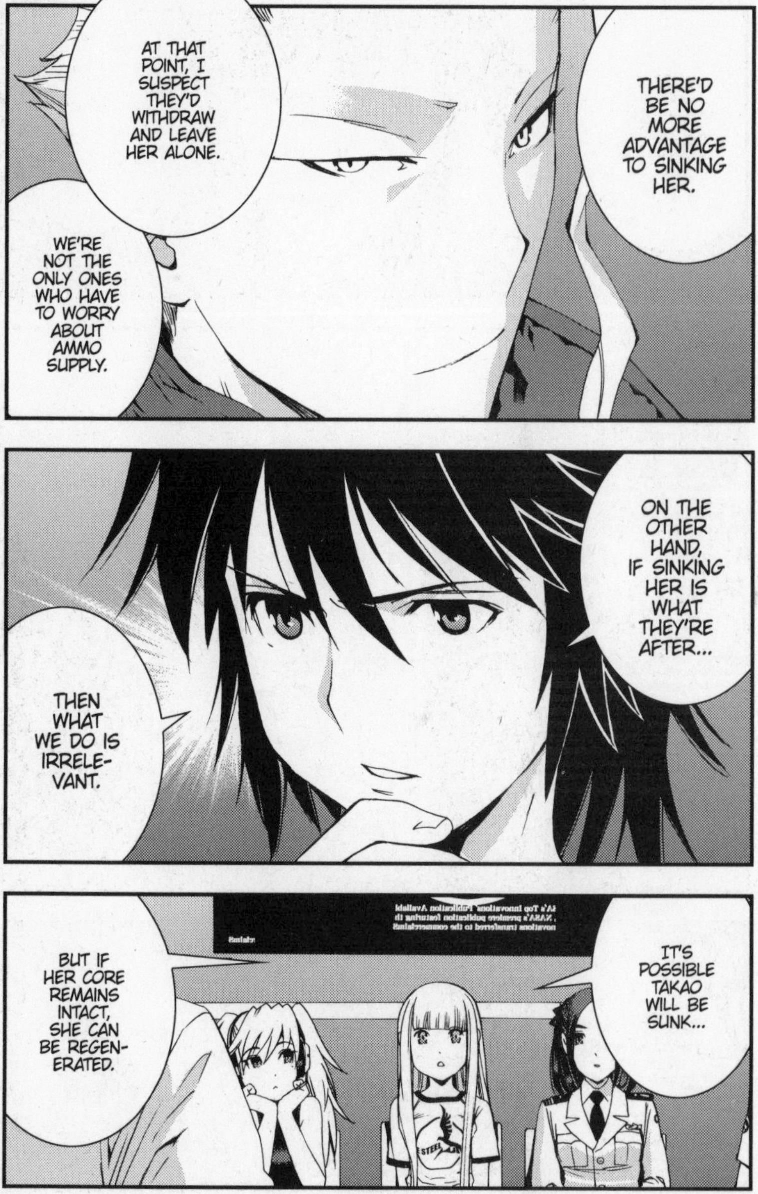
THERE'D BE NO MORE ADVANTAGE TO SINKING HER.
AT THAT POINT, I SUSPECT THEY'D WITHDRAW AND LEAVE HER ALONE.
WE'RE NOT THE ONLY ONES WHO HAVE TO WORRY ABOUT AMMO SUPPLY.
ON THE OTHER HAND, IF SINKING HER IS WHAT THEY'RE AFTER...
THEN WHAT WE DO IS IRRELE-VANT.
IT'S POSSIBLE TAKAO WILL BE SUNK...
BUT IF HER CORE REMAINS INTACT, SHE CAN BE REGENER-ATED.

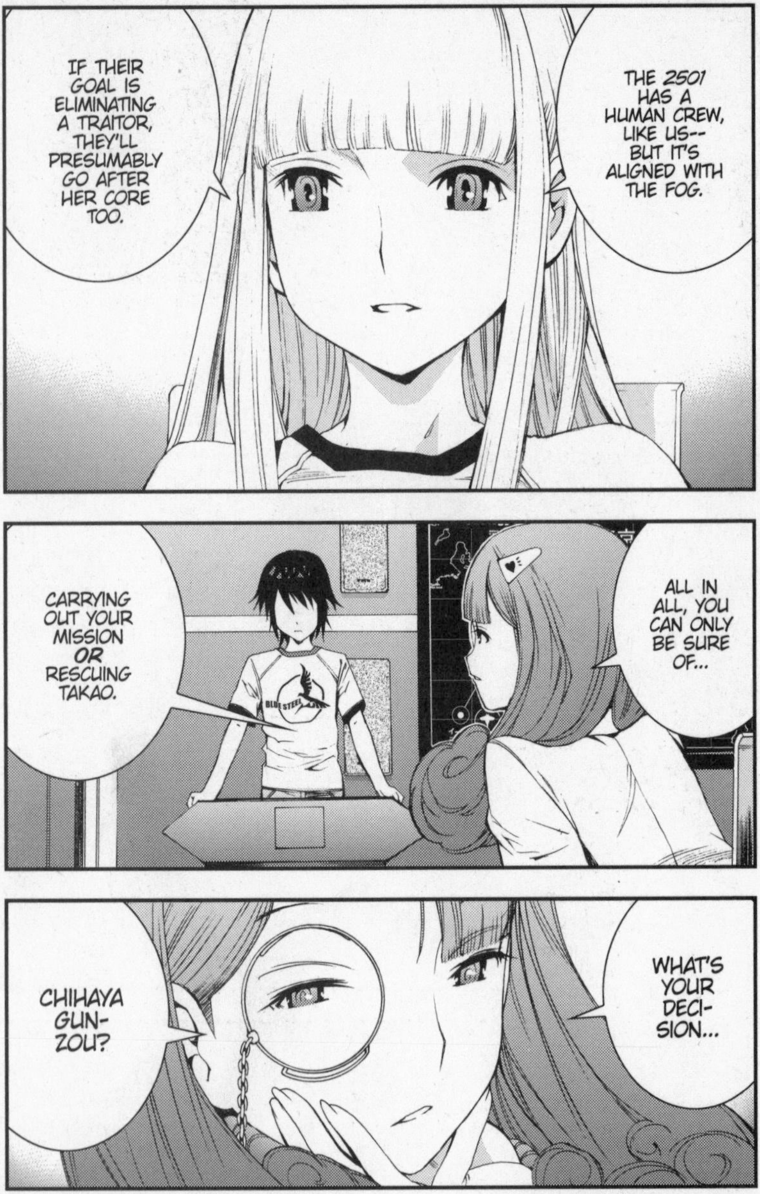
THE 2501 HAS A HUMAN CREW, LIKE US-- BUT IT'S ALIGNED WITH THE FOG.
IF THEIR GOAL IS ELIMINATING A TRAITOR, THEY'LL PRESUMABLY GO AFTER HER CORE TOO.
ALL IN ALL, YOU CAN ONLY BE SURE OF...
CARRYING OUT YOUR MISSION *OR* RESCUING TAKAO.
BLUE STEEL
WHAT'S YOUR DECI-SION...
CHIHAYA GUN-ZOU?

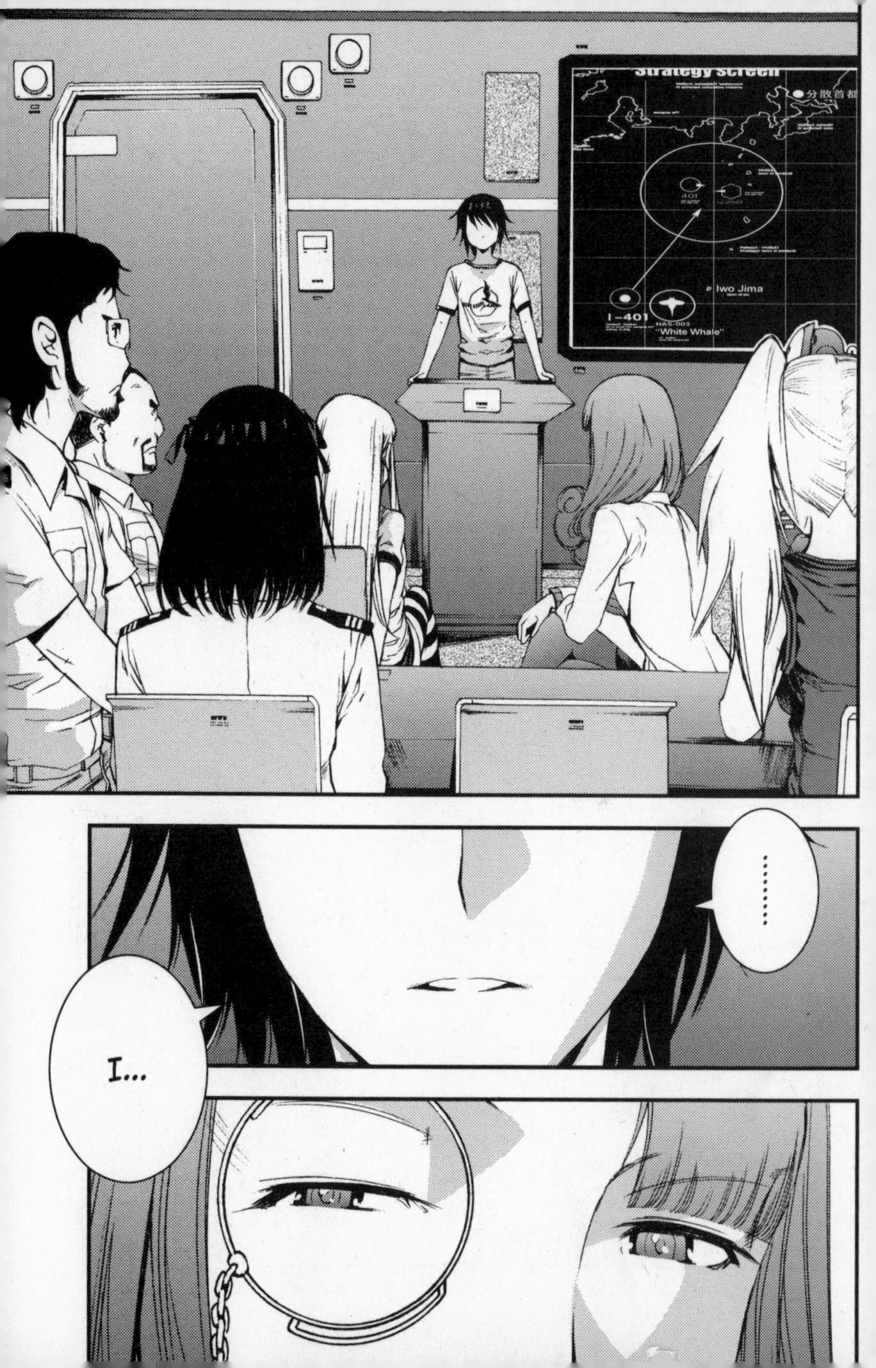
Strategy Screen
分散首都
401
U-2501
Iwo Jima
I-401
HA5-003
"White Whale"
......
I...

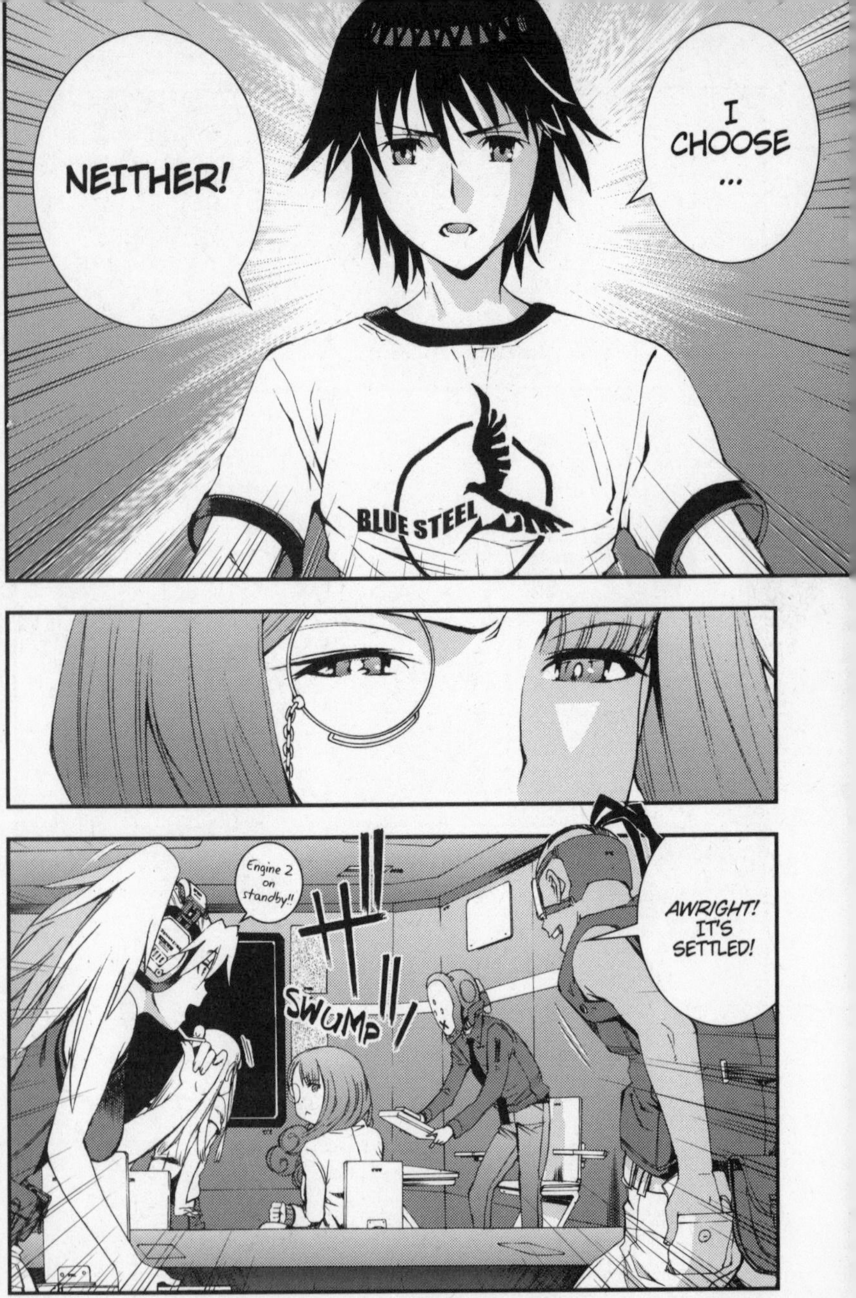
I CHOOSE ...
NEITHER!
BLUE STEEL
AWRIGHT! IT'S SETTLED!
Engine 2 on standby!!
SWUMP

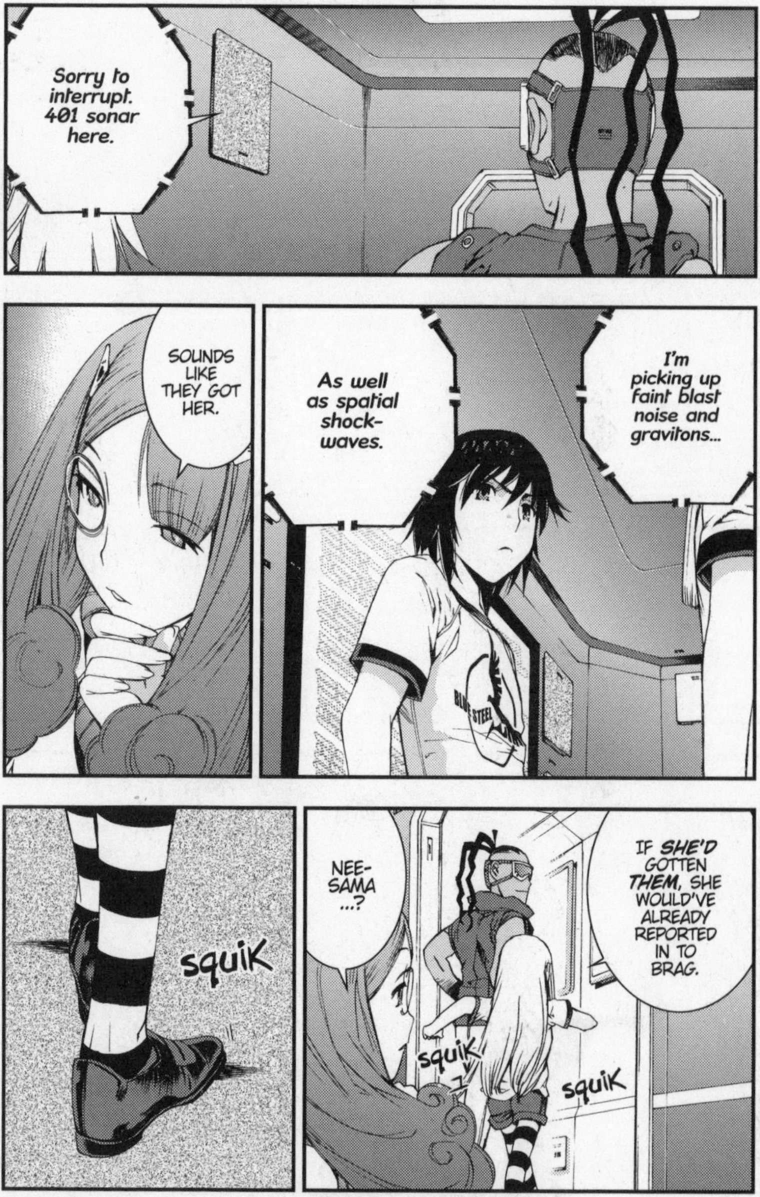
Sorry to interrupt. 401 sonar here.
I'm picking up faint blast noise and gravitons...
As well as spatial shock-waves.
SOUNDS LIKE THEY GOT HER.
IF *SHE'D* GOTTEN *THEM*, SHE WOULD'VE ALREADY REPORTED IN TO BRAG.
NEE-SAMA...?
squik
squik
squik

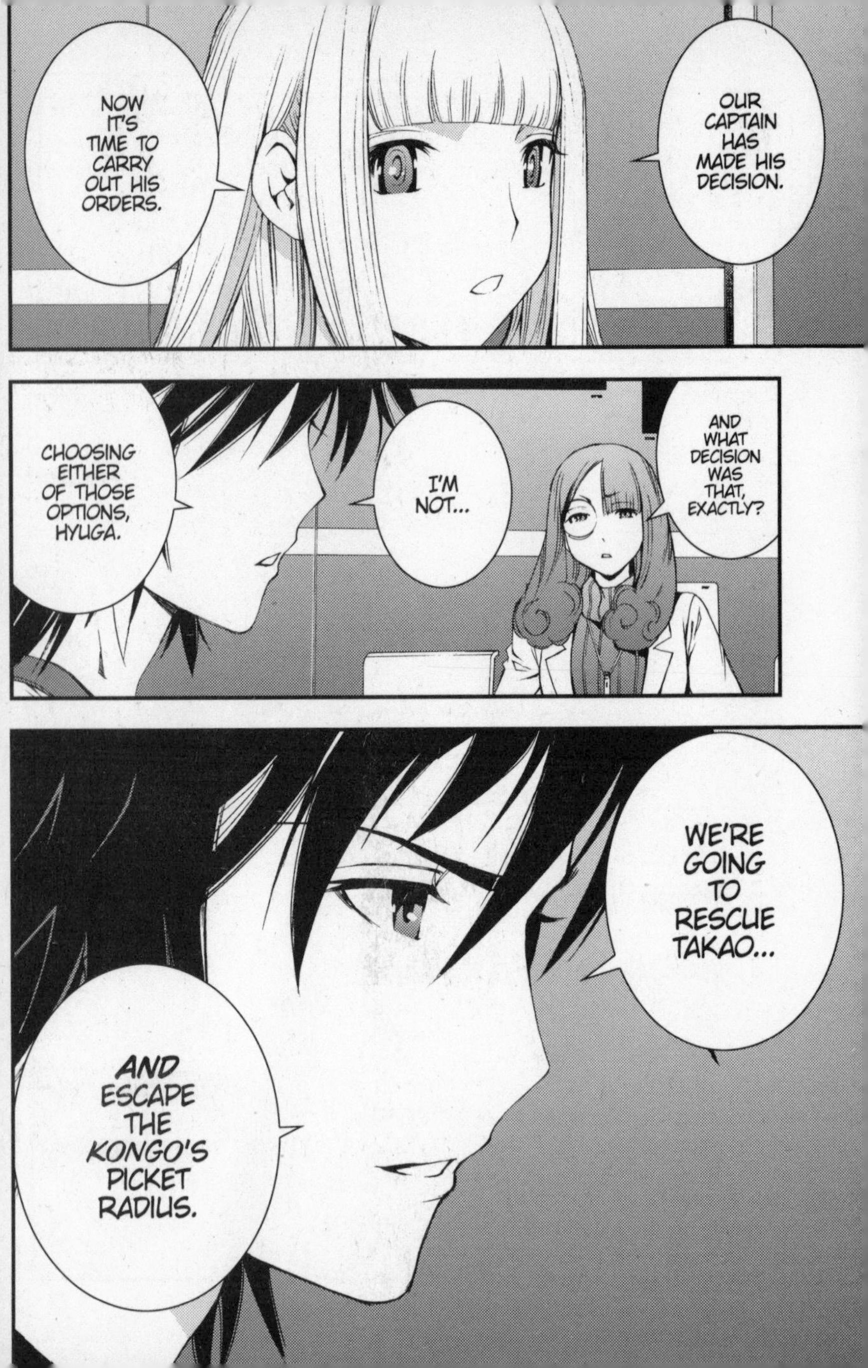
OUR CAPTAIN HAS MADE HIS DECISION.
NOW IT'S TIME TO CARRY OUT HIS ORDERS.
AND WHAT DECISION WAS THAT, EXACTLY?
I'M NOT...
CHOOSING EITHER OF THOSE OPTIONS, HYUGA.
WE'RE GOING TO RESCUE TAKAO...
AND ESCAPE THE *KONGO'S* PICKET RADIUS.

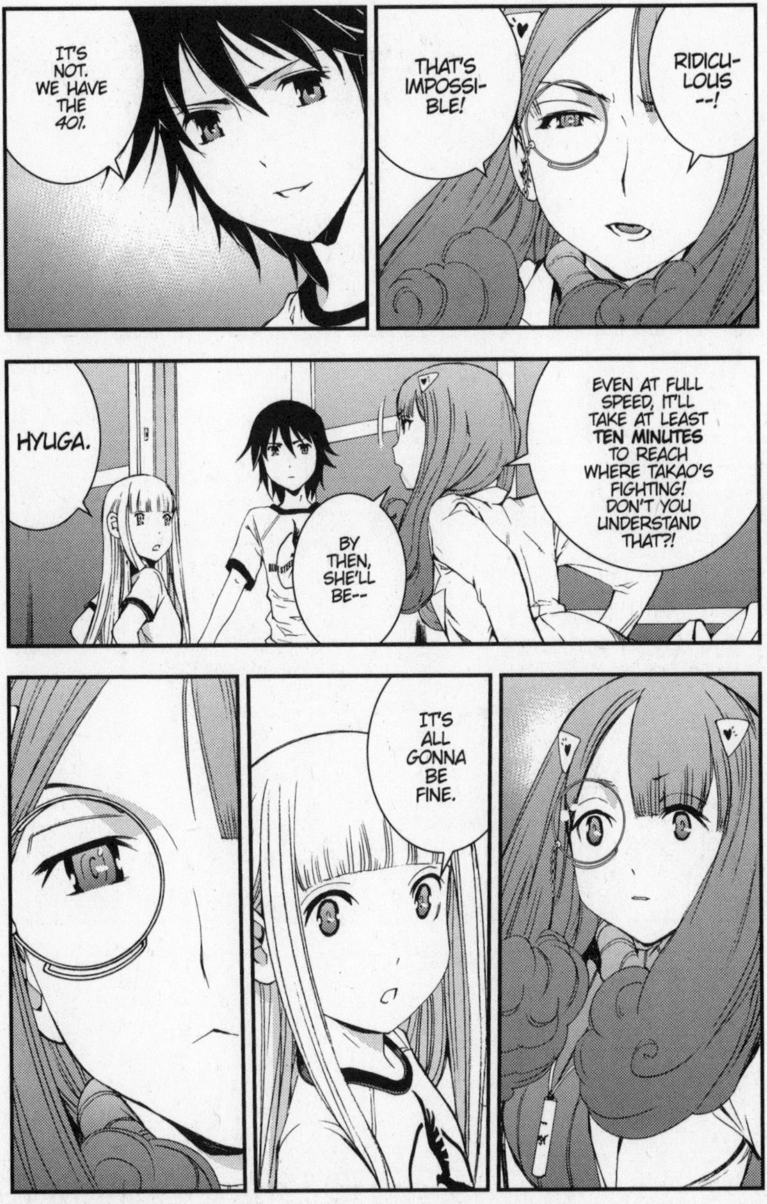
RIDICU-LOUS--!
THAT'S IMPOSSI-BLE!
IT'S NOT. WE HAVE THE 401.
EVEN AT FULL SPEED, IT'LL TAKE AT LEAST **TEN MINUTES** TO REACH WHERE TAKAO'S FIGHTING! DON'T YOU UNDERSTAND THAT?!
BY THEN, SHE'LL BE--
HYUGA.
IT'S ALL GONNA BE FINE.

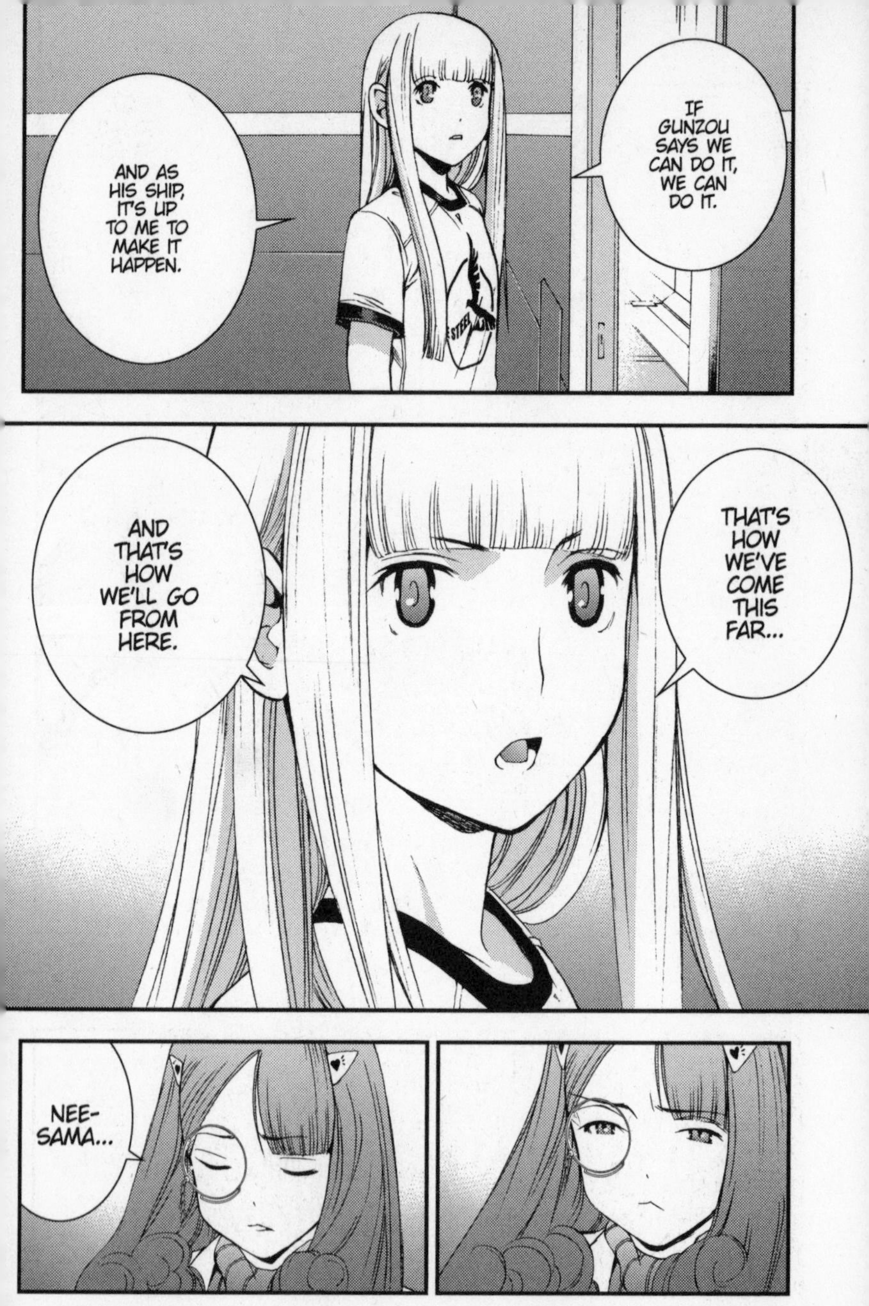
IF GUNZOU SAYS WE CAN DO IT, WE CAN DO IT.
AND AS HIS SHIP, IT'S UP TO ME TO MAKE IT HAPPEN.
THAT'S HOW WE'VE COME THIS FAR...
AND THAT'S HOW WE'LL GO FROM HERE.
NEE-SAMA...

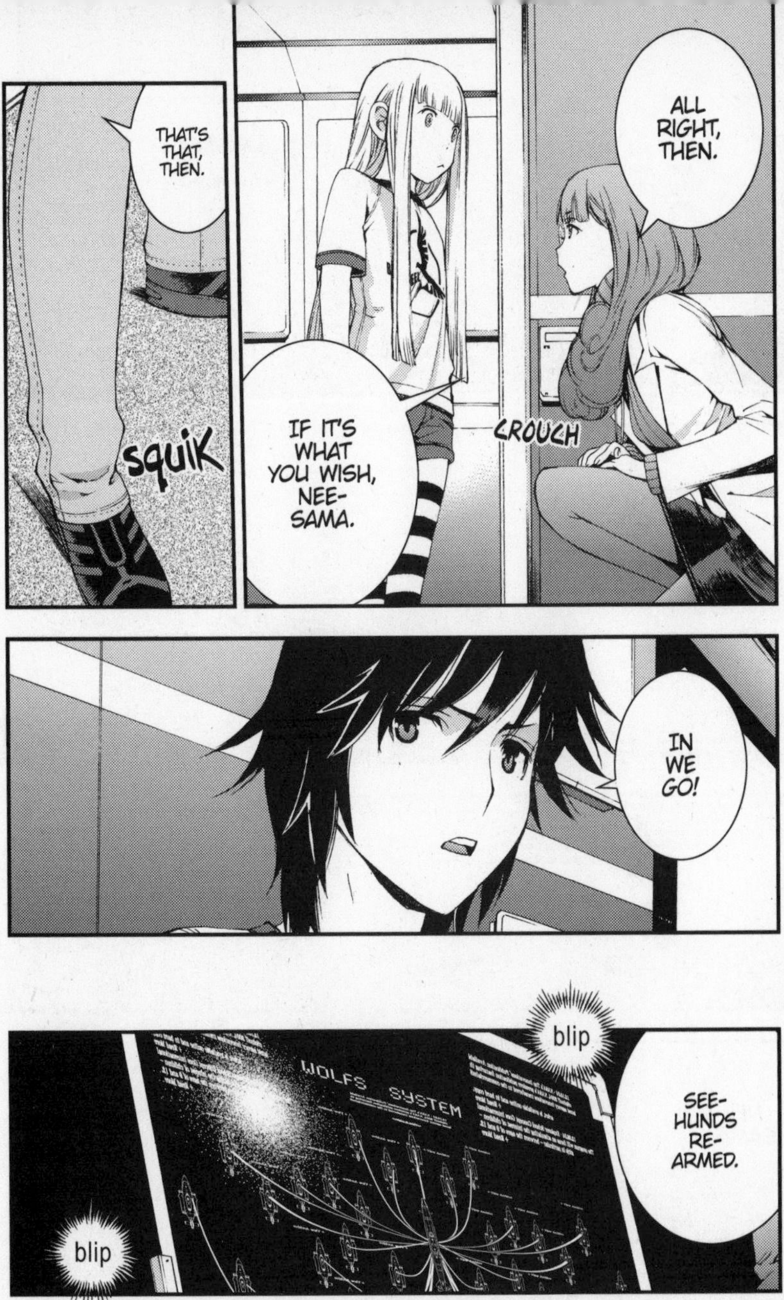
ALL RIGHT, THEN.
IF IT'S WHAT YOU WISH, NEE-SAMA.
CROUCH
THAT'S THAT, THEN.
SQUIK
IN WE GO!
blip
SEE-HUNDS RE-ARMED.
WOLFS SYSTEM
blip

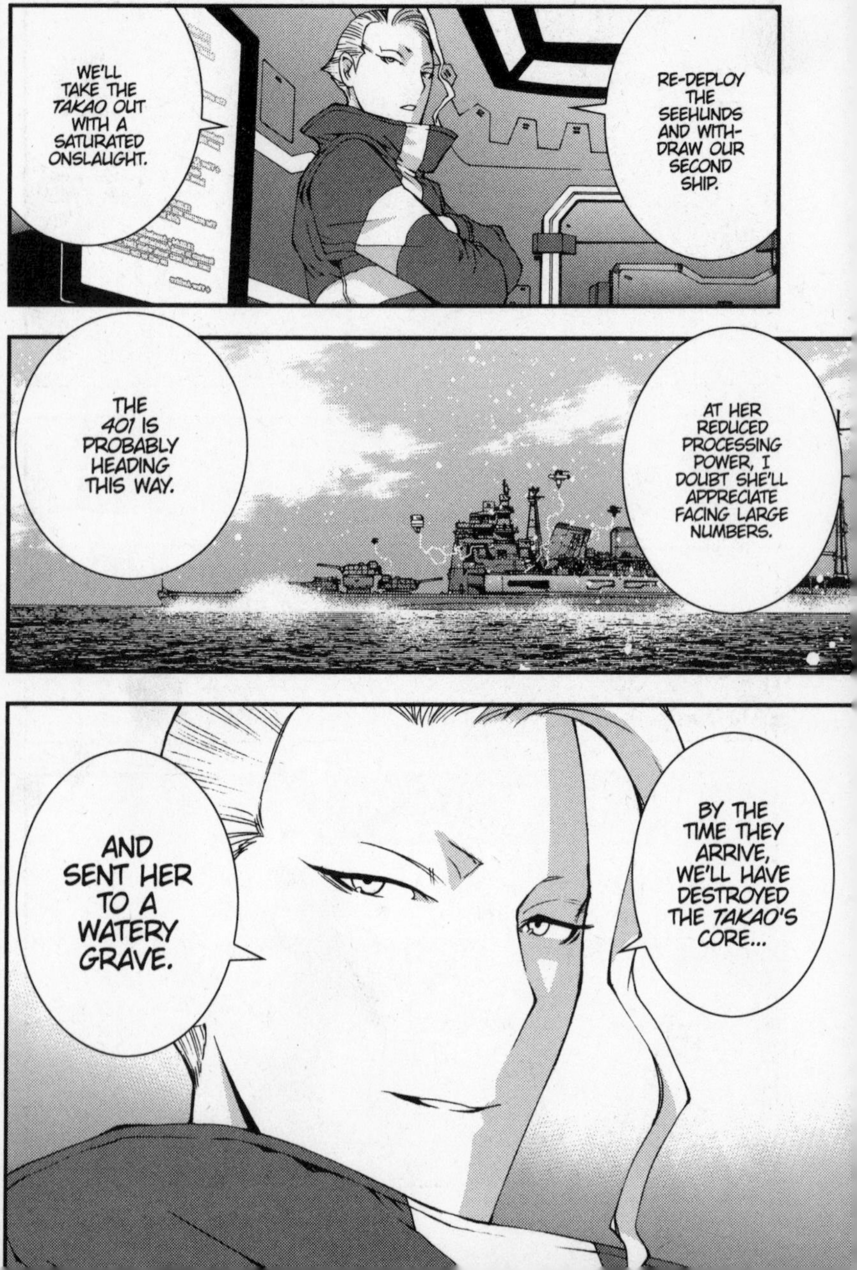
RE-DEPLOY THE SEEHUNDS AND WITH-DRAW OUR SECOND SHIP.
WE'LL TAKE THE *TAKAO* OUT WITH A SATURATED ONSLAUGHT.
AT HER REDUCED PROCESSING POWER, I DOUBT SHE'LL APPRECIATE FACING LARGE NUMBERS.
THE *401* IS PROBABLY HEADING THIS WAY.
BY THE TIME THEY ARRIVE, WE'LL HAVE DESTROYED THE *TAKAO*'S CORE...
AND SENT HER TO A WATERY GRAVE.

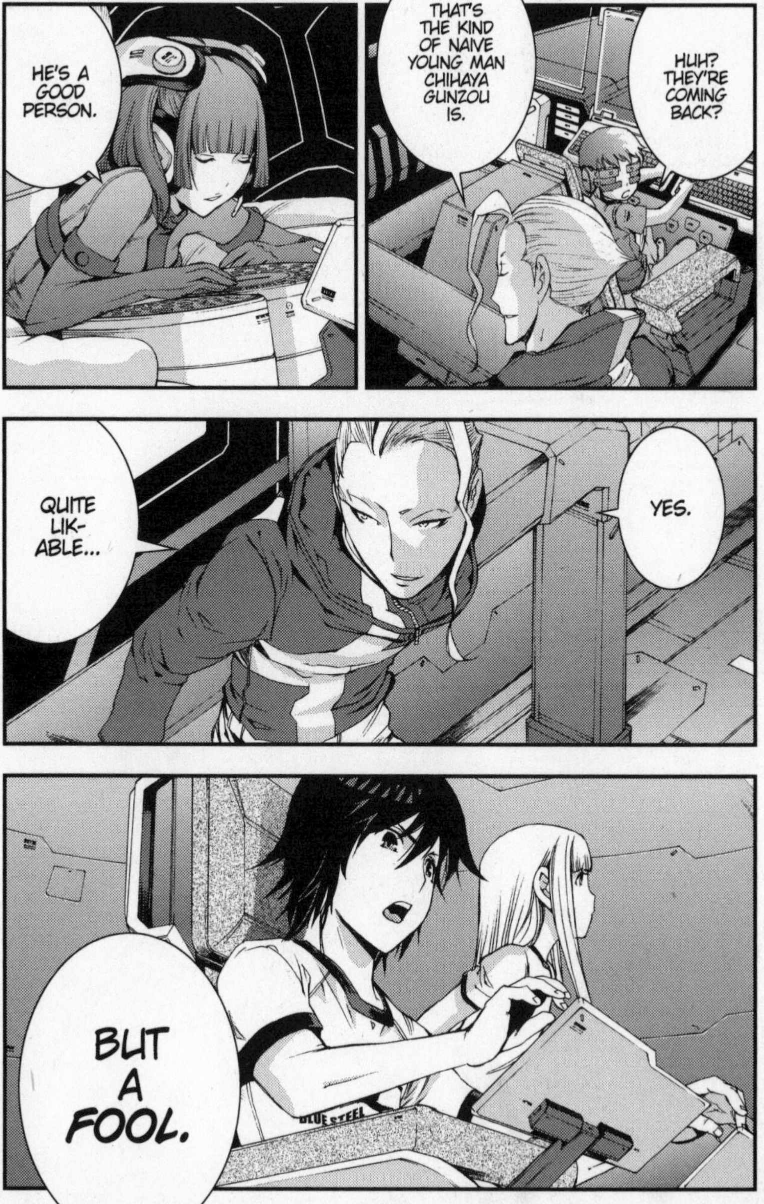
HUH? THEY'RE COMING BACK?
THAT'S THE KIND OF NAIVE YOUNG MAN CHIHAYA GUNZOU IS.
HE'S A GOOD PERSON.
YES.
QUITE LIK-ABLE...
BLUE STEEL
BUT A FOOL.

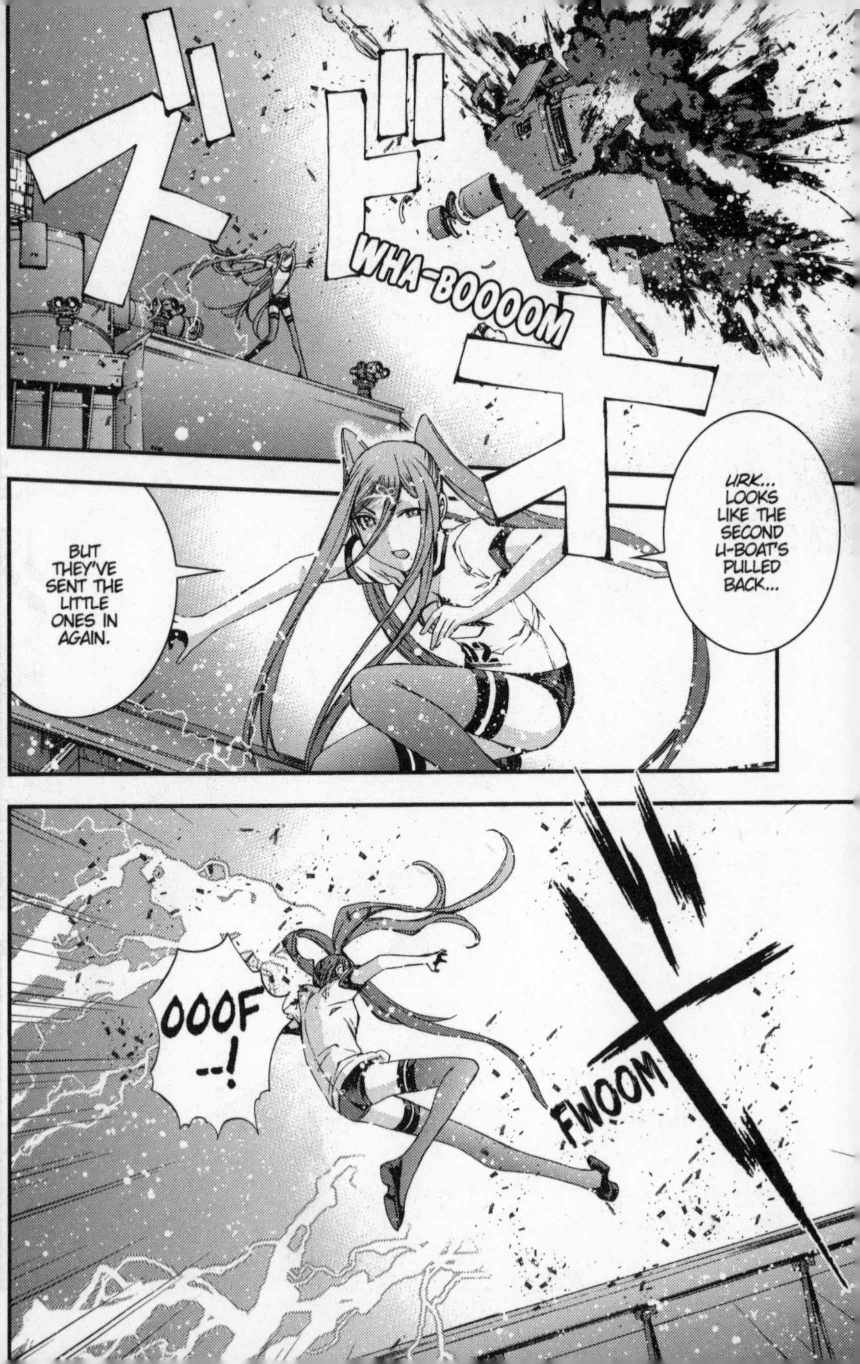
WHA-BOOOOM
URK... LOOKS LIKE THE SECOND U-BOAT'S PULLED BACK...
BUT THEY'VE SENT THE LITTLE ONES IN AGAIN.
FWOOM
OOOF --!

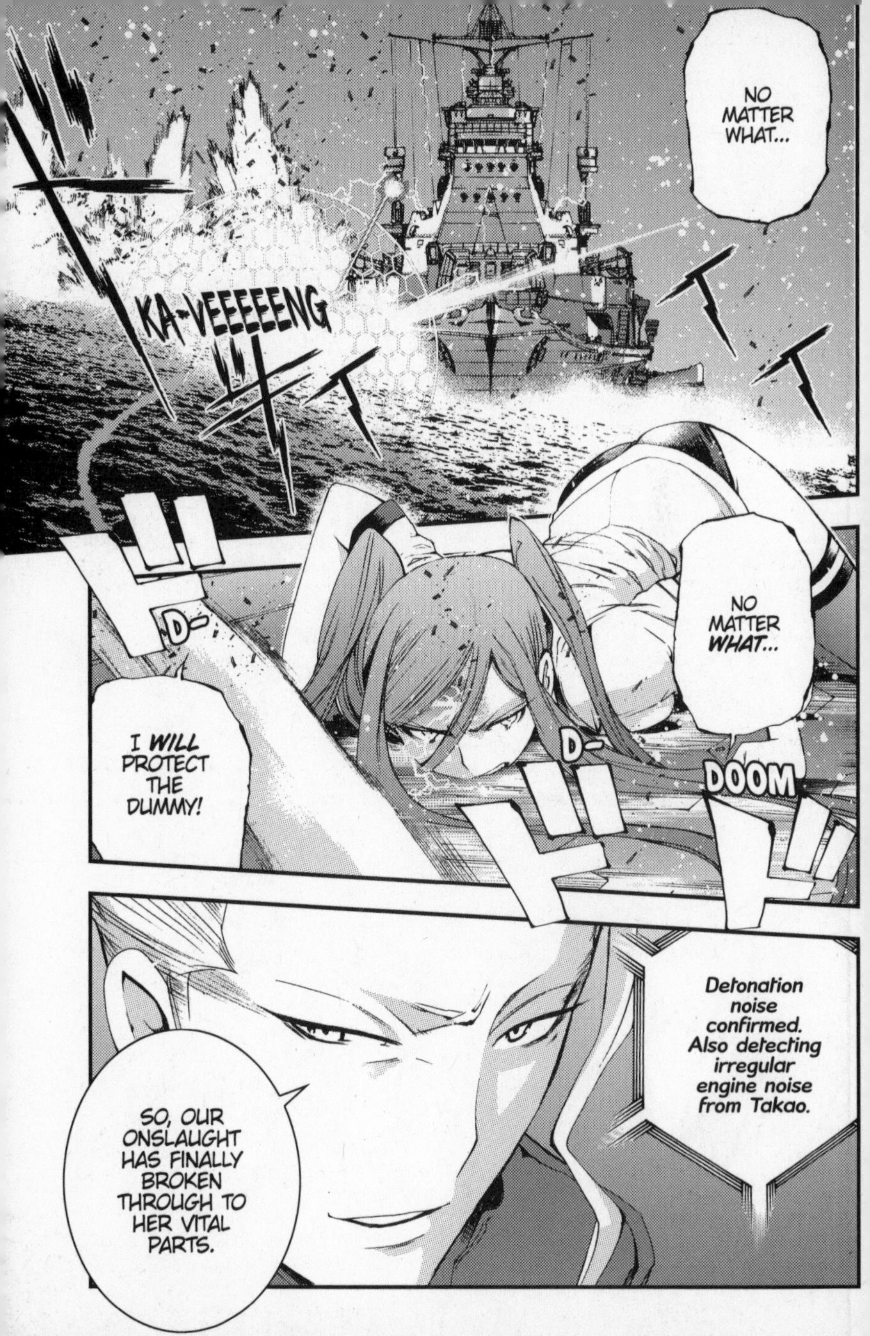
NO MATTER WHAT...
KA-VEEEEEENG
NO MATTER WHAT...
D-
D-
DOOM
I WILL PROTECT THE DUMMY!
Detonation noise confirmed. Also detecting irregular engine noise from Takao.
SO, OUR ONSLAUGHT HAS FINALLY BROKEN THROUGH TO HER VITAL PARTS.

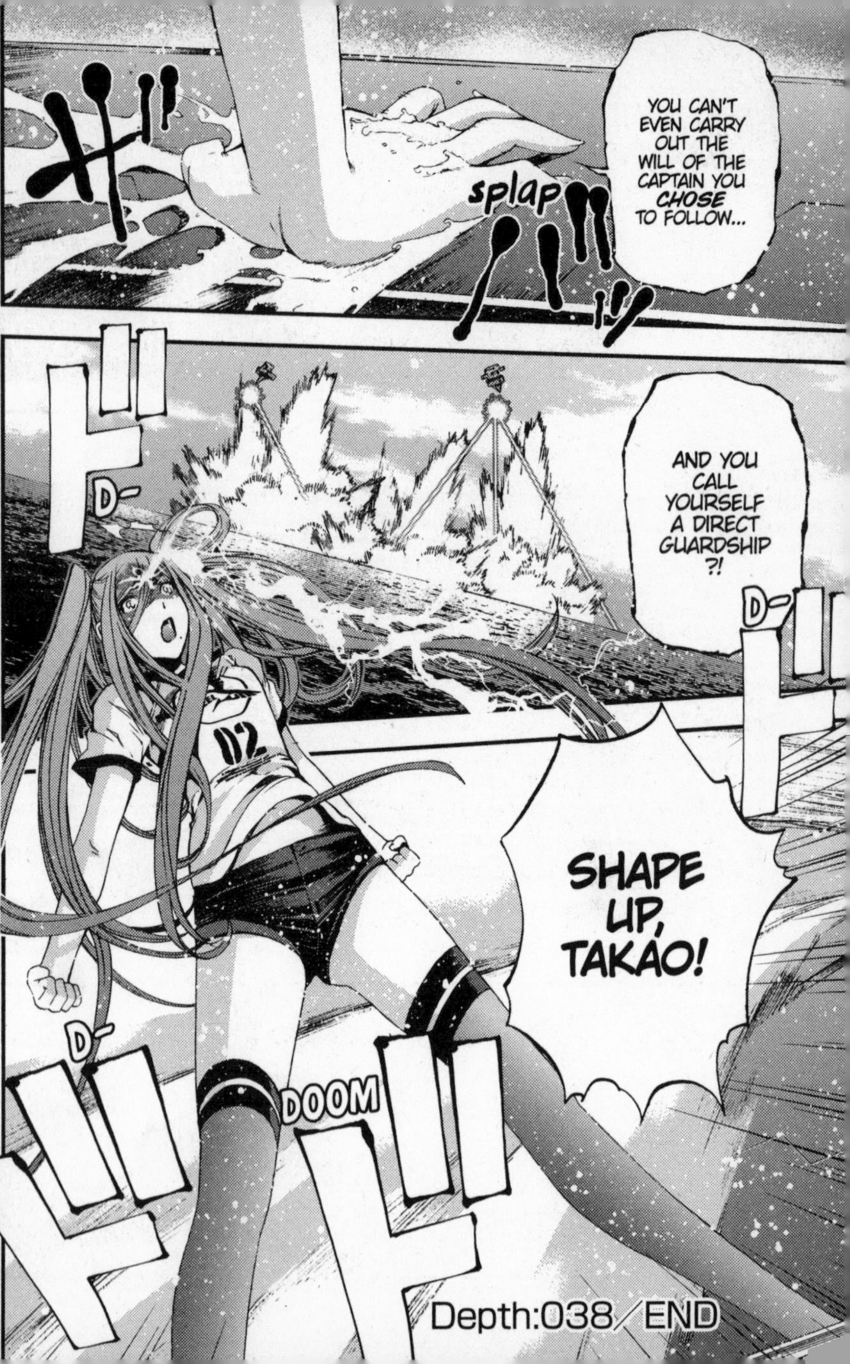
YOU CAN'T EVEN CARRY OUT THE WILL OF THE CAPTAIN YOU CHOSE TO FOLLOW...
splap
AND YOU CALL YOURSELF A DIRECT GUARDSHIP ?!
D-
SHAPE UP, TAKAO!
D-
D-
DOOM

Depth:038/END

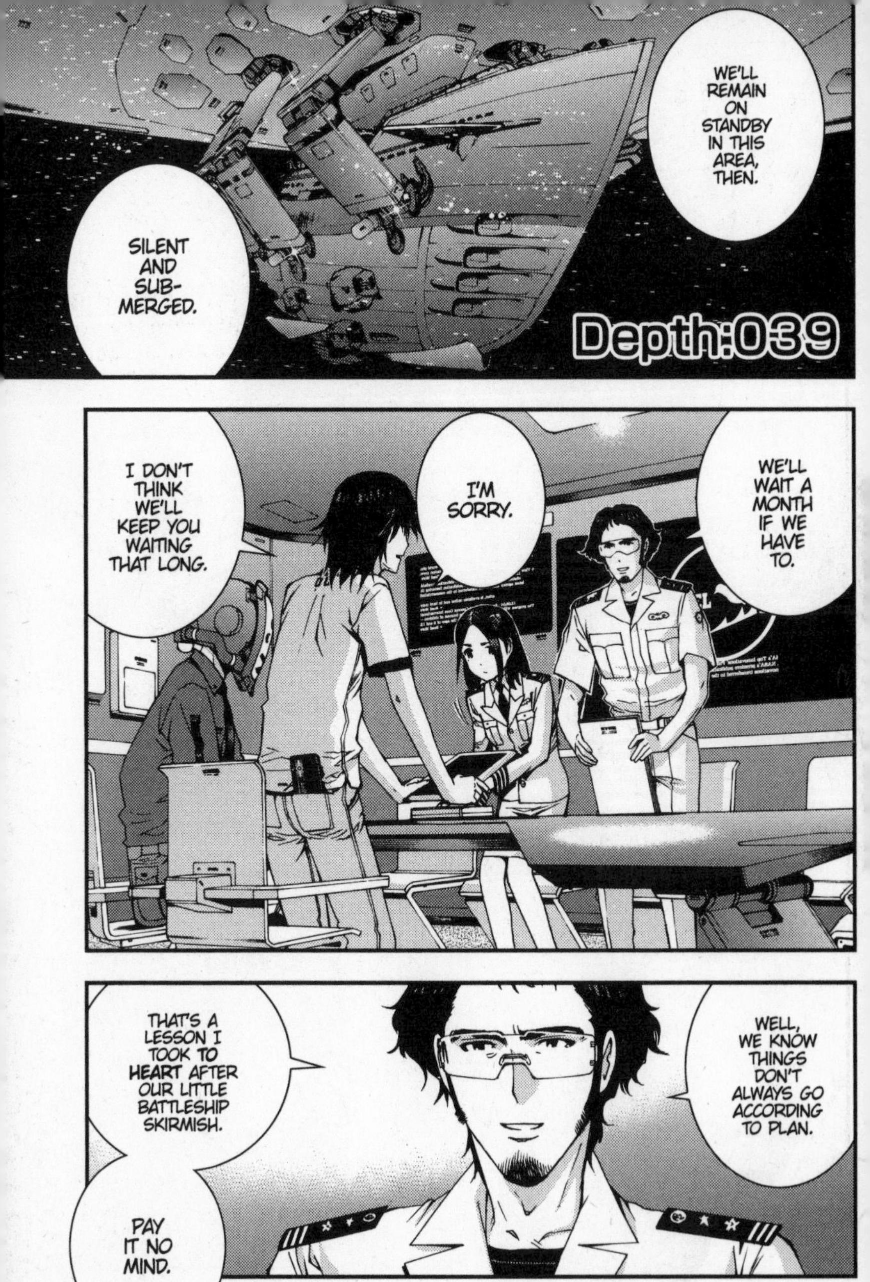
WE'LL REMAIN ON STANDBY IN THIS AREA, THEN.
SILENT AND SUB-MERGED.
Depth:039
WE'LL WAIT A MONTH IF WE HAVE TO.
I'M SORRY.
I DON'T THINK WE'LL KEEP YOU WAITING THAT LONG.
WELL, WE KNOW THINGS DON'T ALWAYS GO ACCORDING TO PLAN.
THAT'S A LESSON I TOOK TO **HEART** AFTER OUR LITTLE BATTLESHIP SKIRMISH.
PAY IT NO MIND.

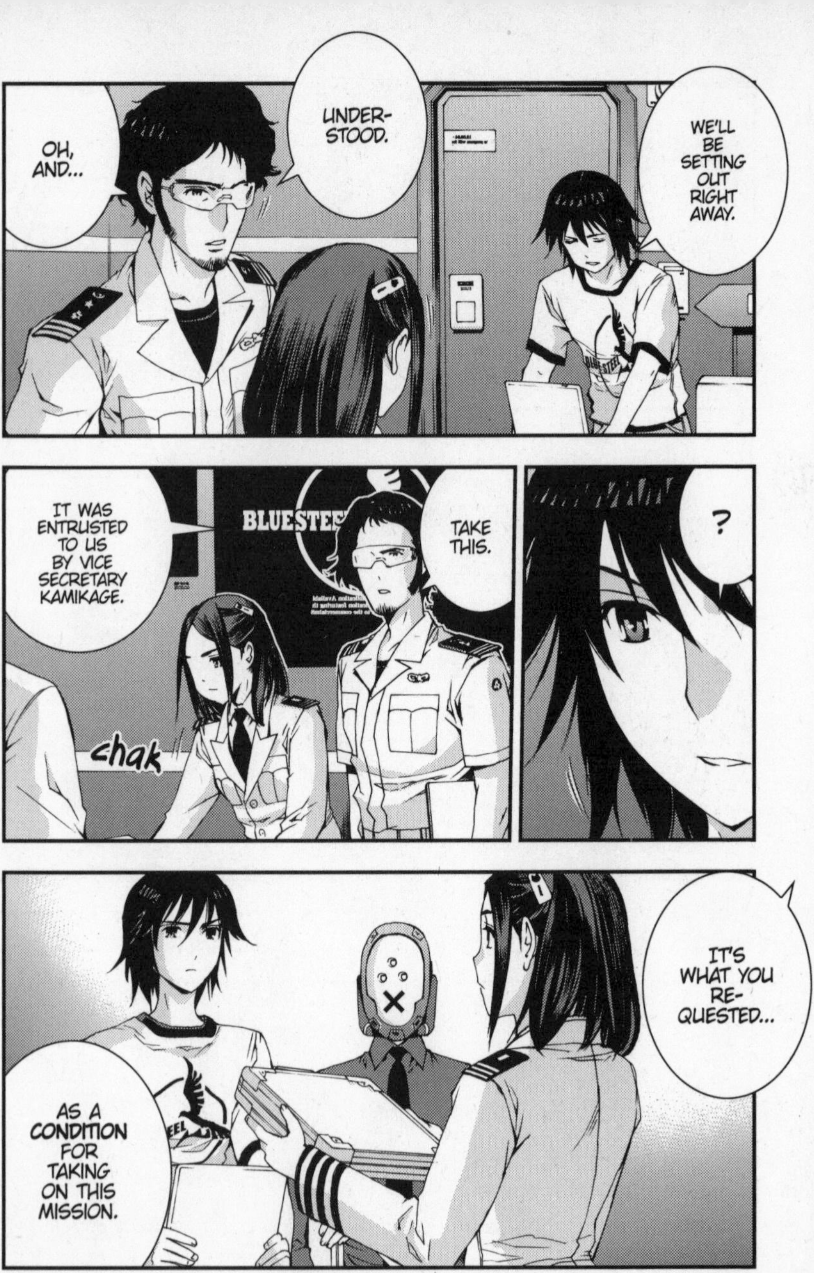
WE'LL BE SETTING OUT RIGHT AWAY.
UNDER-STOOD.
OH, AND...
?
TAKE THIS.
IT WAS ENTRUSTED TO US BY VICE SECRETARY KAMIKAGE.
chak
IT'S WHAT YOU RE-QUESTED...
AS A CONDITION FOR TAKING ON THIS MISSION.

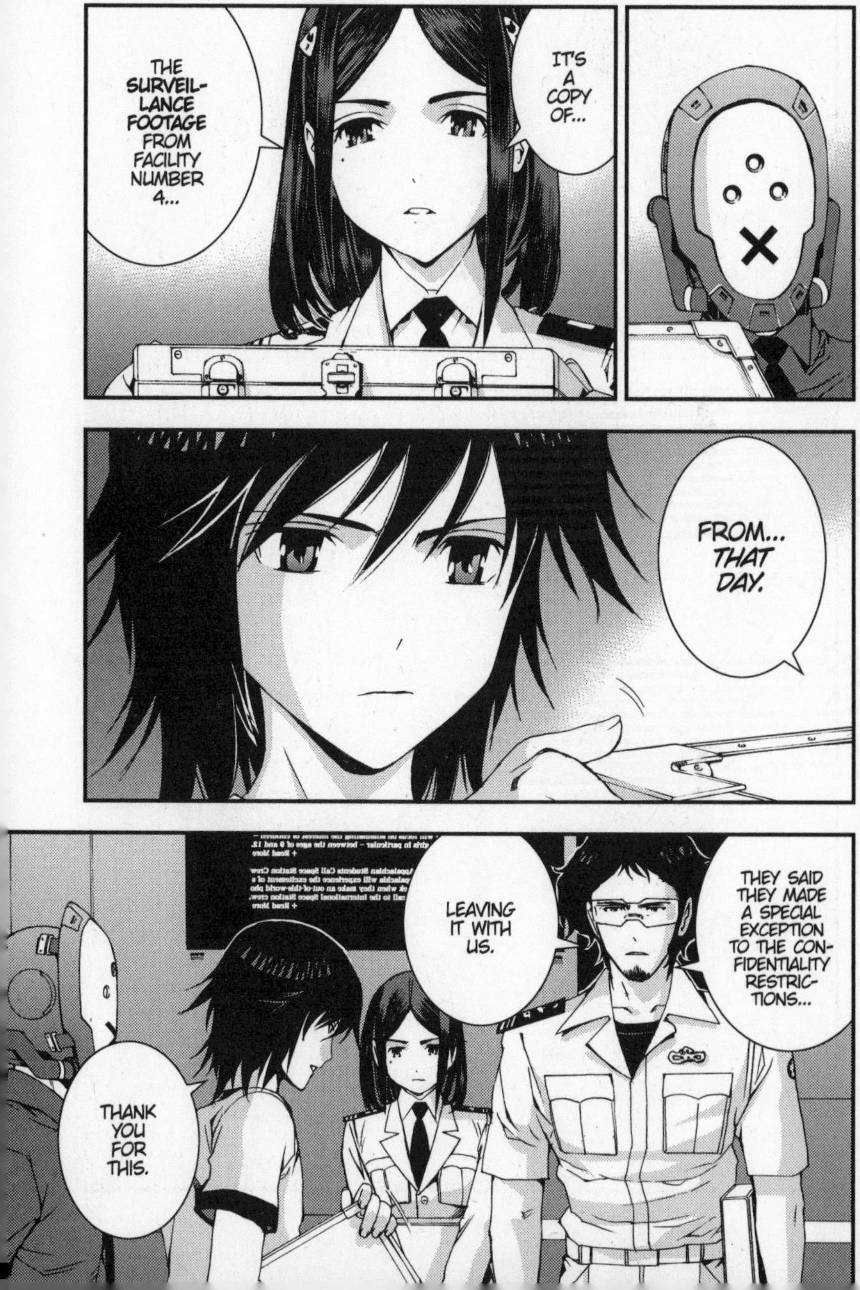
IT'S A COPY OF...
THE SURVEIL-LANCE FOOTAGE FROM FACILITY NUMBER 4...
FROM... THAT DAY.
THEY SAID THEY MADE A SPECIAL EXCEPTION TO THE CON-FIDENTIALITY RESTRIC-TIONS...
LEAVING IT WITH US.
THANK YOU FOR THIS.

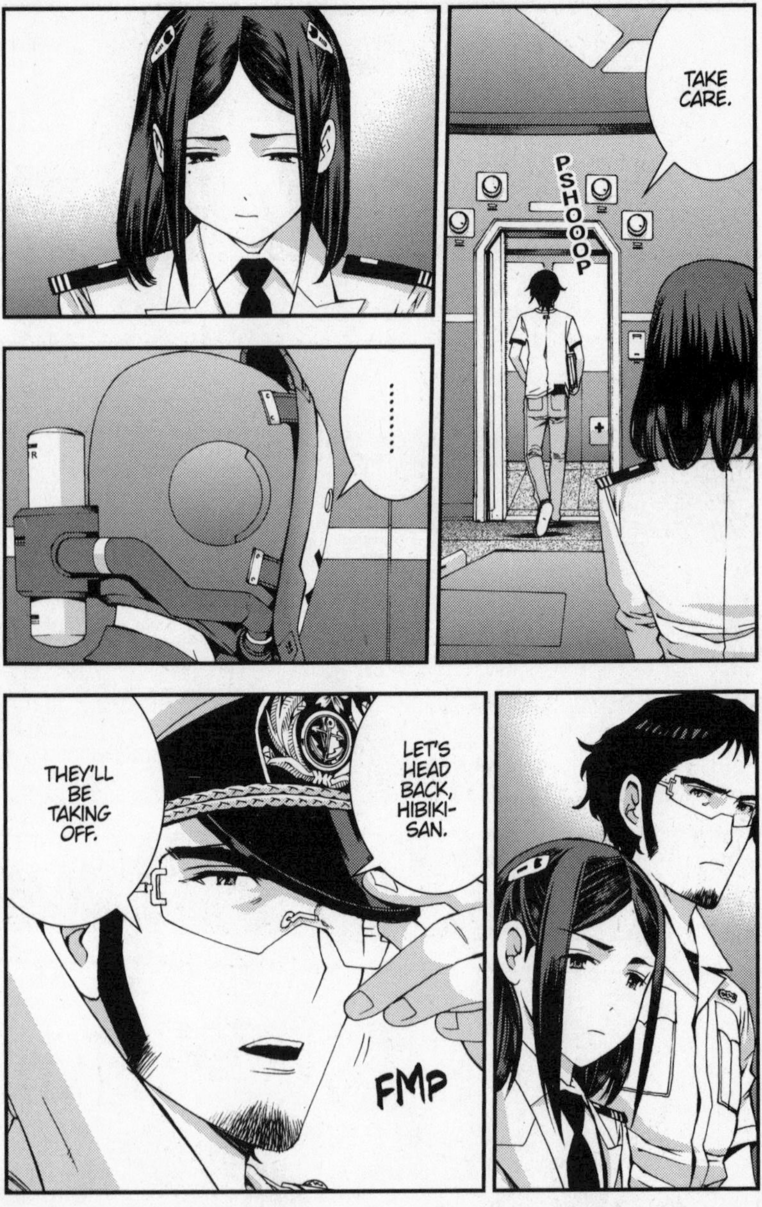
TAKE CARE.
PSHOOOP
......
LET'S HEAD BACK, HIBIKI-SAN.
THEY'LL BE TAKING OFF.
FMP

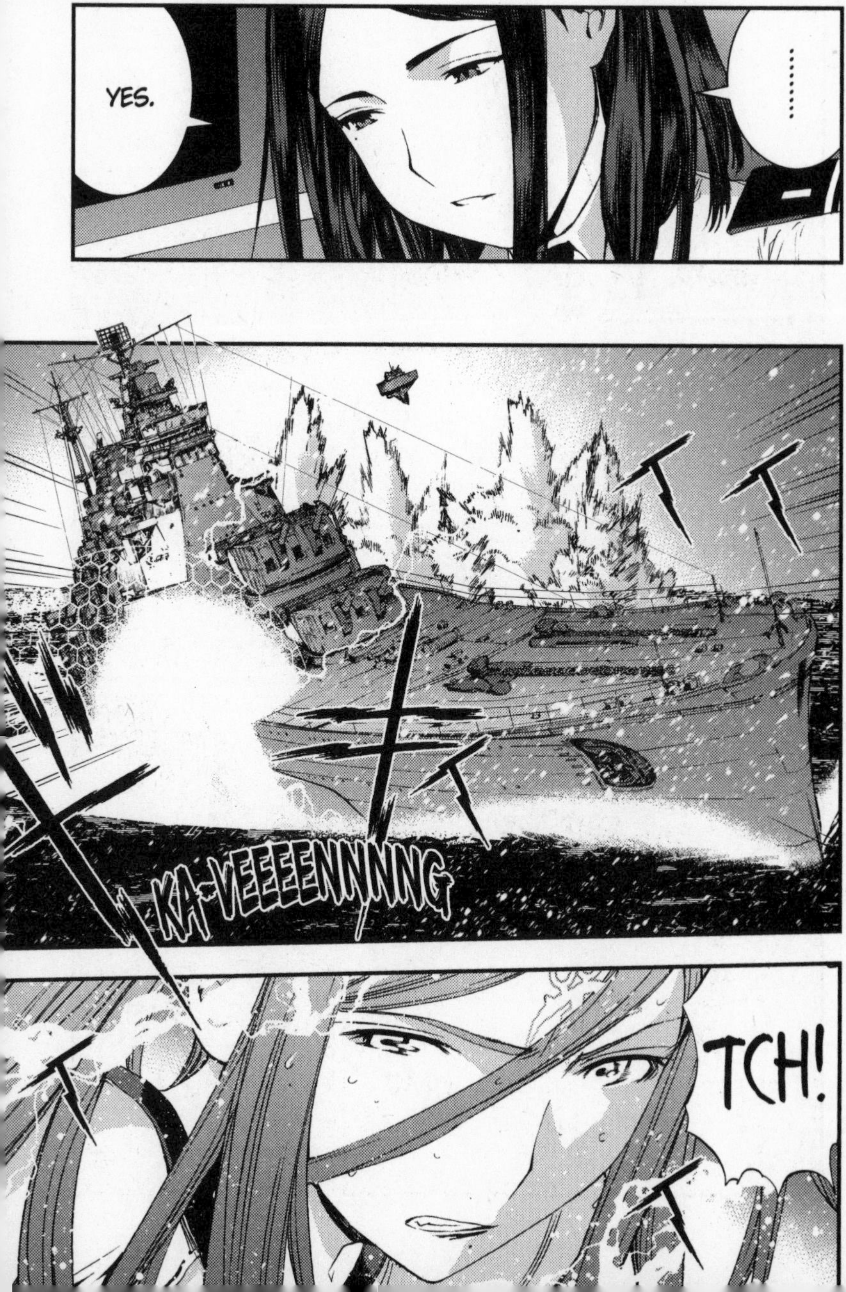
......
YES.
KA-VEEEENNNNG
TCH!

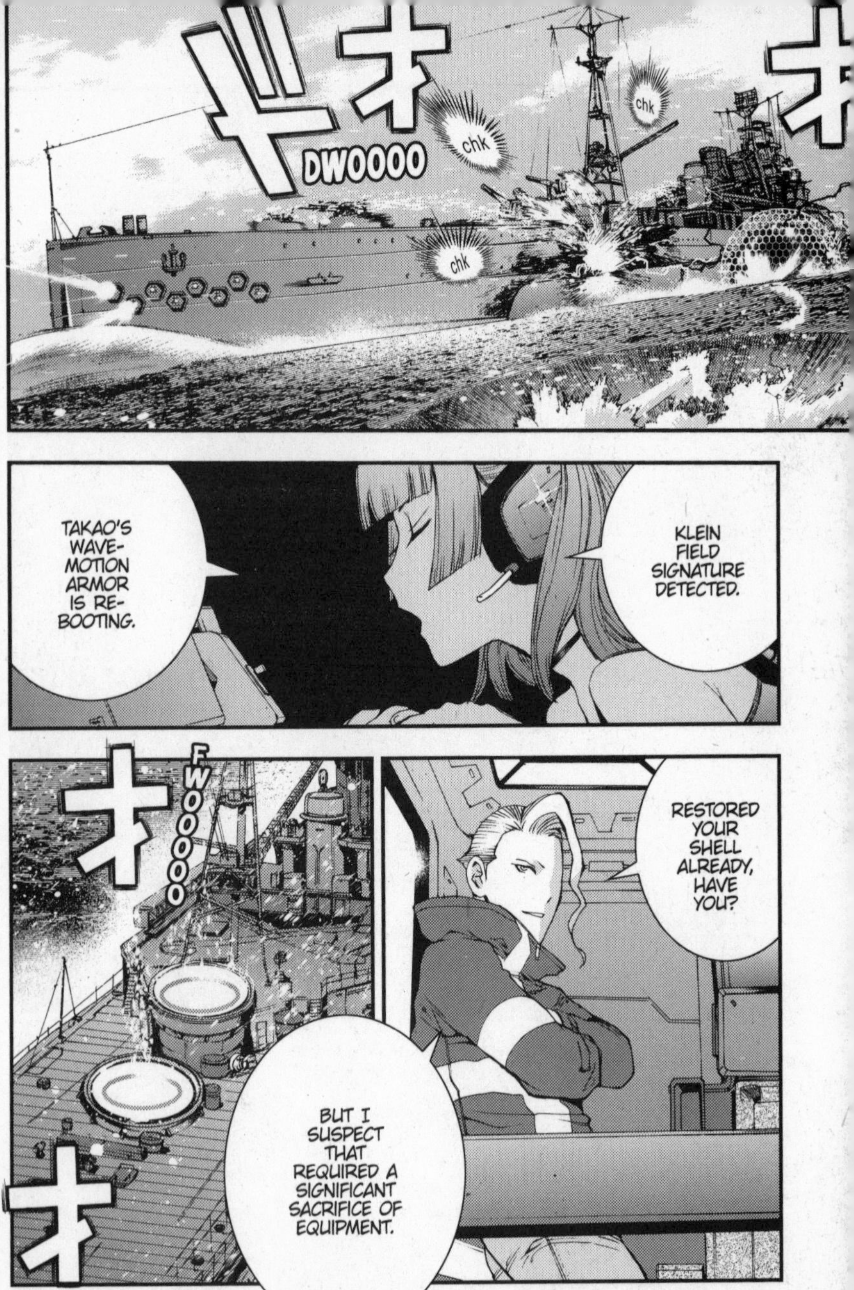
ドオオ
DWOOOO
chk
chk
chk
KLEIN FIELD SIGNATURE DETECTED.
TAKAO'S WAVE-MOTION ARMOR IS RE-BOOTING.
RESTORED YOUR SHELL ALREADY, HAVE YOU?
BUT I SUSPECT THAT REQUIRED A SIGNIFICANT SACRIFICE OF EQUIPMENT.
FWOOOOOO
オオ

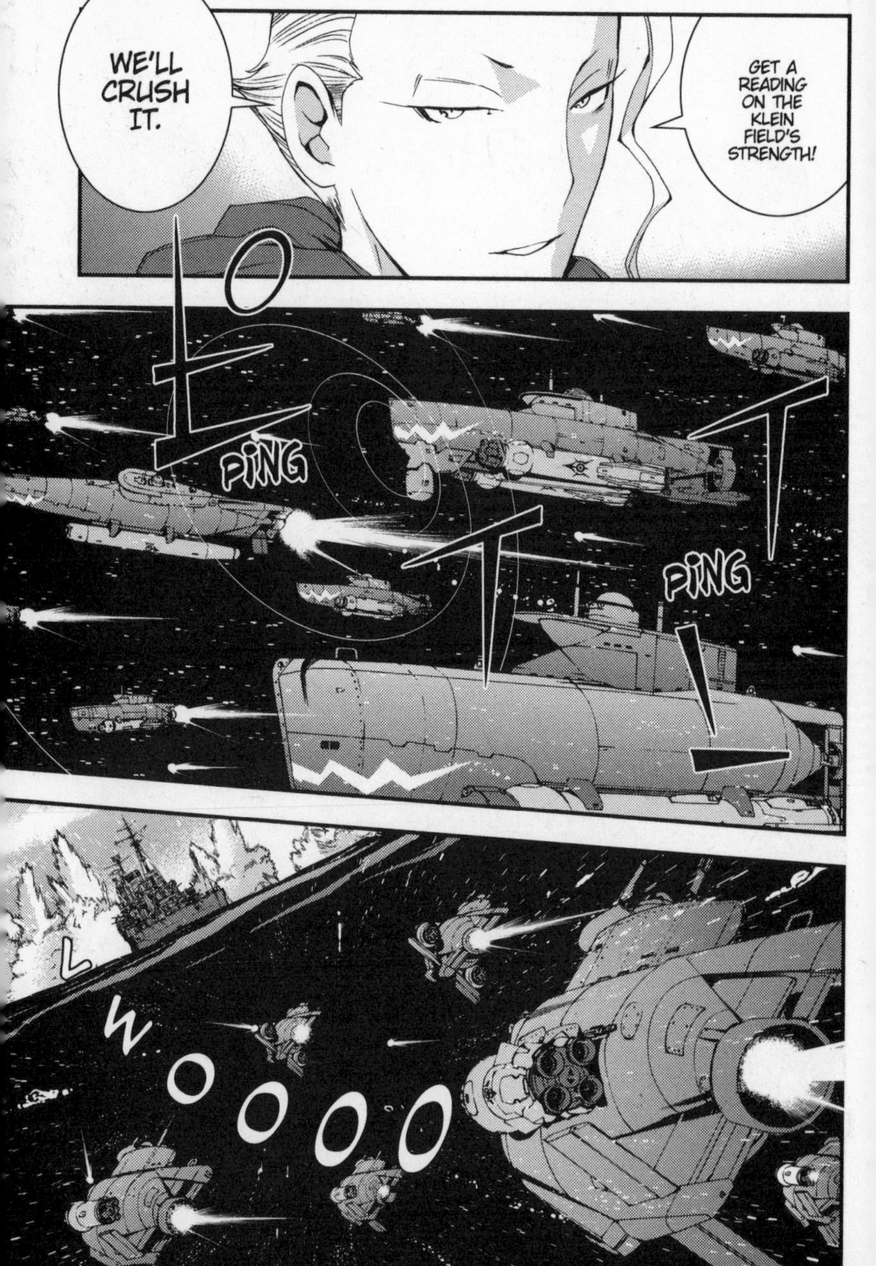
GET A READING ON THE KLEIN FIELD'S STRENGTH!
WE'LL CRUSH IT.
PING
PING
WOOOOO

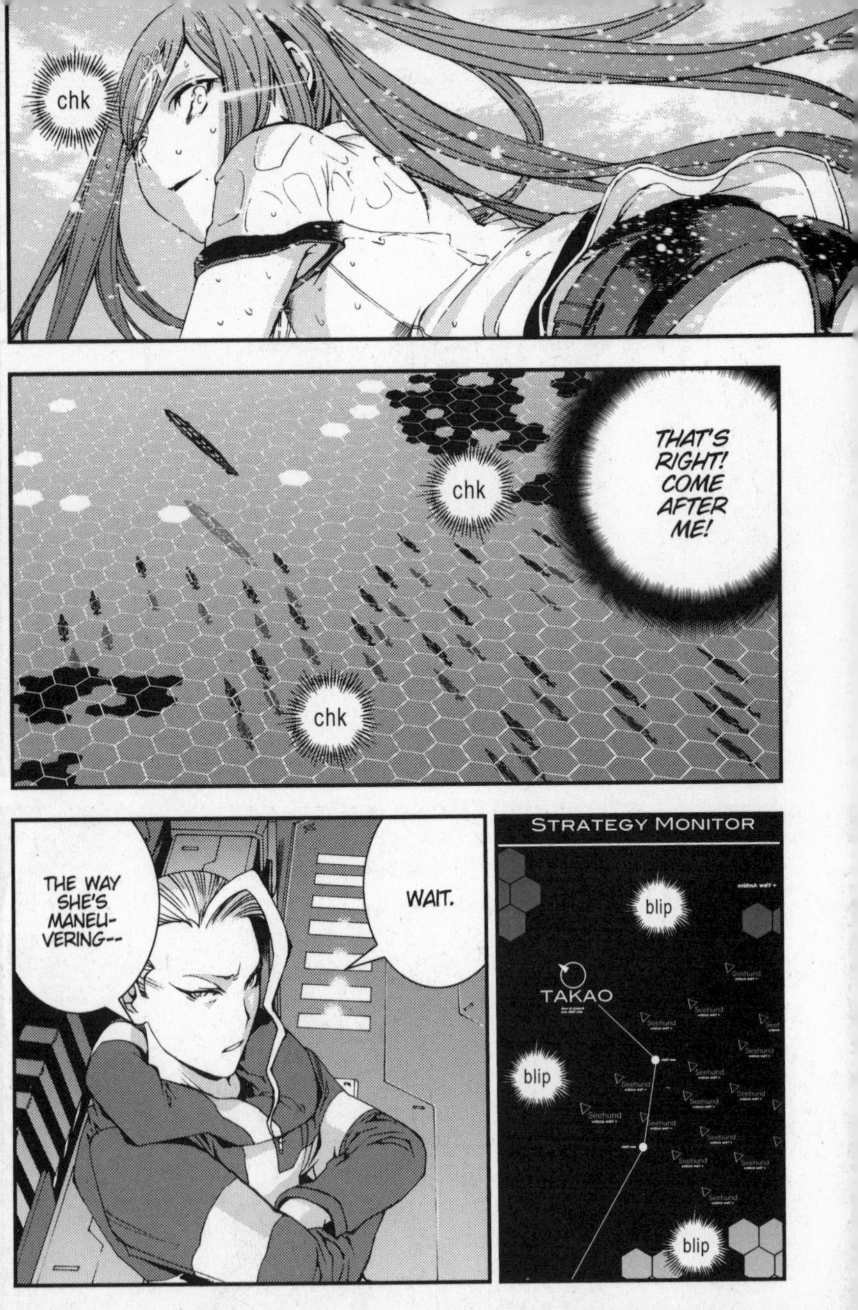
chk
THAT'S RIGHT! COME AFTER ME!
chk
chk
STRATEGY MONITOR
blip
TAKAO
blip
blip
WAIT.
THE WAY SHE'S MANEU-VERING--

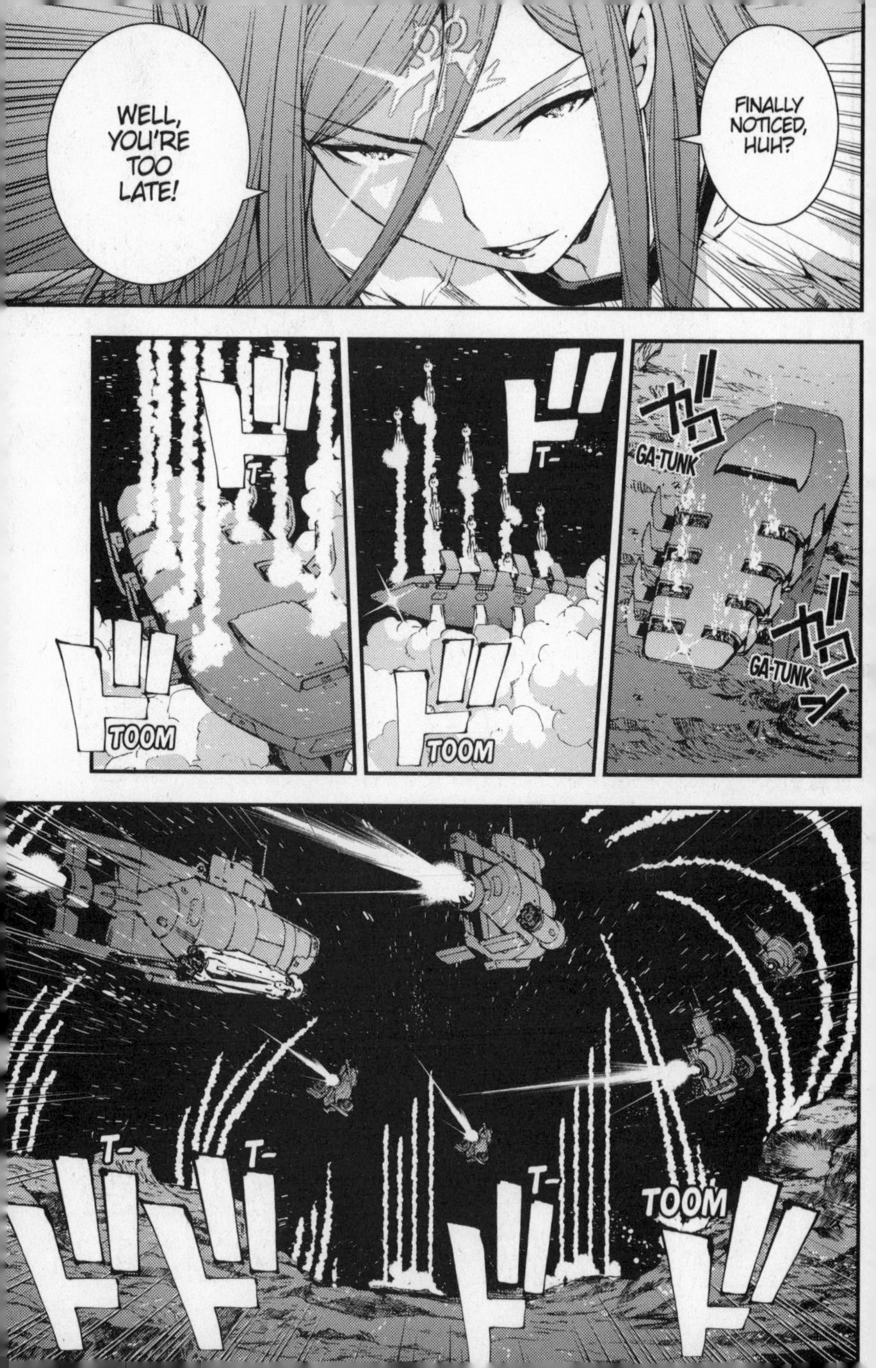
FINALLY NOTICED, HUH?
WELL, YOU'RE TOO LATE!
GA-TUNK
GA-TUNK
T-
TOOM
T-
TOOM
TOOM
T-
T-
T-

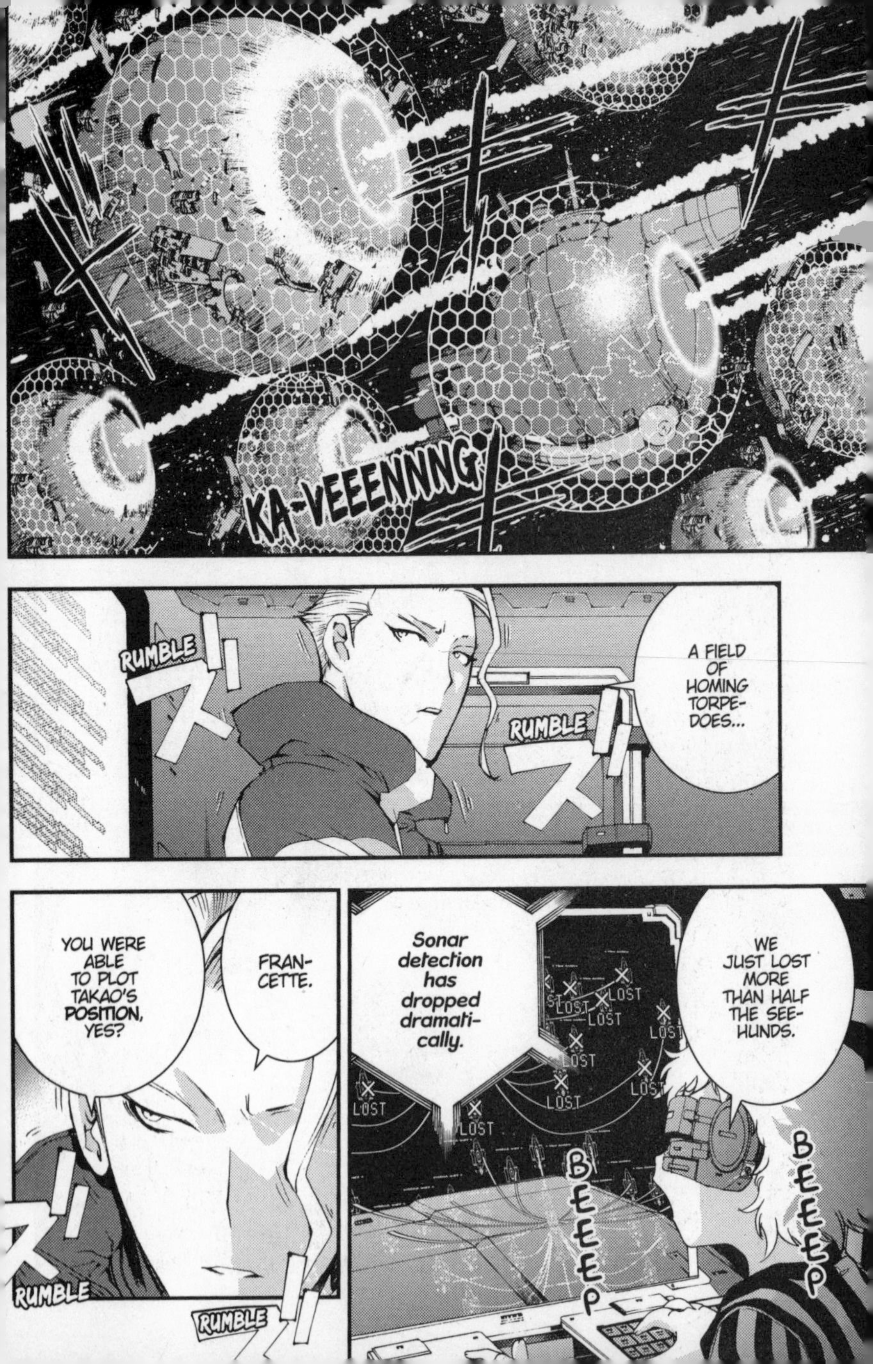
KA-VEEENNNG
RUMBLE
RUMBLE
A FIELD OF HOMING TORPE-DOES...
WE JUST LOST MORE THAN HALF THE SEE-HUNDS.
Sonar detection has dropped dramati-cally.
BEEEP
BEEEP
FRAN-CETTE.
YOU WERE ABLE TO PLOT TAKAO'S POSITION, YES?
RUMBLE
RUMBLE

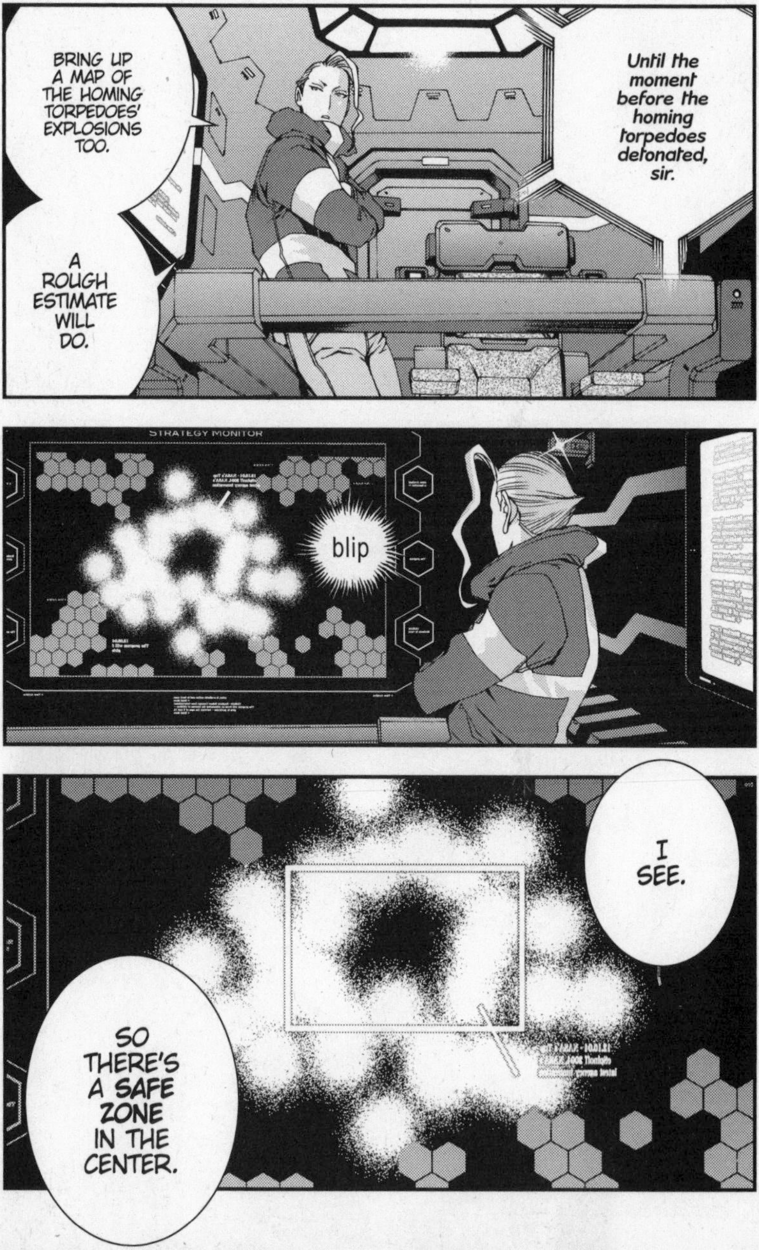
Until the moment before the homing torpedoes detonated, sir.
BRING UP A MAP OF THE HOMING TORPEDOES' EXPLOSIONS TOO.
A ROUGH ESTIMATE WILL DO.
STRATEGY MONITOR
blip
I SEE.
SO THERE'S A SAFE ZONE IN THE CENTER.

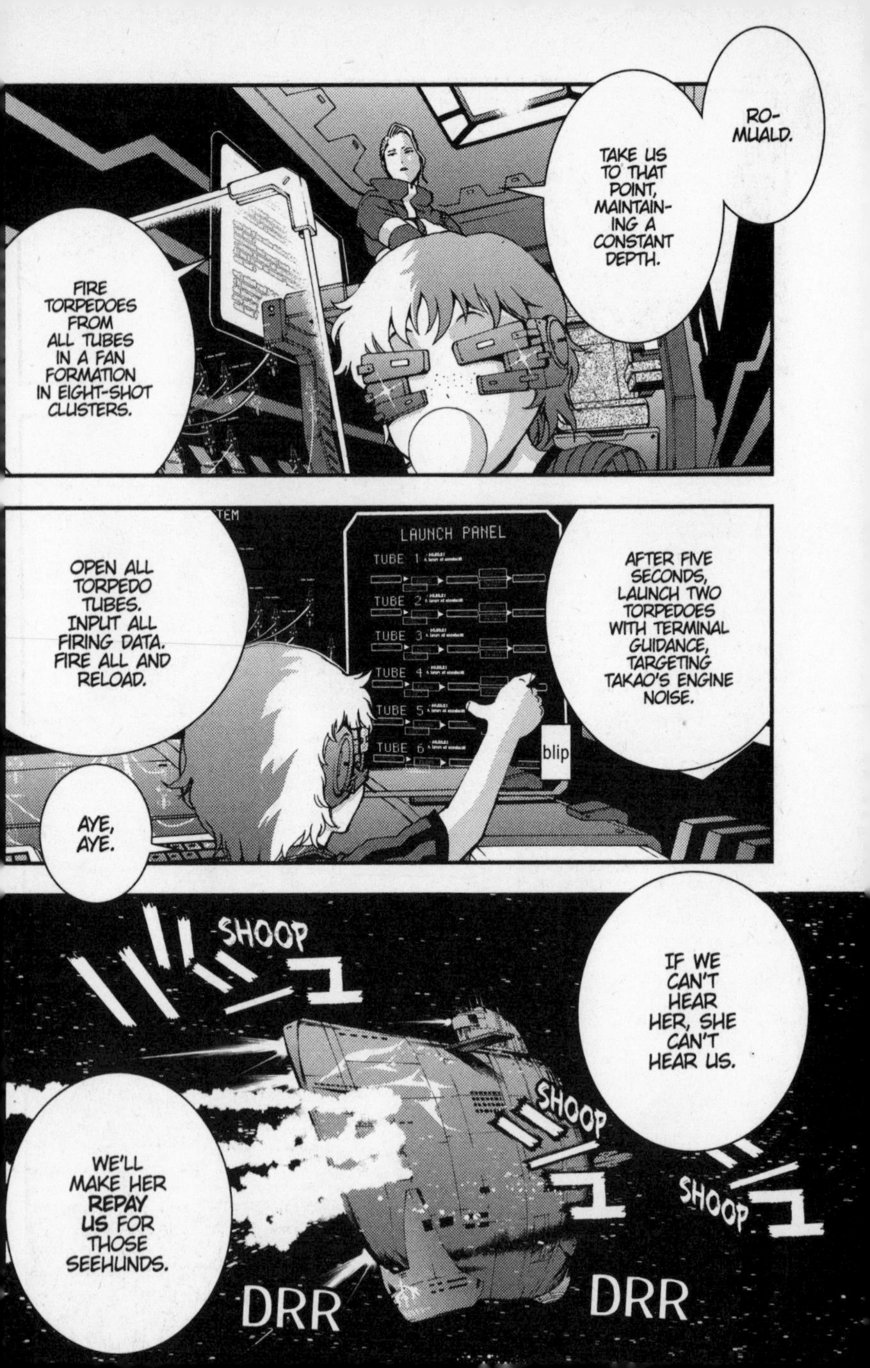
RO-MUALD.
TAKE US TO THAT POINT, MAINTAINING A CONSTANT DEPTH.
FIRE TORPEDOES FROM ALL TUBES IN A FAN FORMATION IN EIGHT-SHOT CLUSTERS.
AFTER FIVE SECONDS, LAUNCH TWO TORPEDOES WITH TERMINAL GUIDANCE, TARGETING TAKAO'S ENGINE NOISE.
LAUNCH PANEL
TUBE 1
TUBE 2
TUBE 3
TUBE 4
TUBE 5
TUBE 6
blip
OPEN ALL TORPEDO TUBES. INPUT ALL FIRING DATA. FIRE ALL AND RELOAD.
AYE, AYE.
IF WE CAN'T HEAR HER, SHE CAN'T HEAR US.
SHOOP
WE'LL MAKE HER REPAY US FOR THOSE SEEHUNDS.
SHOOP
SHOOP
DRR
DRR

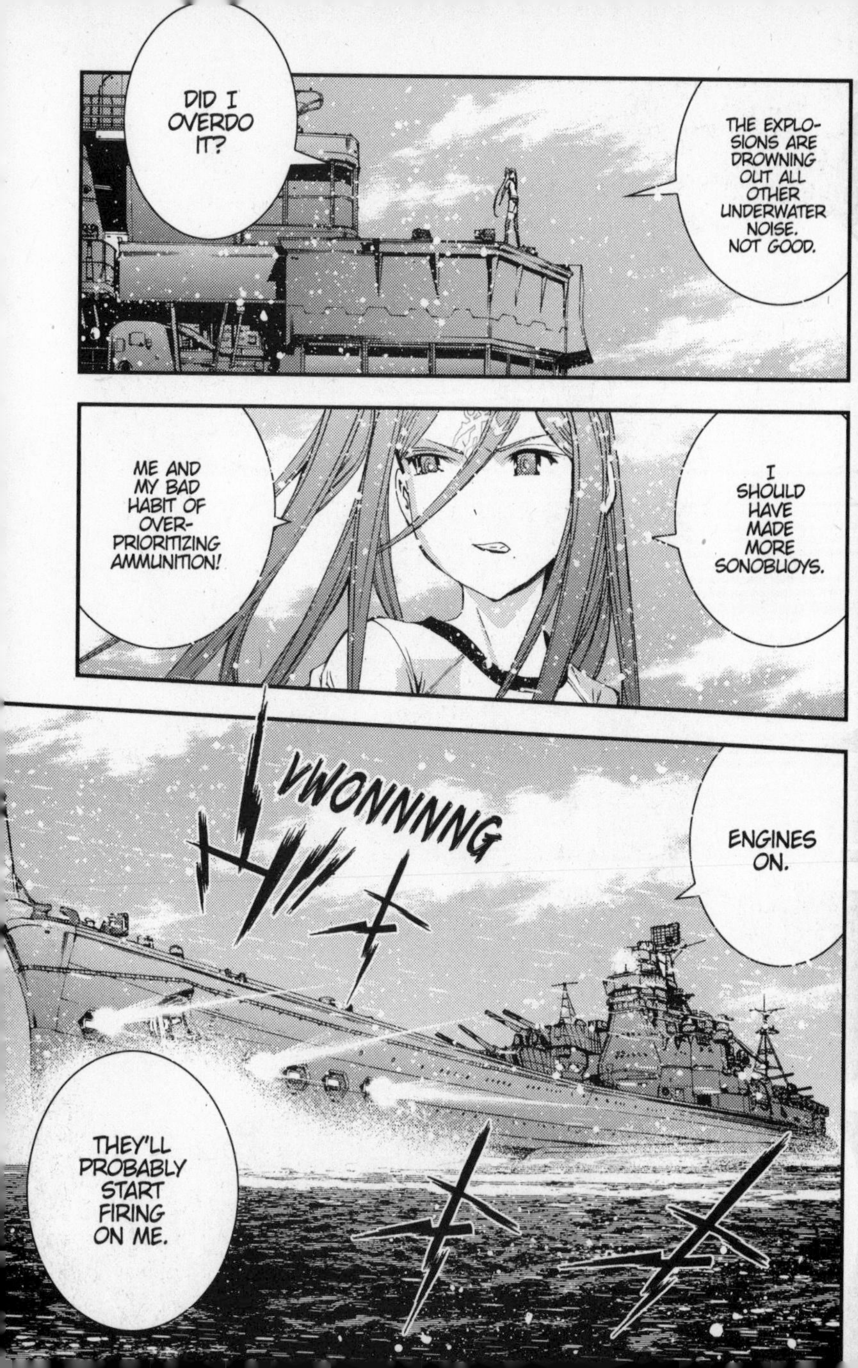
THE EXPLOSIONS ARE DROWNING OUT ALL OTHER UNDERWATER NOISE. NOT GOOD.
DID I OVERDO IT?
I SHOULD HAVE MADE MORE SONOBUOYS.
ME AND MY BAD HABIT OF OVER-PRIORITIZING AMMUNITION!
ENGINES ON.
VWONNNNG
THEY'LL PROBABLY START FIRING ON ME.

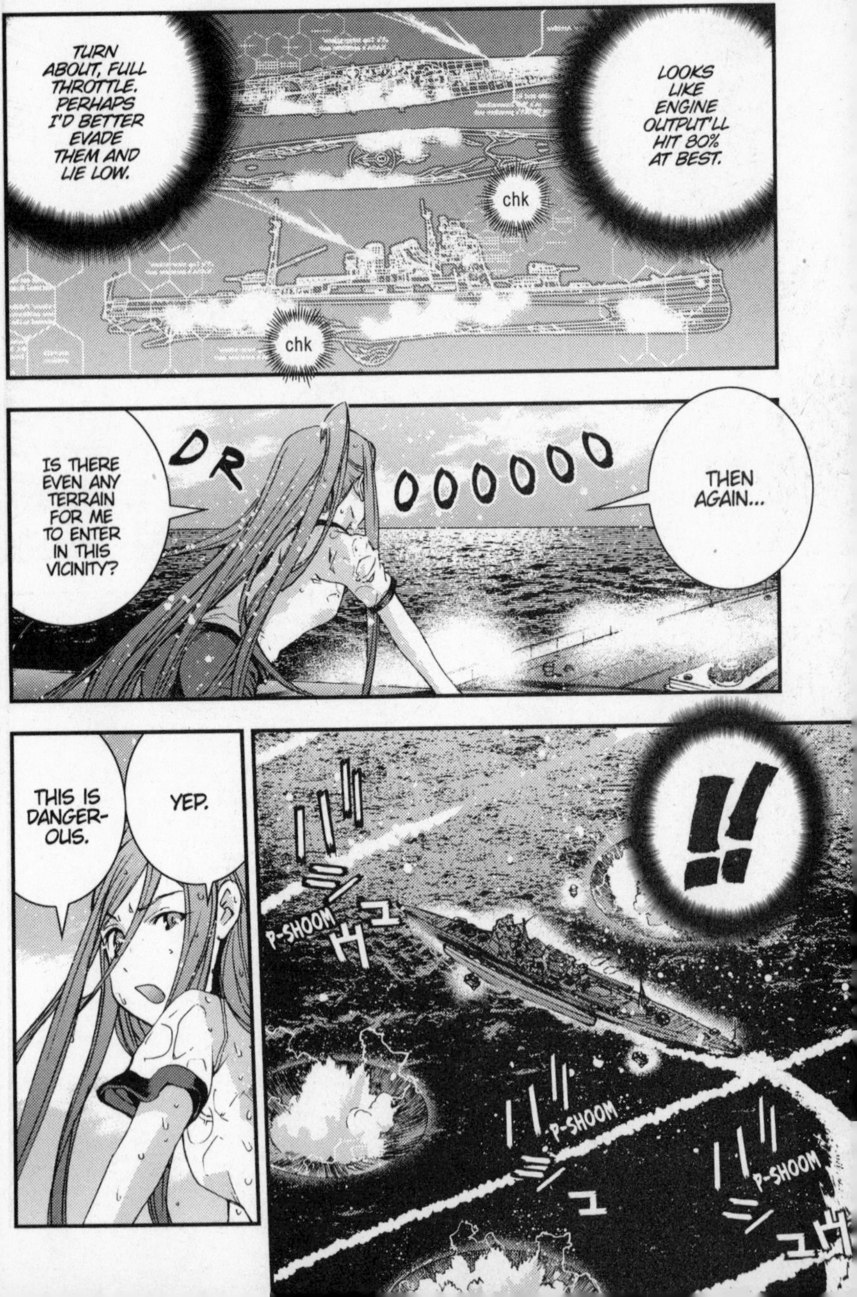
LOOKS LIKE ENGINE OUTPUT'LL HIT 80% AT BEST.
TURN ABOUT, FULL THROTTLE. PERHAPS I'D BETTER EVADE THEM AND LIE LOW.
chk
chk
THEN AGAIN...
DROOOOOOO
IS THERE EVEN ANY TERRAIN FOR ME TO ENTER IN THIS VICINITY?
!!
P-SHOOM
P-SHOOM
P-SHOOM
YEP.
THIS IS DANGER-OUS.

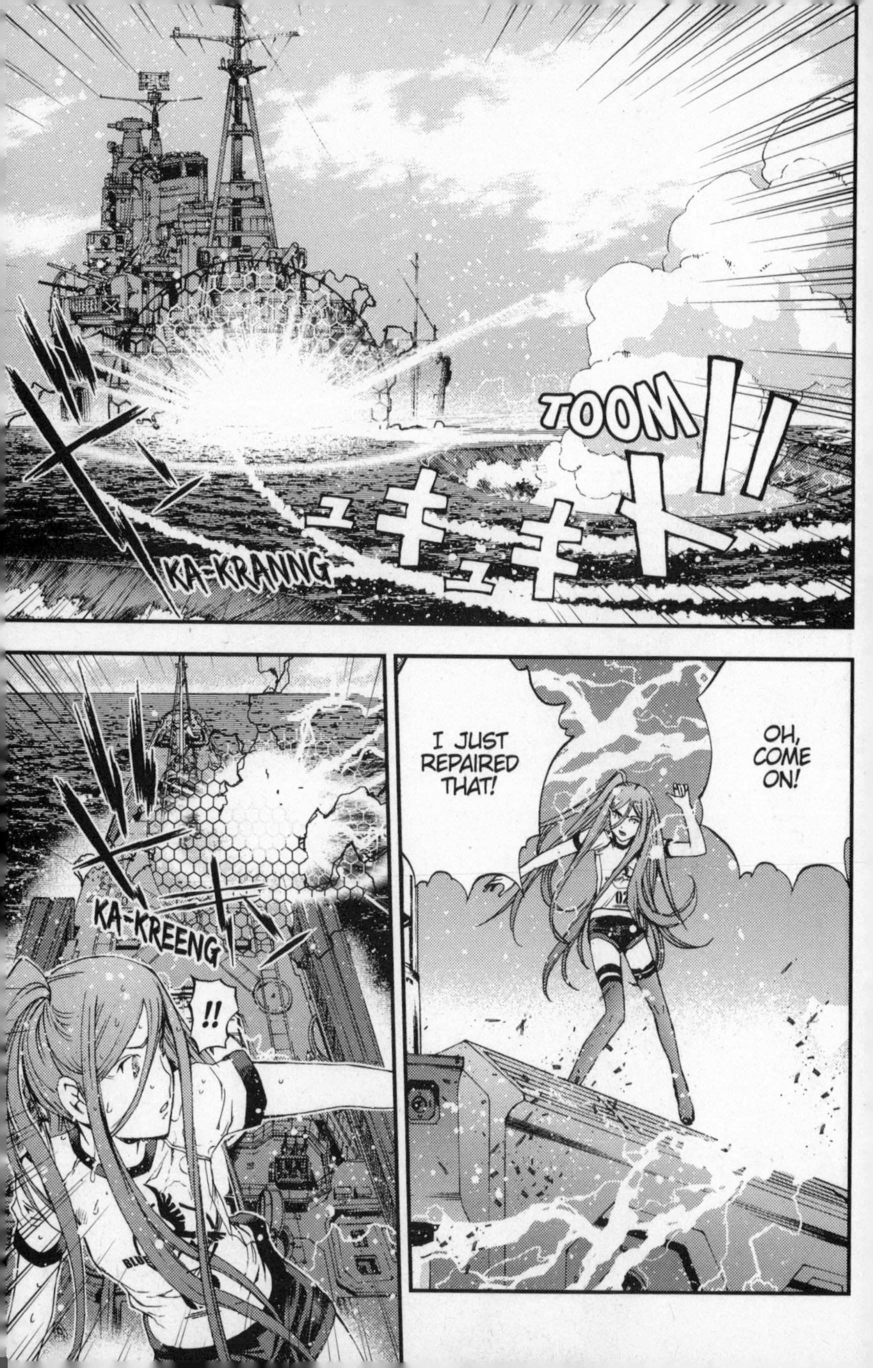
TOOM
KA-KRANNG
ュキュキト
OH, COME ON!
I JUST REPAIRED THAT!
KA-KREENG
!!

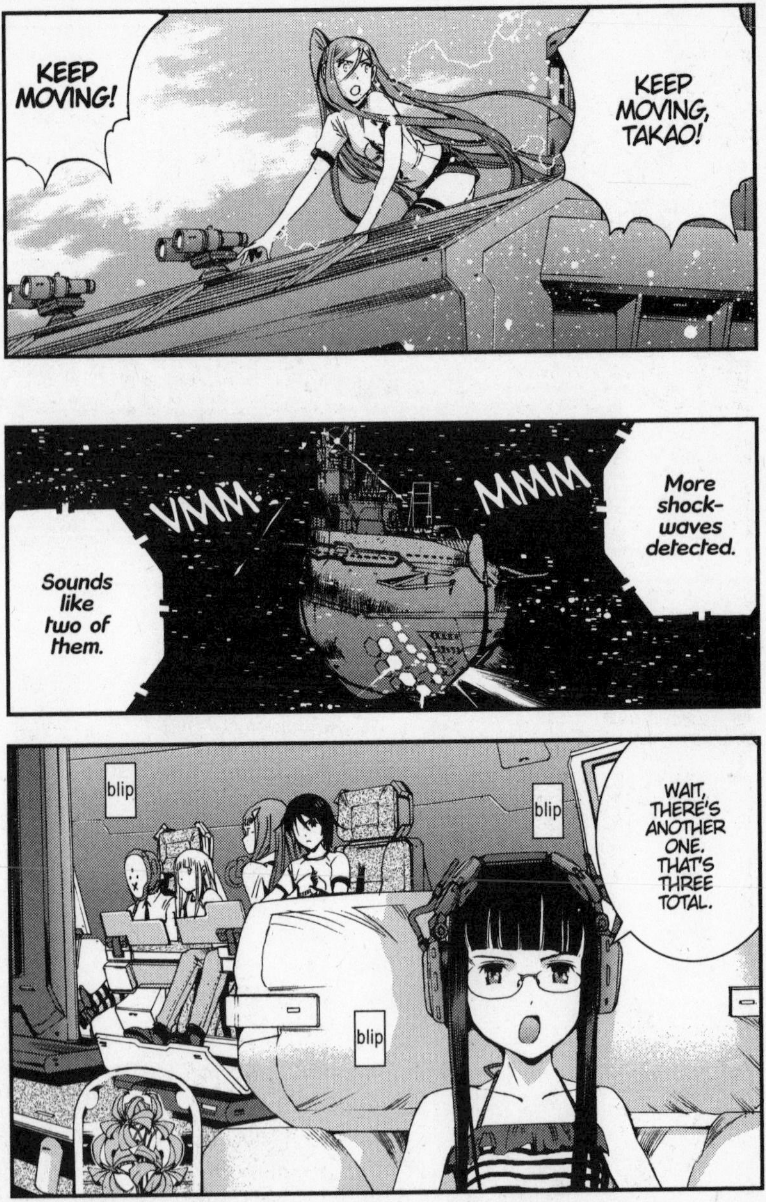
KEEP MOVING, TAKAO!
KEEP MOVING!
More shock-waves detected.
VMM MMM
Sounds like two of them.
blip
blip
blip
WAIT, THERE'S ANOTHER ONE. THAT'S THREE TOTAL.

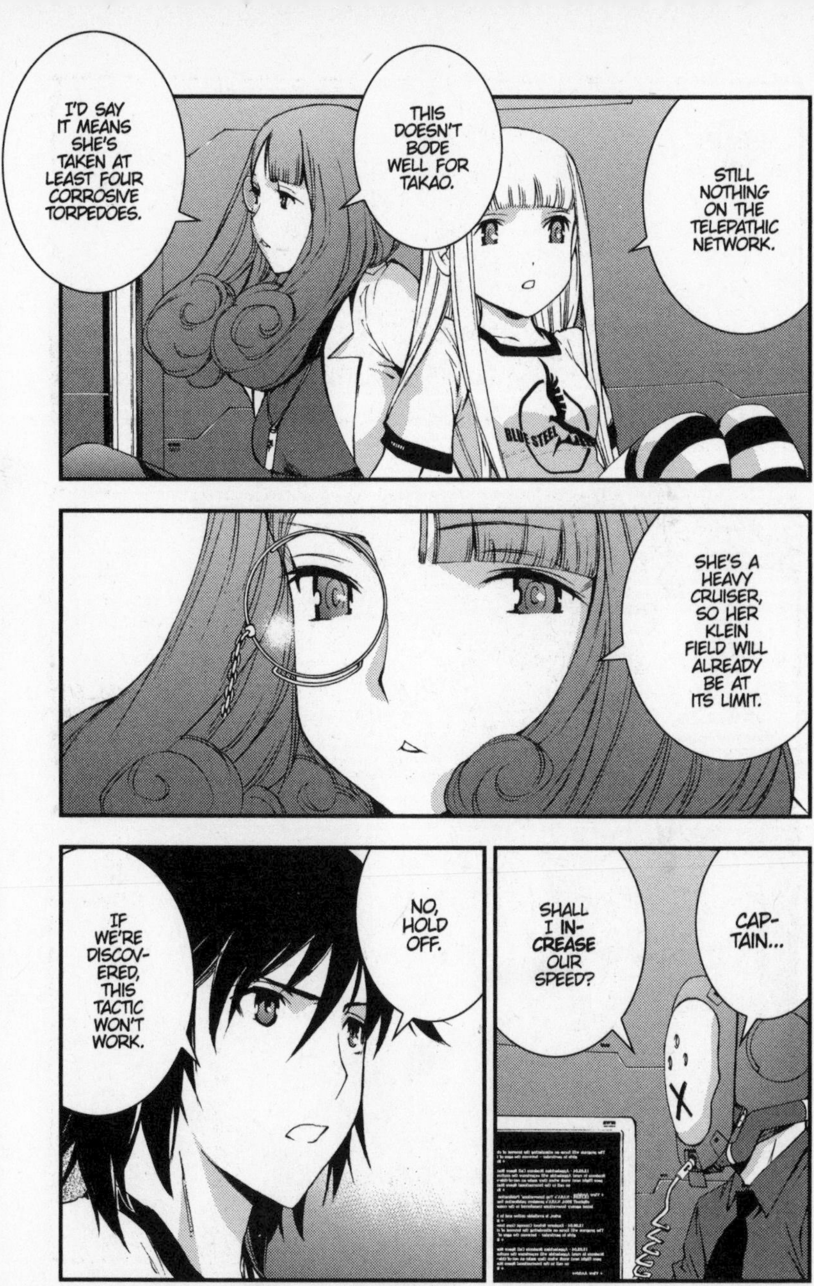
STILL NOTHING ON THE TELEPATHIC NETWORK.
THIS DOESN'T BODE WELL FOR TAKAO.
BLUE STEEL
I'D SAY IT MEANS SHE'S TAKEN AT LEAST FOUR CORROSIVE TORPEDOES.
SHE'S A HEAVY CRUISER, SO HER KLEIN FIELD WILL ALREADY BE AT ITS LIMIT.
CAP-TAIN...
SHALL I IN-CREASE OUR SPEED?
NO, HOLD OFF.
IF WE'RE DISCOV-ERED, THIS TACTIC WON'T WORK.

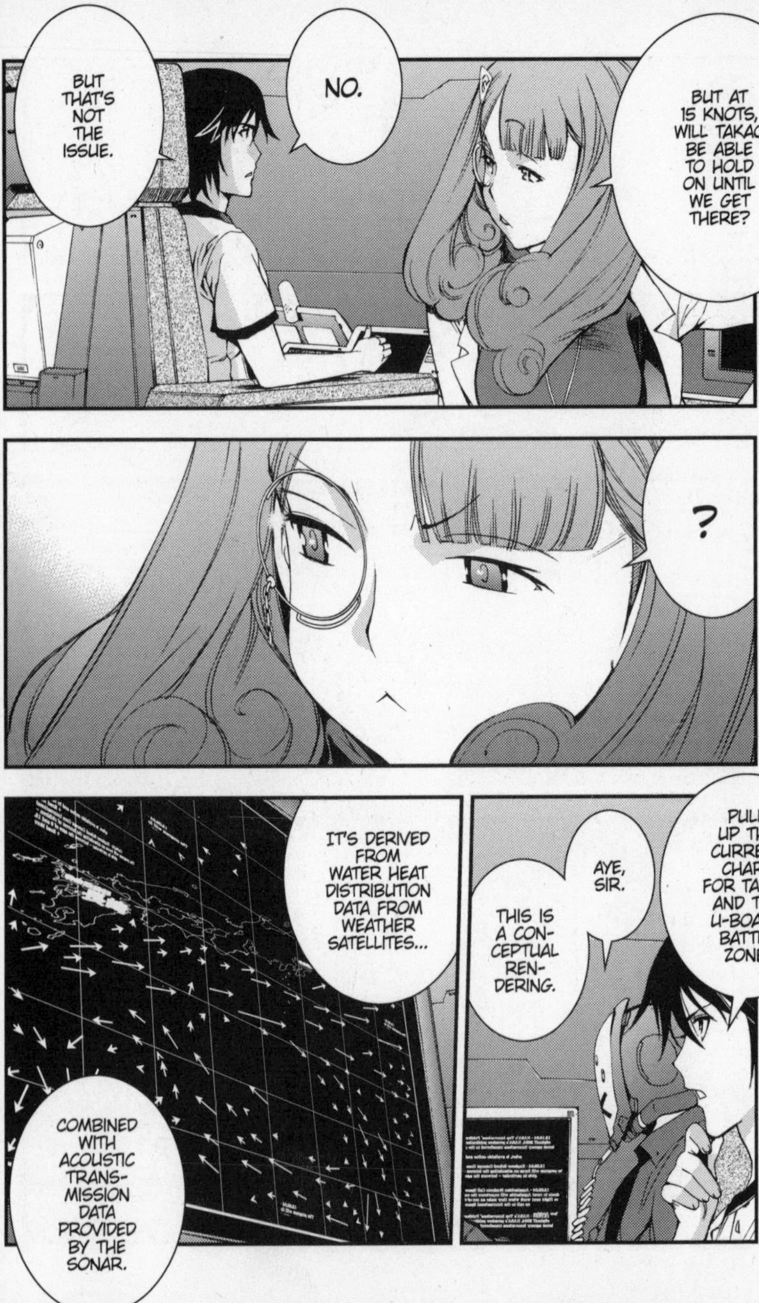
BUT AT 15 KNOTS, WILL TAKAO BE ABLE TO HOLD ON UNTIL WE GET THERE?
NO.
BUT THAT'S NOT THE ISSUE.
?
PULL UP THE CURRENT CHART FOR TAKAO AND THE U-BOAT'S BATTLE ZONE.
AYE, SIR.
THIS IS A CON-CEPTUAL REN-DERING.
IT'S DERIVED FROM WATER HEAT DISTRIBUTION DATA FROM WEATHER SATELLITES...
COMBINED WITH ACOUSTIC TRANS-MISSION DATA PROVIDED BY THE SONAR.

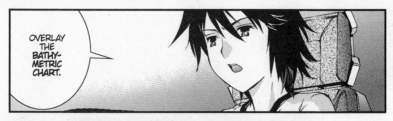

OVERLAY THE BATHY-METRIC CHART.
DEEP SEA MAP
blip
THIS DATA IS EIGHTEEN YEARS OLD.
BUT THERE'S NOTHING TO SUGGEST THE REGION HAS ENCOUNTERED ANY MAJOR SEISMIC ACTIVITY IN THAT TIME.
IT'S UNLIKELY THAT THE CURRENT TOPOGRAPHY IS DRAMATICALLY CHANGED FROM WHAT'S SHOWN HERE.
DO YOU REMEM-BER...
WHEN THE U-BOAT FIRST AP-PEARED?
YEAH.

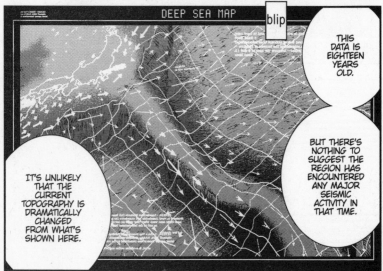

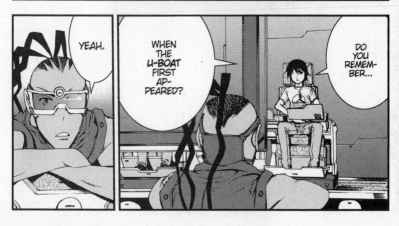

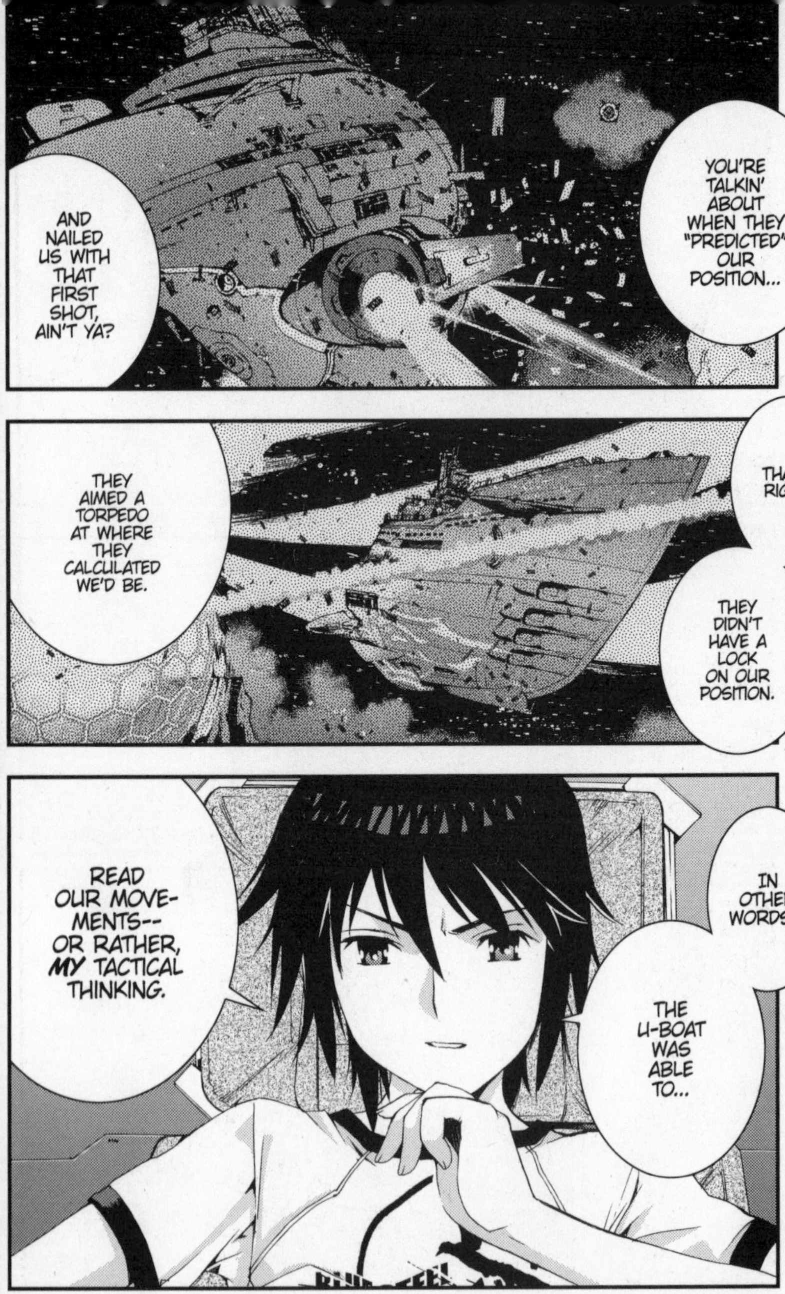
YOU'RE TALKIN' ABOUT WHEN THEY "PREDICTED" OUR POSITION...
AND NAILED US WITH THAT FIRST SHOT, AIN'T YA?
THAT'S RIGHT.
THEY DIDN'T HAVE A LOCK ON OUR POSITION.
THEY AIMED A TORPEDO AT WHERE THEY CALCULATED WE'D BE.
IN OTHER WORDS...
THE U-BOAT WAS ABLE TO...
READ OUR MOVEMENTS-- OR RATHER, *MY* TACTICAL THINKING.

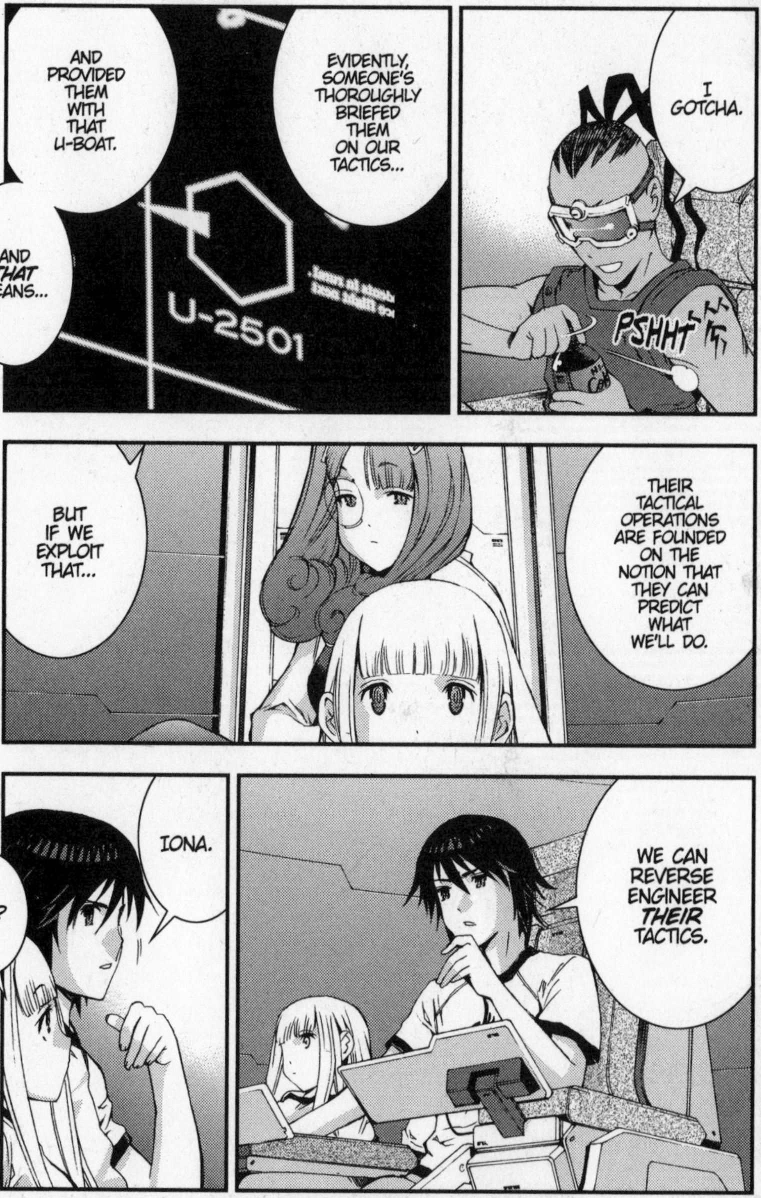
I GOTCHA.
PSHHT
EVIDENTLY, SOMEONE'S THOROUGHLY BRIEFED THEM ON OUR TACTICS...
AND PROVIDED THEM WITH THAT U-BOAT.
U-2501
AND *THAT* MEANS...
THEIR TACTICAL OPERATIONS ARE FOUNDED ON THE NOTION THAT THEY CAN PREDICT WHAT WE'LL DO.
BUT IF WE EXPLOIT THAT...
WE CAN REVERSE ENGINEER *THEIR* TACTICS.
IONA.
MM?

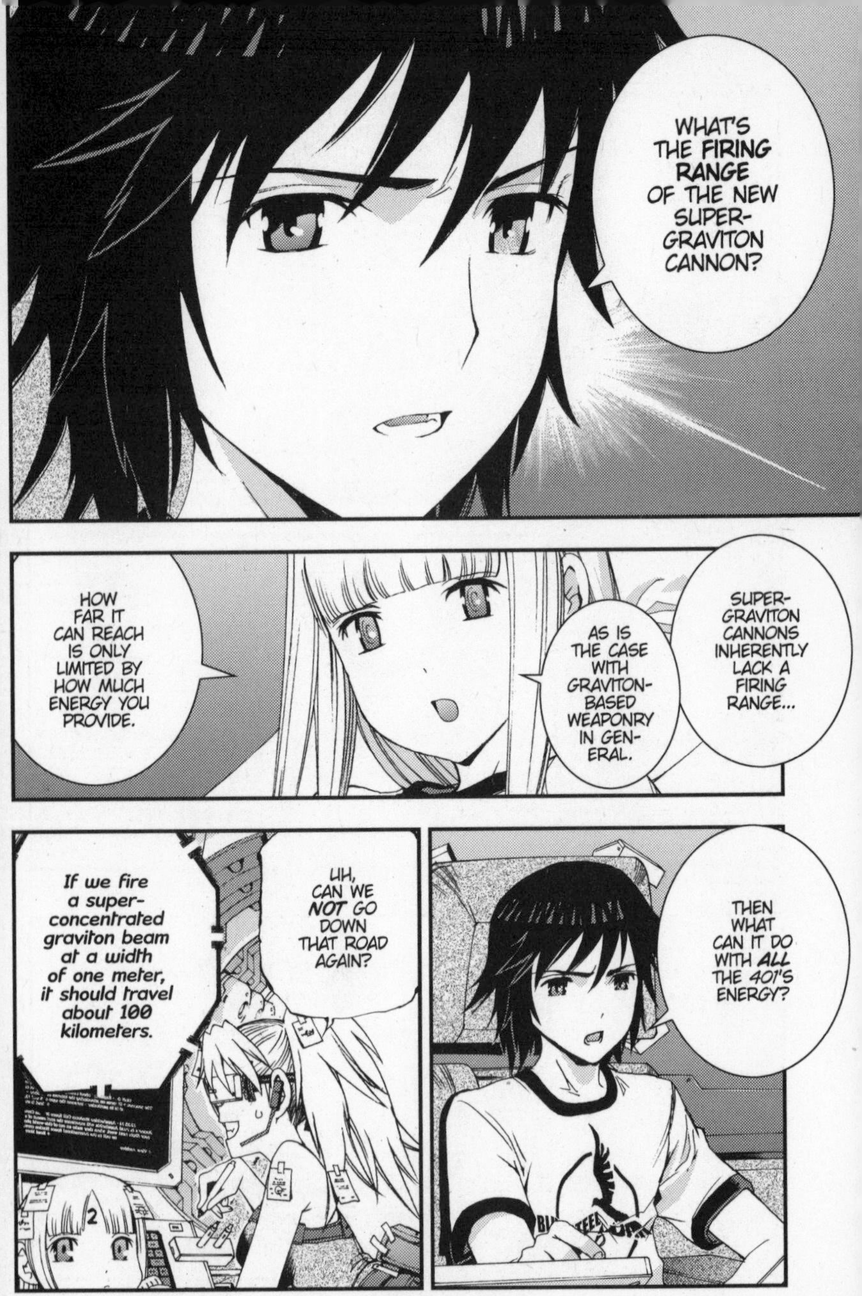
WHAT'S THE FIRING RANGE OF THE NEW SUPER-GRAVITON CANNON?
SUPER-GRAVITON CANNONS INHERENTLY LACK A FIRING RANGE...
AS IS THE CASE WITH GRAVITON-BASED WEAPONRY IN GENERAL.
HOW FAR IT CAN REACH IS ONLY LIMITED BY HOW MUCH ENERGY YOU PROVIDE.
THEN WHAT CAN IT DO WITH ALL THE 401'S ENERGY?
UH, CAN WE NOT GO DOWN THAT ROAD AGAIN?
If we fire a super-concentrated graviton beam at a width of one meter, it should travel about 100 kilometers.

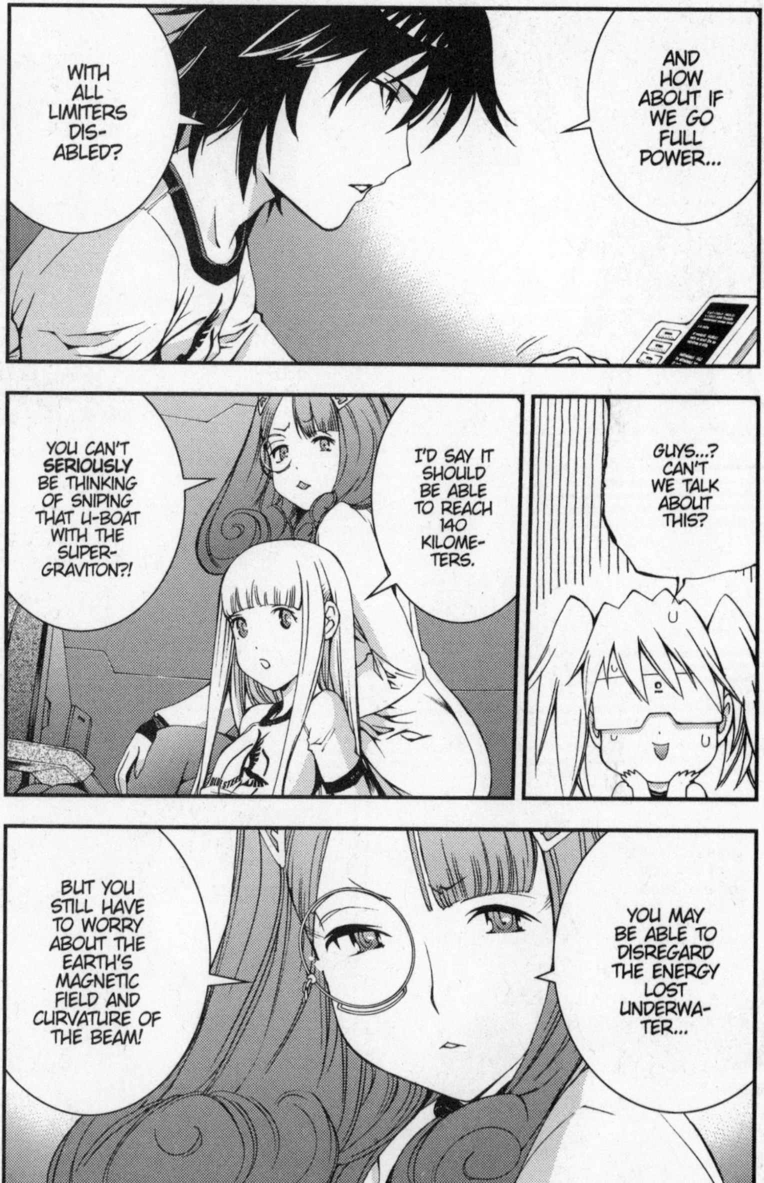
AND HOW ABOUT IF WE GO FULL POWER...
WITH ALL LIMITERS DIS-ABLED?
GUYS...? CAN'T WE TALK ABOUT THIS?
I'D SAY IT SHOULD BE ABLE TO REACH 140 KILOME-TERS.
YOU CAN'T **SERIOUSLY** BE THINKING OF SNIPING THAT U-BOAT WITH THE SUPER-GRAVITON?!
YOU MAY BE ABLE TO DISREGARD THE ENERGY LOST UNDERWA-TER...
BUT YOU STILL HAVE TO WORRY ABOUT THE EARTH'S MAGNETIC FIELD AND CURVATURE OF THE BEAM!

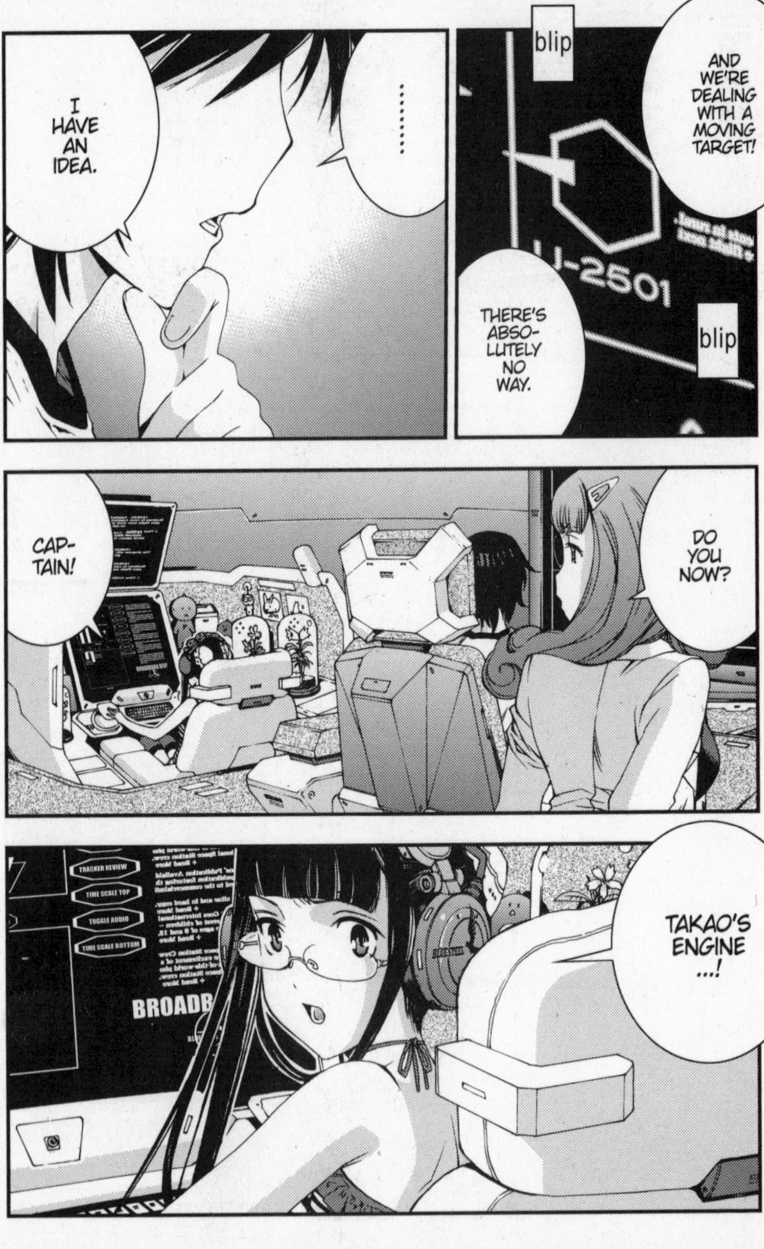
blip
AND WE'RE DEALING WITH A MOVING TARGET!
U-2501
THERE'S ABSOLUTELY NO WAY.
blip
......
I HAVE AN IDEA.
DO YOU NOW?
CAP-TAIN!
TAKAO'S ENGINE ...!
TRACKER REVIEW
TIME SCALE TOP
TOGGLE AUDIO
TIME SCALE BOTTOM
BROADB
BLUESTEEL

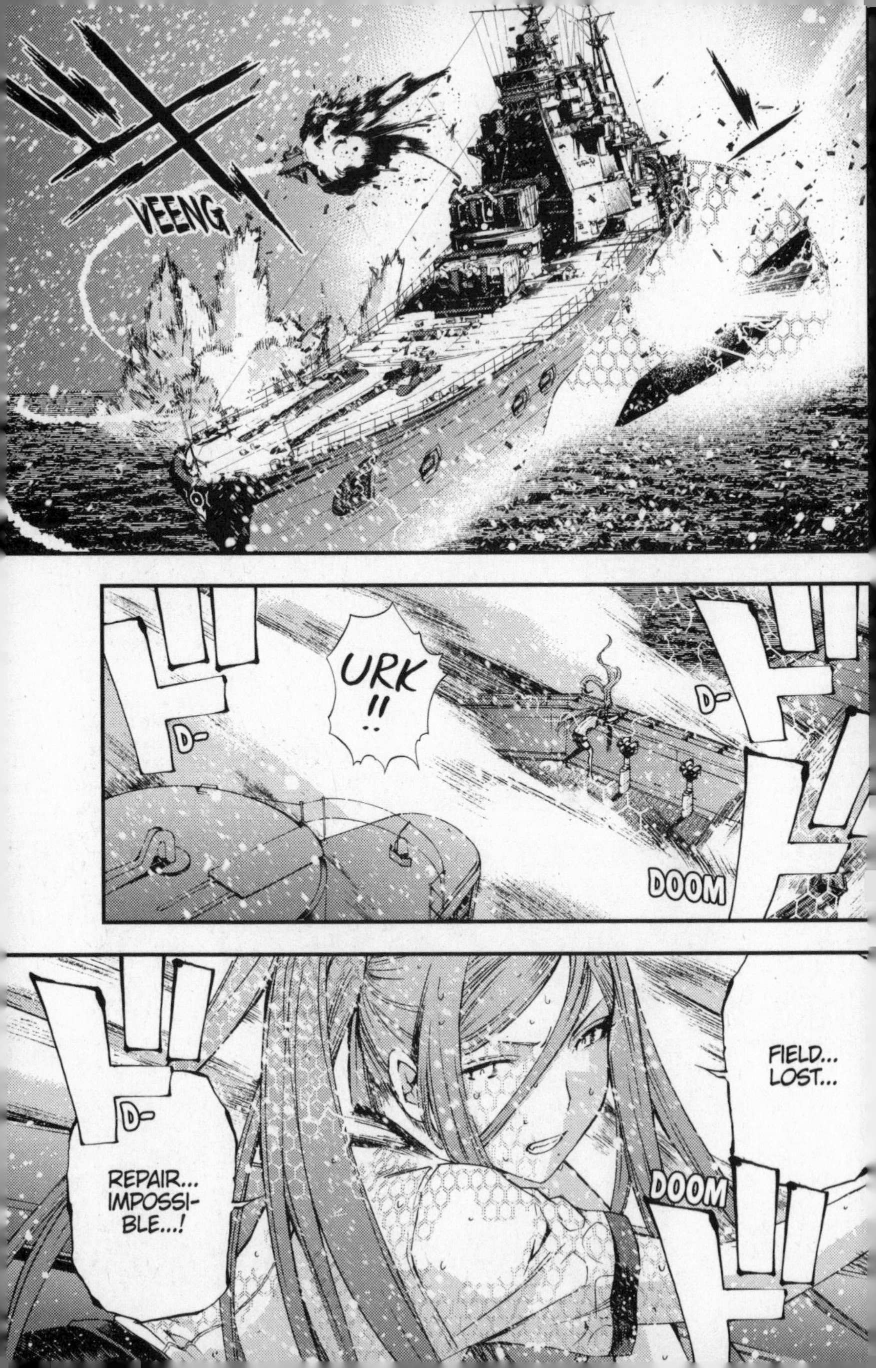
VEENG
D-
DOOM
URK!!
D-
FIELD... LOST...
DOOM
D-
REPAIR... IMPOSSI-BLE...!

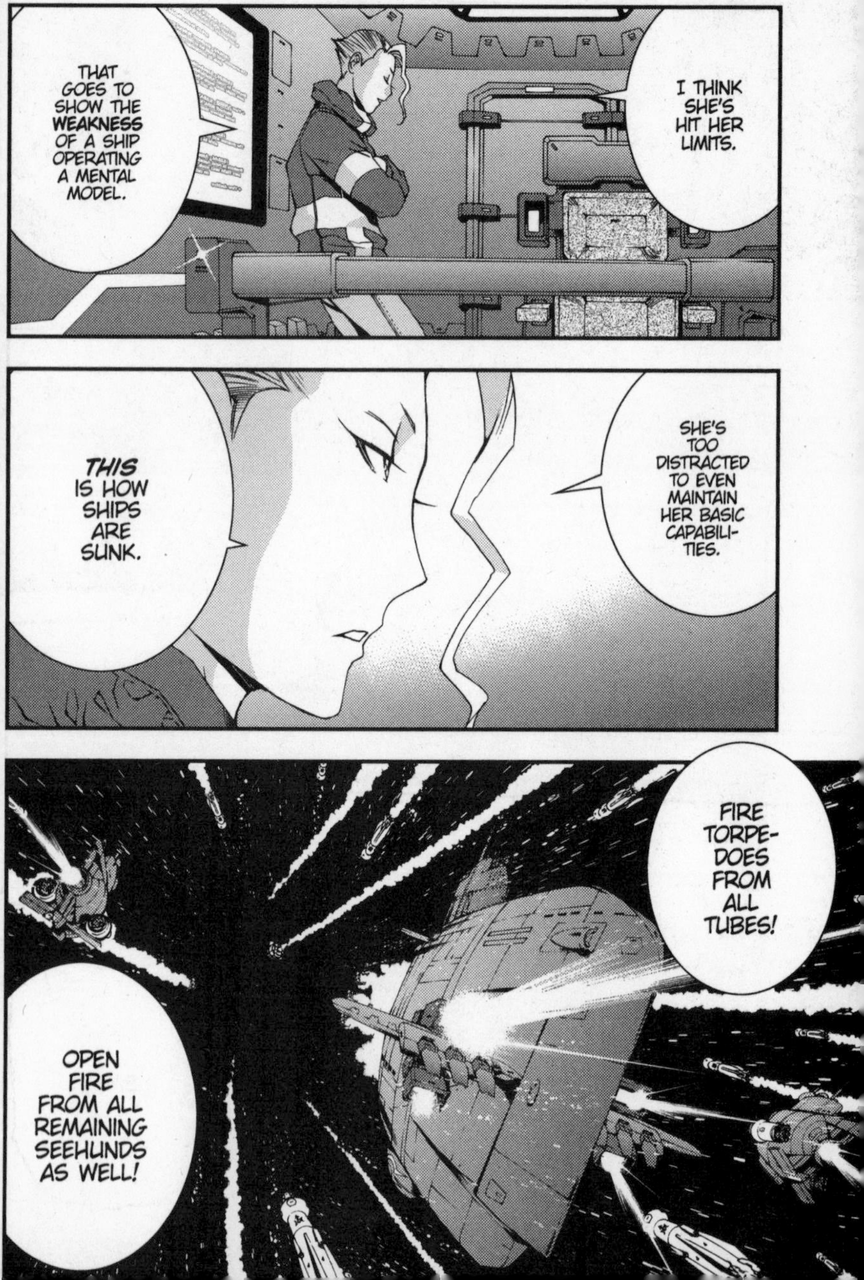
I THINK SHE'S HIT HER LIMITS.
THAT GOES TO SHOW THE WEAKNESS OF A SHIP OPERATING A MENTAL MODEL.
SHE'S TOO DISTRACTED TO EVEN MAINTAIN HER BASIC CAPABILI-TIES.
THIS IS HOW SHIPS ARE SUNK.
FIRE TORPE-DOES FROM ALL TUBES!
OPEN FIRE FROM ALL REMAINING SEEHUNDS AS WELL!

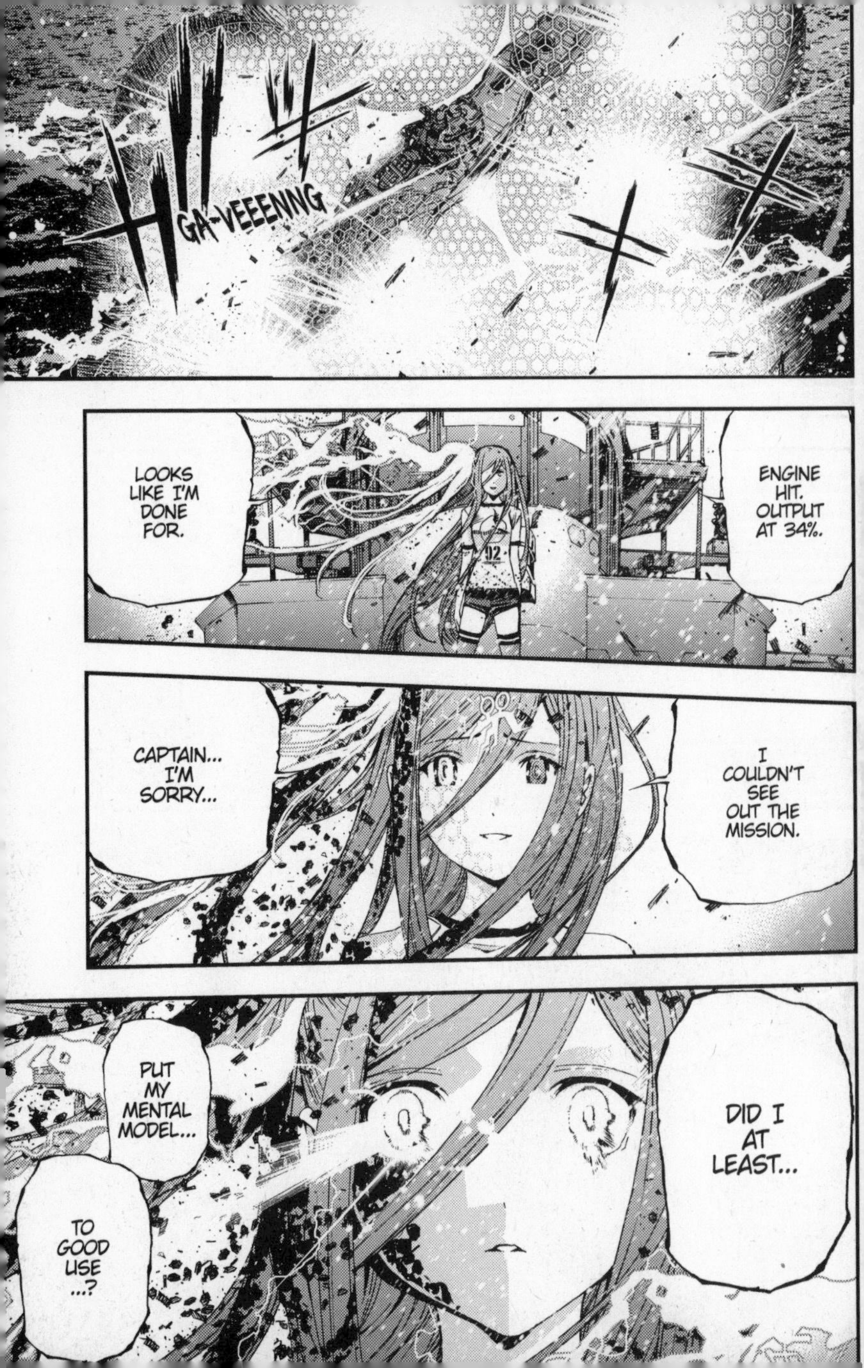
GA-VEEENING
ENGINE HIT. OUTPUT AT 34%.
LOOKS LIKE I'M DONE FOR.
I COULDN'T SEE OUT THE MISSION.
CAPTAIN... I'M SORRY...
DID I AT LEAST...
PUT MY MENTAL MODEL...
TO GOOD USE ...?

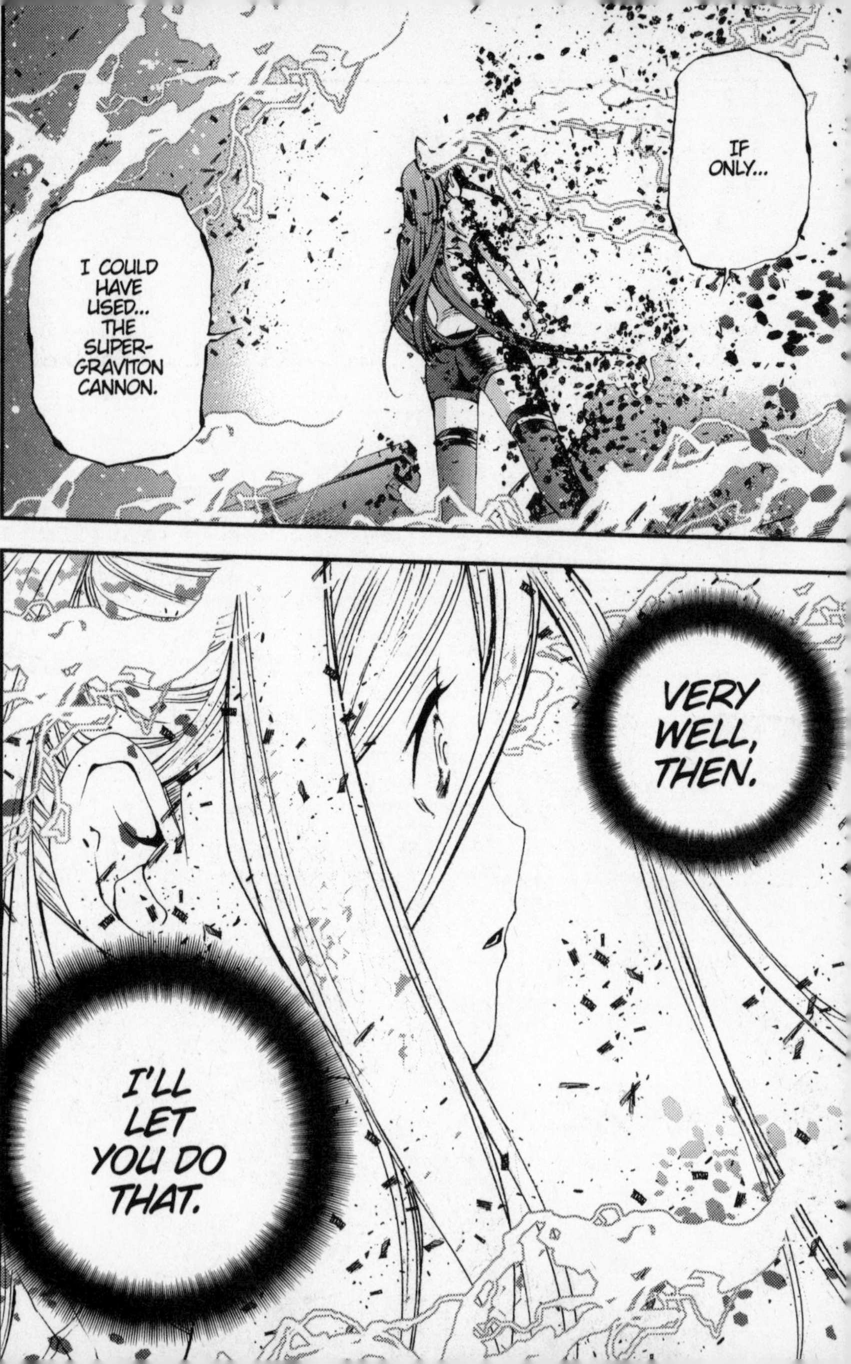
IF ONLY...
I COULD HAVE USED... THE SUPER-GRAVITON CANNON.
VERY WELL, THEN.
I'LL LET YOU DO THAT.

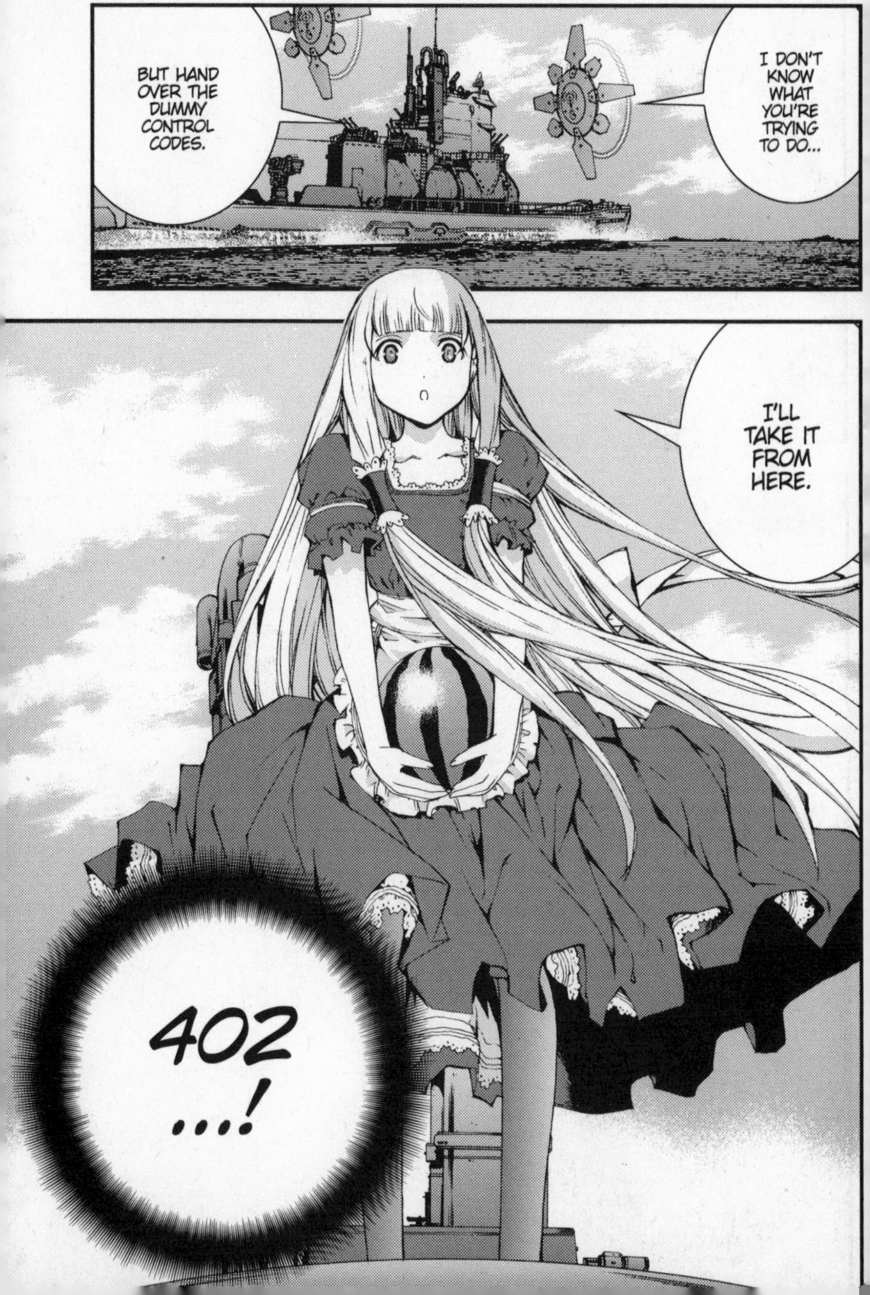
I DON'T KNOW WHAT YOU'RE TRYING TO DO...
BUT HAND OVER THE DUMMY CONTROL CODES.
I'LL TAKE IT FROM HERE.
402 ...!

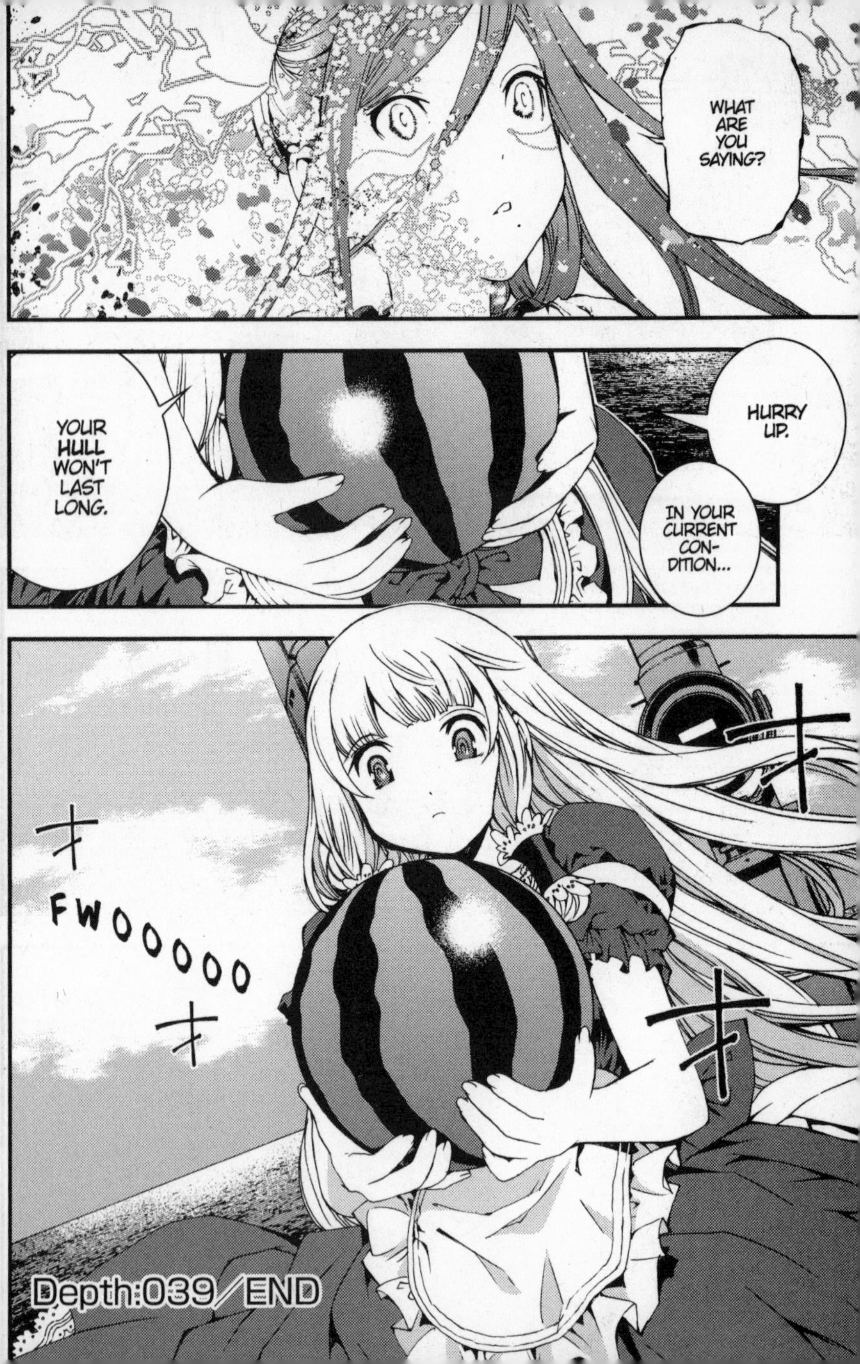
WHAT ARE YOU SAYING?
HURRY UP.
IN YOUR CURRENT CON-DITION...
YOUR HULL WON'T LAST LONG.
FWOOOOOO
Depth:039／END

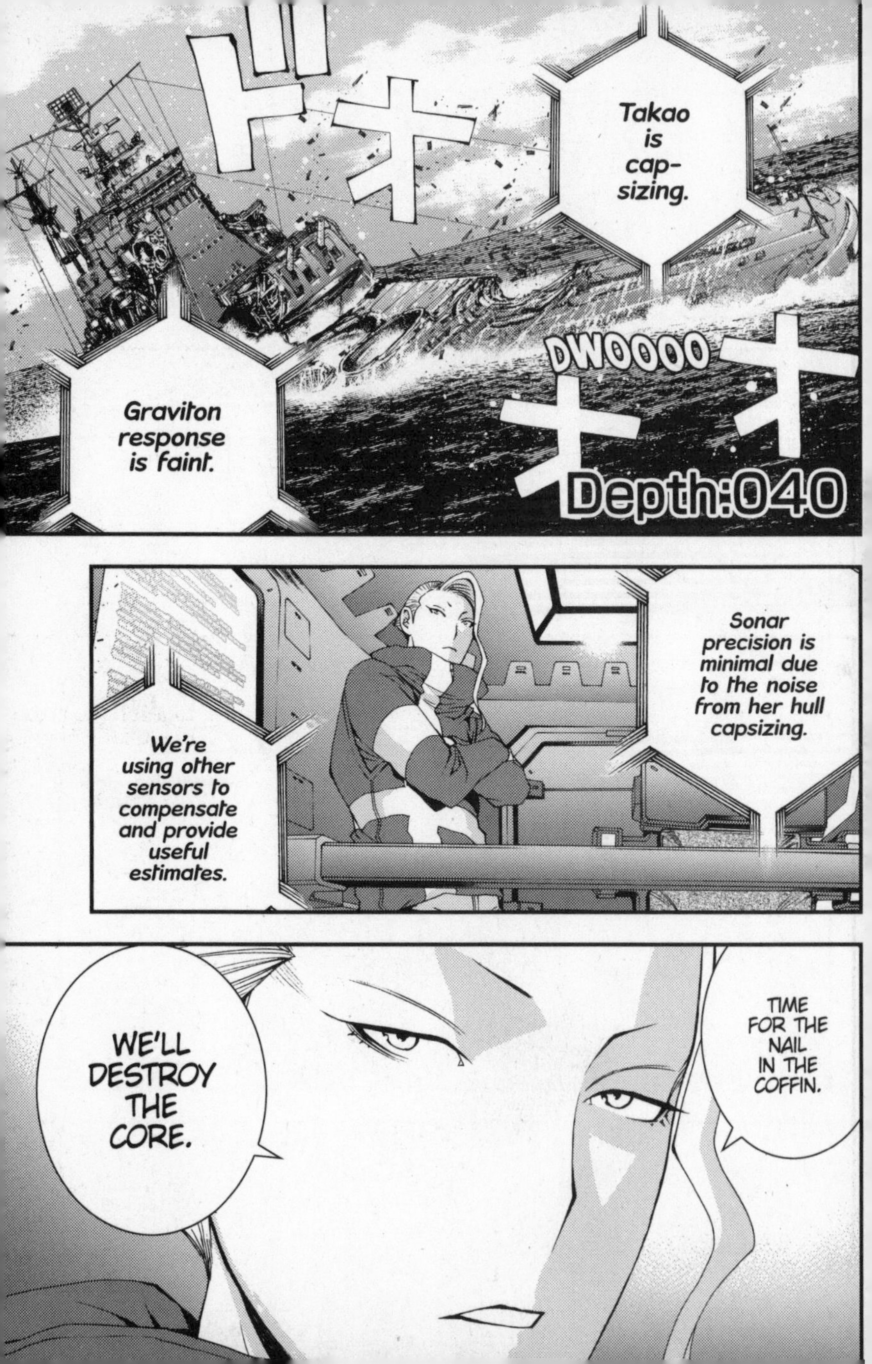
Takao is cap-sizing.
DWOOOO
Graviton response is faint.
Depth:040
Sonar precision is minimal due to the noise from her hull capsizing.
We're using other sensors to compensate and provide useful estimates.
TIME FOR THE NAIL IN THE COFFIN.
WE'LL DESTROY THE CORE.

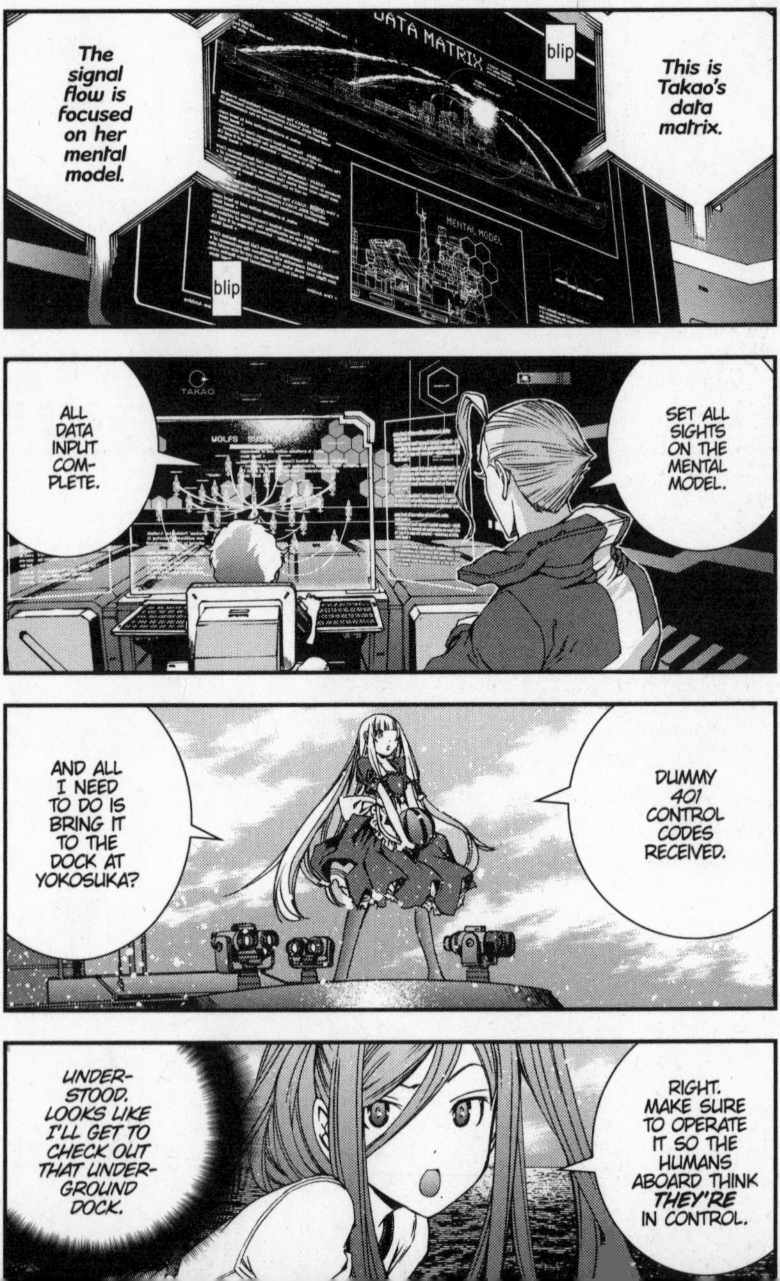
blip
This is Takao's data matrix.
The signal flow is focused on her mental model.
blip
SET ALL SIGHTS ON THE MENTAL MODEL.
ALL DATA INPUT COMPLETE.
DUMMY 401 CONTROL CODES RECEIVED.
AND ALL I NEED TO DO IS BRING IT TO THE DOCK AT YOKOSUKA?
RIGHT. MAKE SURE TO OPERATE IT SO THE HUMANS ABOARD THINK *THEY'RE* IN CONTROL.
UNDERSTOOD. LOOKS LIKE I'LL GET TO CHECK OUT THAT UNDERGROUND DOCK.

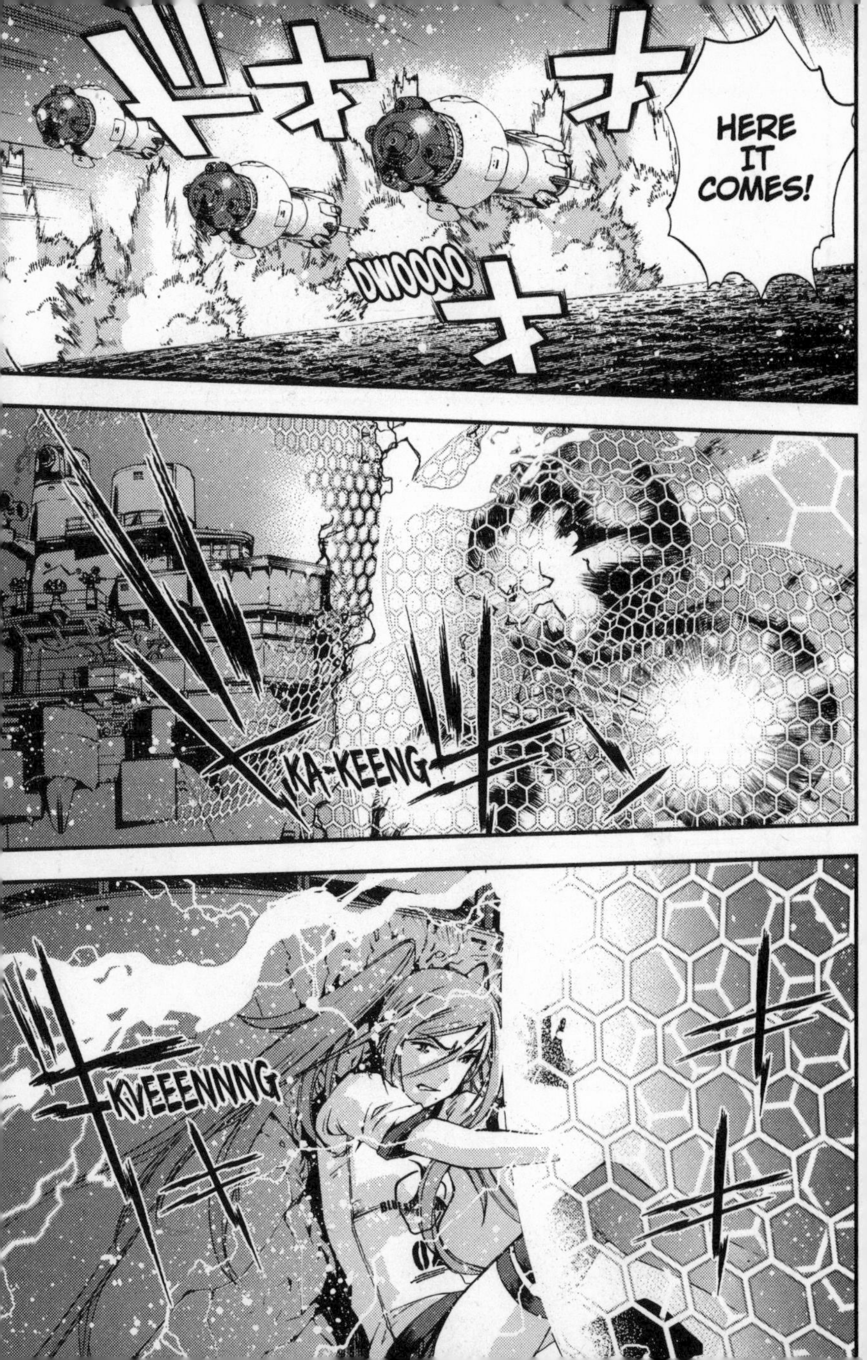
HERE IT COMES!
DWOOOO
KA-KEENG
KVEEENNNG

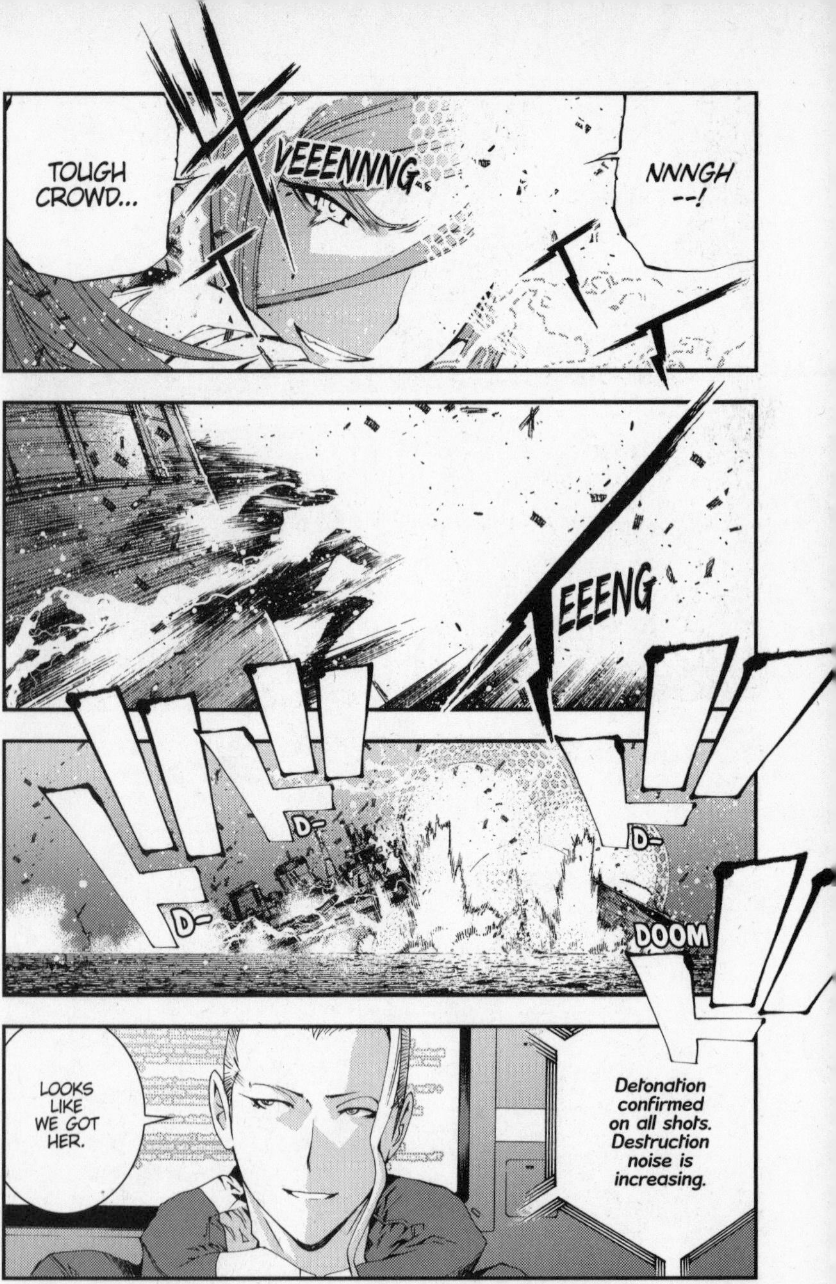
NNNGH --!
VEEENNNG
TOUGH CROWD...
EEEENG
D-
D-
DOOM
D-
Detonation confirmed on all shots. Destruction noise is increasing.
LOOKS LIKE WE GOT HER.

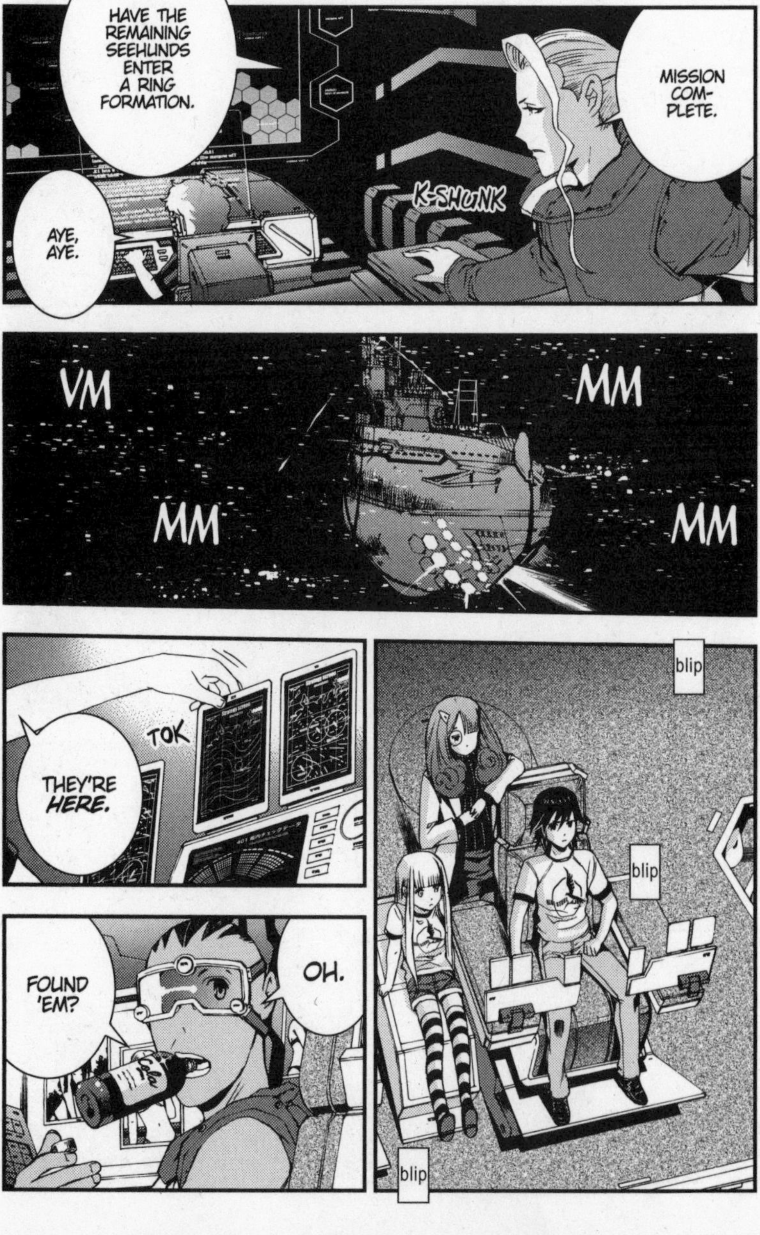
MISSION COMPLETE.
HAVE THE REMAINING SEEHUNDS ENTER A RING FORMATION.
K-SHUNK
AYE, AYE.
MM
VM
MM
MM
blip
blip
blip
TOK
THEY'RE *HERE.*
OH.
FOUND 'EM?

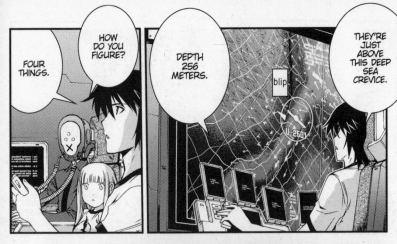

THEY'RE JUST ABOVE THIS DEEP SEA CREVICE.
DEPTH 256 METERS.
blip
U-2501
HOW DO YOU FIGURE?
FOUR THINGS.
FIRST...
THIS REGION EXPERIENCES CHAOTIC CURRENT PATTERNS YEAR ROUND.
blip
Speed of Current
U-2501
Estimated position
Depth···250m
EXCEPT IN THIS ONE SPOT, THE CUR-RENT IS *STABLE.*
SEC-OND...
IN AN EMERGENCY, THEY COULD ENTER THIS CREVICE.
U-2501
U-2501
blip
THAT WOULD MAKE THEM HARD TO DETECT, EVEN WITH ACTIVE SONAR.
THIRD, THIS REGION HAS A LAYER DEPTH OF ABOUT 1500 METERS.
1200
1300
1400
depth···1500
blip
THAT'S THE YEARLY AVERAGE.

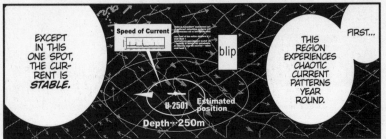

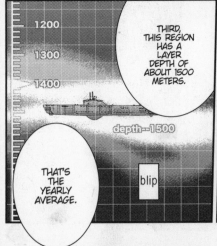

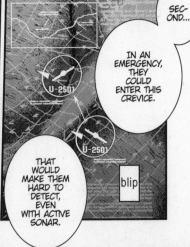

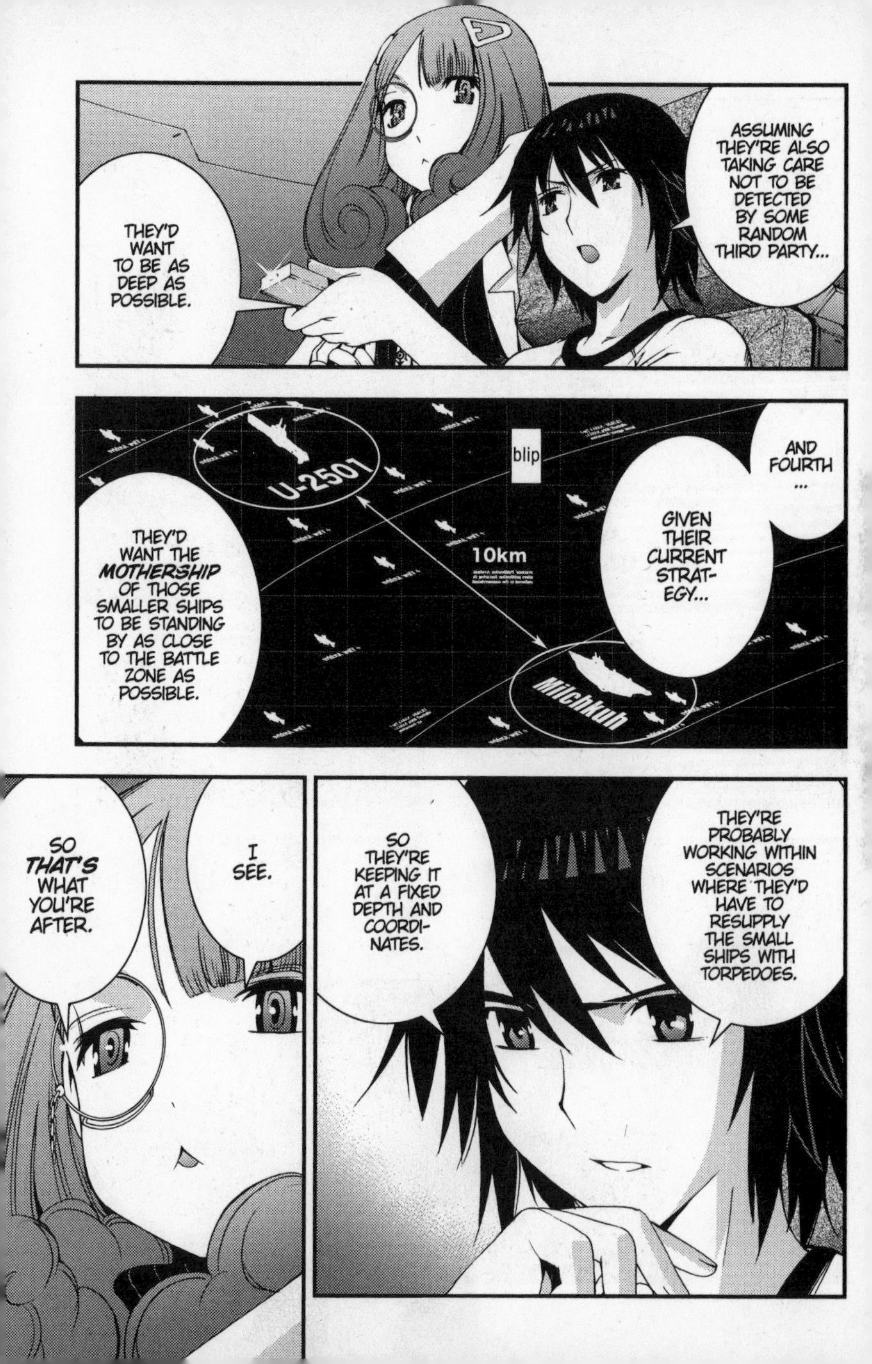
ASSUMING THEY'RE ALSO TAKING CARE NOT TO BE DETECTED BY SOME RANDOM THIRD PARTY...
THEY'D WANT TO BE AS DEEP AS POSSIBLE.
AND FOURTH ...
GIVEN THEIR CURRENT STRAT-EGY...
blip
U-2501
10km
Milchkuh
THEY'D WANT THE *MOTHERSHIP* OF THOSE SMALLER SHIPS TO BE STANDING BY AS CLOSE TO THE BATTLE ZONE AS POSSIBLE.
THEY'RE PROBABLY WORKING WITHIN SCENARIOS WHERE THEY'D HAVE TO RESUPPLY THE SMALL SHIPS WITH TORPEDOES.
SO THEY'RE KEEPING IT AT A FIXED DEPTH AND COORDI-NATES.
I SEE.
SO *THAT'S* WHAT YOU'RE AFTER.

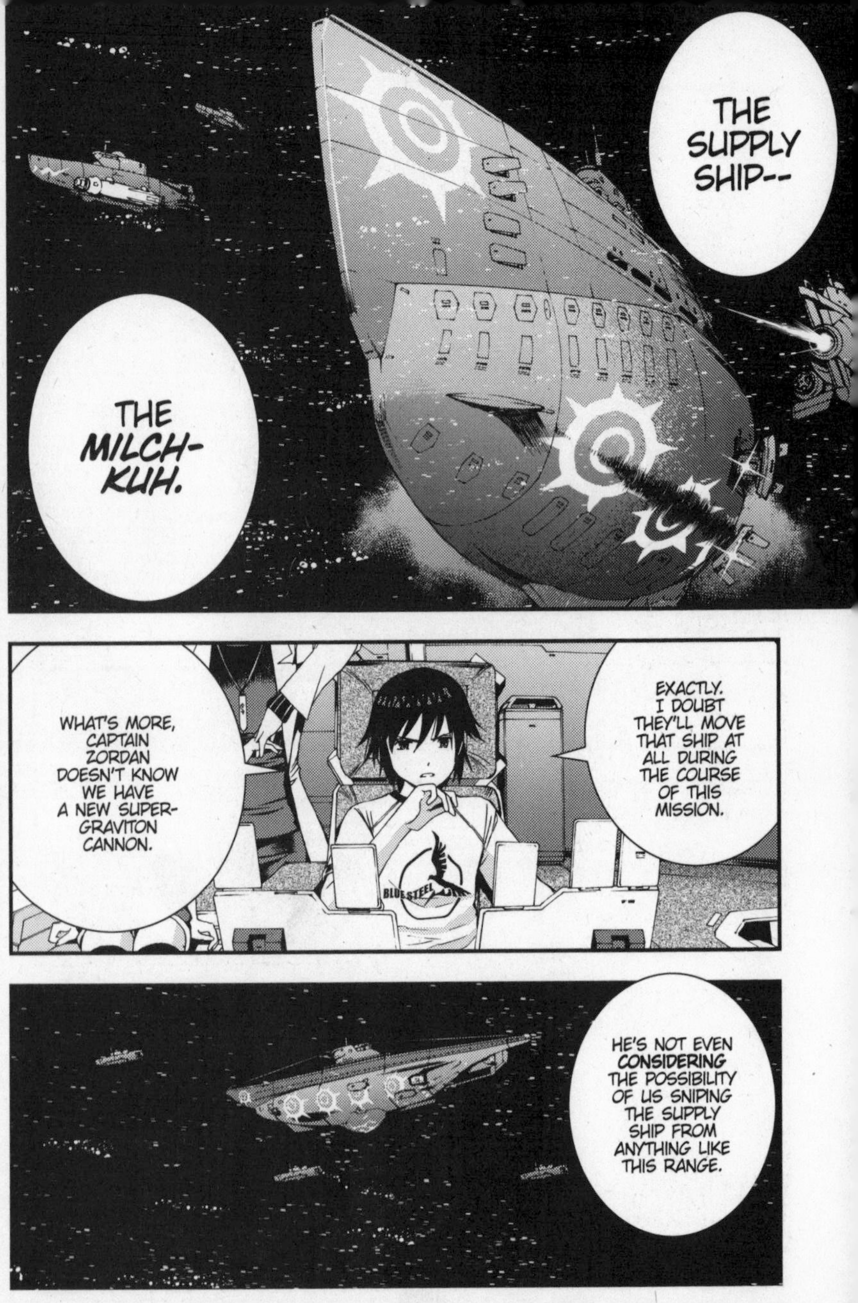
THE SUPPLY SHIP--
THE *MILCH-KUH.*
EXACTLY. I DOUBT THEY'LL MOVE THAT SHIP AT ALL DURING THE COURSE OF THIS MISSION.
WHAT'S MORE, CAPTAIN ZORDAN DOESN'T KNOW WE HAVE A NEW SUPER-GRAVITON CANNON.
HE'S NOT EVEN **CONSIDERING** THE POSSIBILITY OF US SNIPING THE SUPPLY SHIP FROM ANYTHING LIKE THIS RANGE.

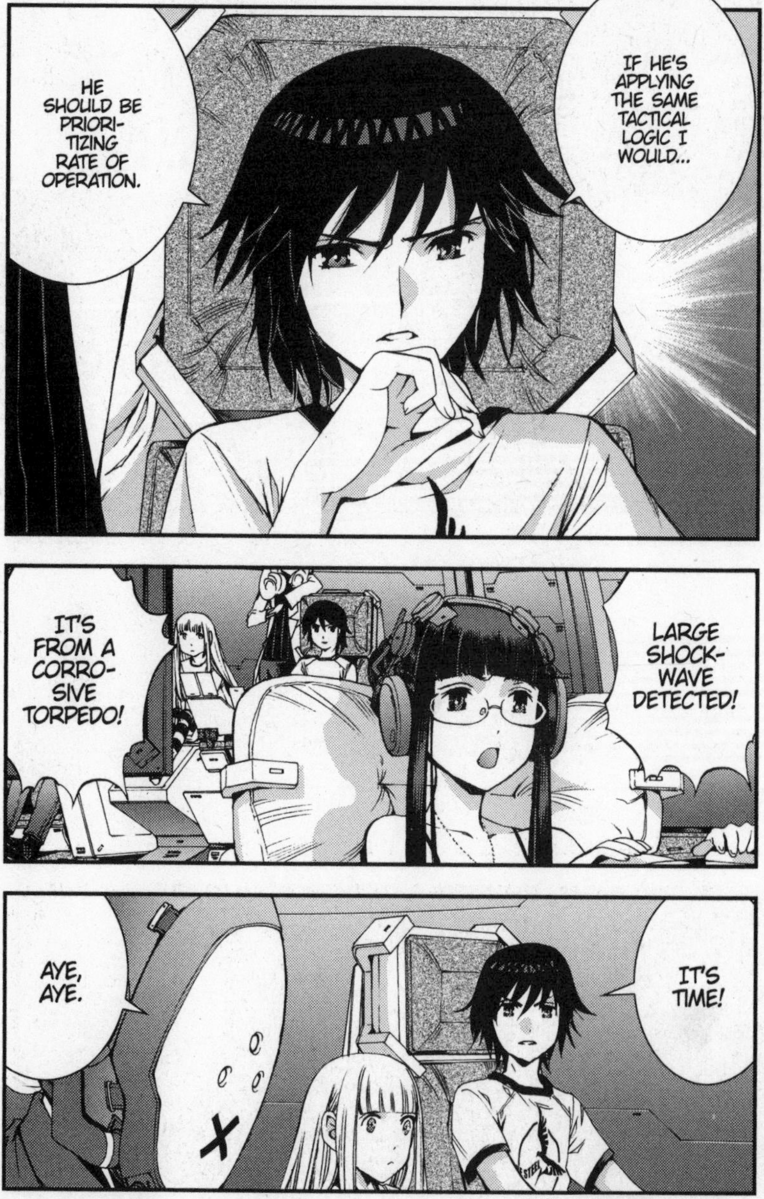
IF HE'S APPLYING THE SAME TACTICAL LOGIC I WOULD...
HE SHOULD BE PRIORI-TIZING RATE OF OPERATION.
LARGE SHOCK-WAVE DETECTED!
IT'S FROM A CORRO-SIVE TORPEDO!
IT'S TIME!
AYE, AYE.

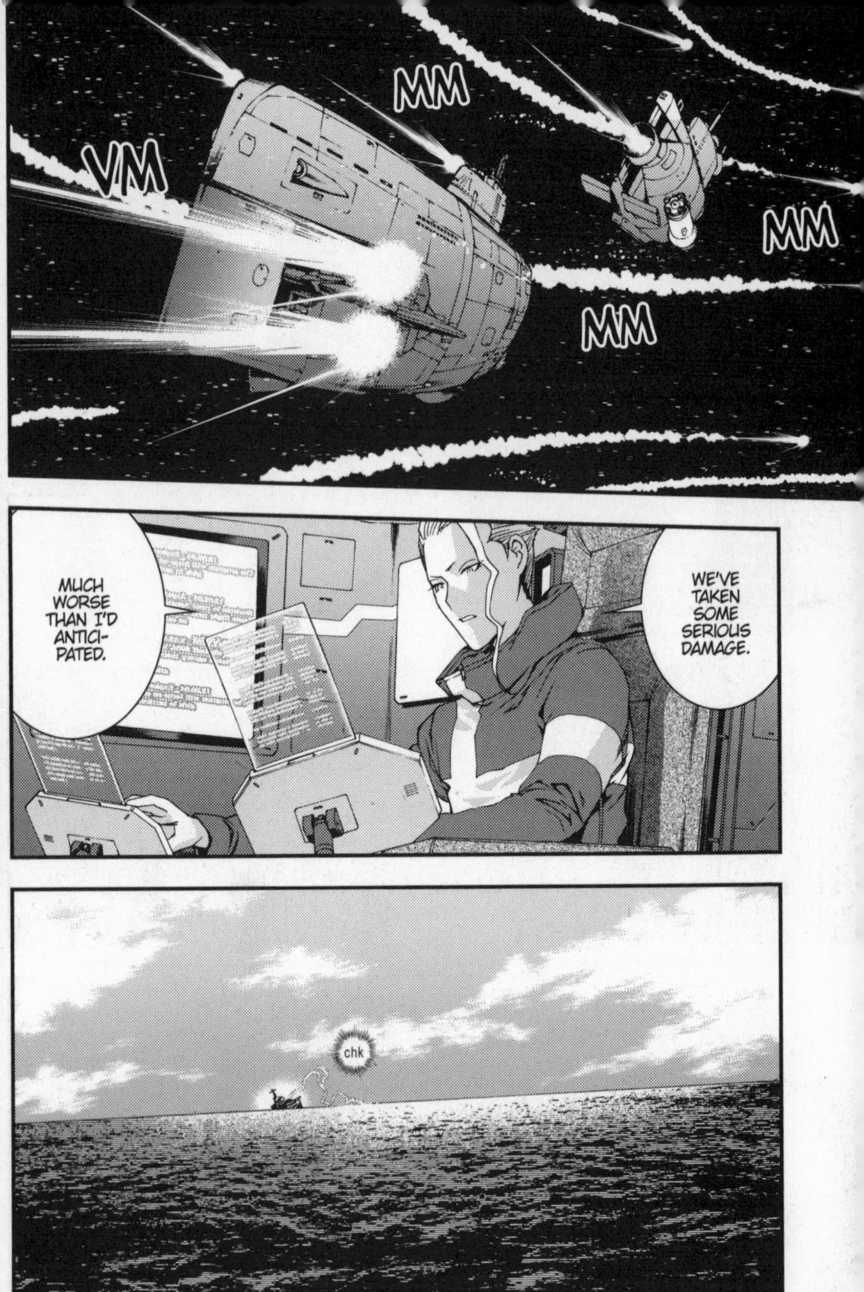
MM
MM
VM
MM
WE'VE TAKEN SOME SERIOUS DAMAGE.
MUCH WORSE THAN I'D ANTICI-PATED.
chk

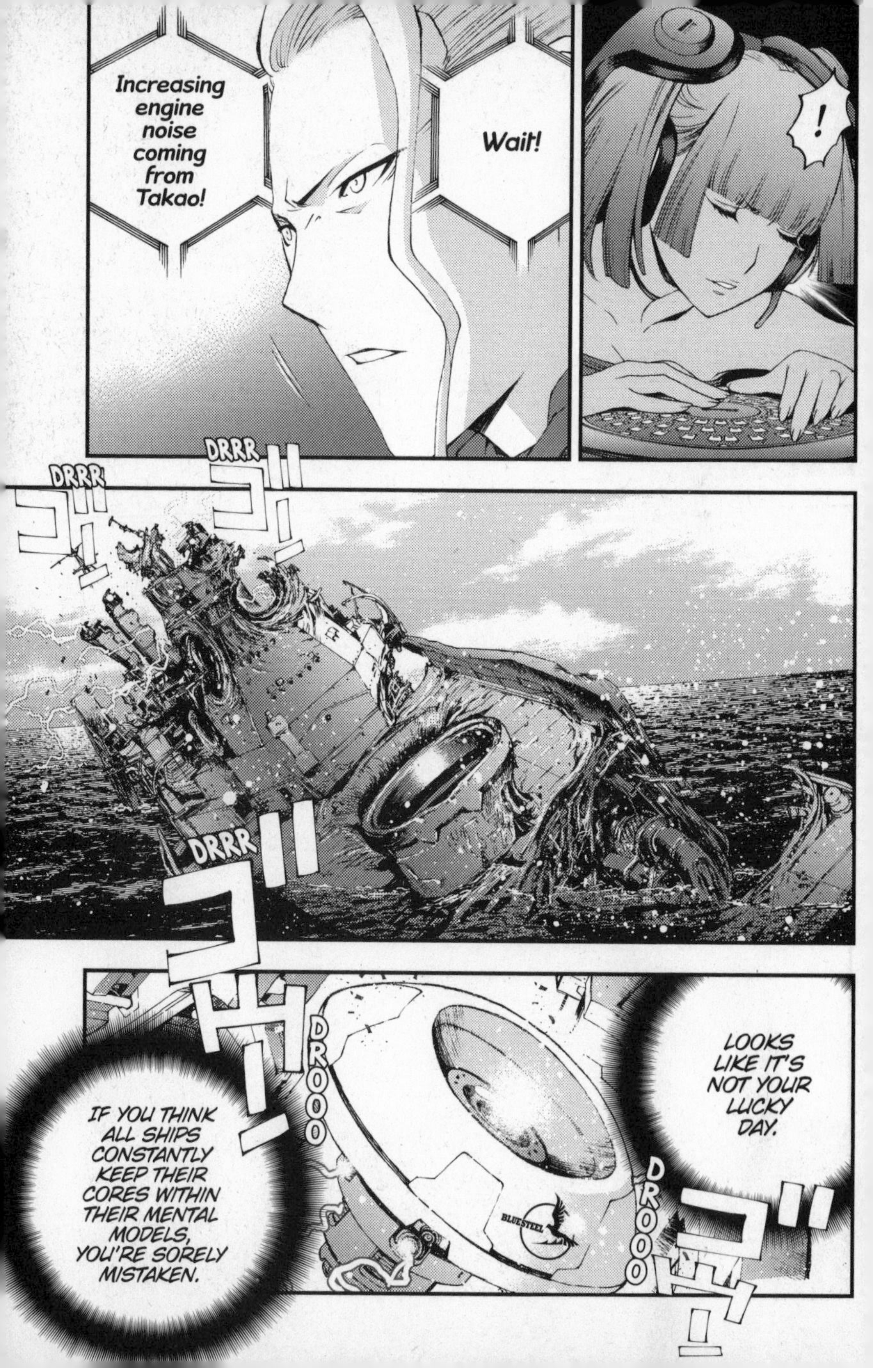
!
Wait!
Increasing engine noise coming from Takao!
DRRR
DRRR
DRRR
LOOKS LIKE IT'S NOT YOUR LUCKY DAY.
DROOO
BLUESTEEL
DROOO
IF YOU THINK ALL SHIPS CONSTANTLY KEEP THEIR CORES WITHIN THEIR MENTAL MODELS, YOU'RE SORELY MISTAKEN.

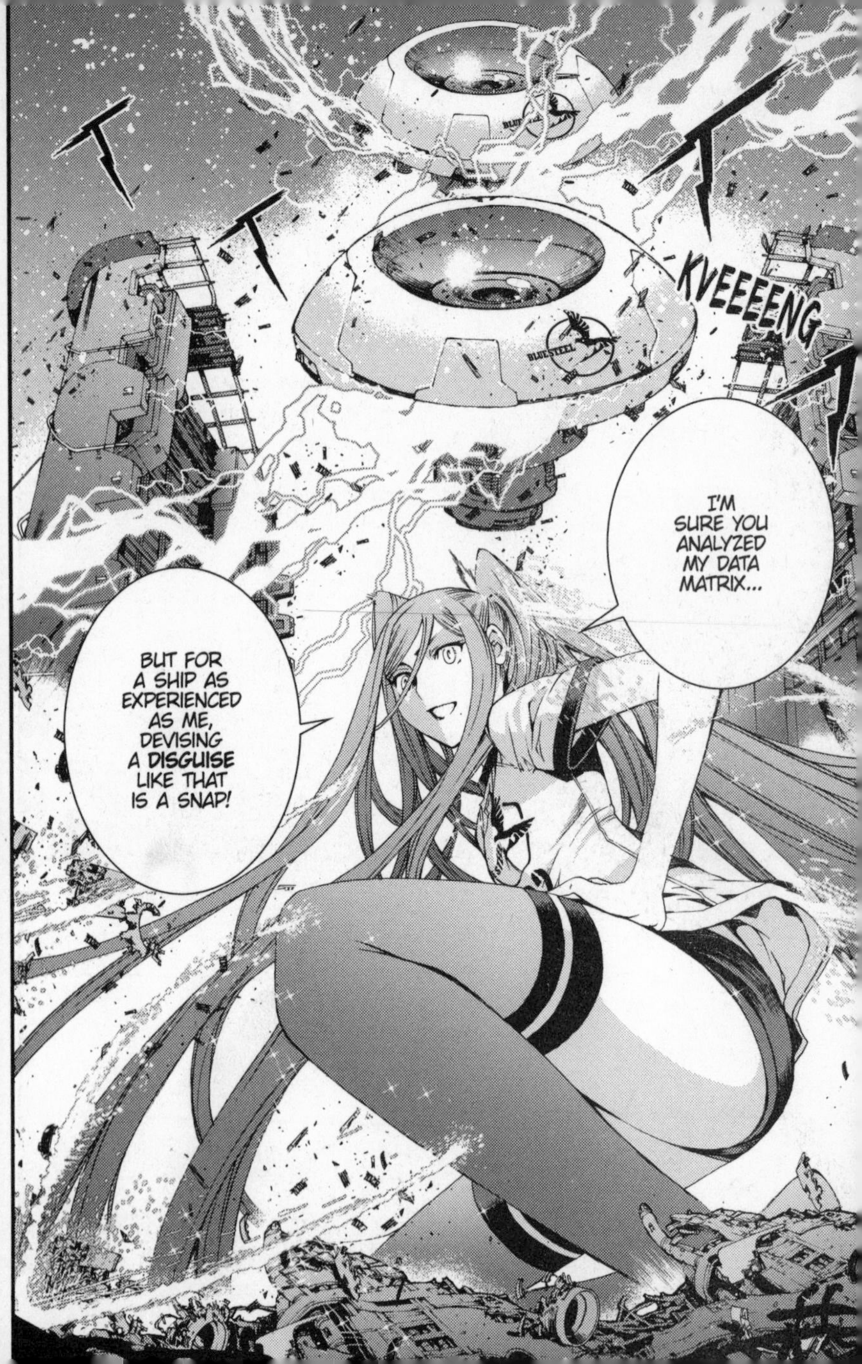
KVEEEEENG
I'M SURE YOU ANALYZED MY DATA MATRIX...
BUT FOR A SHIP AS EXPERIENCED AS ME, DEVISING A DISGUISE LIKE THAT IS A SNAP!

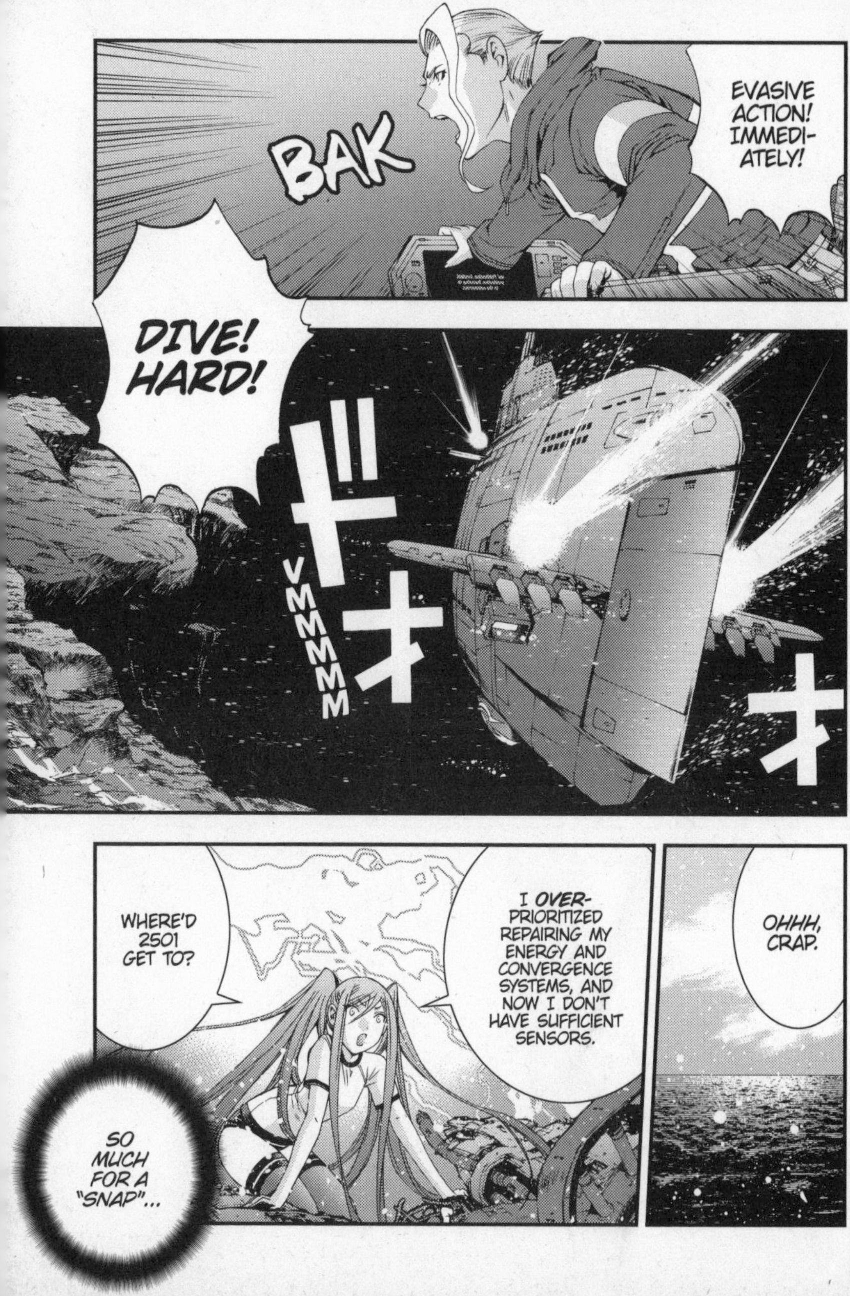
EVASIVE ACTION! IMMEDI-ATELY!
BAK
DIVE! HARD!
VMMMMM
OHHH, CRAP.
I OVER-PRIORITIZED REPAIRING MY ENERGY AND CONVERGENCE SYSTEMS, AND NOW I DON'T HAVE SUFFICIENT SENSORS.
WHERE'D 2501 GET TO?
SO MUCH FOR A "SNAP"...

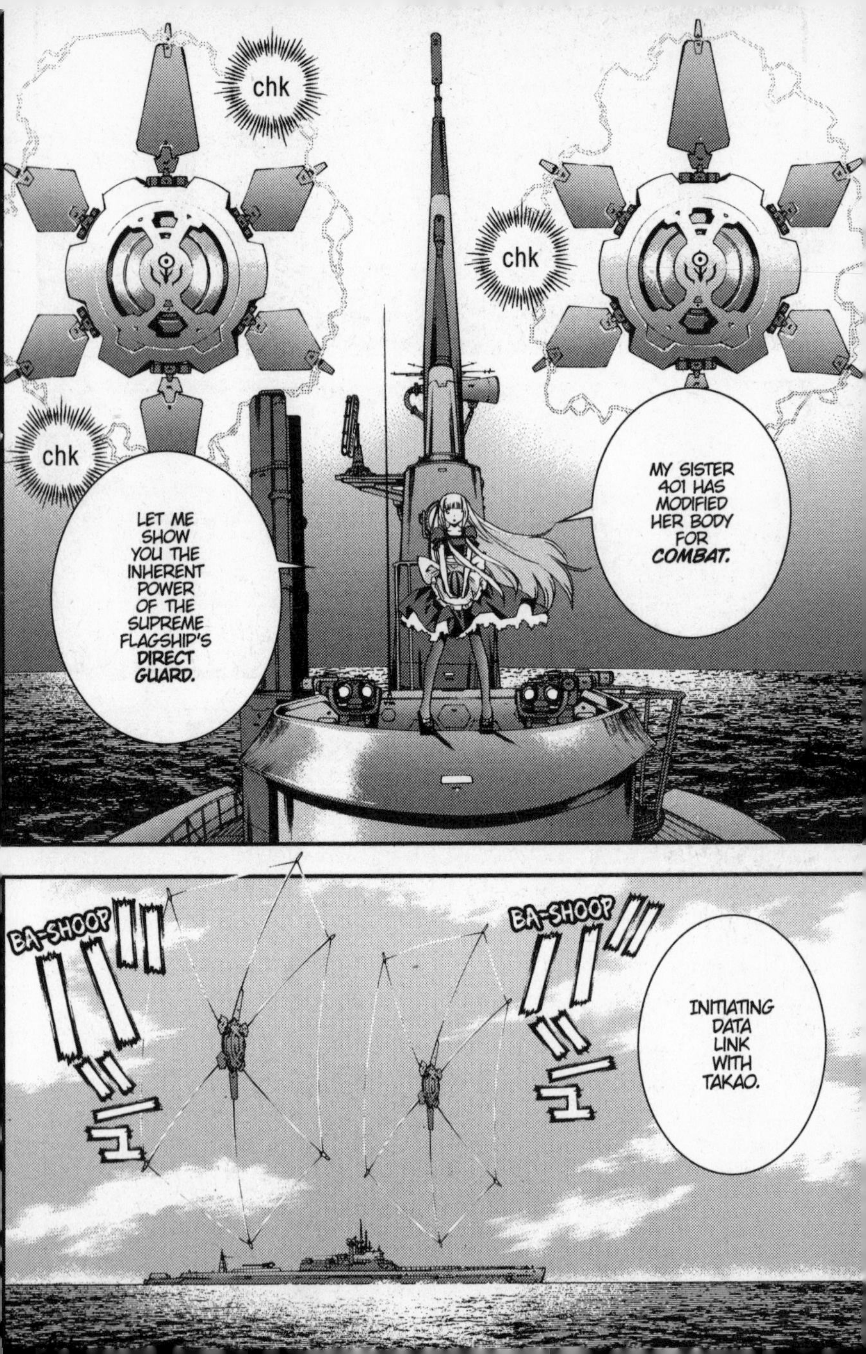
chk
chk
MY SISTER 401 HAS MODIFIED HER BODY FOR COMBAT.
chk
LET ME SHOW YOU THE INHERENT POWER OF THE SUPREME FLAGSHIP'S DIRECT GUARD.
INITIATING DATA LINK WITH TAKAO.
BA-SHOOP
BA-SHOOP

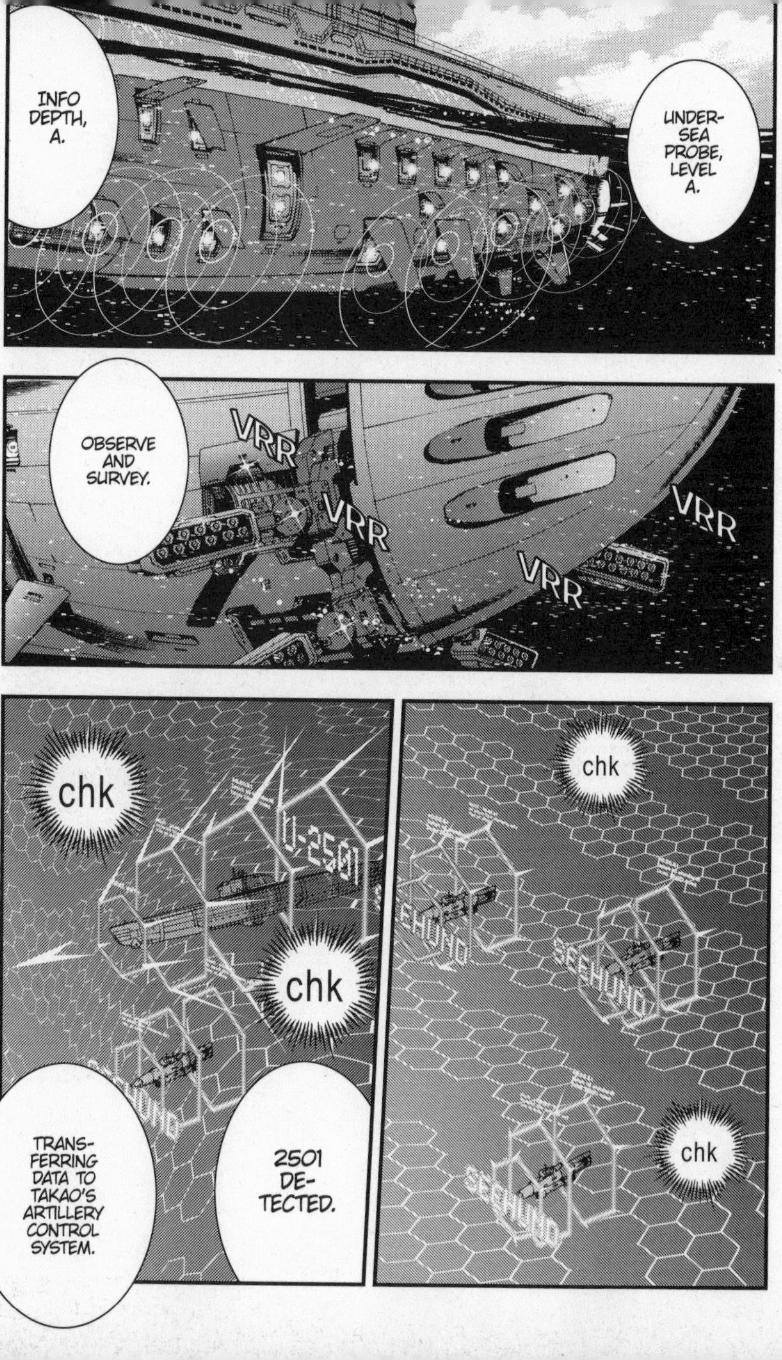
UNDER-SEA PROBE, LEVEL A.
INFO DEPTH, A.
VRR
VRR
VRR
VRR
OBSERVE AND SURVEY.
chk
SEEHUND
SEEHUND
chk
SEEHUND
chk
U-2501
chk
SEEHUND
2501 DETECTED.
TRANSFERRING DATA TO TAKAO'S ARTILLERY CONTROL SYSTEM.

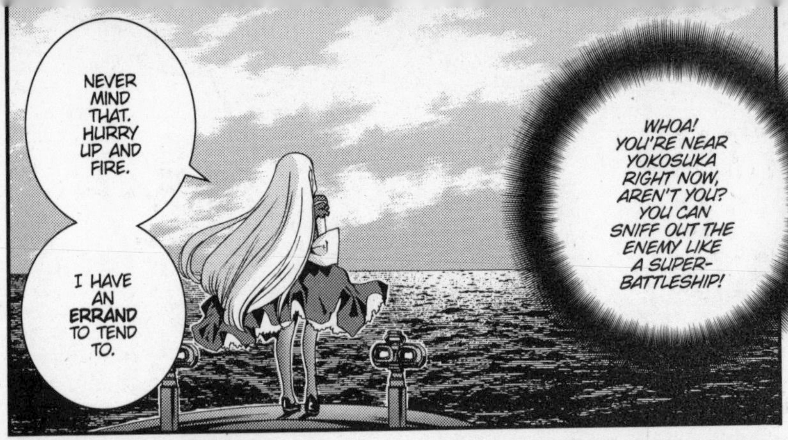
WHOA! YOU'RE NEAR YOKOSUKA RIGHT NOW, AREN'T YOU? YOU CAN SNIFF OUT THE ENEMY LIKE A SUPER-BATTLESHIP!
NEVER MIND THAT. HURRY UP AND FIRE.
I HAVE AN ERRAND TO TEND TO.
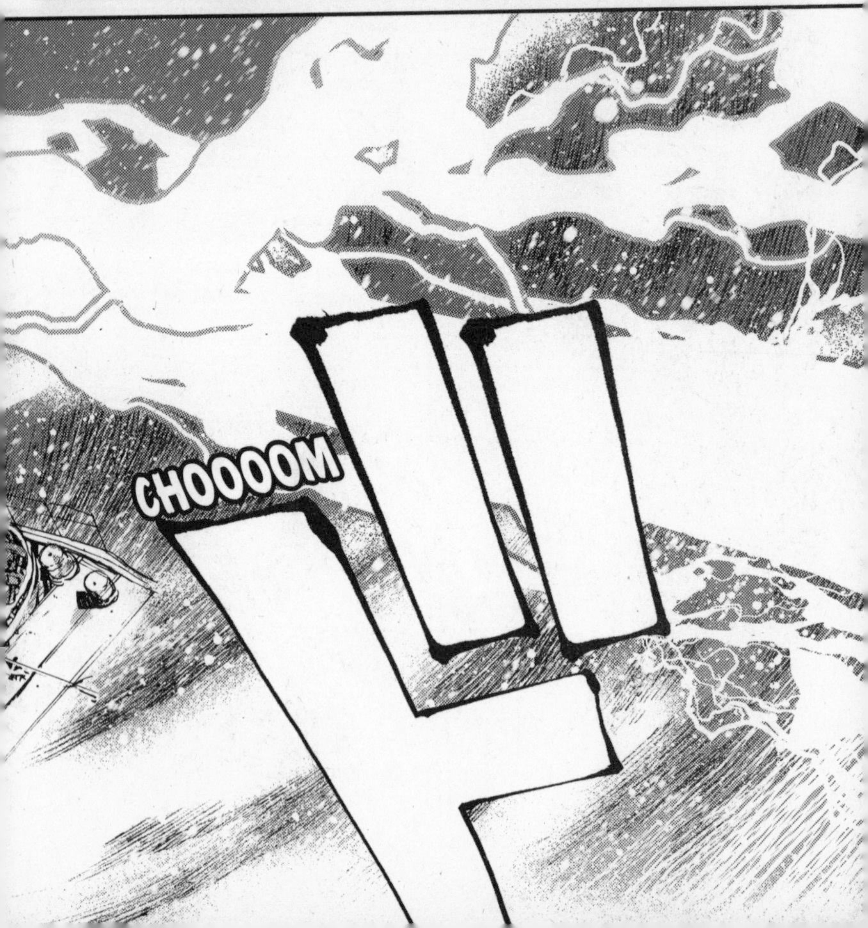
CHOOOOM

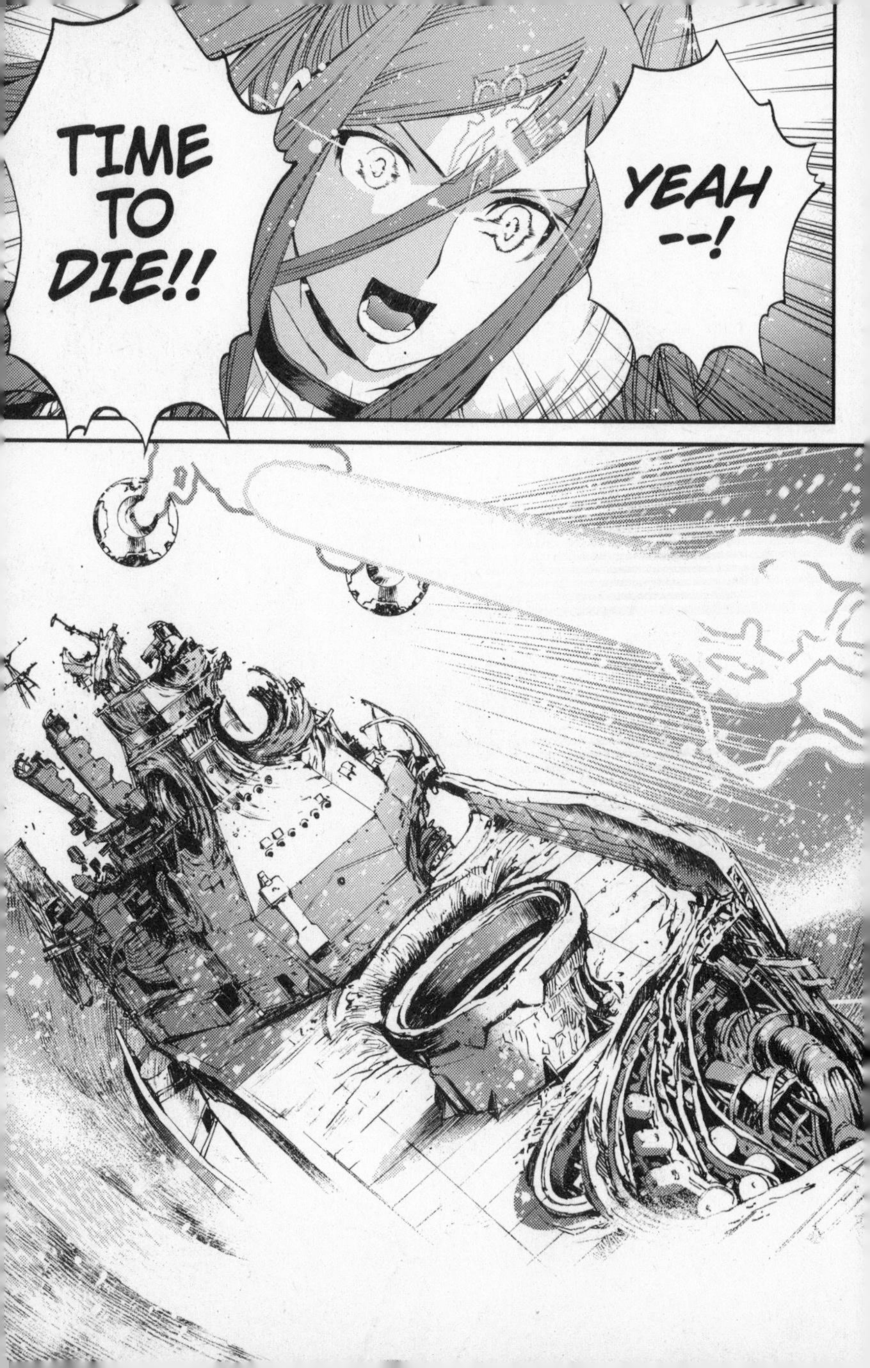
YEAH --!
TIME TO DIE!!

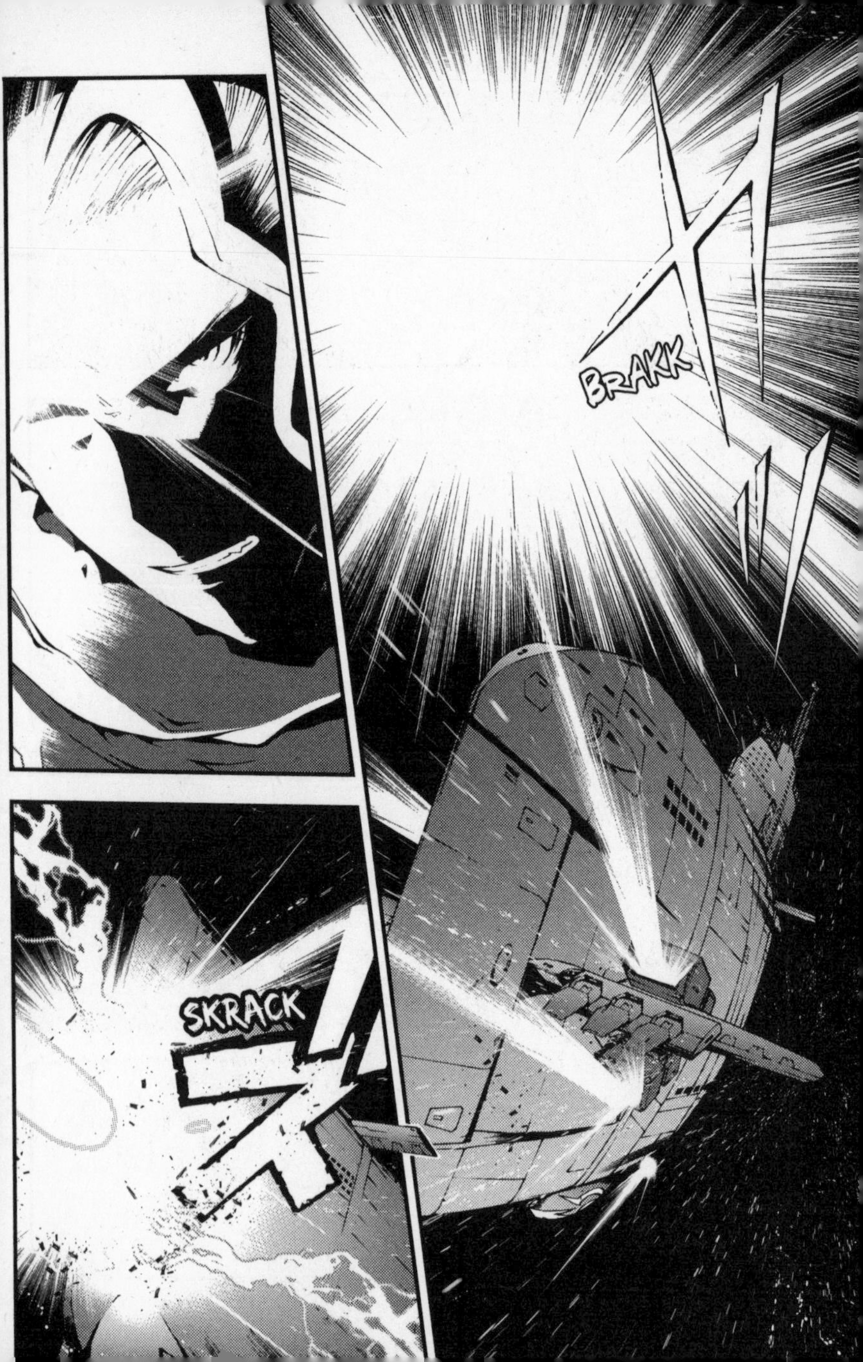
BRAKK
SKRACK

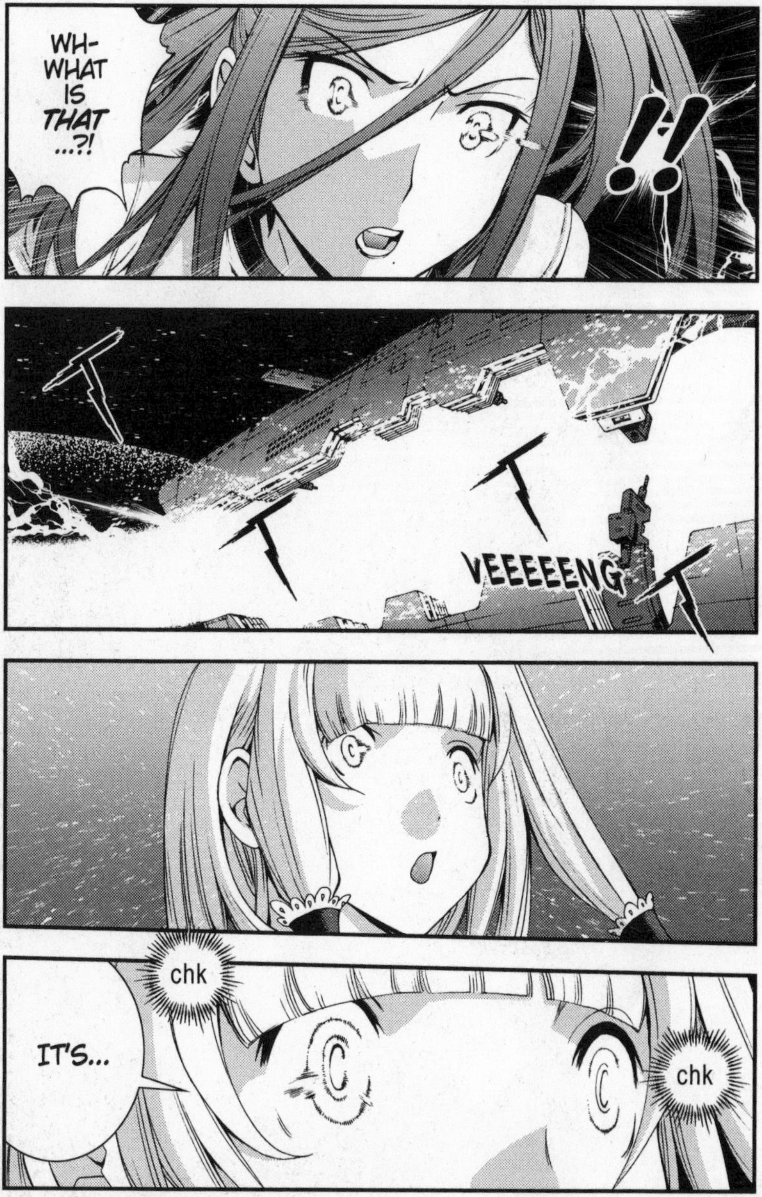

!!
WH-WHAT IS THAT ...?!
VEEEEENG
chk
chk
IT'S...

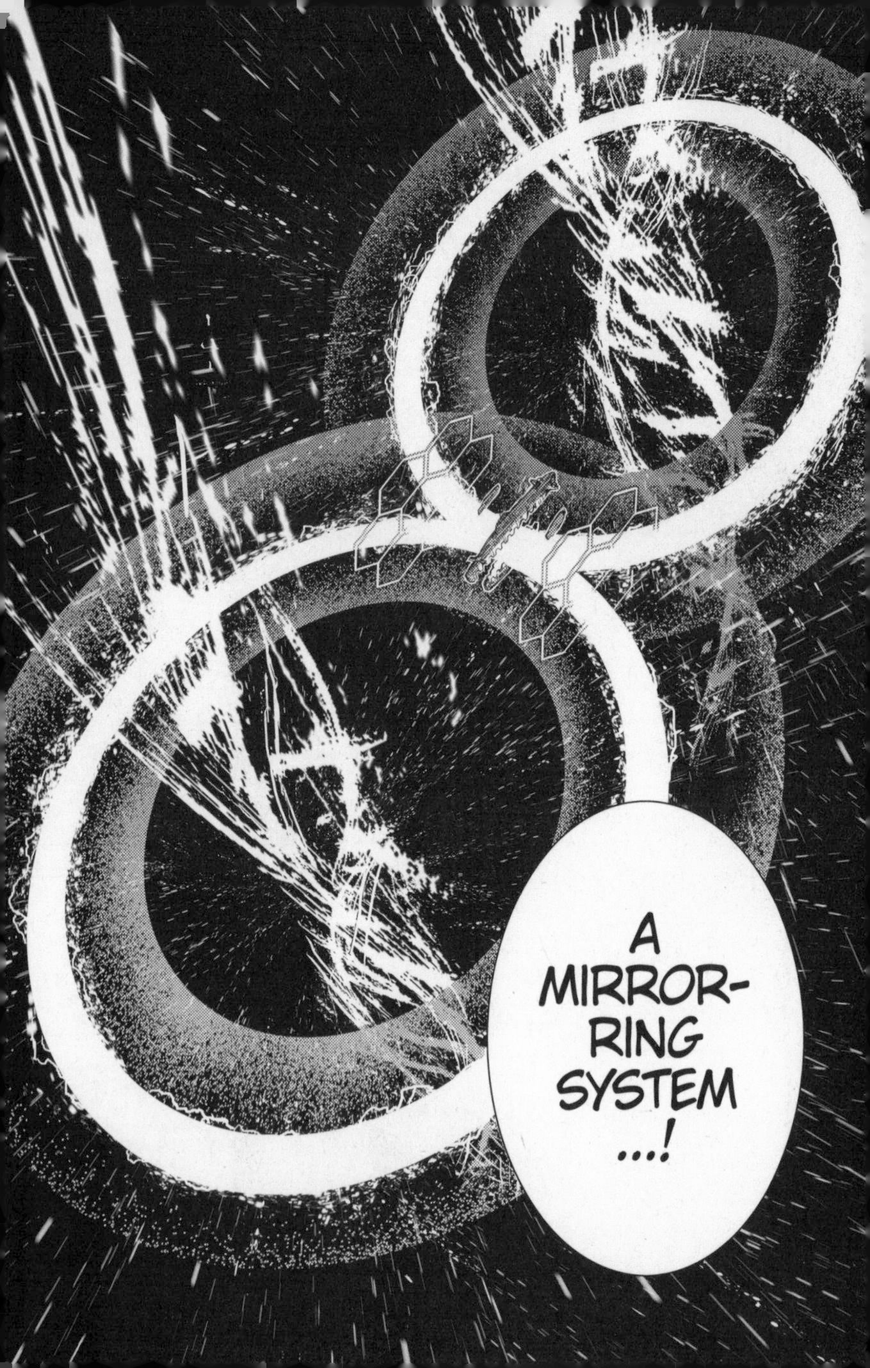
A MIRROR-RING SYSTEM ...!

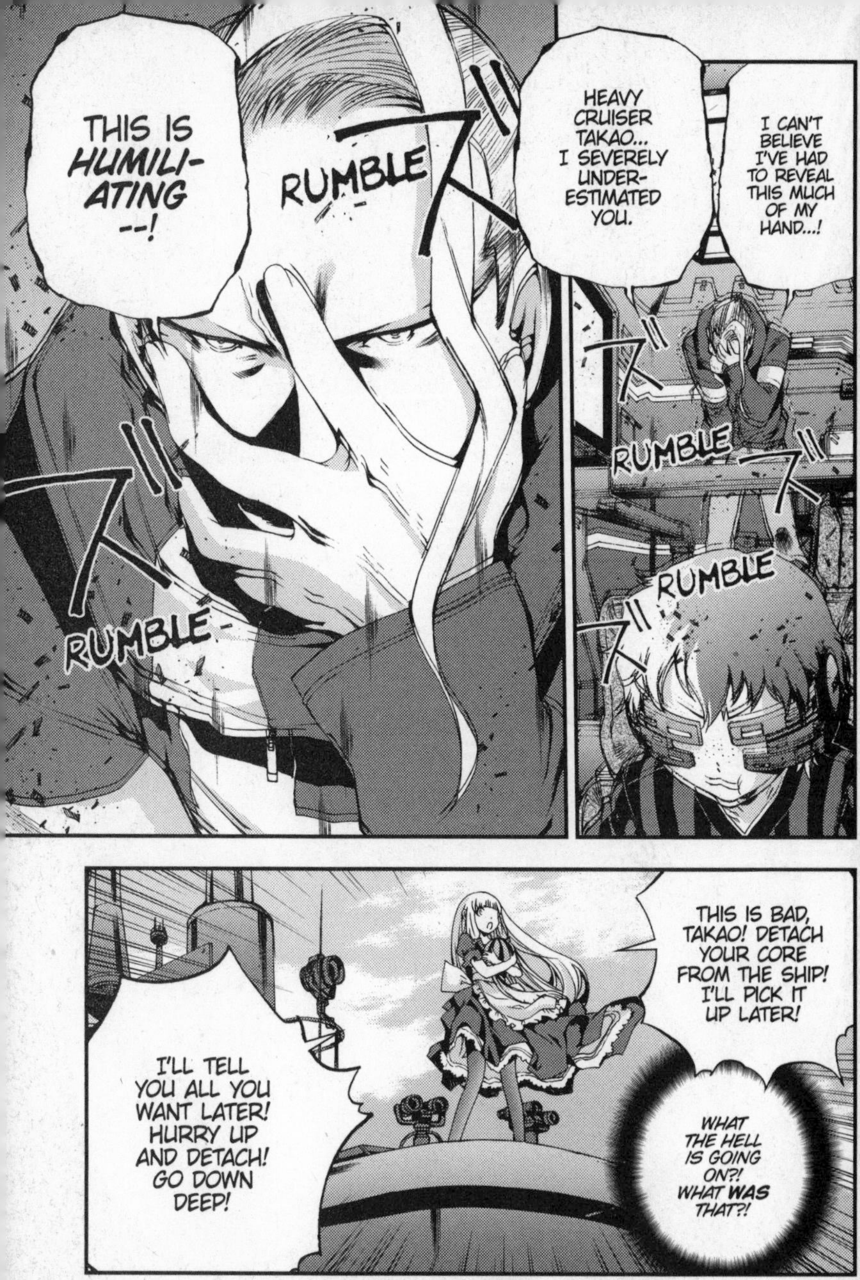
I CAN'T BELIEVE I'VE HAD TO REVEAL THIS MUCH OF MY HAND...!
HEAVY CRUISER TAKAO... I SEVERELY UNDER-ESTIMATED YOU.
RUMBLE
RUMBLE
THIS IS HUMILI-ATING --!
RUMBLE
RUMBLE
THIS IS BAD, TAKAO! DETACH YOUR CORE FROM THE SHIP! I'LL PICK IT UP LATER!
WHAT THE HELL IS GOING ON?! WHAT WAS THAT?!
I'LL TELL YOU ALL YOU WANT LATER! HURRY UP AND DETACH! GO DOWN DEEP!

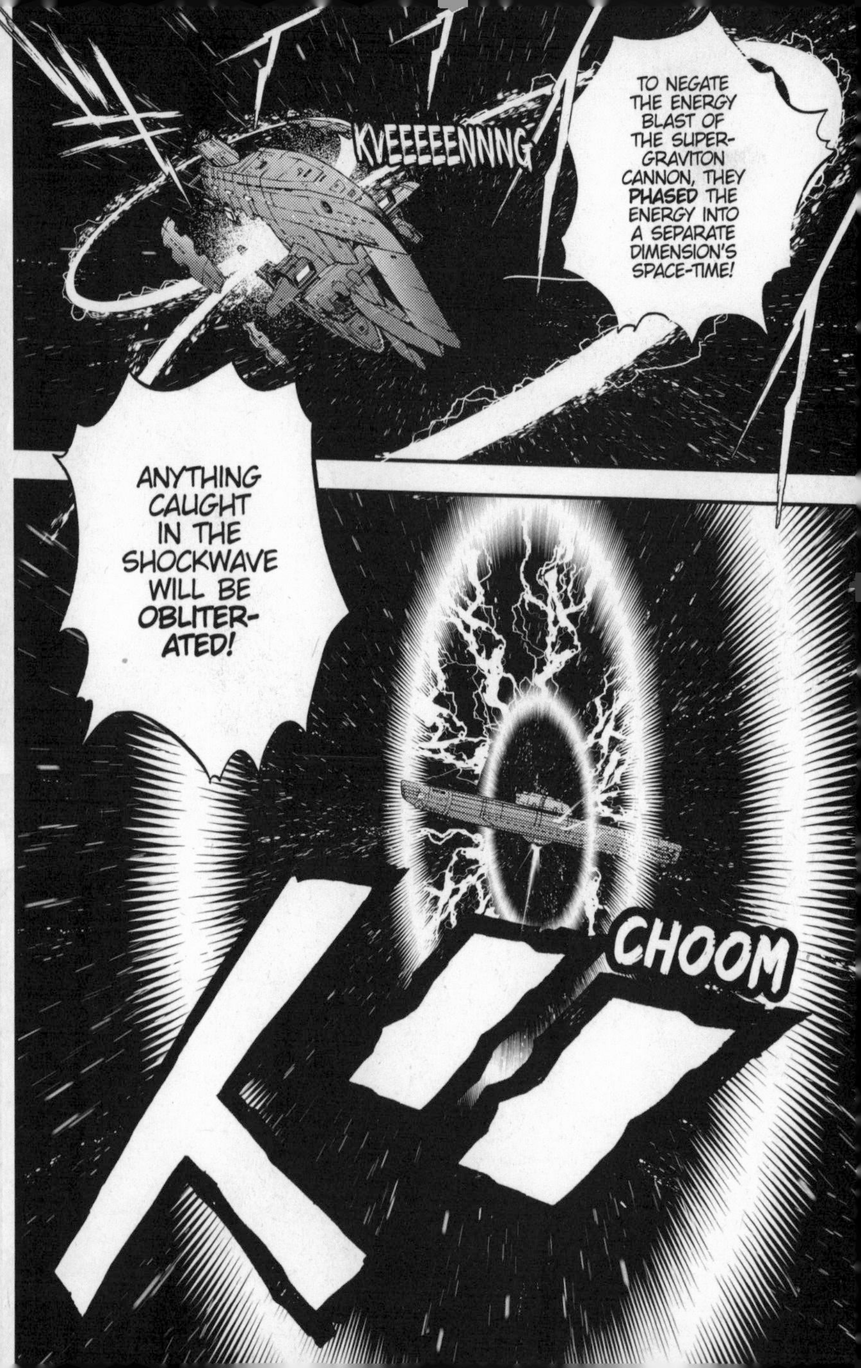
TO NEGATE THE ENERGY BLAST OF THE SUPER-GRAVITON CANNON, THEY **PHASED** THE ENERGY INTO A SEPARATE DIMENSION'S SPACE-TIME!
KVEEEEENNNG
ANYTHING CAUGHT IN THE SHOCKWAVE WILL BE OBLITERATED!
CHOOM

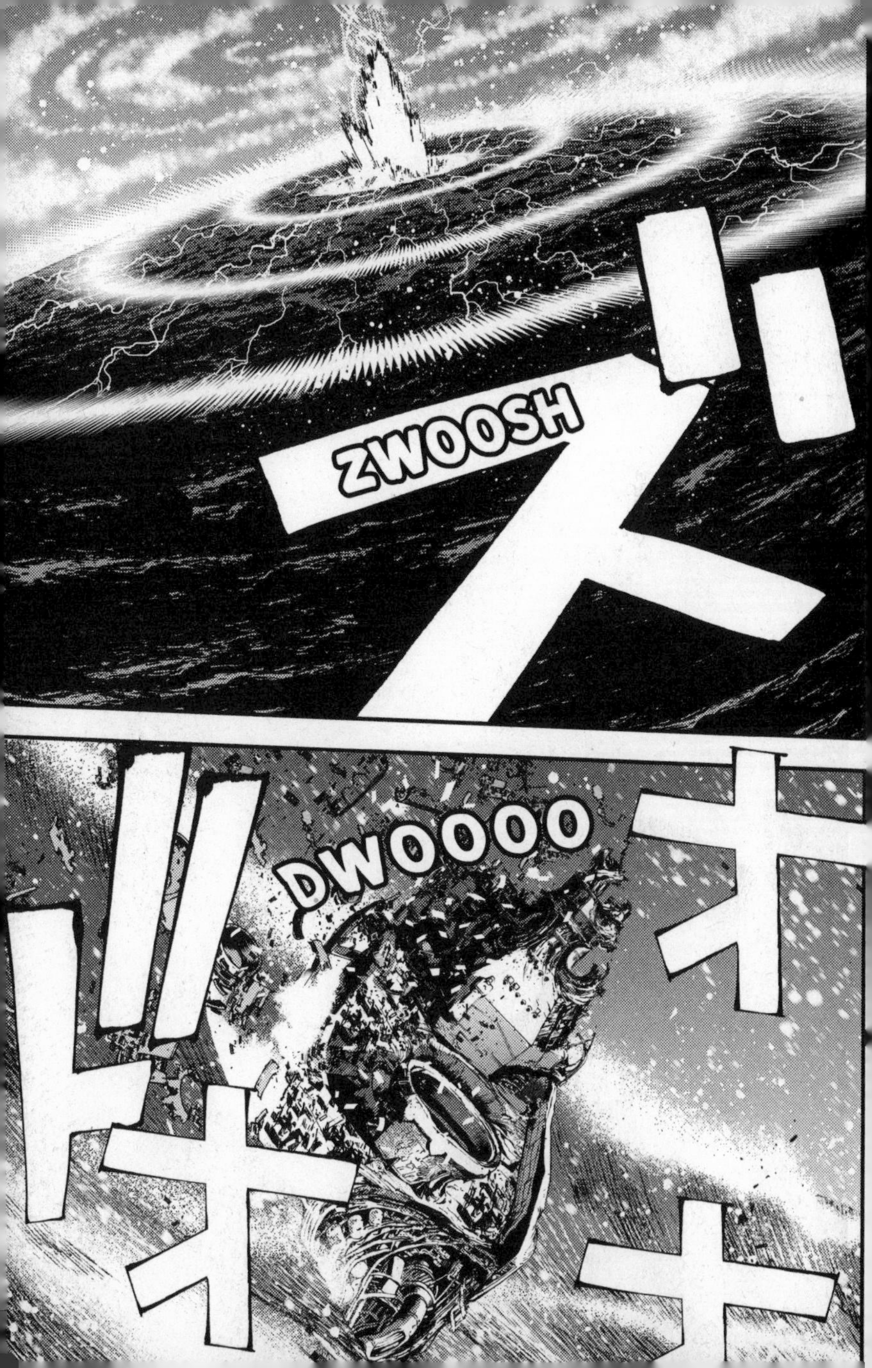
ZWOOSH
ズ
DWOOOO
ドオオオ

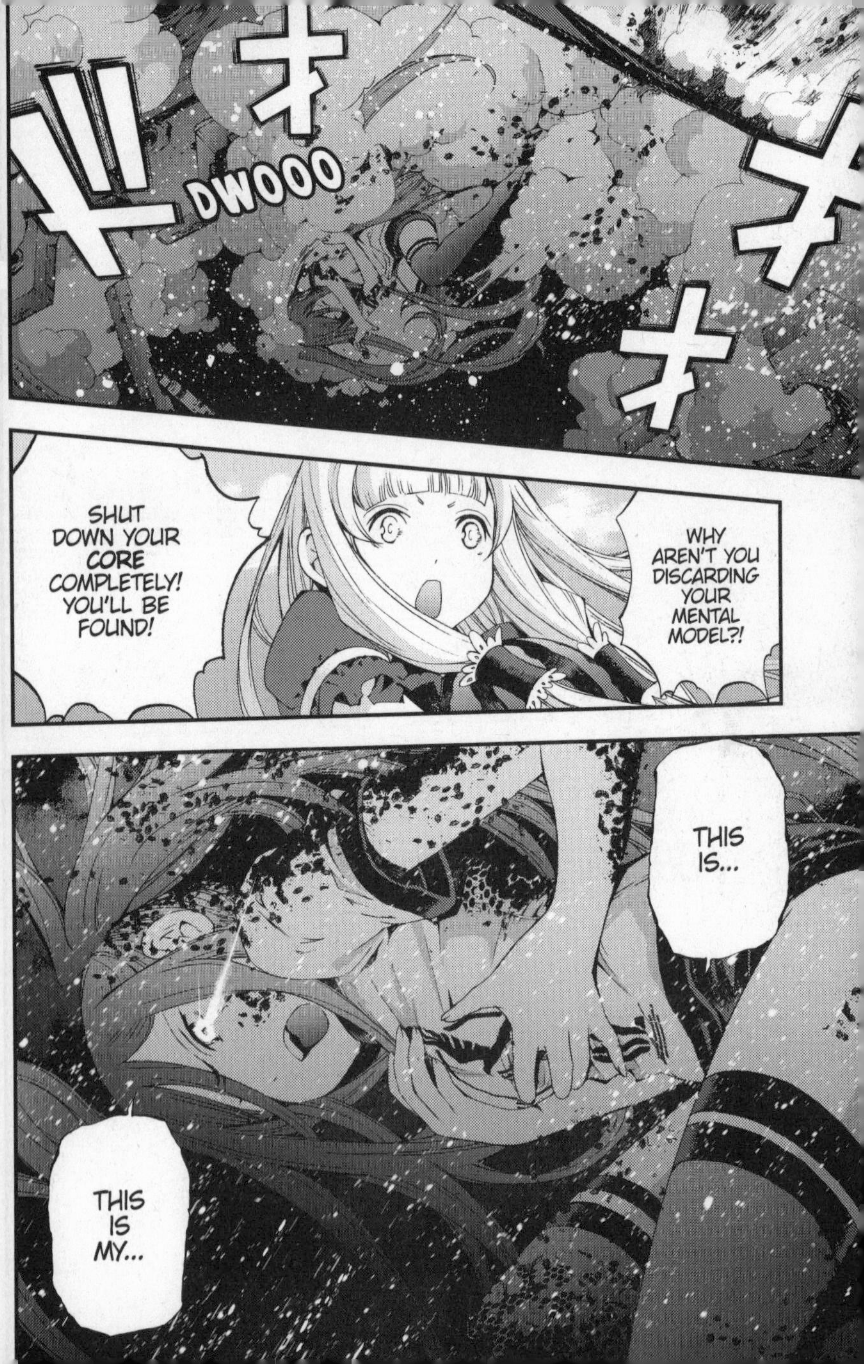
DWOOO
WHY AREN'T YOU DISCARDING YOUR MENTAL MODEL?!
SHUT DOWN YOUR CORE COMPLETELY! YOU'LL BE FOUND!
THIS IS...
THIS IS MY...

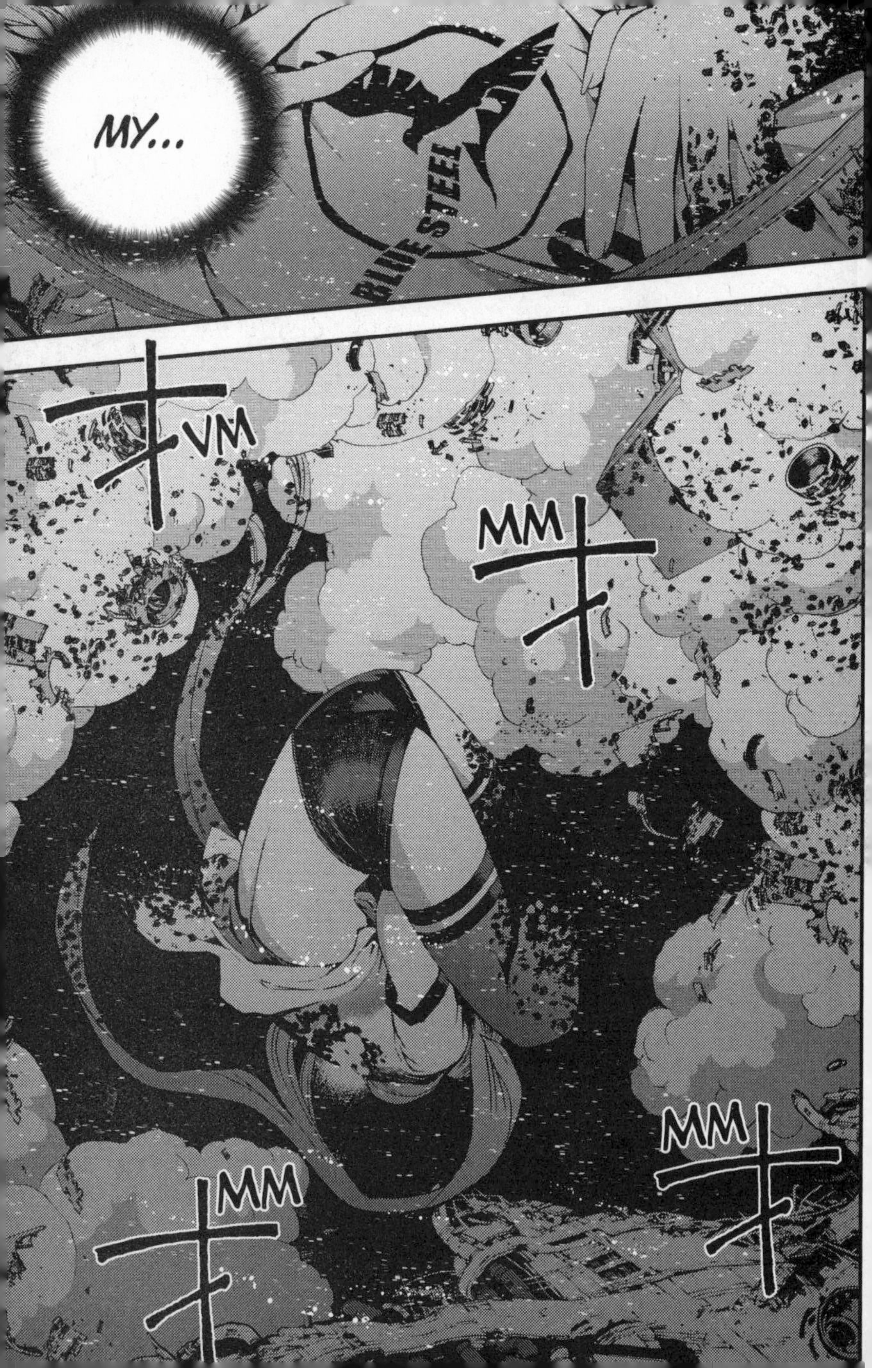
MY...
BLUE STEEL
MM
VM
MM
MM

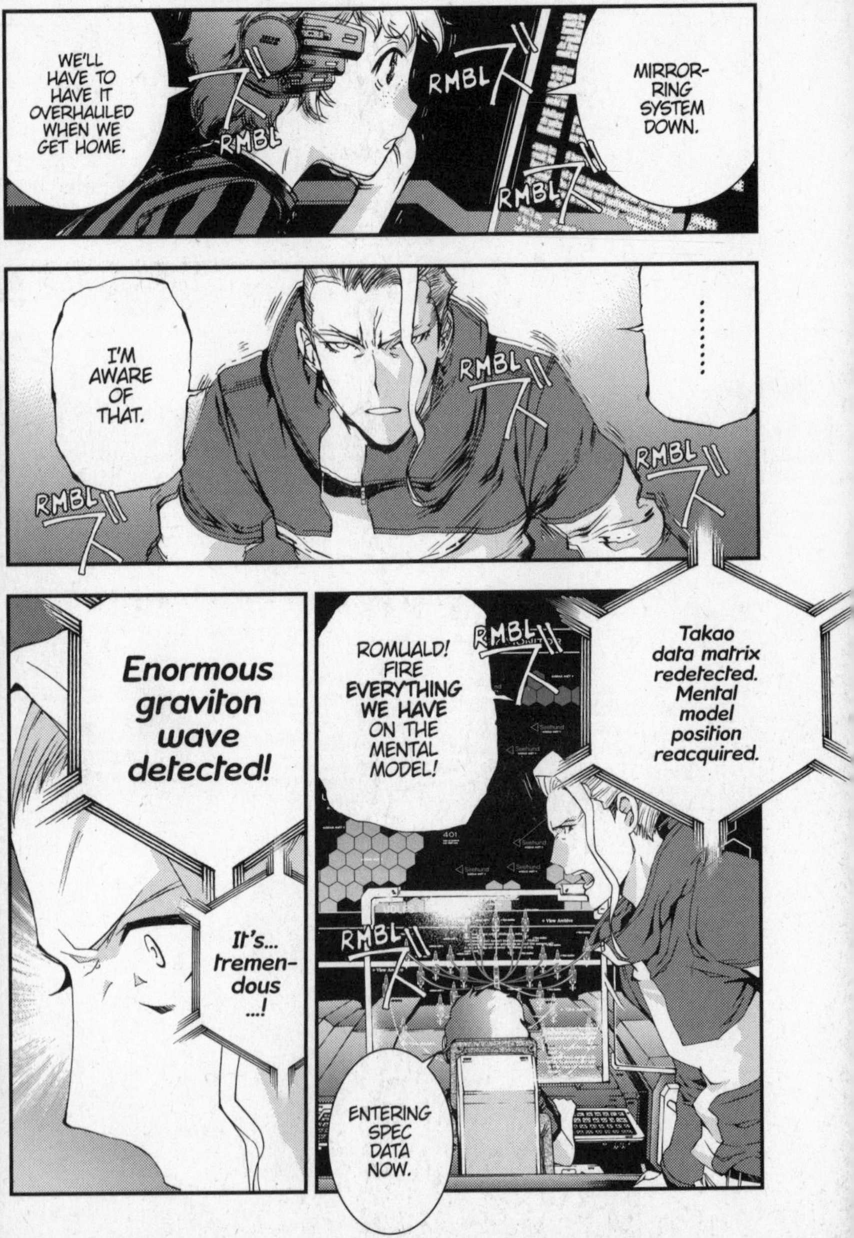
MIRROR-RING SYSTEM DOWN.
RMBL
RMBL
WE'LL HAVE TO HAVE IT OVERHAULED WHEN WE GET HOME.
RMBL
......
RMBL
RMBL
I'M AWARE OF THAT.
RMBL
Takao data matrix redetected. Mental model position reacquired.
RMBL
ROMUALD! FIRE EVERYTHING WE HAVE ON THE MENTAL MODEL!
RMBL
ENTERING SPEC DATA NOW.
Enormous graviton wave detected!
It's... tremen-dous ...!

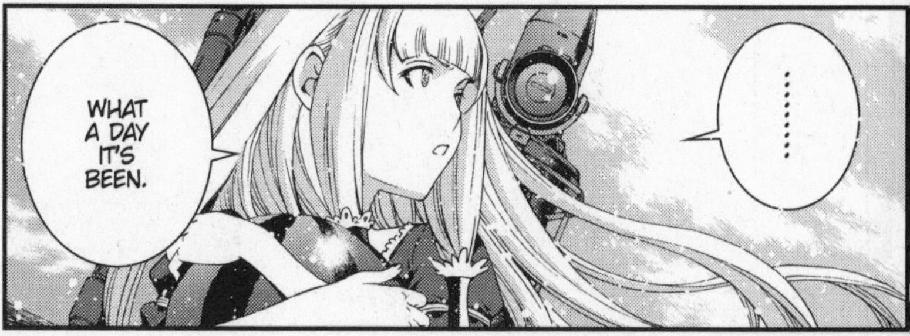
......
WHAT A DAY IT'S BEEN.

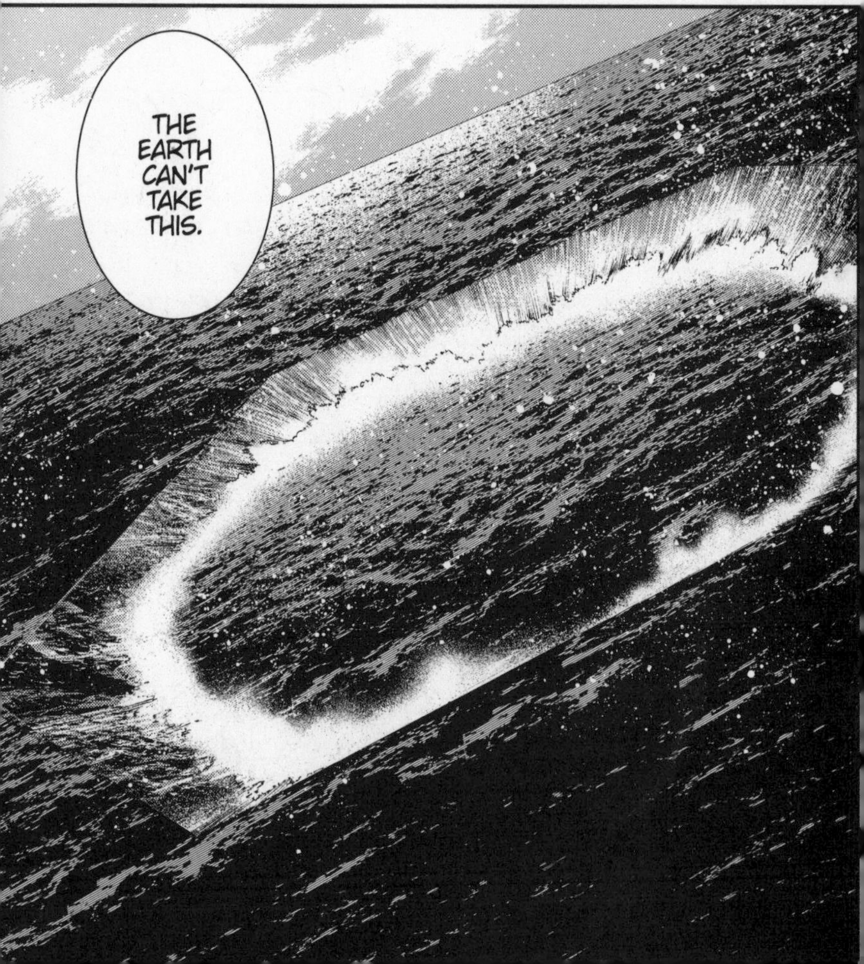
THE EARTH CAN'T TAKE THIS.

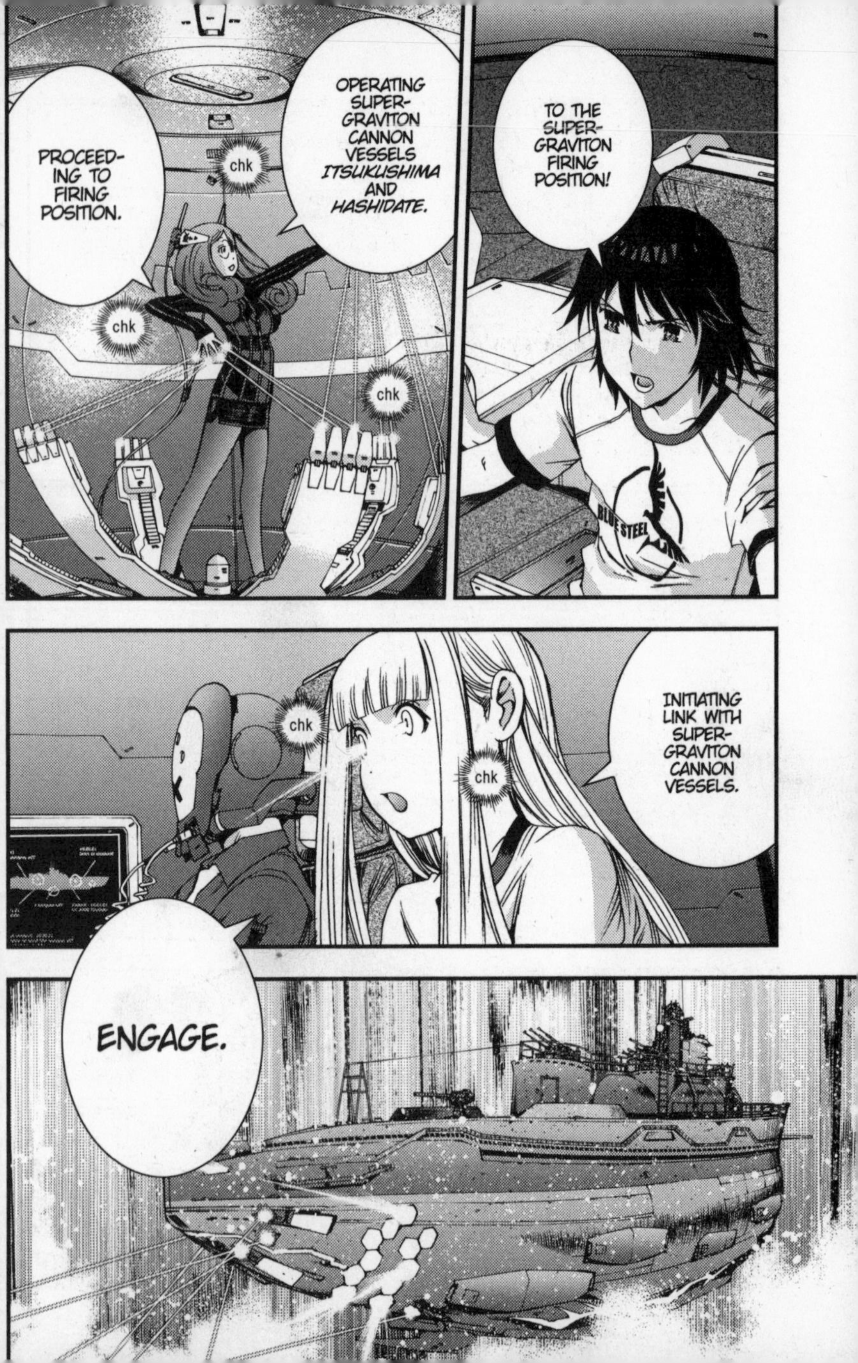
TO THE SUPER-GRAVITON FIRING POSITION!
OPERATING SUPER-GRAVITON CANNON VESSELS *ITSUKUSHIMA* AND *HASHIDATE.*
chk
PROCEED-ING TO FIRING POSITION.
chk
chk
INITIATING LINK WITH SUPER-GRAVITON CANNON VESSELS.
chk
chk
ENGAGE.

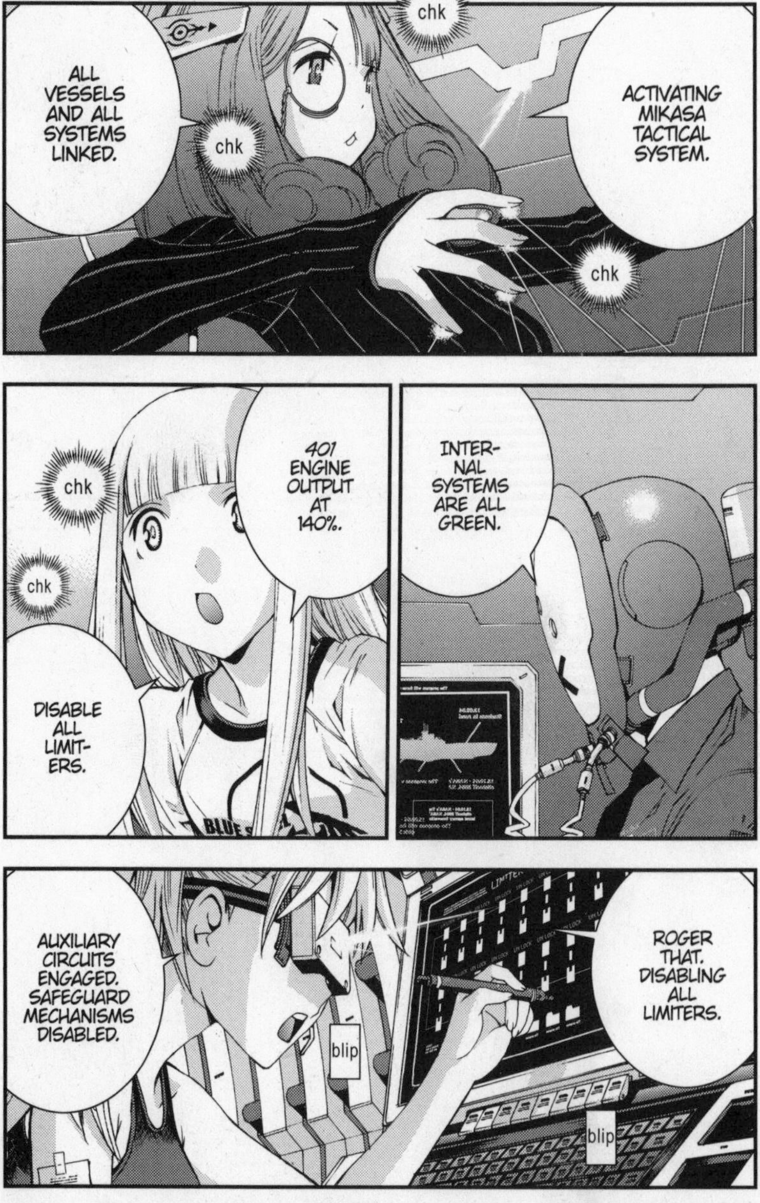
chk
ACTIVATING MIKASA TACTICAL SYSTEM.
ALL VESSELS AND ALL SYSTEMS LINKED.
chk
chk
INTER-NAL SYSTEMS ARE ALL GREEN.
401 ENGINE OUTPUT AT 140%.
chk
chk
DISABLE ALL LIMIT-ERS.
ROGER THAT. DISABLING ALL LIMITERS.
AUXILIARY CIRCUITS ENGAGED. SAFEGUARD MECHANISMS DISABLED.
blip
blip

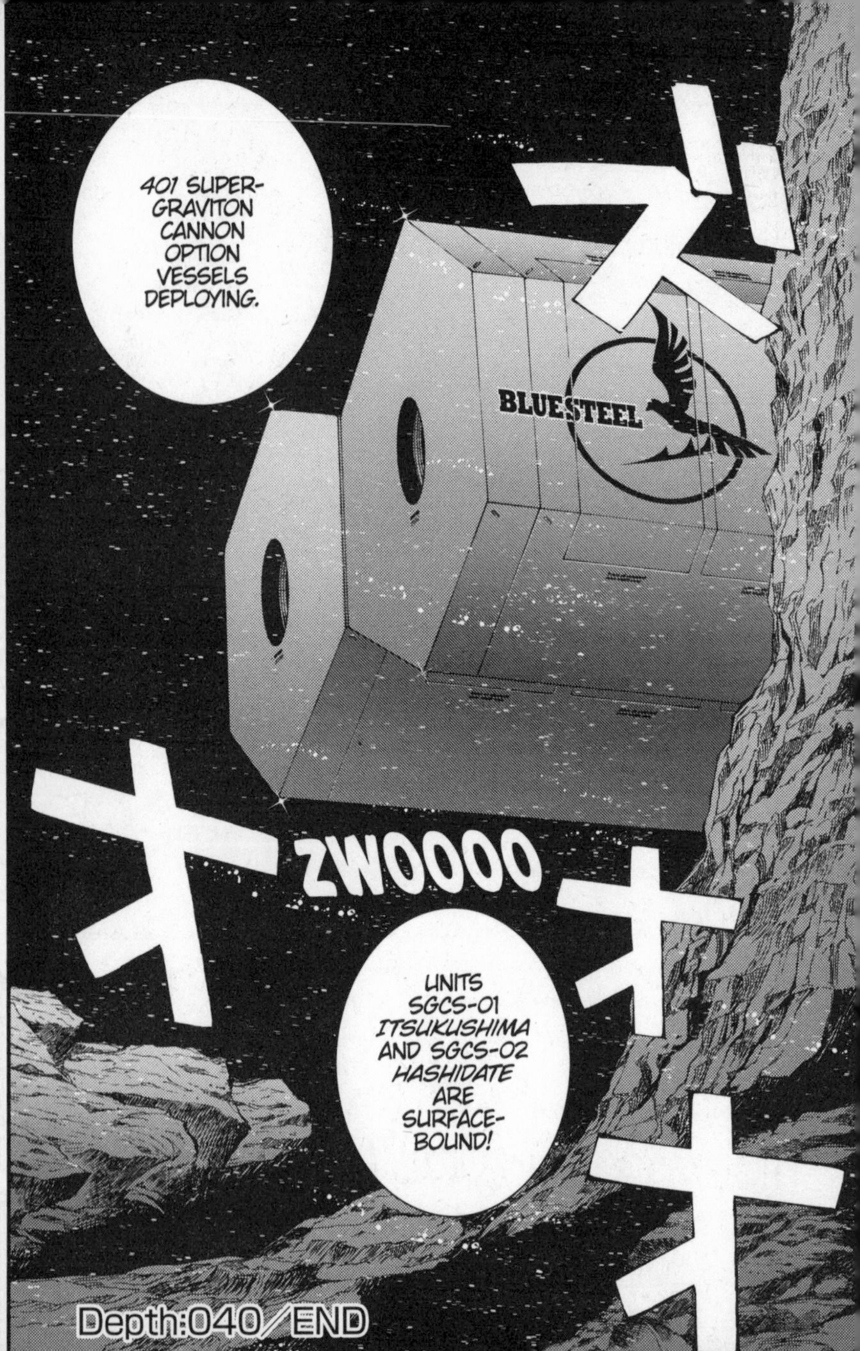
401 SUPER-GRAVITON CANNON OPTION VESSELS DEPLOYING.
BLUESTEEL
ズオオオオ
ZWOOOO
UNITS SGCS-01 ITSUKUSHIMA AND SGCS-02 HASHIDATE ARE SURFACE-BOUND!
Depth:040／END

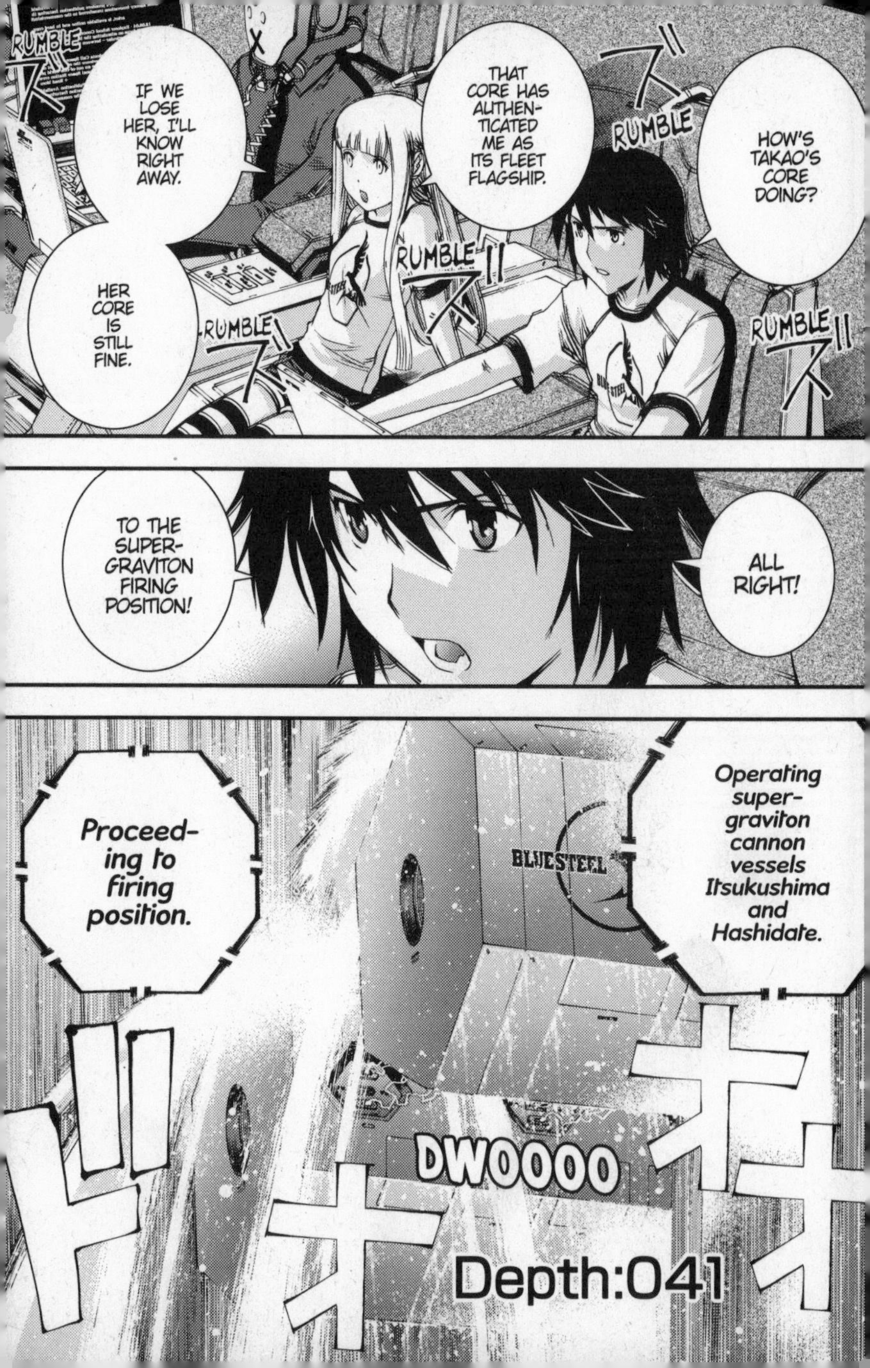
HOW'S TAKAO'S CORE DOING?
RUMBLE
THAT CORE HAS AUTHENTICATED ME AS ITS FLEET FLAGSHIP.
RUMBLE
RUMBLE
IF WE LOSE HER, I'LL KNOW RIGHT AWAY.
RUMBLE
RUMBLE
HER CORE IS STILL FINE.
ALL RIGHT!
TO THE SUPER-GRAVITON FIRING POSITION!
Operating super-graviton cannon vessels Itsukushima and Hashidate.
BLUESTEEL
Proceeding to firing position.
DWOOOO
Depth:041

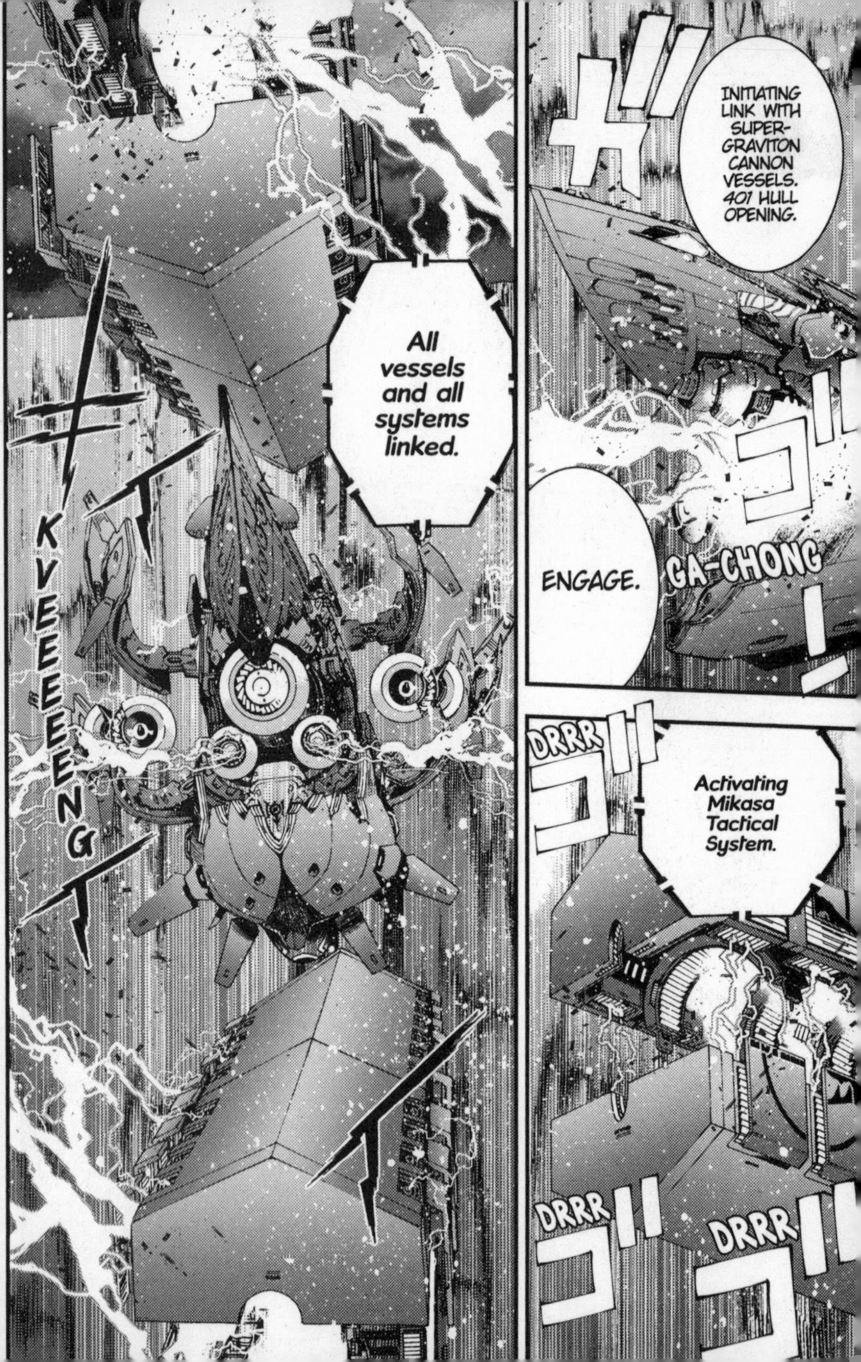
INITIATING LINK WITH SUPER-GRAVITON CANNON VESSELS. 401 HULL OPENING.
GA-CHONG
ENGAGE.
Activating Mikasa Tactical System.
DRRR
DRRR
DRRR
All vessels and all systems linked.
KVEEEEEENG

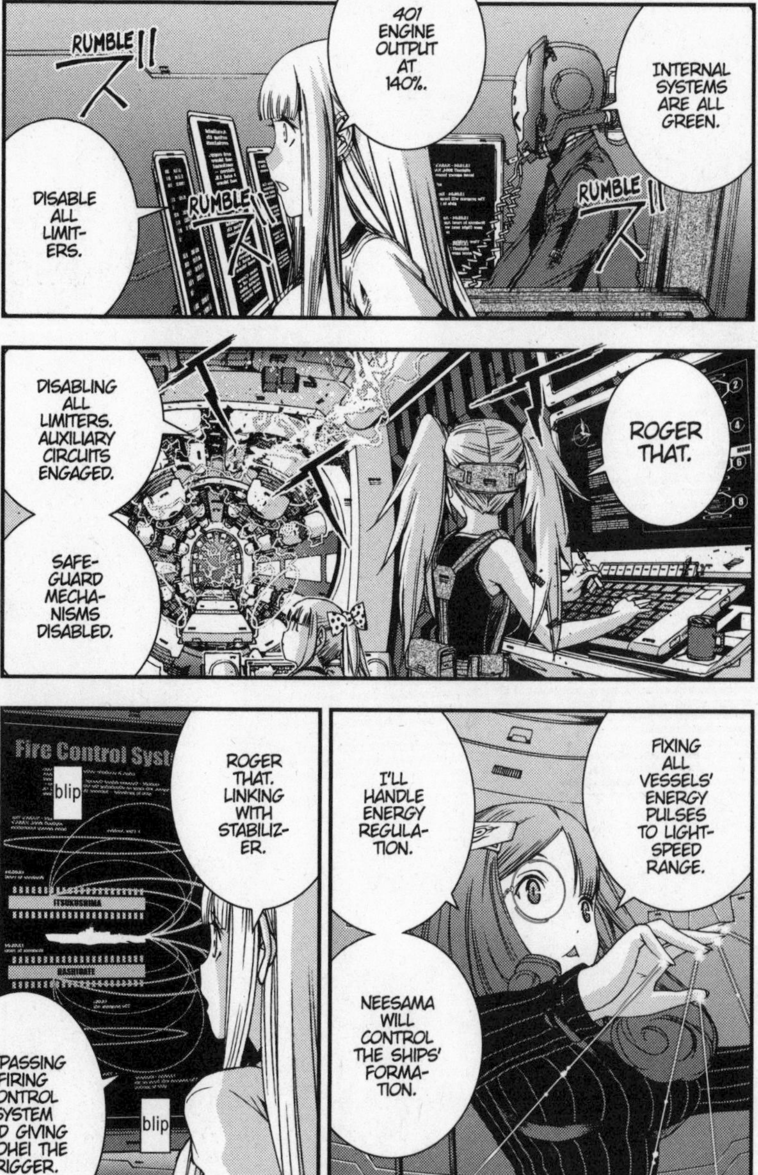

INTERNAL SYSTEMS ARE ALL GREEN.
401 ENGINE OUTPUT AT 140%.
RUMBLE
RUMBLE
DISABLE ALL LIMIT-ERS.
RUMBLE
ROGER THAT.
DISABLING ALL LIMITERS. AUXILIARY CIRCUITS ENGAGED.
SAFE-GUARD MECHA-NISMS DISABLED.
FIXING ALL VESSELS' ENERGY PULSES TO LIGHT-SPEED RANGE.
I'LL HANDLE ENERGY REGULA-TION.
NEESAMA WILL CONTROL THE SHIPS' FORMA-TION.
ROGER THAT. LINKING WITH STABILIZ-ER.
Fire Control Syst
blip
ITSUKUSHIMA
HASHIDATE
BYPASSING FIRING CONTROL SYSTEM AND GIVING KYOHEI THE TRIGGER.
blip

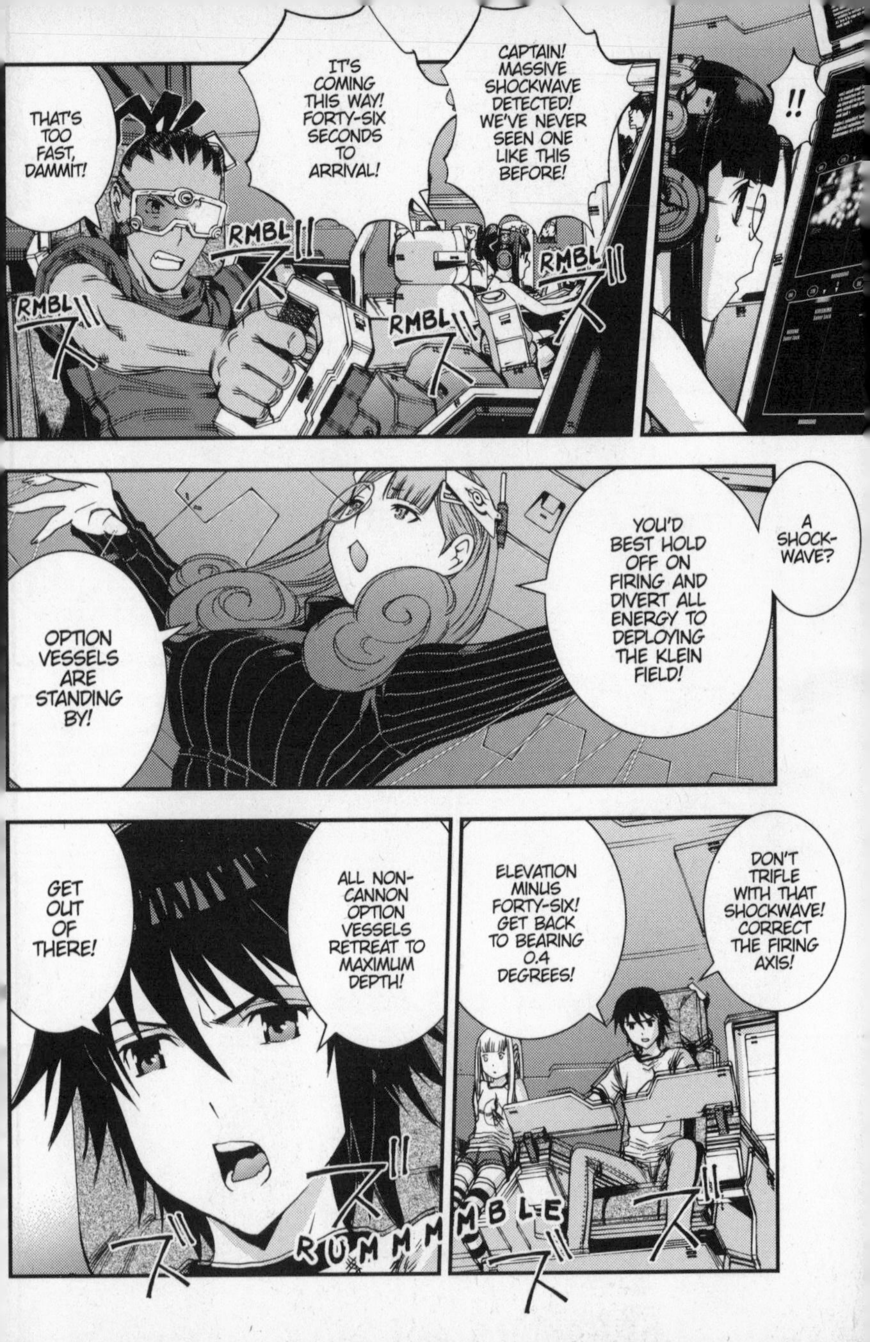
!!
CAPTAIN! MASSIVE SHOCKWAVE DETECTED! WE'VE NEVER SEEN ONE LIKE THIS BEFORE!
IT'S COMING THIS WAY! FORTY-SIX SECONDS TO ARRIVAL!
RMBL
RMBL
RMBL
THAT'S TOO FAST, DAMMIT!
RMBL
A SHOCK-WAVE?
YOU'D BEST HOLD OFF ON FIRING AND DIVERT ALL ENERGY TO DEPLOYING THE KLEIN FIELD!
OPTION VESSELS ARE STANDING BY!
DON'T TRIFLE WITH THAT SHOCKWAVE! CORRECT THE FIRING AXIS!
ELEVATION MINUS FORTY-SIX! GET BACK TO BEARING 0.4 DEGREES!
ALL NON-CANNON OPTION VESSELS RETREAT TO MAXIMUM DEPTH!
GET OUT OF THERE!
RUMMMMBLE

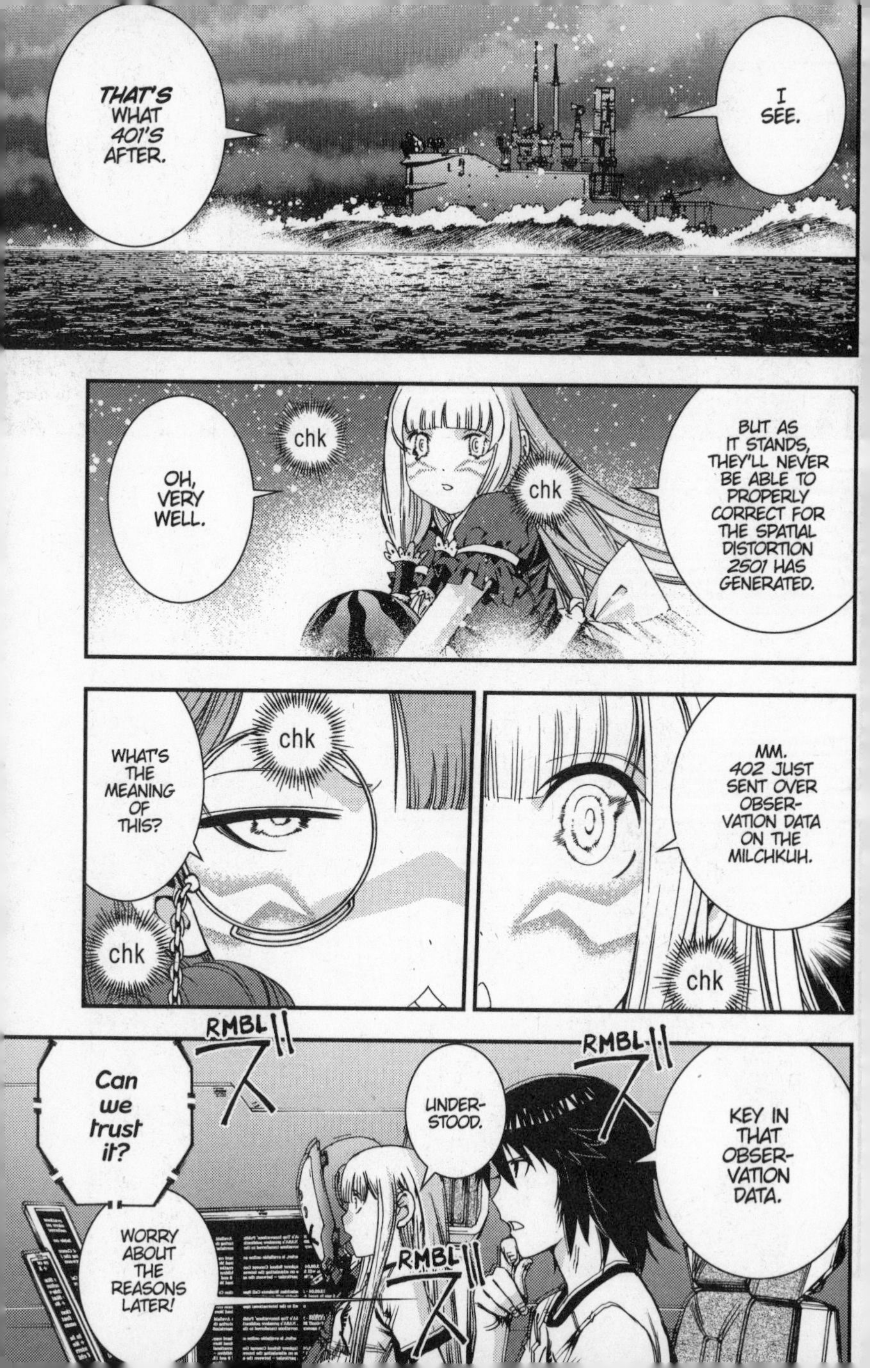
I SEE.
THAT'S WHAT 401'S AFTER.
BUT AS IT STANDS, THEY'LL NEVER BE ABLE TO PROPERLY CORRECT FOR THE SPATIAL DISTORTION 2501 HAS GENERATED.
chk
chk
OH, VERY WELL.
MM. 402 JUST SENT OVER OBSER-VATION DATA ON THE MILCHKUH.
chk
chk
WHAT'S THE MEANING OF THIS?
chk
RMBL
KEY IN THAT OBSER-VATION DATA.
UNDER-STOOD.
RMBL
Can we trust it?
WORRY ABOUT THE REASONS LATER!
RMBL

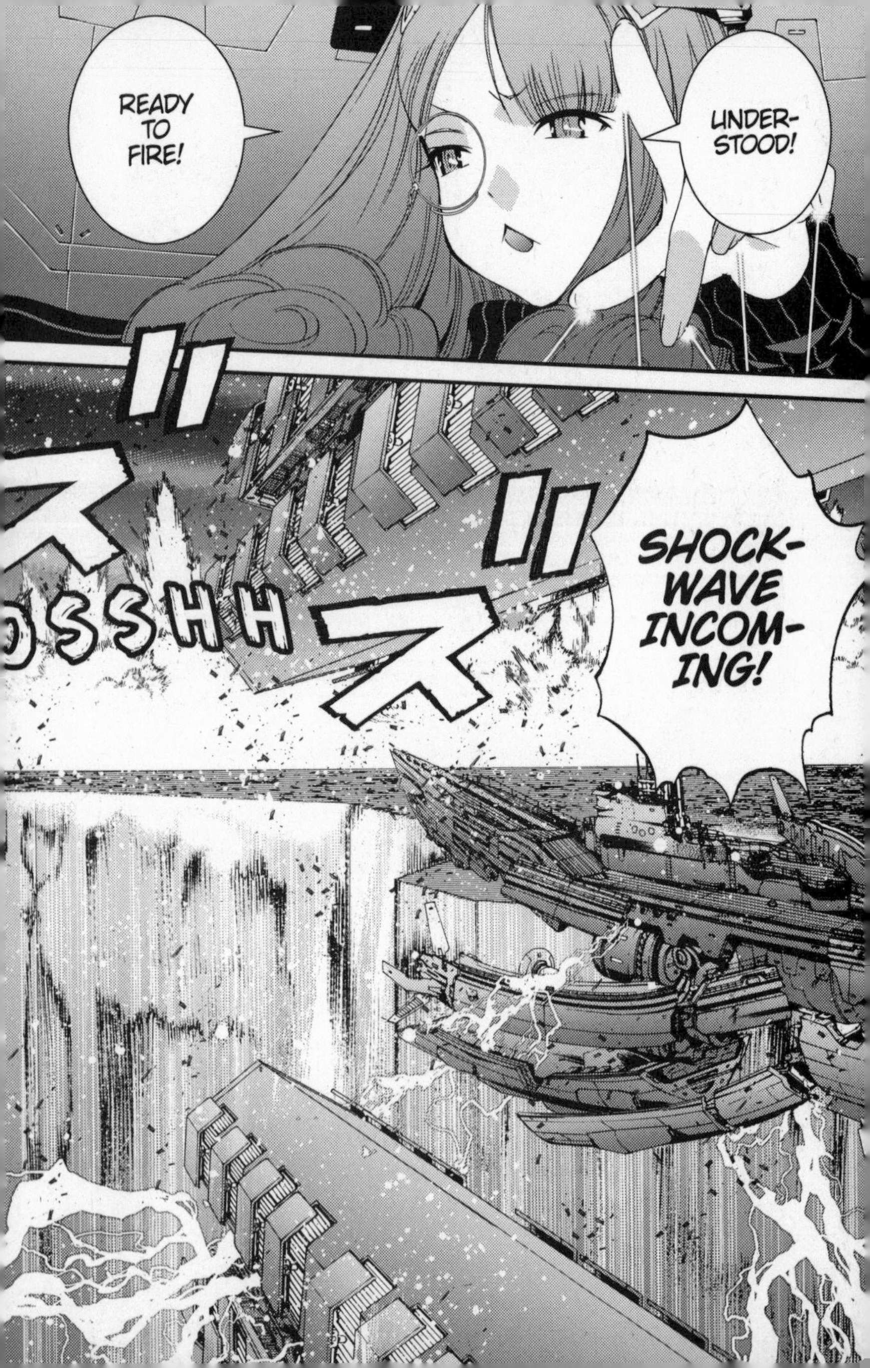
UNDER-STOOD!
READY TO FIRE!
SHOCK-WAVE INCOM-ING!
OSSHH

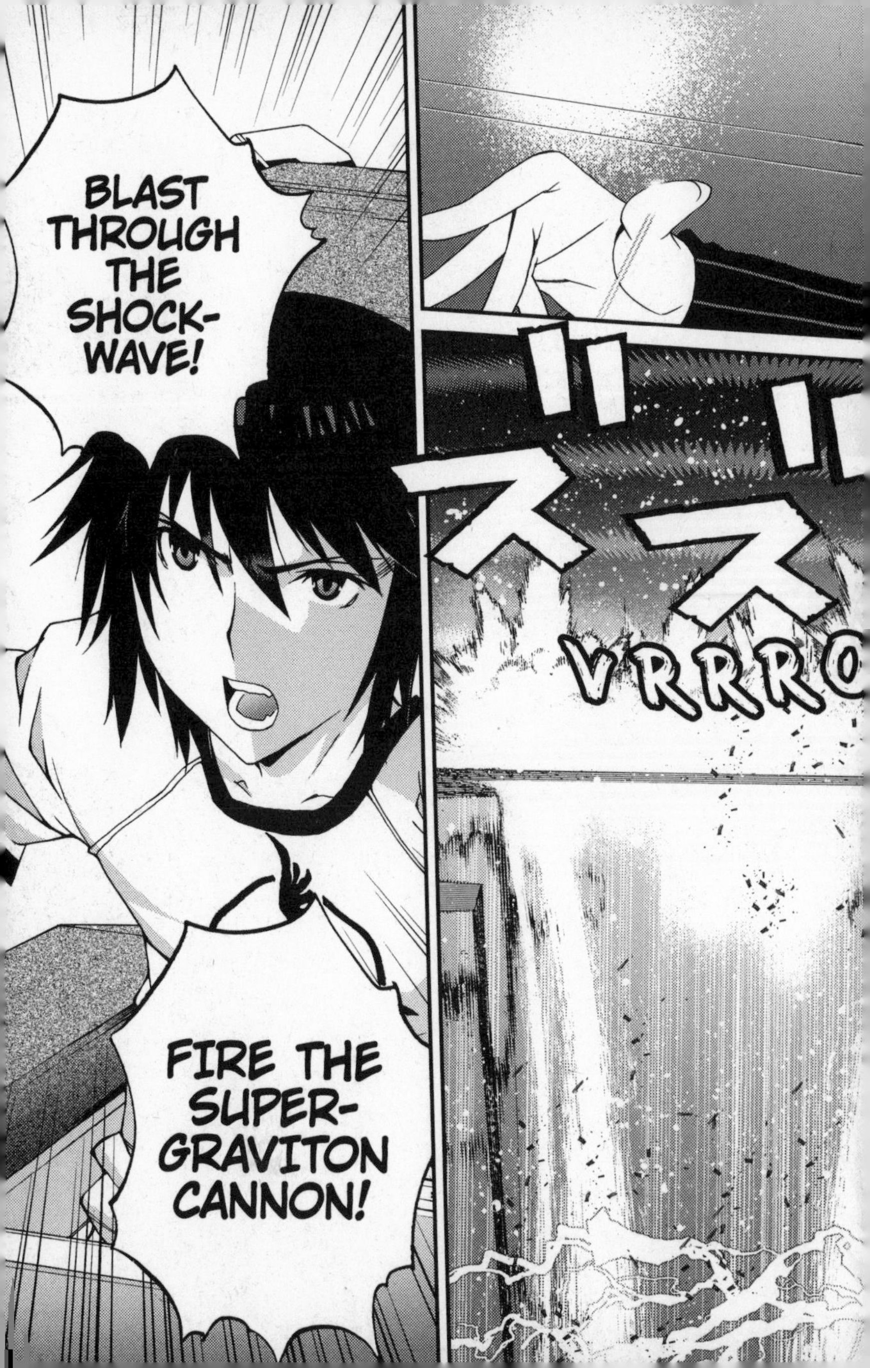
ズズ
VRRRO
BLAST THROUGH THE SHOCK-WAVE!
FIRE THE SUPER-GRAVITON CANNON!

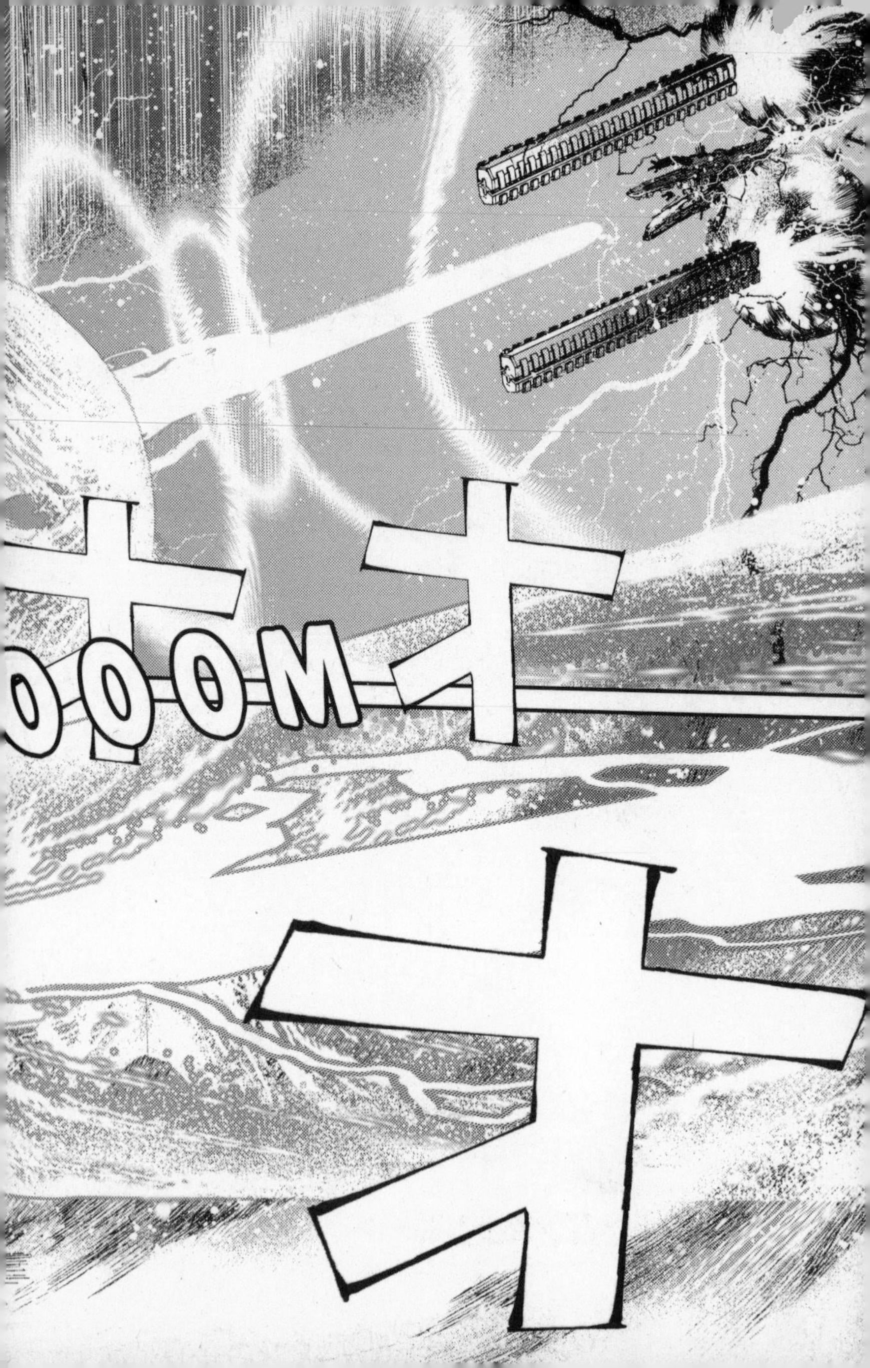
オオオ
OOOM

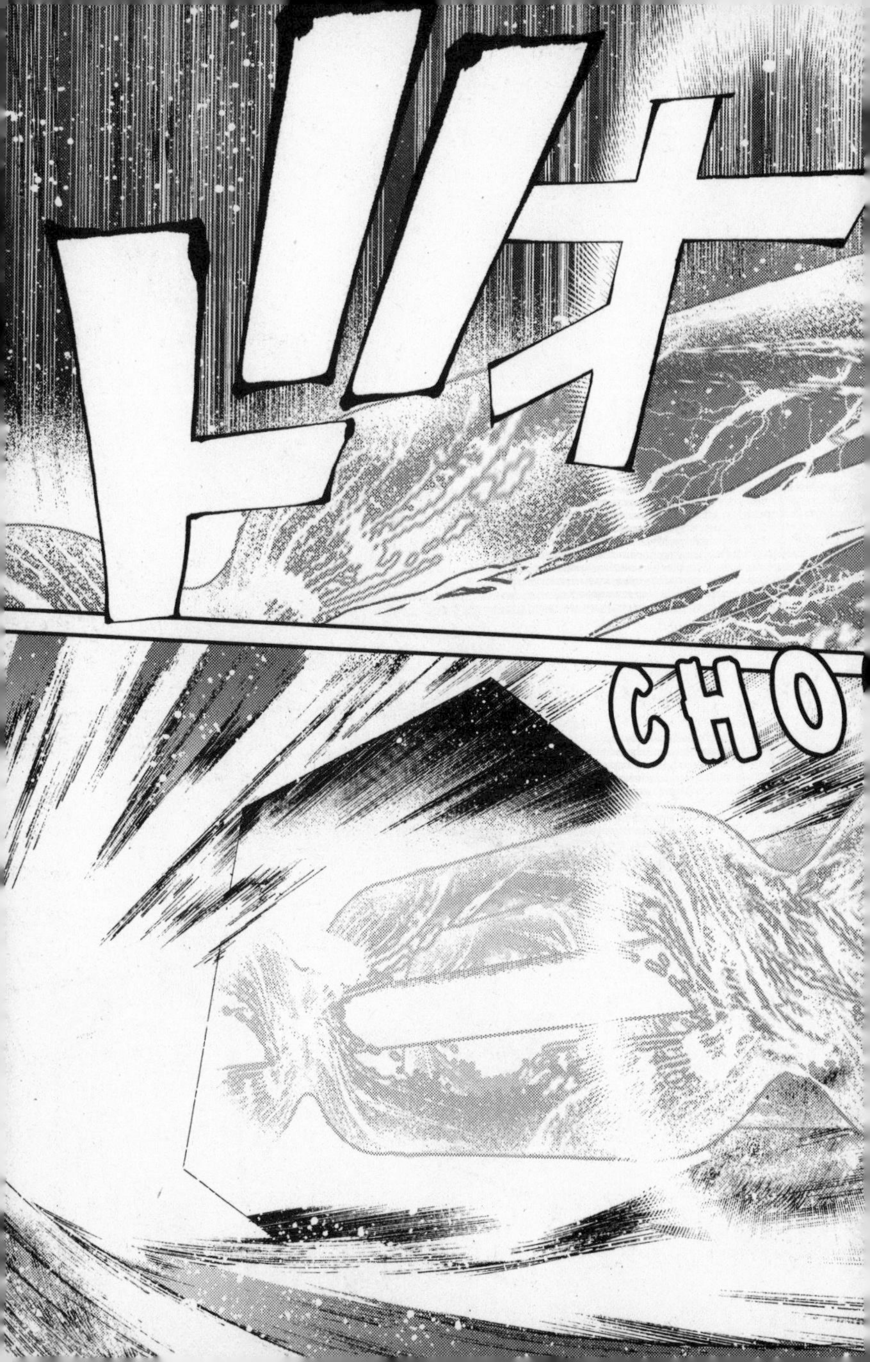
ドオ
CHO

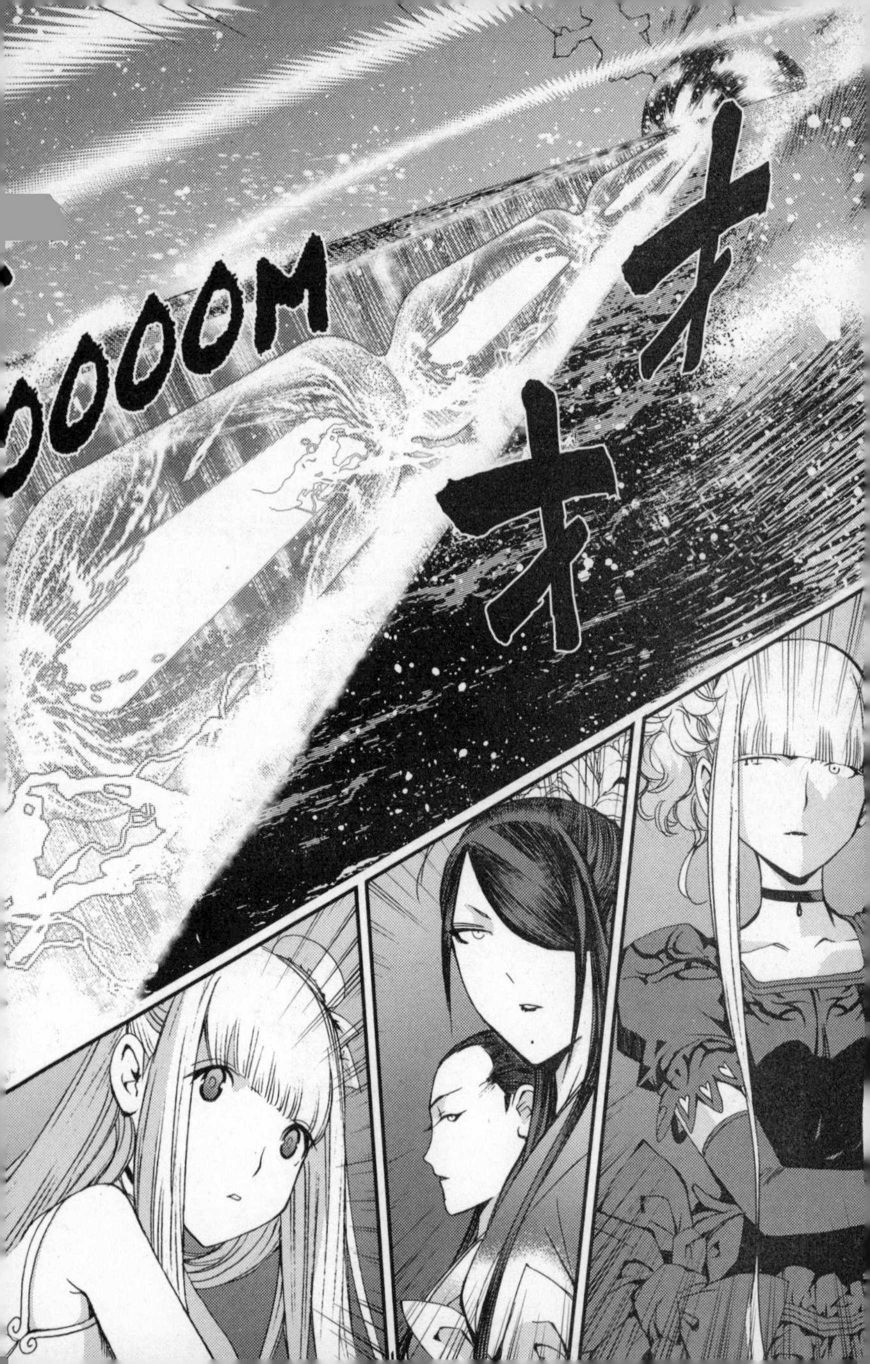
DOOOOM
オオ

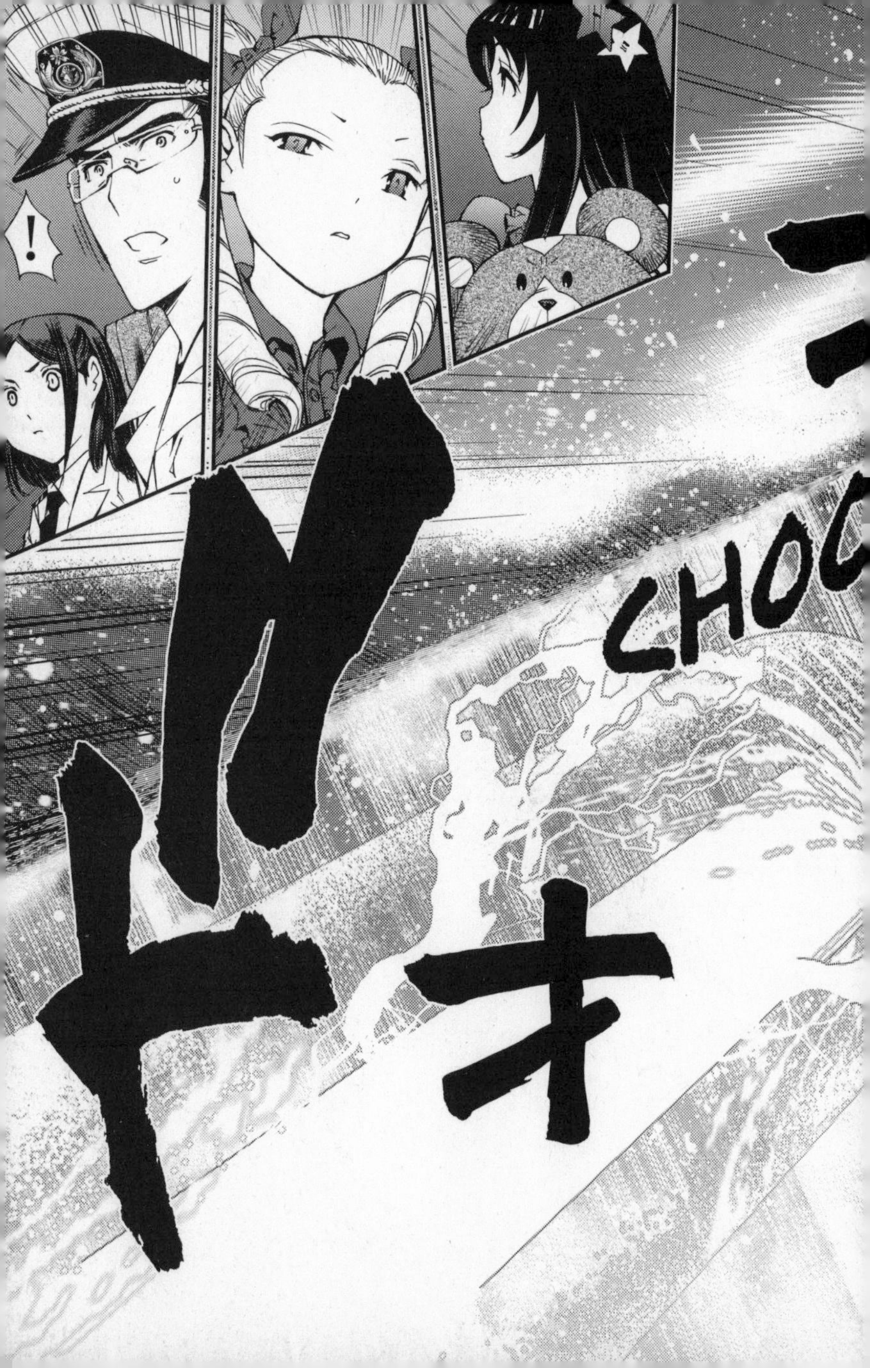
ドオ
CHO
!

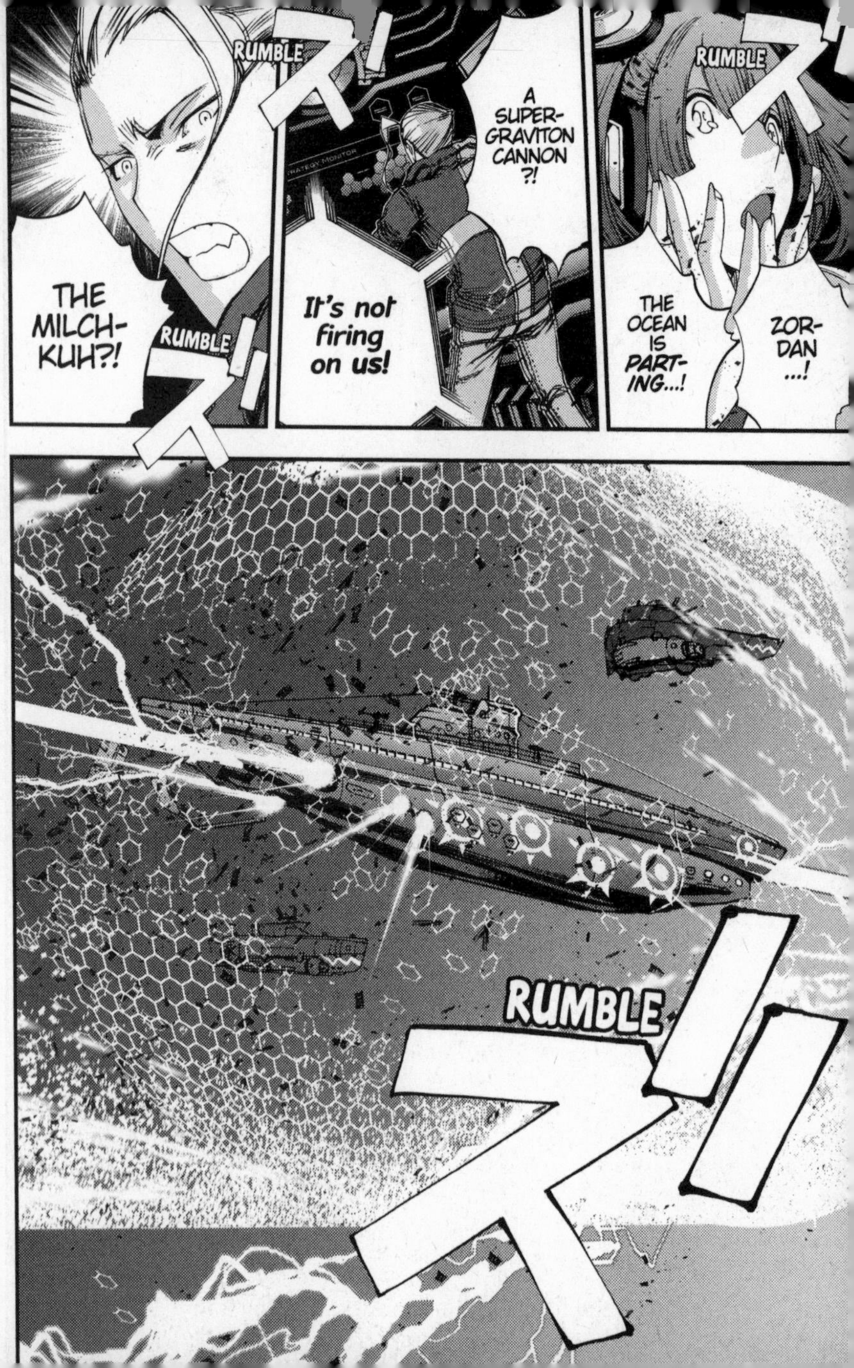
RUMBLE
ZOR-DAN ...!
THE OCEAN IS PARTING...!
A SUPER-GRAVITON CANNON ?!
It's not firing on us!
RUMBLE
THE MILCH-KUH?!
RUMBLE
RUMBLE

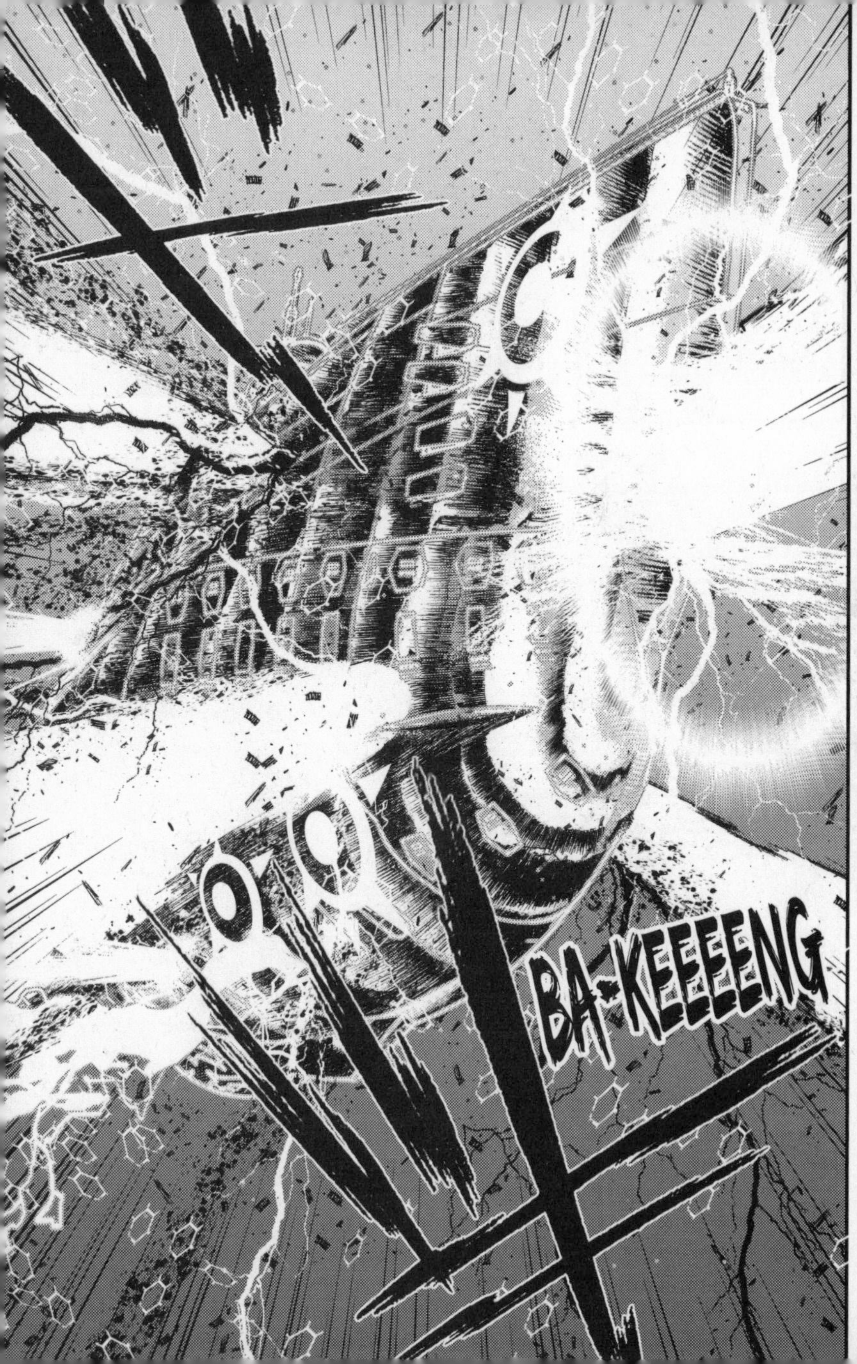
BA-KEEEENG

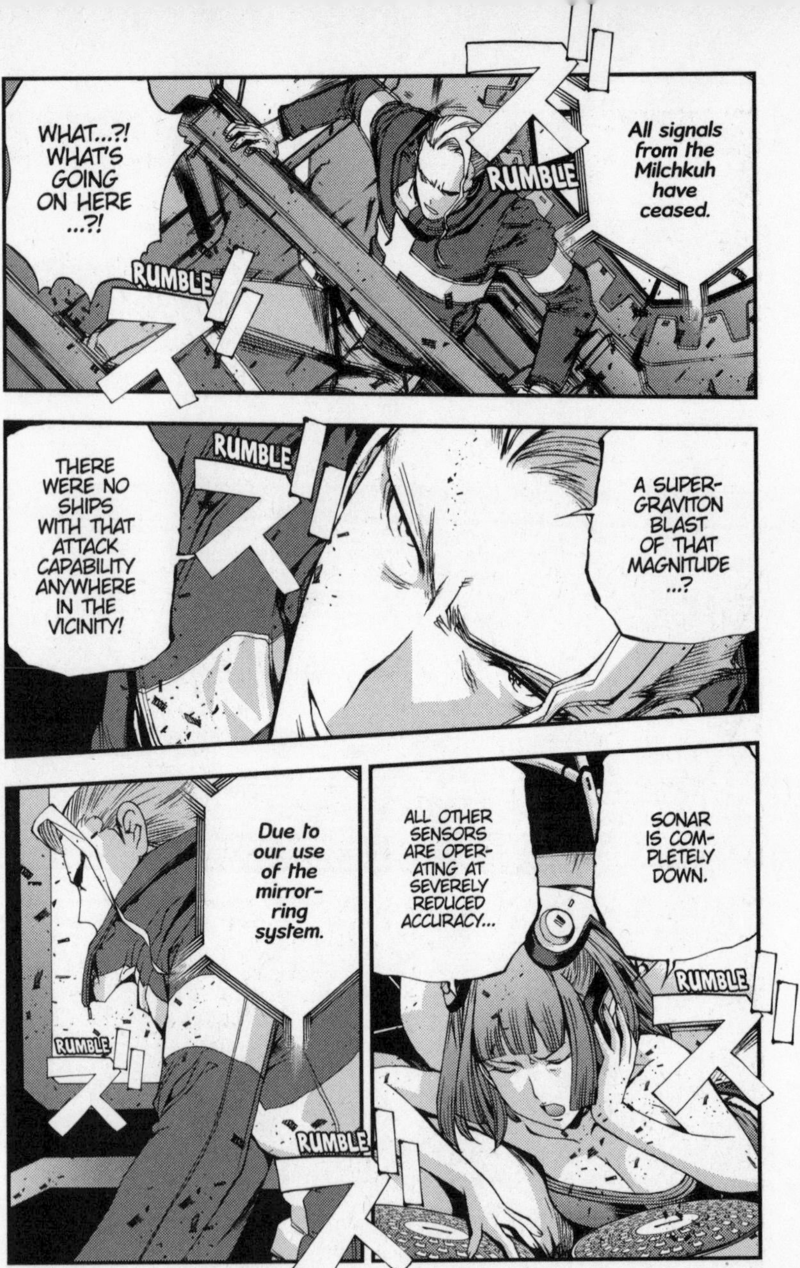
All signals from the Milchkuh have ceased.
RUMBLE
WHAT...?! WHAT'S GOING ON HERE ...?!
RUMBLE
A SUPER-GRAVITON BLAST OF THAT MAGNITUDE ...?
RUMBLE
THERE WERE NO SHIPS WITH THAT ATTACK CAPABILITY ANYWHERE IN THE VICINITY!
SONAR IS COMPLETELY DOWN.
ALL OTHER SENSORS ARE OPERATING AT SEVERELY REDUCED ACCURACY...
RUMBLE
RUMBLE
Due to our use of the mirroring system.
RUMBLE

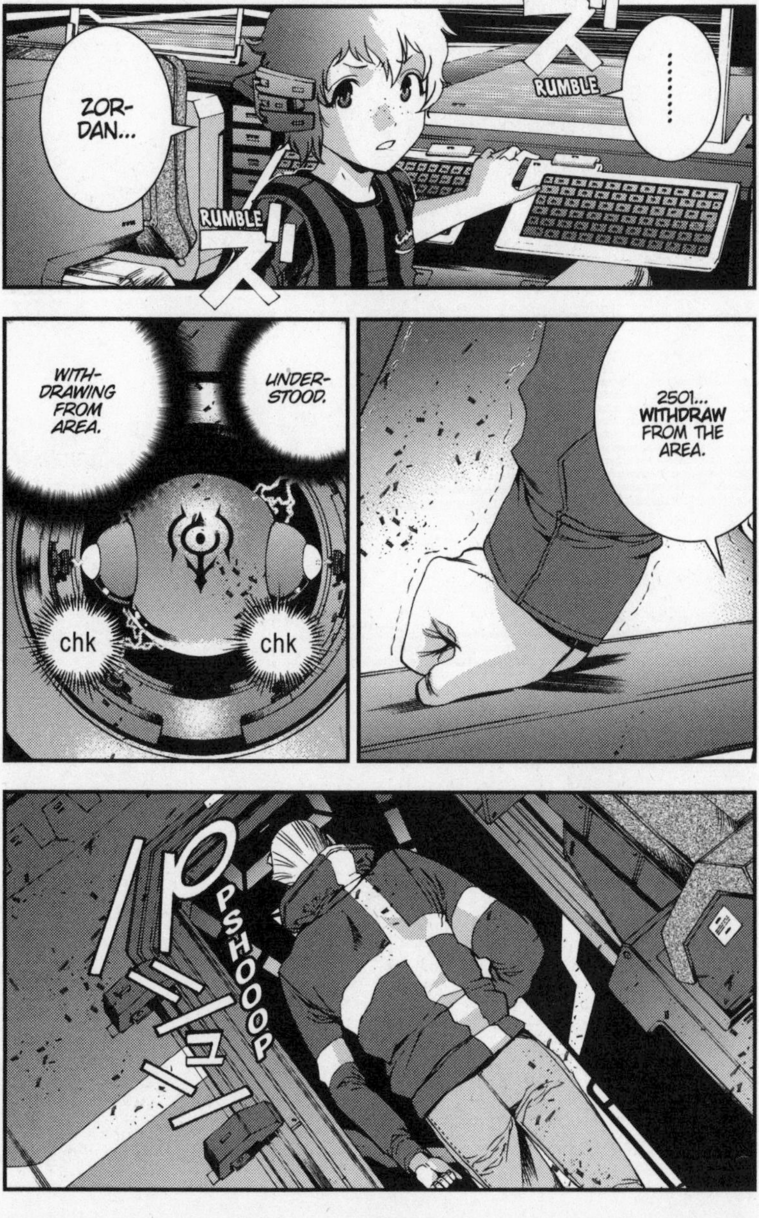
RUMBLE
......
ZOR-DAN...
RUMBLE
2501... WITHDRAW FROM THE AREA.
UNDER-STOOD.
WITH-DRAWING FROM AREA.
chk
chk
PSHOOOOP

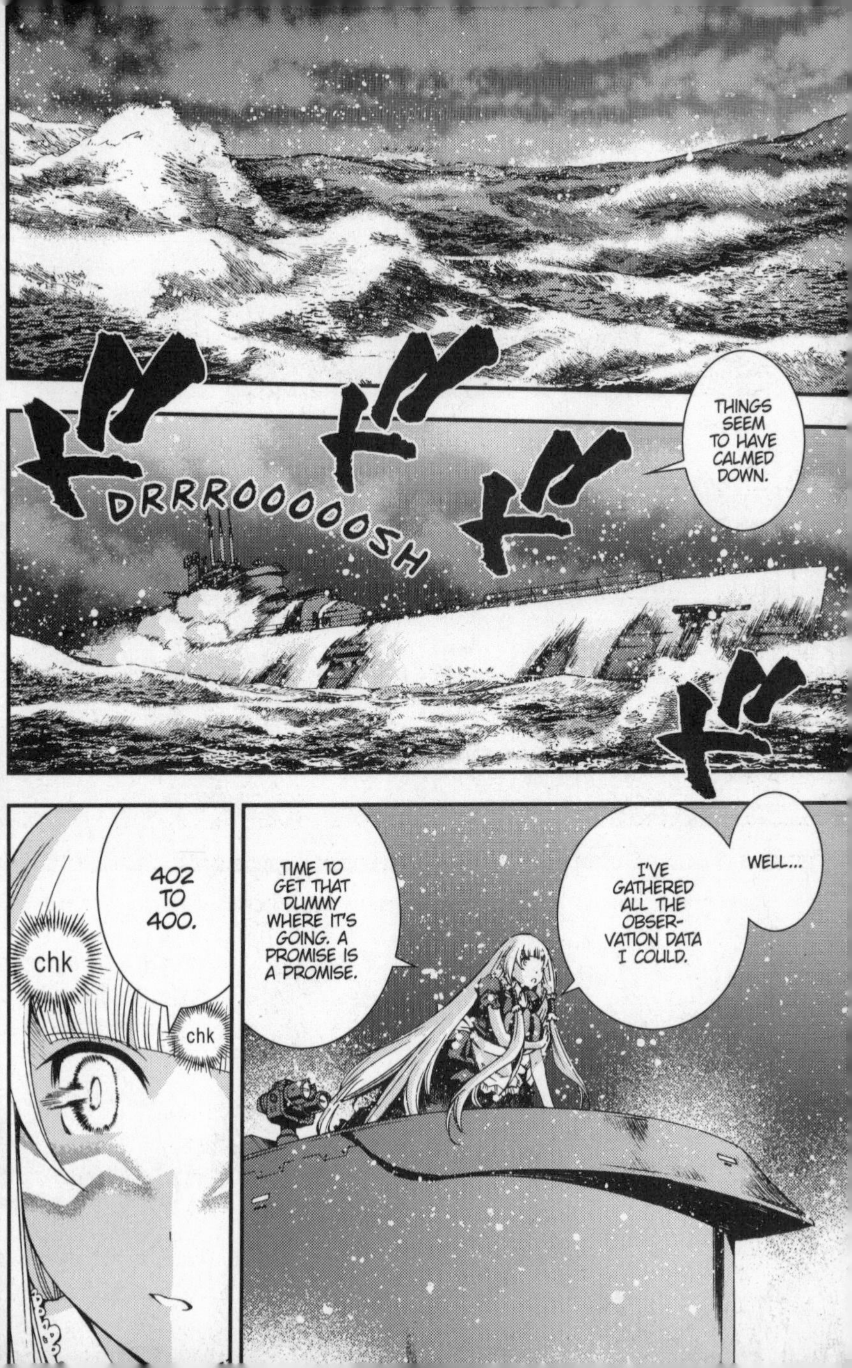
ドドドド
DRRROOOOOOSH
THINGS SEEM TO HAVE CALMED DOWN.
WELL...
I'VE GATHERED ALL THE OBSERVATION DATA I COULD.
TIME TO GET THAT DUMMY WHERE IT'S GOING. A PROMISE IS A PROMISE.
402 TO 400.
chk
chk

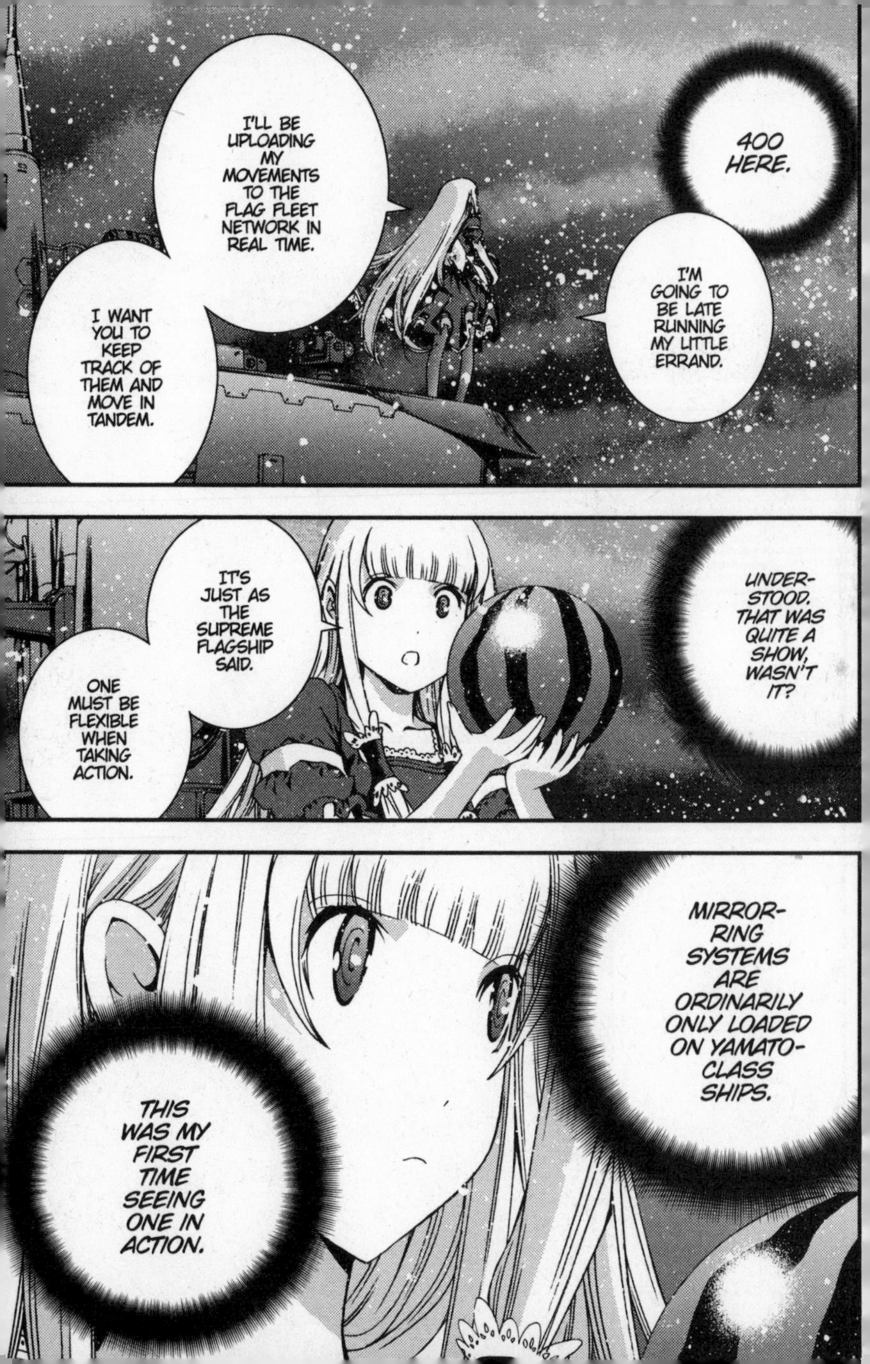
400 HERE.
I'M GOING TO BE LATE RUNNING MY LITTLE ERRAND.
I'LL BE UPLOADING MY MOVEMENTS TO THE FLAG FLEET NETWORK IN REAL TIME.
I WANT YOU TO KEEP TRACK OF THEM AND MOVE IN TANDEM.
UNDERSTOOD. THAT WAS QUITE A SHOW, WASN'T IT?
IT'S JUST AS THE SUPREME FLAGSHIP SAID.
ONE MUST BE FLEXIBLE WHEN TAKING ACTION.
MIRROR-RING SYSTEMS ARE ORDINARILY ONLY LOADED ON YAMATO-CLASS SHIPS.
THIS WAS MY FIRST TIME SEEING ONE IN ACTION.

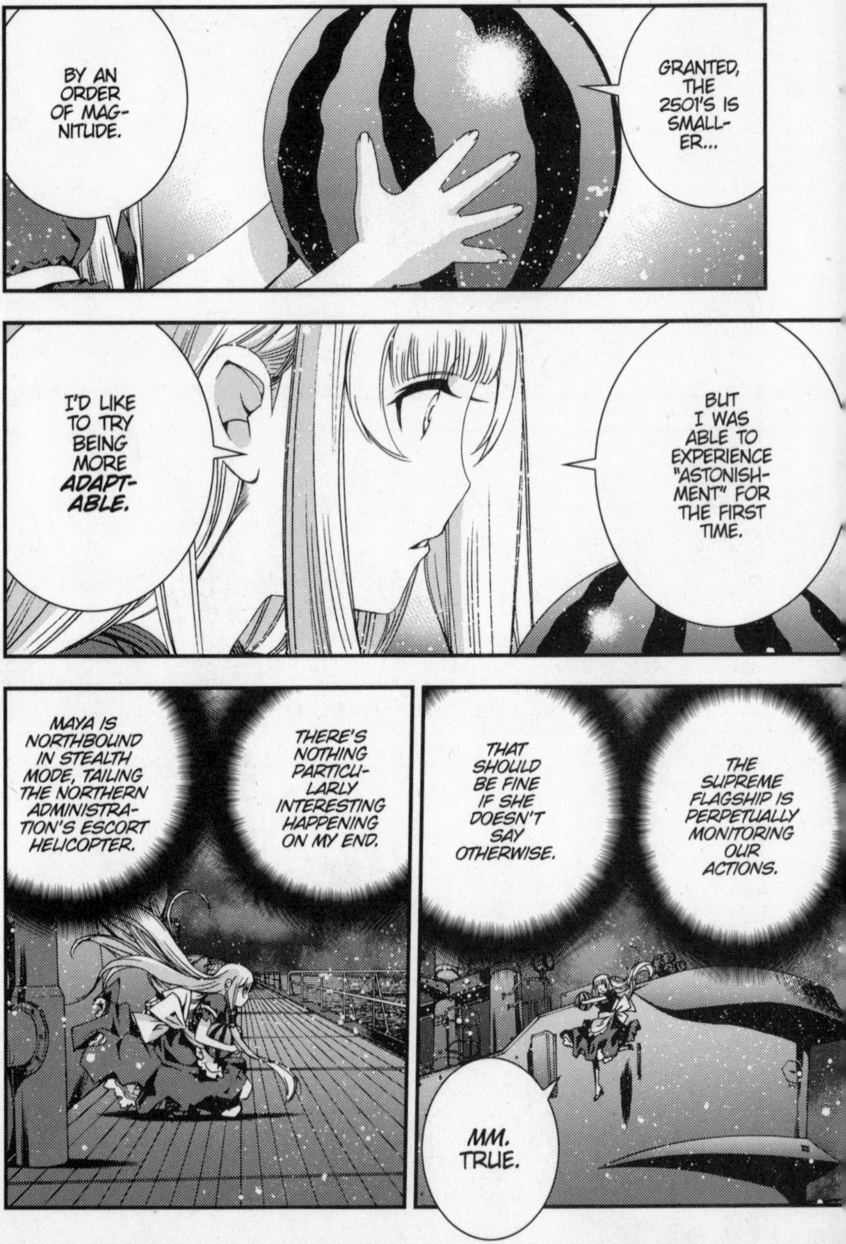
GRANTED, THE 2501'S IS SMALLER...
BY AN ORDER OF MAGNITUDE.
BUT I WAS ABLE TO EXPERIENCE "ASTONISHMENT" FOR THE FIRST TIME.
I'D LIKE TO TRY BEING MORE **ADAPTABLE.**
THE SUPREME FLAGSHIP IS PERPETUALLY MONITORING OUR ACTIONS.
THAT SHOULD BE FINE IF SHE DOESN'T SAY OTHERWISE.
MM. TRUE.
THERE'S NOTHING PARTICULARLY INTERESTING HAPPENING ON MY END.
MAYA IS NORTHBOUND IN STEALTH MODE, TAILING THE NORTHERN ADMINISTRATION'S ESCORT HELICOPTER.

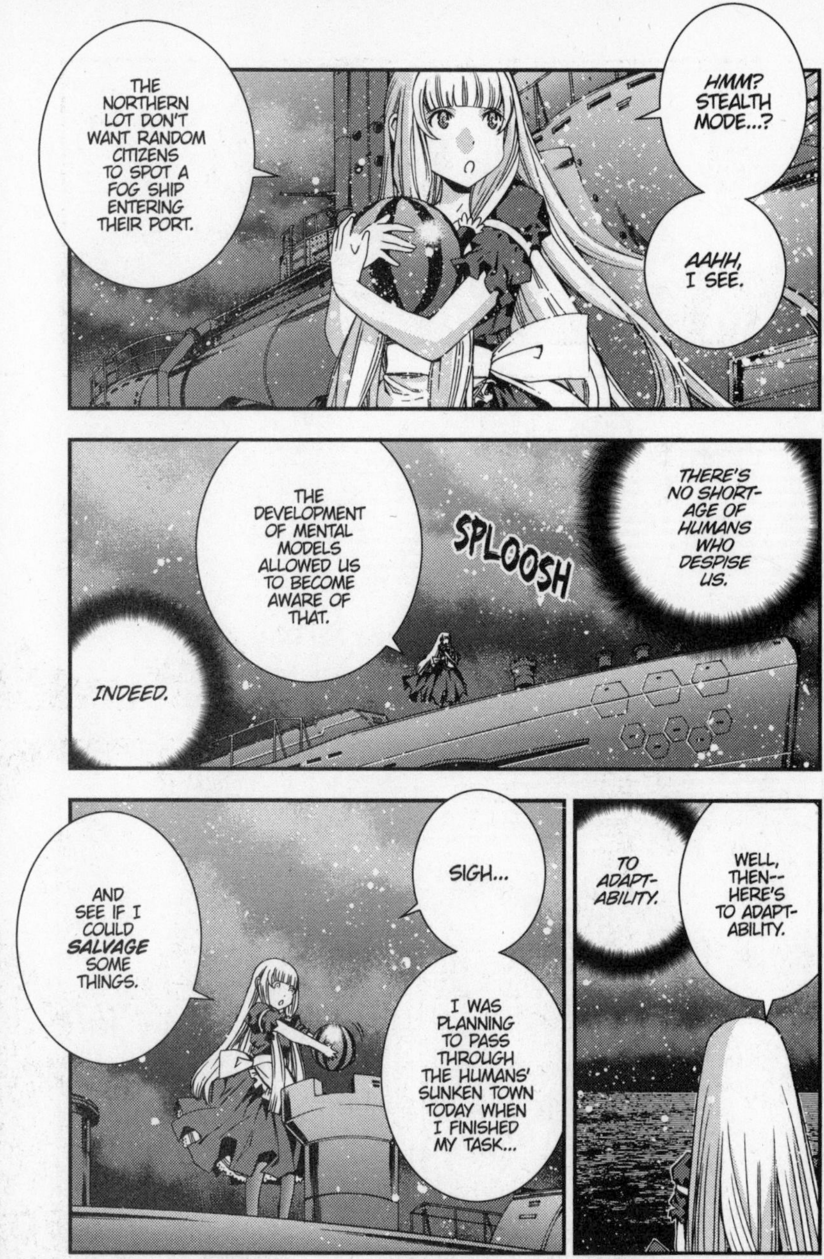
HMM? STEALTH MODE...?
AAHH, I SEE.
THE NORTHERN LOT DON'T WANT RANDOM CITIZENS TO SPOT A FOG SHIP ENTERING THEIR PORT.
THERE'S NO SHORTAGE OF HUMANS WHO DESPISE US.
SPLOOSH
THE DEVELOPMENT OF MENTAL MODELS ALLOWED US TO BECOME AWARE OF THAT.
INDEED.
WELL, THEN-- HERE'S TO ADAPTABILITY.
TO ADAPTABILITY.
SIGH...
I WAS PLANNING TO PASS THROUGH THE HUMANS' SUNKEN TOWN TODAY WHEN I FINISHED MY TASK...
AND SEE IF I COULD **SALVAGE** SOME THINGS.

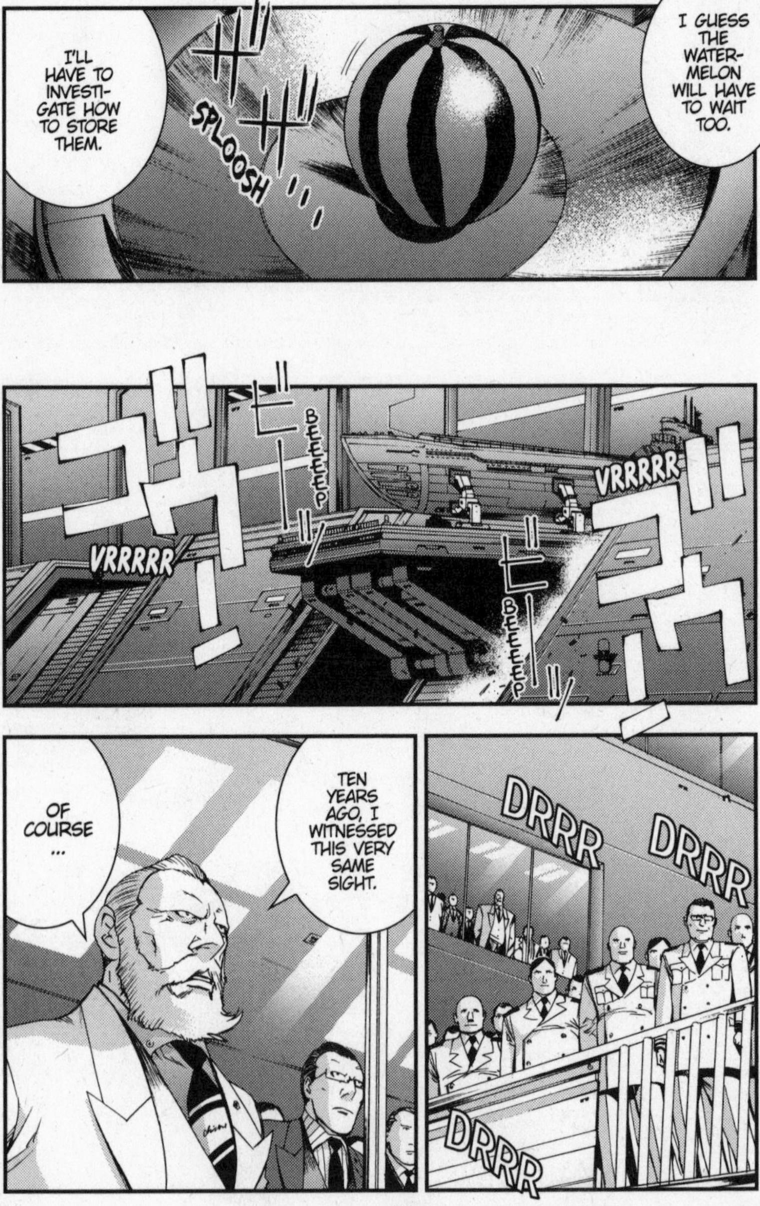

I GUESS THE WATER-MELON WILL HAVE TO WAIT TOO.
SPLOOSH
I'LL HAVE TO INVESTI-GATE HOW TO STORE THEM.
VRRRRR
BEEEEP
BEEEEP
VRRRRR
DRRRR
DRRR
DRRRR
TEN YEARS AGO, I WITNESSED THIS VERY SAME SIGHT.
OF COURSE ...

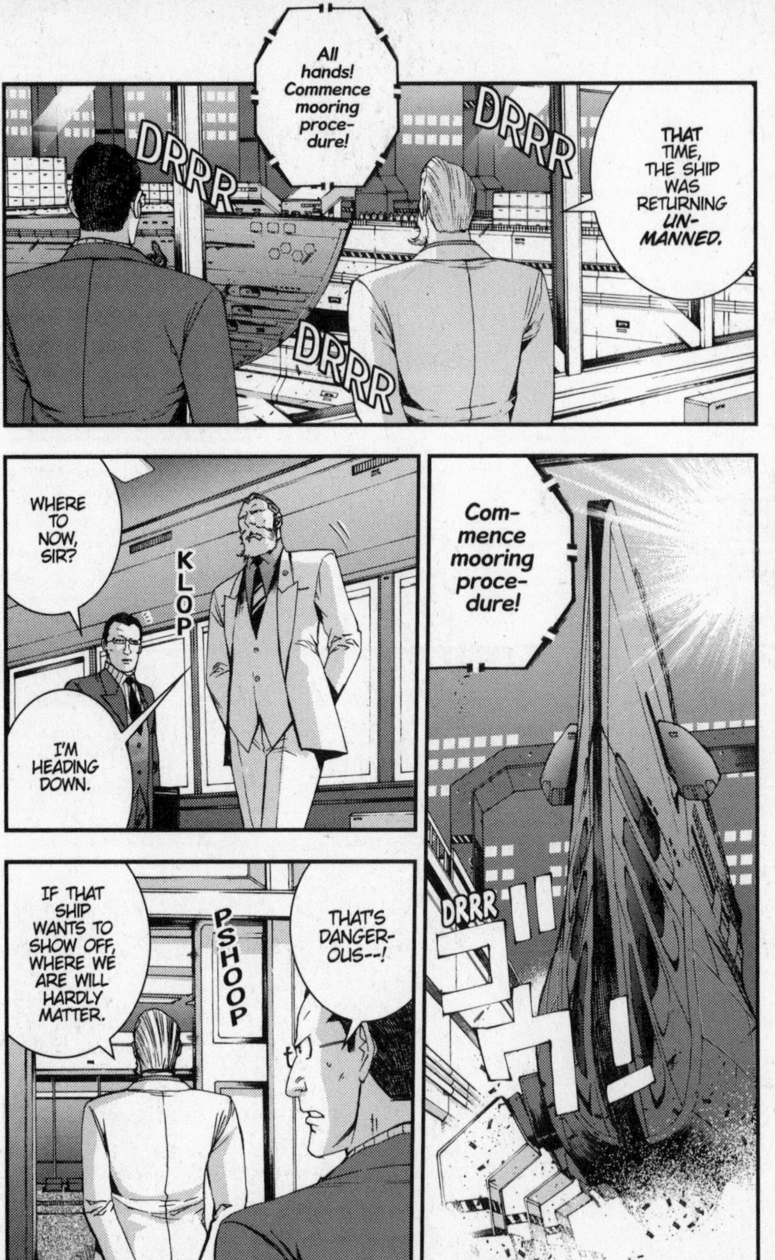
All hands! Commence mooring procedure!
DRRR
THAT TIME, THE SHIP WAS RETURNING UN-MANNED.
DRRR
DRRRR
Com-mence mooring proce-dure!
DRRR
WHERE TO NOW, SIR?
KLOP
I'M HEADING DOWN.
THAT'S DANGER-OUS--!
PSHOOP
IF THAT SHIP WANTS TO SHOW OFF, WHERE WE ARE WILL HARDLY MATTER.

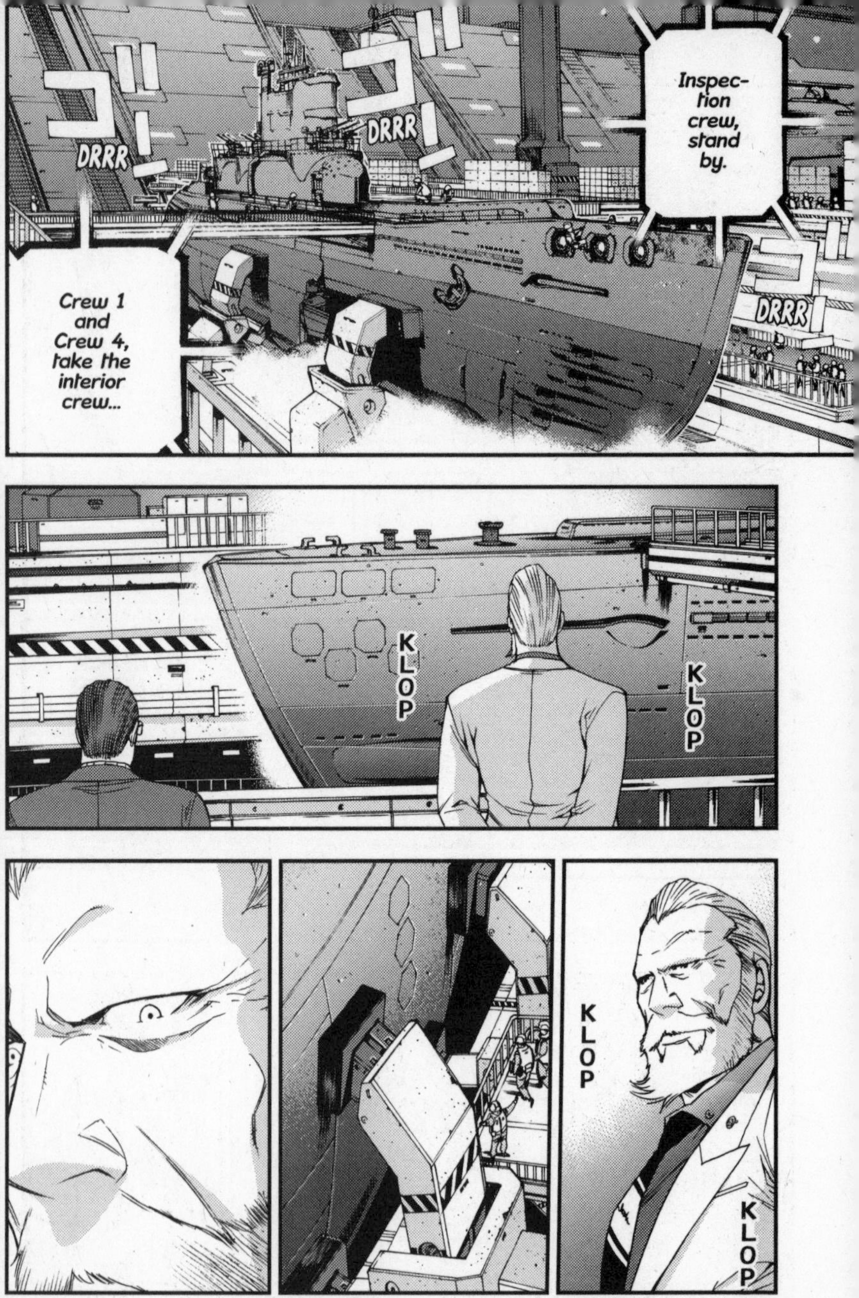
DRRR
Inspection crew, stand by.
DRRR
DRRR
Crew 1 and Crew 4, take the interior crew...
KLOP
KLOP
KLOP
KLOP

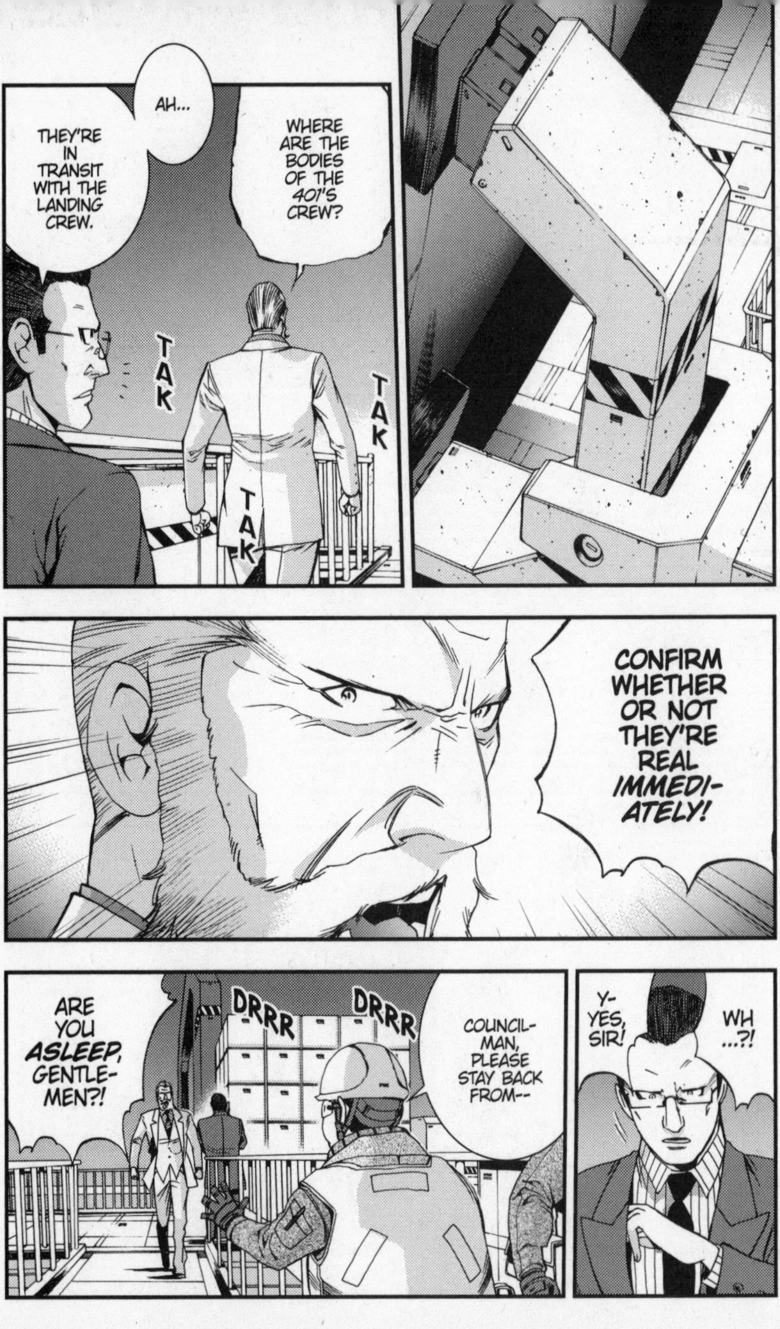
WHERE ARE THE BODIES OF THE 401'S CREW?
AH...
THEY'RE IN TRANSIT WITH THE LANDING CREW.
TAK
TAK
TAK
CONFIRM WHETHER OR NOT THEY'RE REAL IMMEDIATELY!
WH...?!
Y-YES, SIR!
COUNCILMAN, PLEASE STAY BACK FROM--
DRRR
DRRR
ARE YOU ASLEEP, GENTLEMEN?!

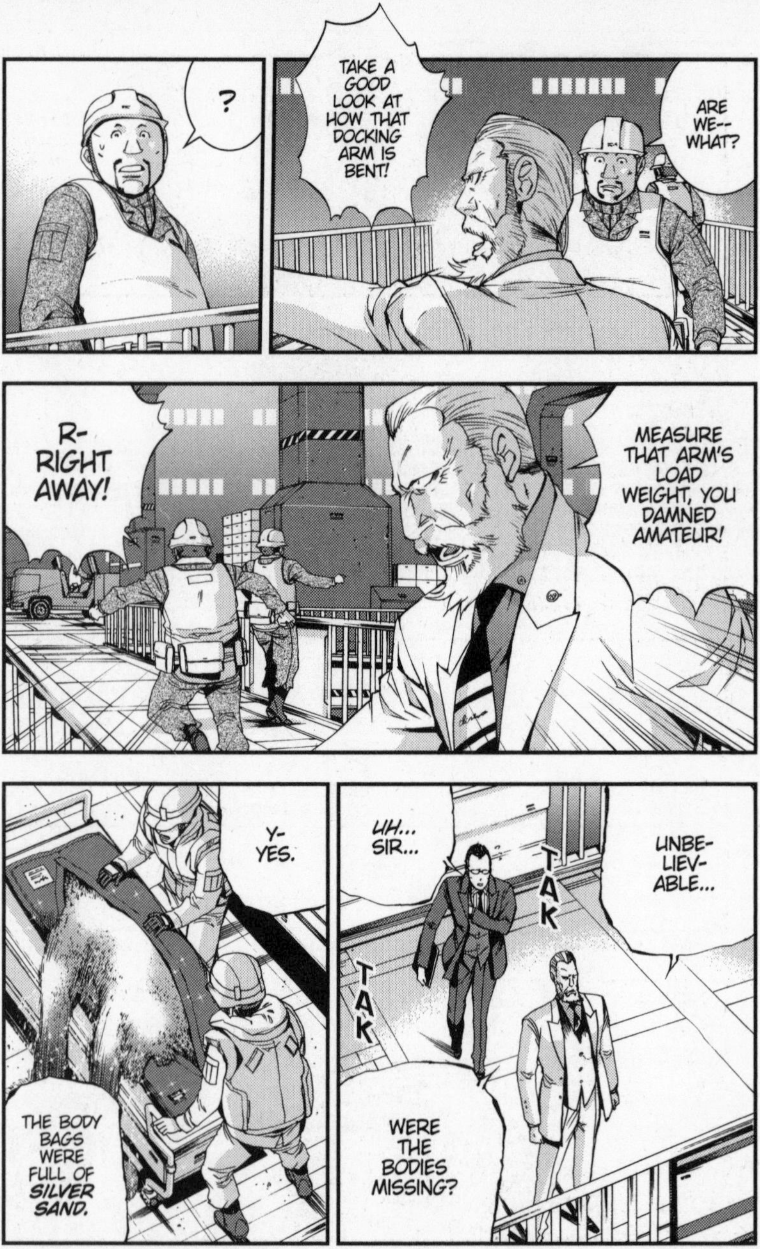
ARE WE-- WHAT?
TAKE A GOOD LOOK AT HOW THAT DOCKING ARM IS BENT!
?
MEASURE THAT ARM'S LOAD WEIGHT, YOU DAMNED AMATEUR!
R-RIGHT AWAY!
UNBE-LIEV-ABLE...
TAK
UH... SIR...
TAK
WERE THE BODIES MISSING?
Y-YES.
THE BODY BAGS WERE FULL OF SILVER SAND.

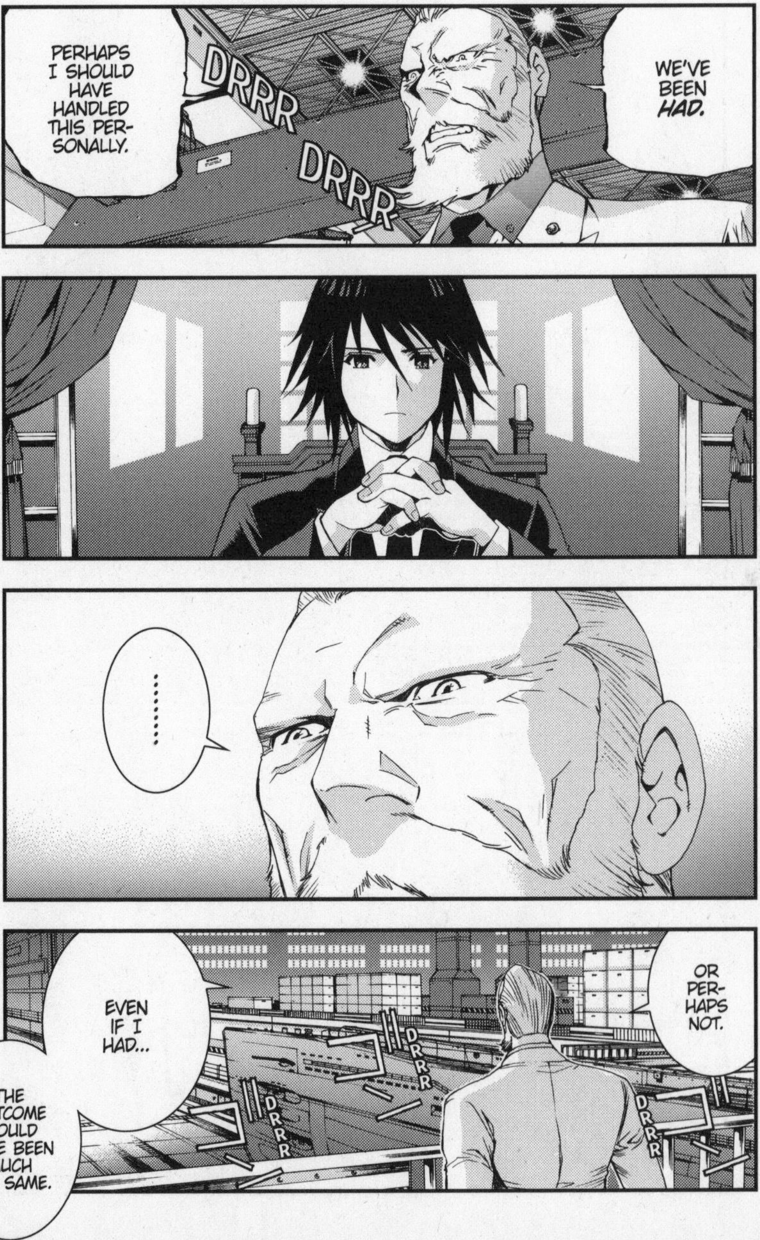
WE'VE BEEN HAD.
DRRR
DRRR
PERHAPS I SHOULD HAVE HANDLED THIS PER-SONALLY.
......
OR PER-HAPS NOT.
DRRR
DRRR
DRRR
EVEN IF I HAD...
THE OUTCOME WOULD HAVE BEEN MUCH THE SAME.

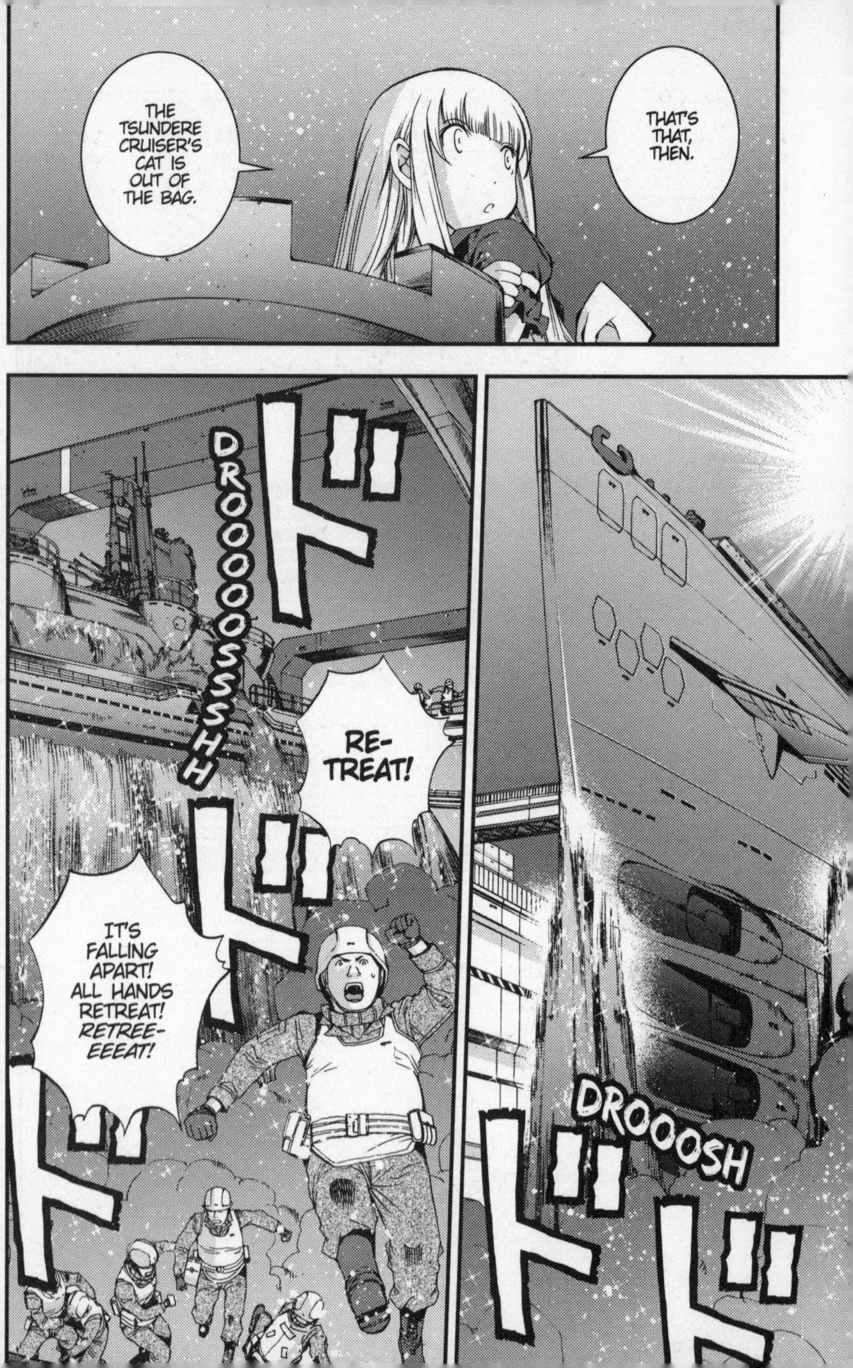
THAT'S THAT, THEN.
THE TSUNDERE CRUISER'S CAT IS OUT OF THE BAG.
DROOOOSH
DROOOOOOSSSHH
RE-TREAT!
IT'S FALLING APART! ALL HANDS RETREAT! RETREE-EEEAT!

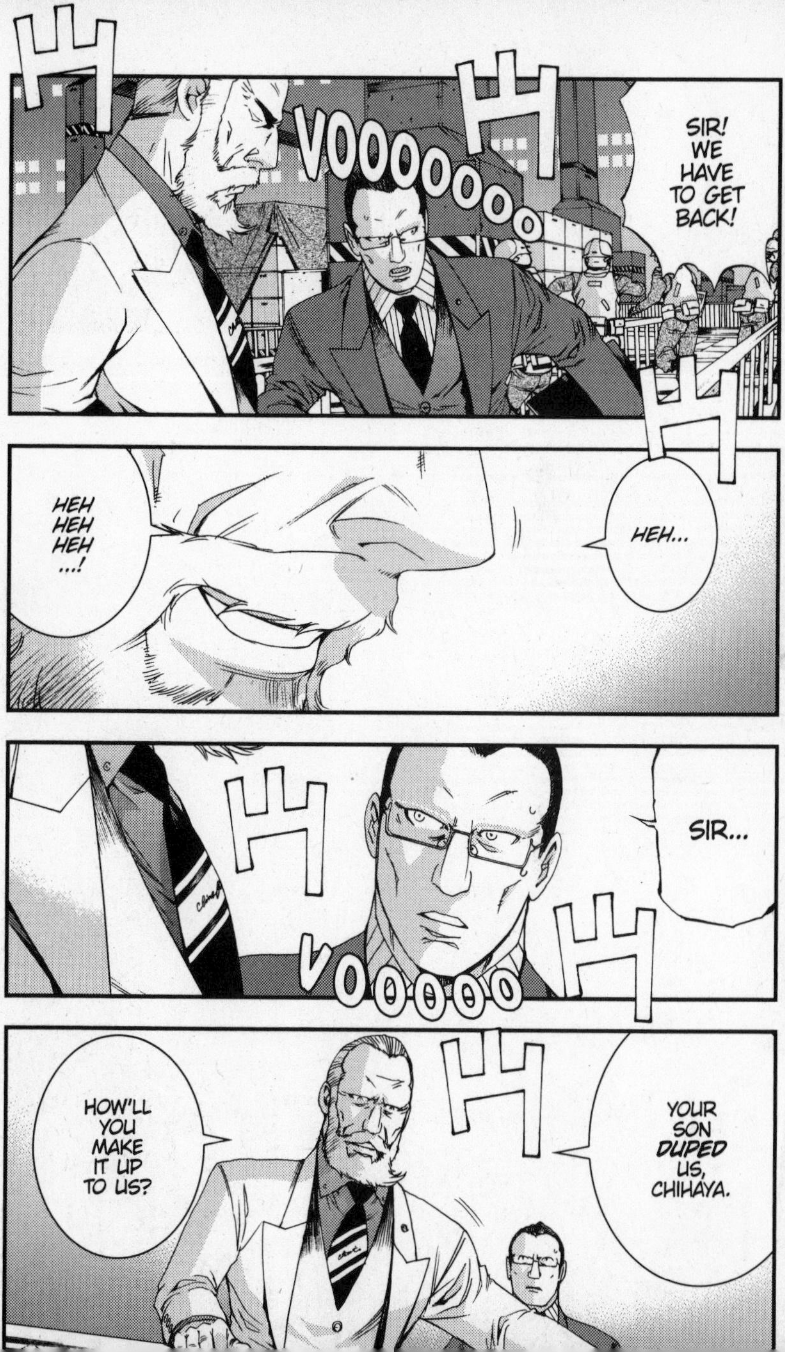
SIR! WE HAVE TO GET BACK!
VOOOOOOOO
HEH...
HEH HEH HEH ...!
SIR...
VOOOOO
YOUR SON *DUPED* US, CHIHAYA.
HOW'LL YOU MAKE IT UP TO US?

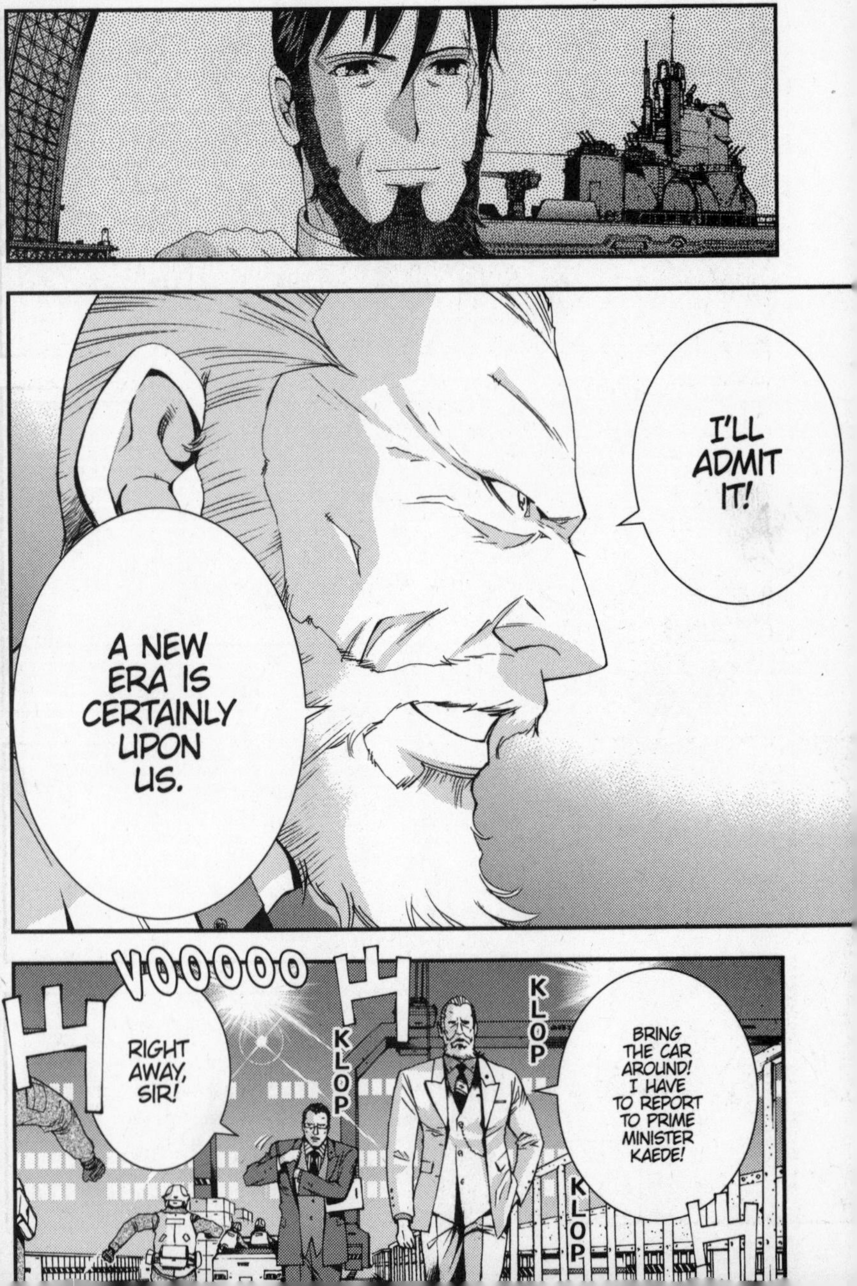
I'LL ADMIT IT!
A NEW ERA IS CERTAINLY UPON US.
KLOP
BRING THE CAR AROUND! I HAVE TO REPORT TO PRIME MINISTER KAEDE!
VOOOOOHH
KLOP
RIGHT AWAY, SIR!
KLOP

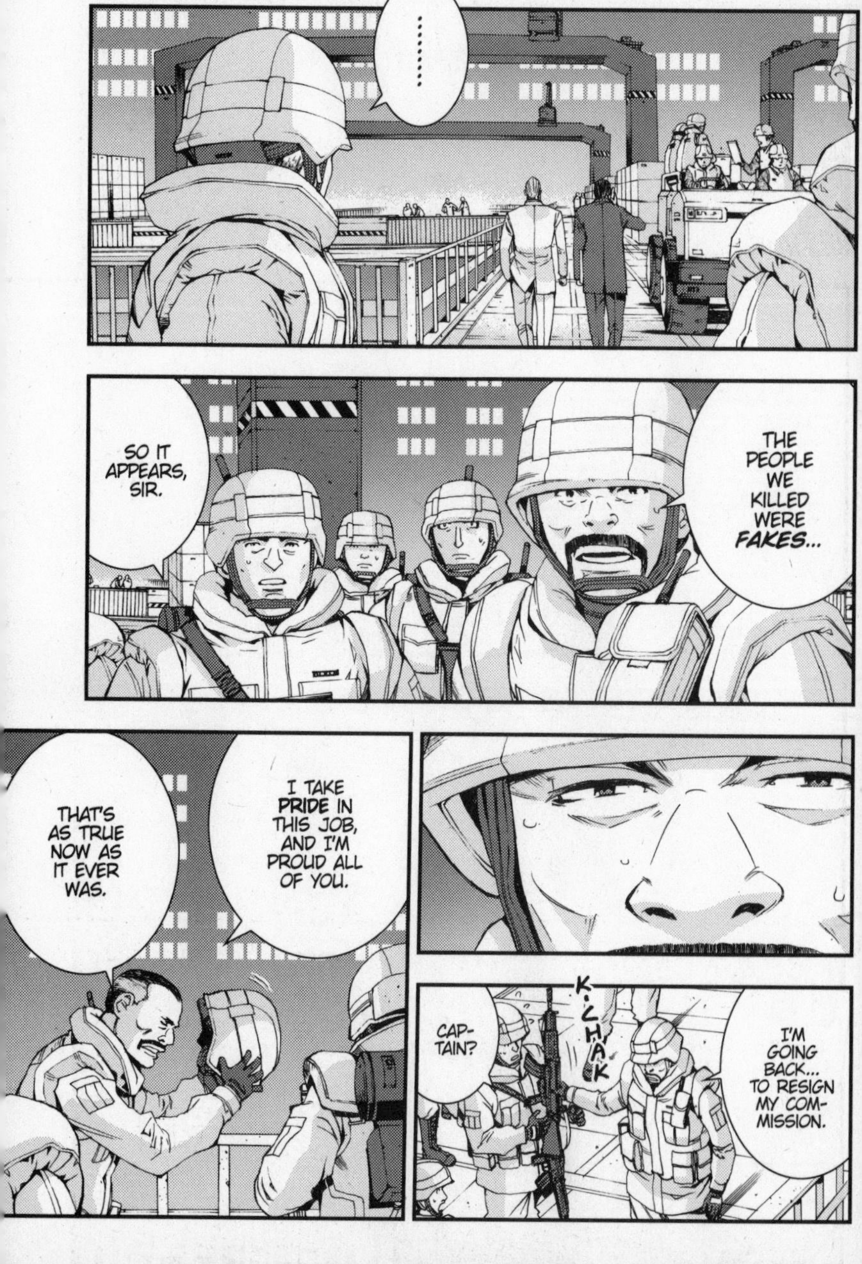
......
THE PEOPLE WE KILLED WERE FAKES...
SO IT APPEARS, SIR.
I'M GOING BACK... TO RESIGN MY COMMISSION.
K-CHAK
CAP-TAIN?
I TAKE PRIDE IN THIS JOB, AND I'M PROUD ALL OF YOU.
THAT'S AS TRUE NOW AS IT EVER WAS.

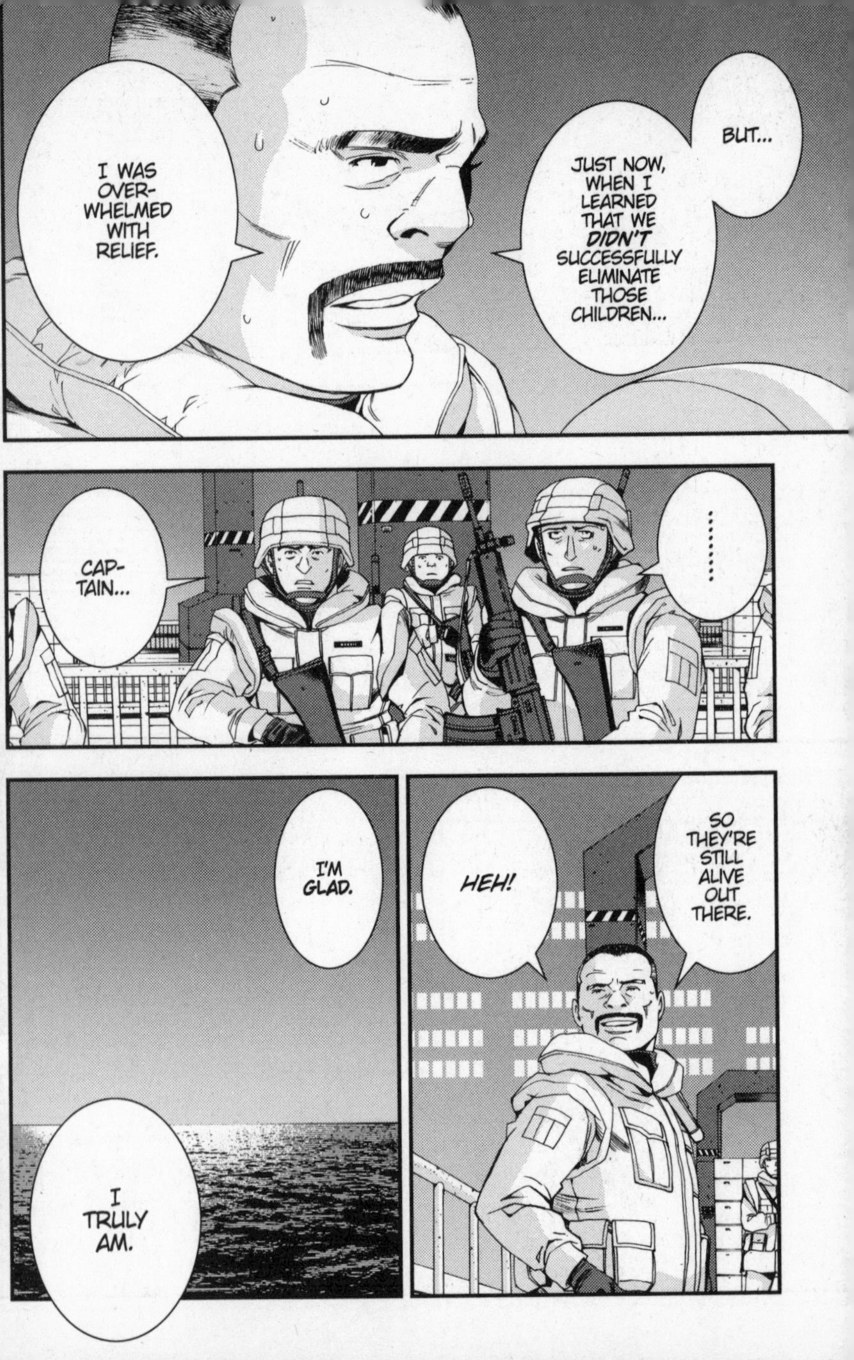
BUT...
JUST NOW, WHEN I LEARNED THAT WE *DIDN'T* SUCCESSFULLY ELIMINATE THOSE CHILDREN...
I WAS OVERWHELMED WITH RELIEF.
......
CAPTAIN...
SO THEY'RE STILL ALIVE OUT THERE.
HEH!
I'M GLAD.
I TRULY AM.

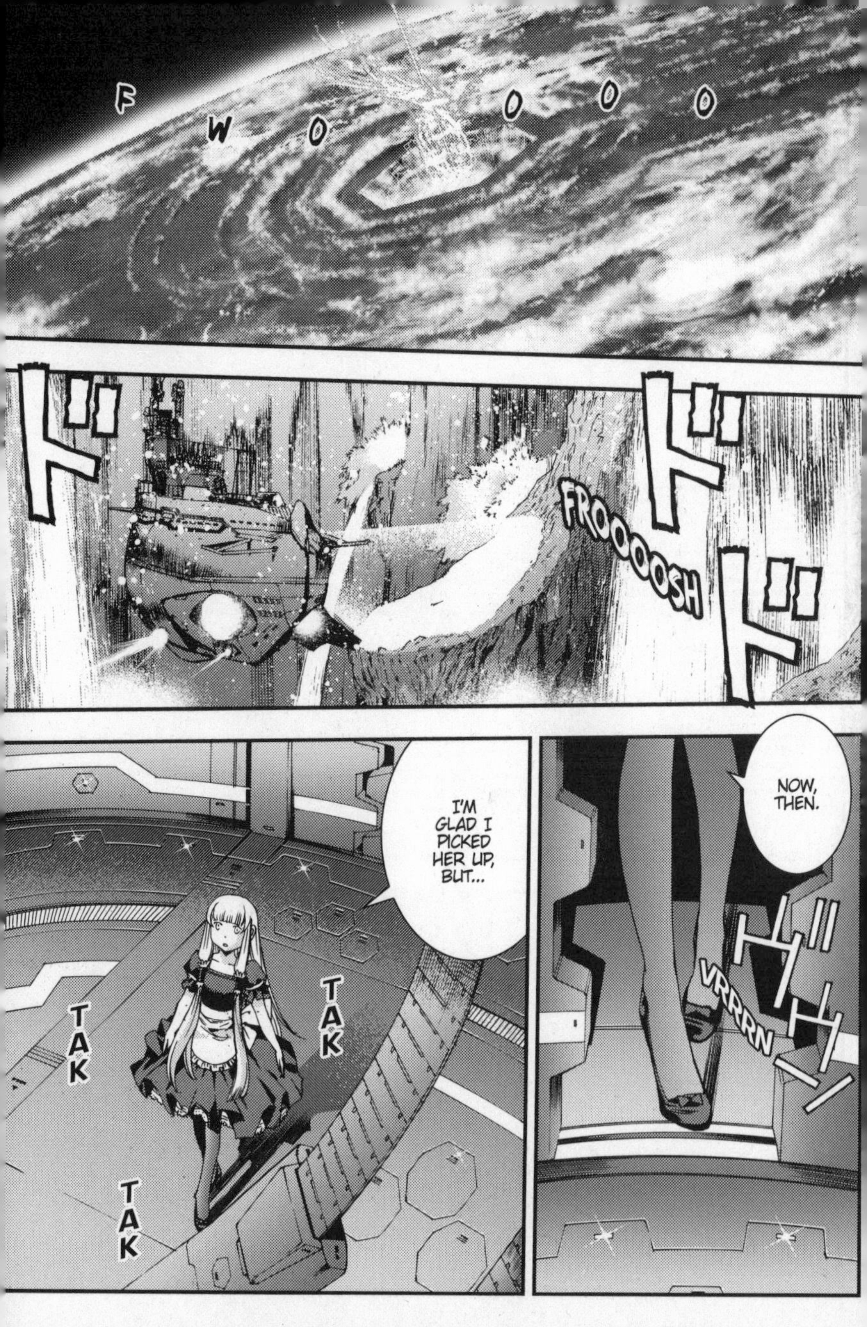
FWOOOO
FROOOOSH
NOW, THEN.
VRRRN
I'M GLAD I PICKED HER UP, BUT...
TAK
TAK
TAK
TAK

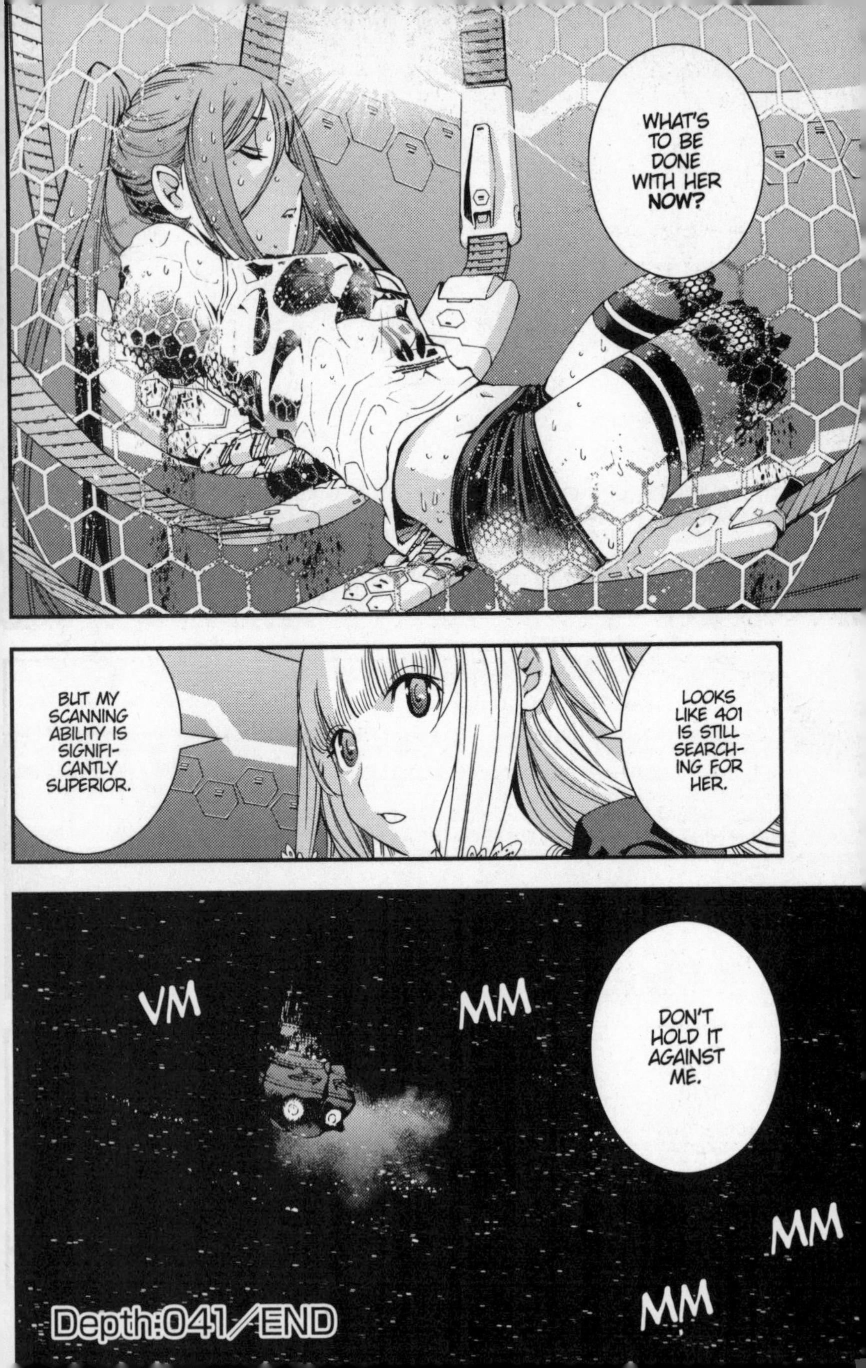
WHAT'S TO BE DONE WITH HER NOW?
LOOKS LIKE 401 IS STILL SEARCHING FOR HER.
BUT MY SCANNING ABILITY IS SIGNIFICANTLY SUPERIOR.
DON'T HOLD IT AGAINST ME.
VM
MM
MM
MM
Depth:041/END

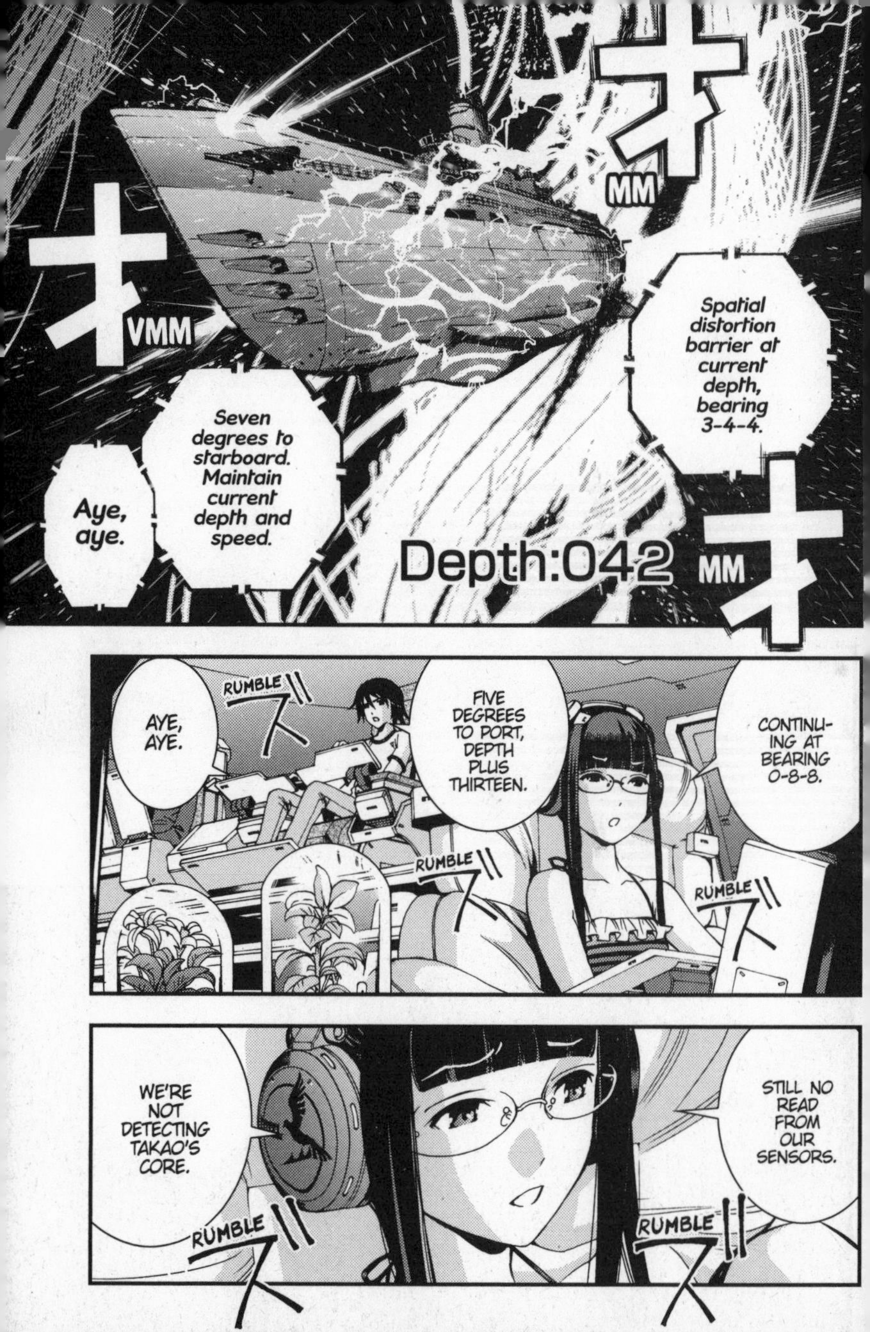
MM
Spatial distortion barrier at current depth, bearing 3-4-4.
VMM
Seven degrees to starboard. Maintain current depth and speed.
Aye, aye.
MM
Depth:042
CONTINU-ING AT BEARING 0-8-8.
RUMBLE
FIVE DEGREES TO PORT, DEPTH PLUS THIRTEEN.
RUMBLE
RUMBLE
AYE, AYE.
STILL NO READ FROM OUR SENSORS.
RUMBLE
WE'RE NOT DETECTING TAKAO'S CORE.
RUMBLE

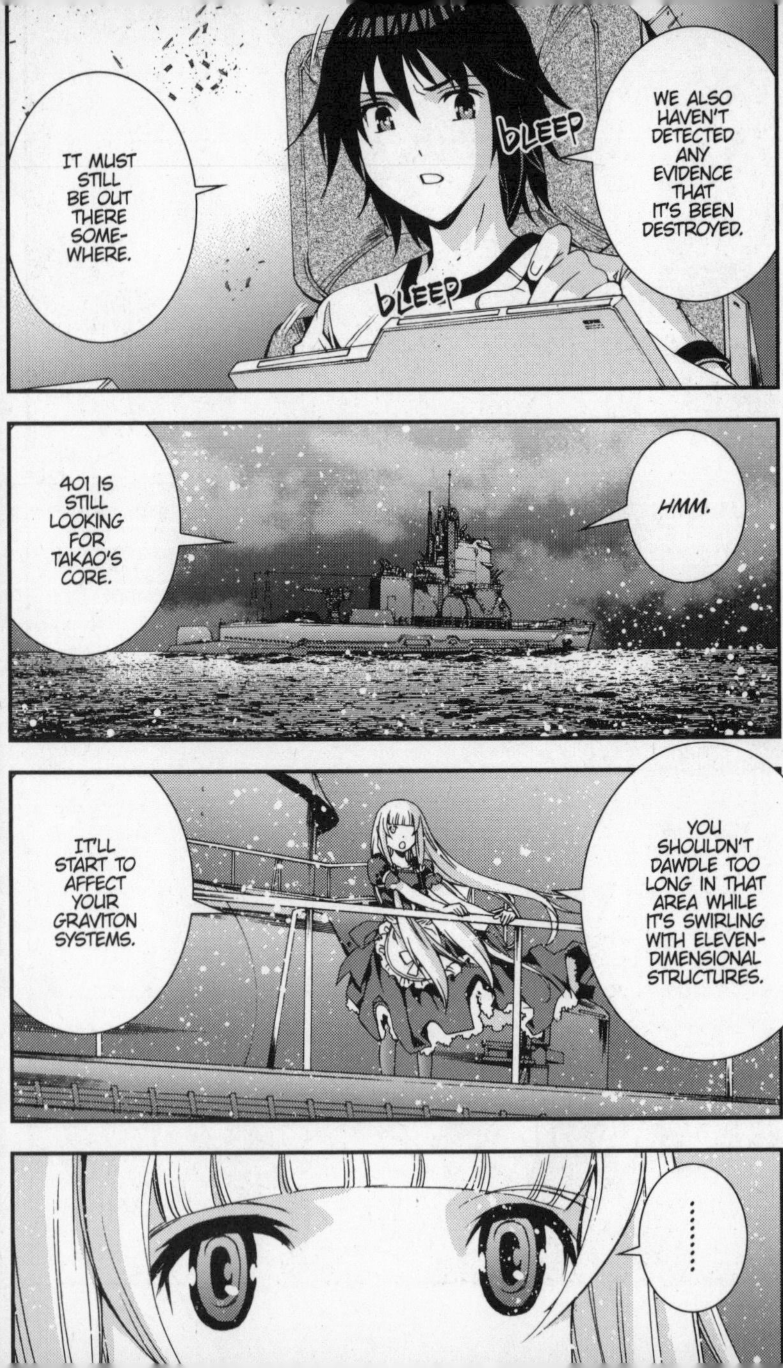
WE ALSO HAVEN'T DETECTED ANY EVIDENCE THAT IT'S BEEN DESTROYED.
BLEEP
BLEEP
IT MUST STILL BE OUT THERE SOME-WHERE.
HMM.
401 IS STILL LOOKING FOR TAKAO'S CORE.
YOU SHOULDN'T DAWDLE TOO LONG IN THAT AREA WHILE IT'S SWIRLING WITH ELEVEN-DIMENSIONAL STRUCTURES.
IT'LL START TO AFFECT YOUR GRAVITON SYSTEMS.
......

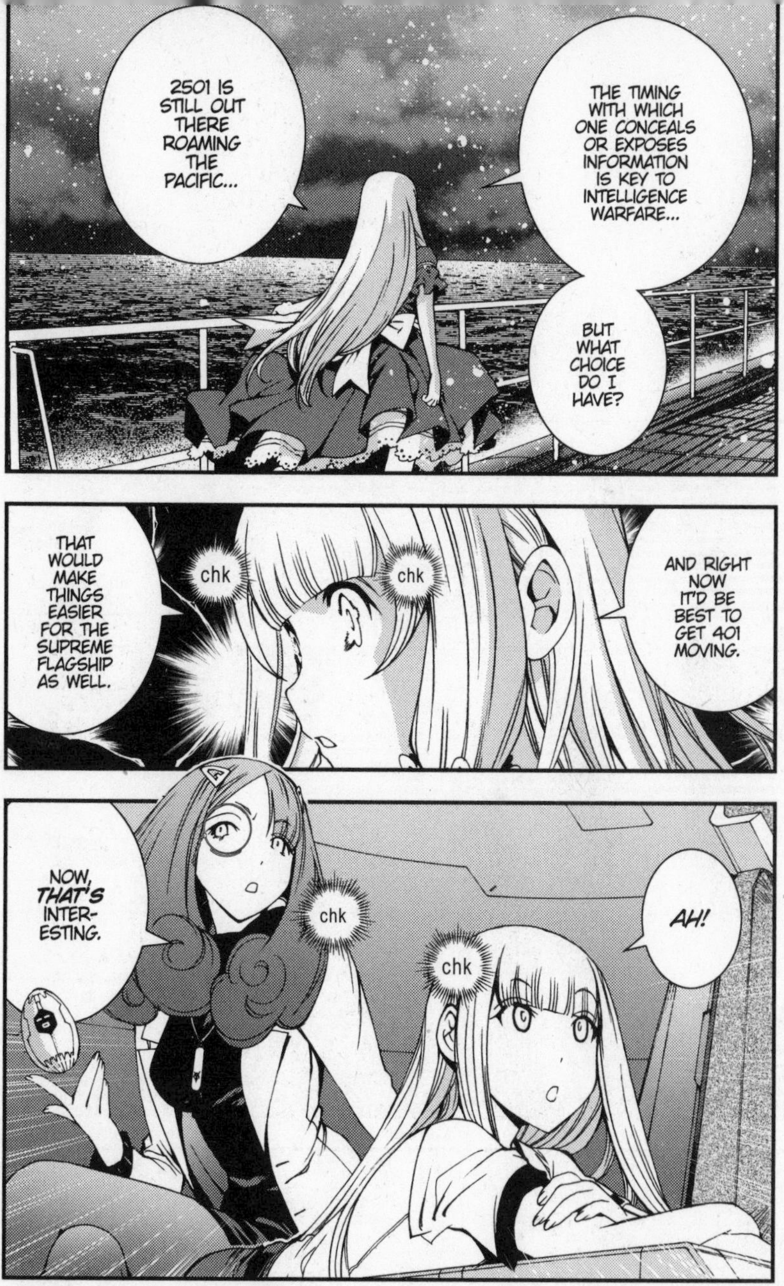
THE TIMING WITH WHICH ONE CONCEALS OR EXPOSES INFORMATION IS KEY TO INTELLIGENCE WARFARE...
BUT WHAT CHOICE DO I HAVE?
2501 IS STILL OUT THERE ROAMING THE PACIFIC...
AND RIGHT NOW IT'D BE BEST TO GET 401 MOVING.
chk
chk
THAT WOULD MAKE THINGS EASIER FOR THE SUPREME FLAGSHIP AS WELL.
AH!
chk
chk
NOW, ***THAT'S*** INTER-ESTING.

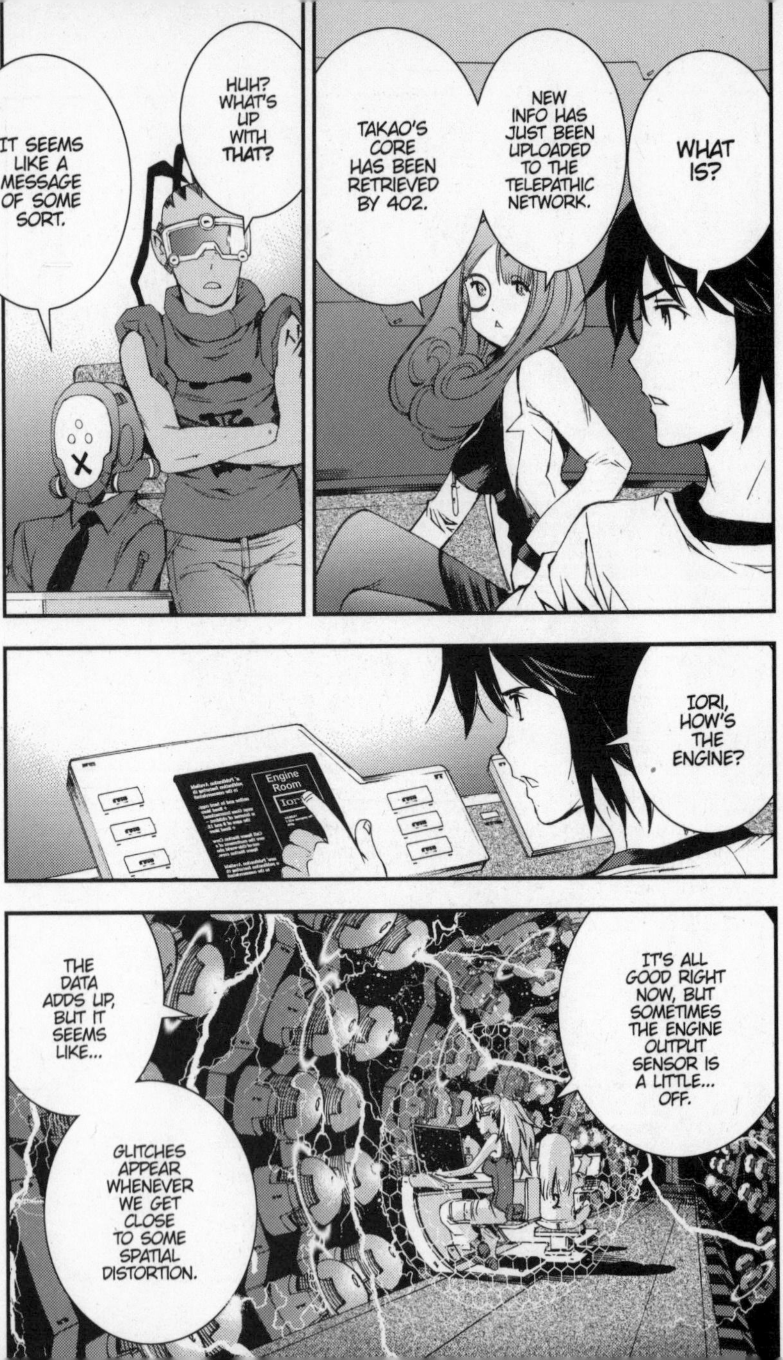
WHAT IS?
NEW INFO HAS JUST BEEN UPLOADED TO THE TELEPATHIC NETWORK.
TAKAO'S CORE HAS BEEN RETRIEVED BY 402.
HUH? WHAT'S UP WITH THAT?
IT SEEMS LIKE A MESSAGE OF SOME SORT.
IORI, HOW'S THE ENGINE?
Engine Room
Iori
IT'S ALL GOOD RIGHT NOW, BUT SOMETIMES THE ENGINE OUTPUT SENSOR IS A LITTLE... OFF.
THE DATA ADDS UP, BUT IT SEEMS LIKE...
GLITCHES APPEAR WHENEVER WE GET CLOSE TO SOME SPATIAL DISTORTION.

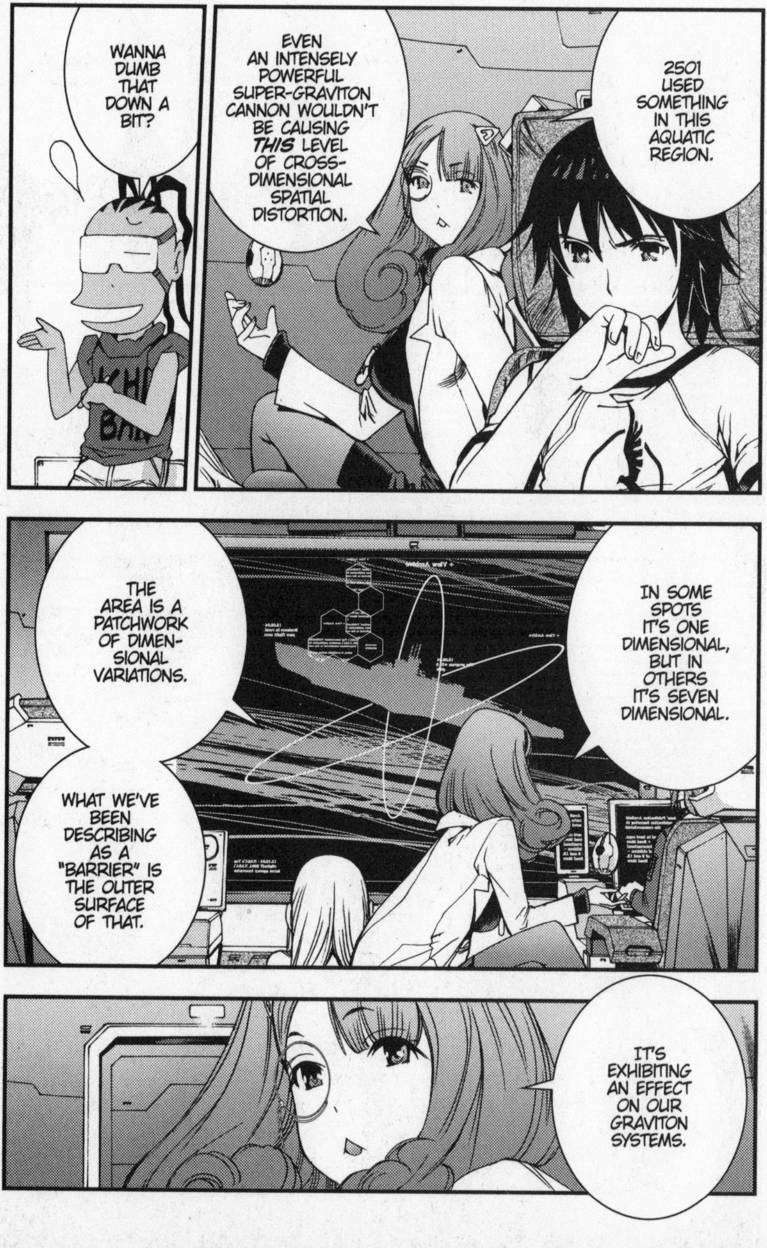
2501 USED SOMETHING IN THIS AQUATIC REGION.
EVEN AN INTENSELY POWERFUL SUPER-GRAVITON CANNON WOULDN'T BE CAUSING *THIS* LEVEL OF CROSS-DIMENSIONAL SPATIAL DISTORTION.
WANNA DUMB THAT DOWN A BIT?
IN SOME SPOTS IT'S ONE DIMENSIONAL, BUT IN OTHERS IT'S SEVEN DIMENSIONAL.
THE AREA IS A PATCHWORK OF DIMEN-SIONAL VARIATIONS.
WHAT WE'VE BEEN DESCRIBING AS A "BARRIER" IS THE OUTER SURFACE OF THAT.
IT'S EXHIBITING AN EFFECT ON OUR GRAVITON SYSTEMS.

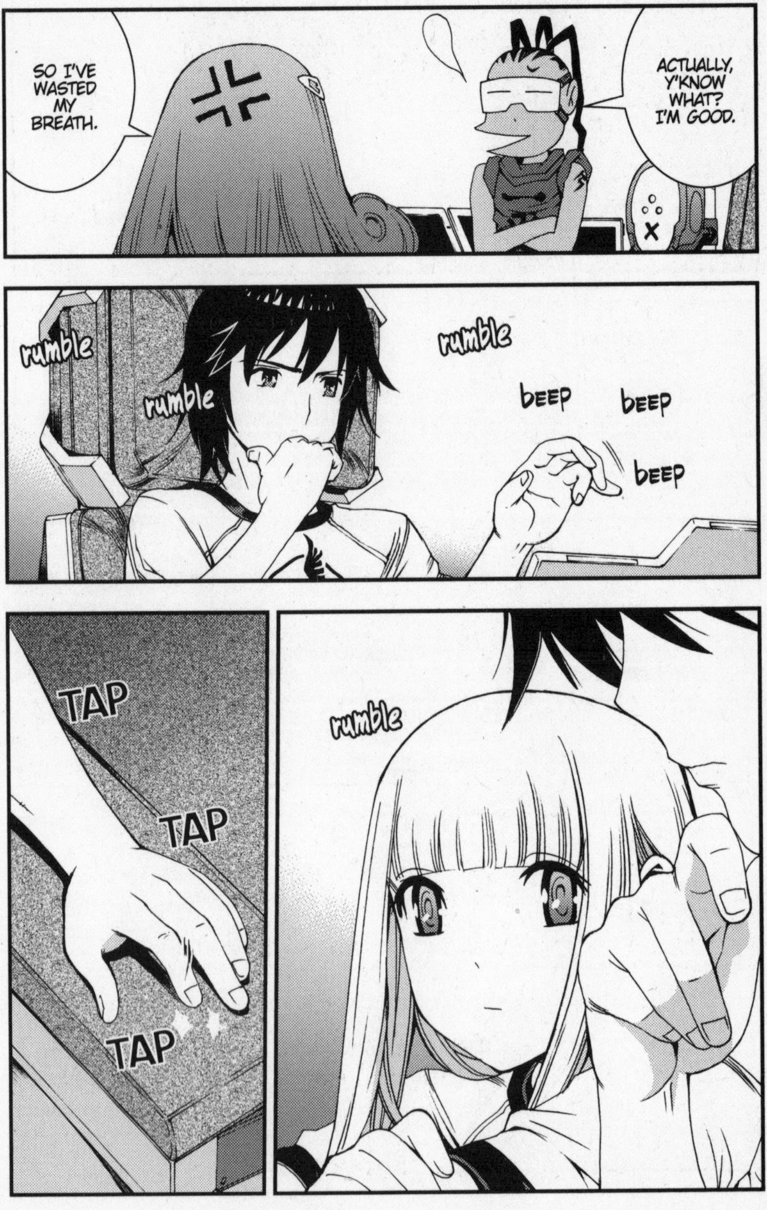
ACTUALLY, Y'KNOW WHAT? I'M GOOD.
SO I'VE WASTED MY BREATH.
rumble
beep
beep
beep
rumble
rumble
rumble
TAP
TAP
TAP

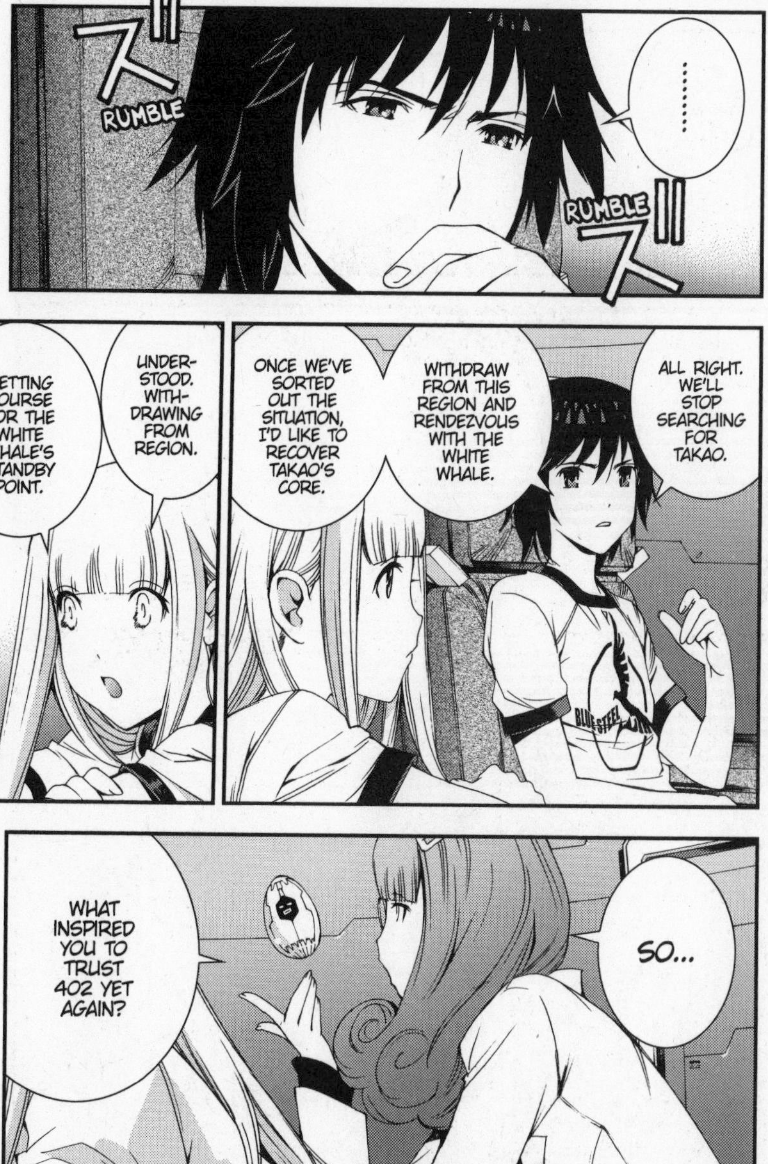
......
RUMBLE
RUMBLE
ALL RIGHT. WE'LL STOP SEARCHING FOR TAKAO.
WITHDRAW FROM THIS REGION AND RENDEZVOUS WITH THE WHITE WHALE.
ONCE WE'VE SORTED OUT THE SITUATION, I'D LIKE TO RECOVER TAKAO'S CORE.
UNDER-STOOD. WITH-DRAWING FROM REGION.
SETTING COURSE FOR THE WHITE WHALE'S STANDBY POINT.
SO...
WHAT INSPIRED YOU TO TRUST 402 YET AGAIN?

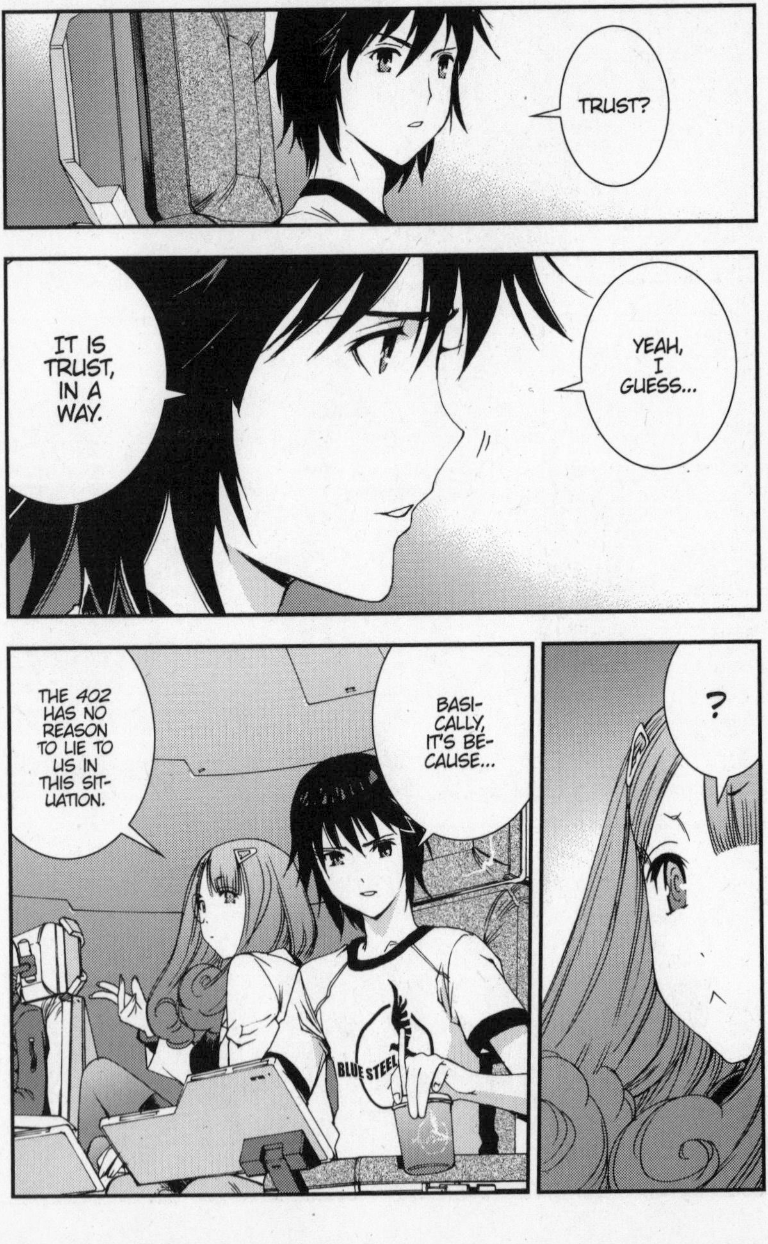
TRUST?
YEAH, I GUESS...
IT IS TRUST, IN A WAY.
?
BASICALLY, IT'S BECAUSE...
THE 402 HAS NO REASON TO LIE TO US IN THIS SITUATION.

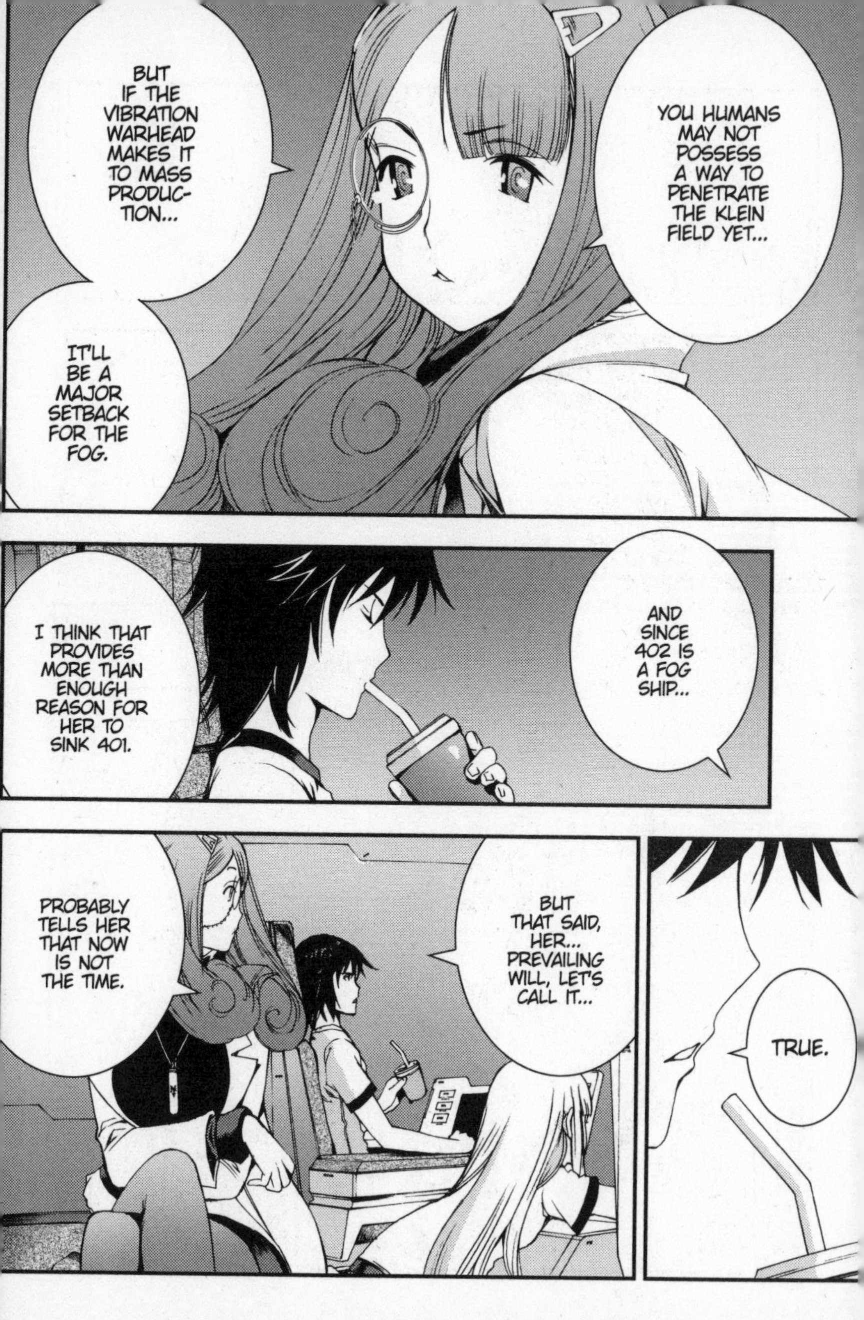
YOU HUMANS MAY NOT POSSESS A WAY TO PENETRATE THE KLEIN FIELD YET...
BUT IF THE VIBRATION WARHEAD MAKES IT TO MASS PRODUC-TION...
IT'LL BE A MAJOR SETBACK FOR THE FOG.
AND SINCE 402 IS A FOG SHIP...
I THINK THAT PROVIDES MORE THAN ENOUGH REASON FOR HER TO SINK 401.
TRUE.
BUT THAT SAID, HER... PREVAILING WILL, LET'S CALL IT...
PROBABLY TELLS HER THAT NOW IS NOT THE TIME.

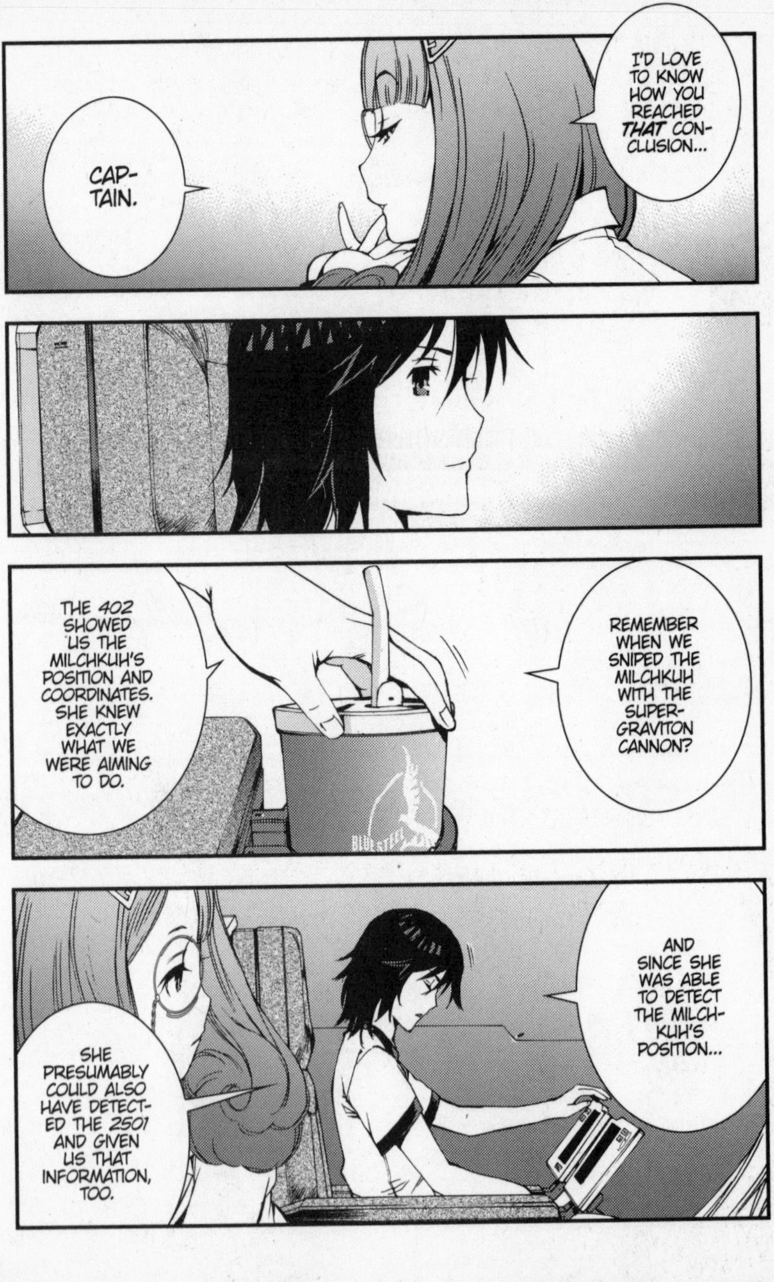
I'D LOVE TO KNOW HOW YOU REACHED *THAT* CON-CLUSION...
CAP-TAIN.
REMEMBER WHEN WE SNIPED THE MILCHKUH WITH THE SUPER-GRAVITON CANNON?
THE 402 SHOWED US THE MILCHKUH'S POSITION AND COORDINATES. SHE KNEW EXACTLY WHAT WE WERE AIMING TO DO.
AND SINCE SHE WAS ABLE TO DETECT THE MILCH-KUH'S POSITION...
SHE PRESUMABLY COULD ALSO HAVE DETECT-ED THE 2501 AND GIVEN US THAT INFORMATION, TOO.

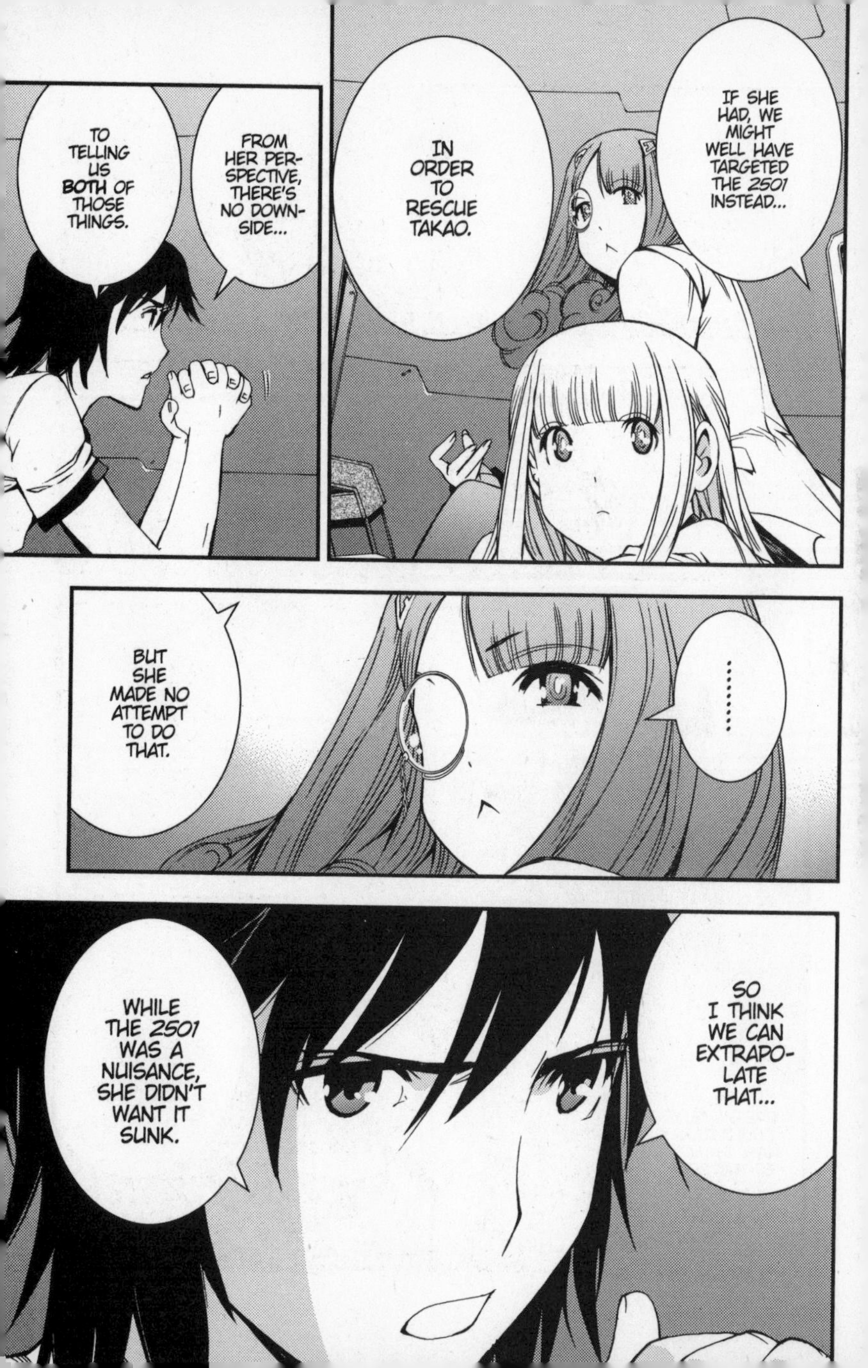
IF SHE HAD, WE MIGHT WELL HAVE TARGETED THE 2501 INSTEAD...
IN ORDER TO RESCUE TAKAO.
FROM HER PERSPECTIVE, THERE'S NO DOWNSIDE...
TO TELLING US BOTH OF THOSE THINGS.
......
BUT SHE MADE NO ATTEMPT TO DO THAT.
SO I THINK WE CAN EXTRAPOLATE THAT...
WHILE THE 2501 WAS A NUISANCE, SHE DIDN'T WANT IT SUNK.

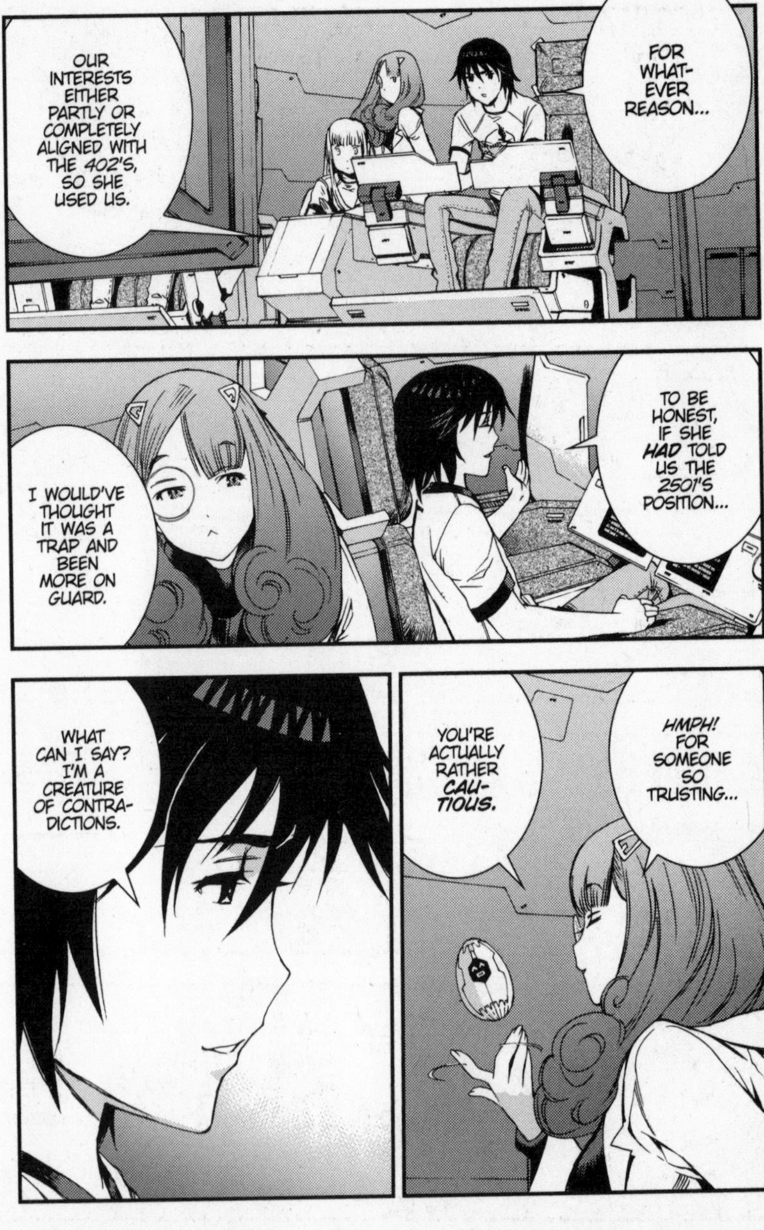
FOR WHAT-EVER REASON...
OUR INTERESTS EITHER PARTLY OR COMPLETELY ALIGNED WITH THE 402'S, SO SHE USED US.
TO BE HONEST, IF SHE *HAD* TOLD US THE 2501'S POSITION...
I WOULD'VE THOUGHT IT WAS A TRAP AND BEEN MORE ON GUARD.
HMPH! FOR SOMEONE SO TRUSTING...
YOU'RE ACTUALLY RATHER *CAU-TIOUS.*
WHAT CAN I SAY? I'M A CREATURE OF CONTRA-DICTIONS.

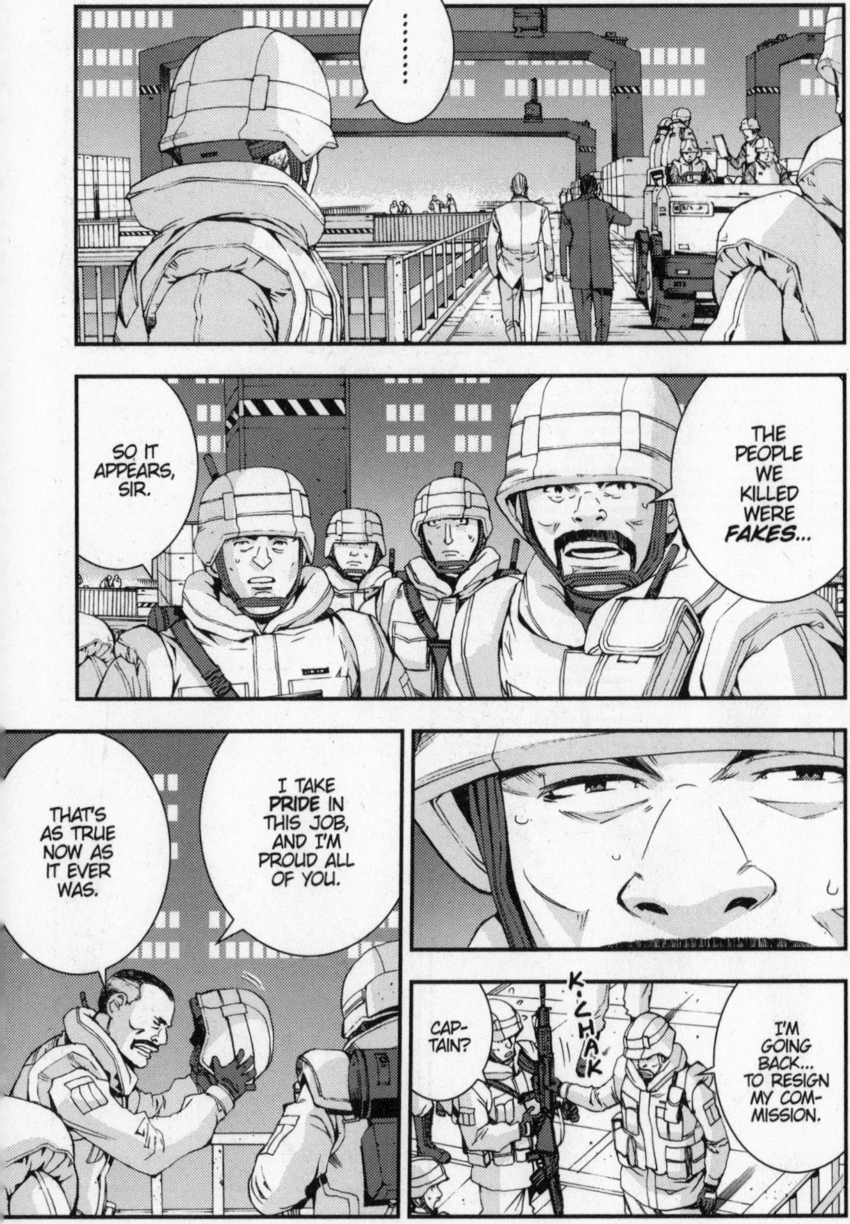
......
THE PEOPLE WE KILLED WERE FAKES...
SO IT APPEARS, SIR.
I'M GOING BACK... TO RESIGN MY COMMISSION.
K-CHAK
CAP-TAIN?
I TAKE PRIDE IN THIS JOB, AND I'M PROUD ALL OF YOU.
THAT'S AS TRUE NOW AS IT EVER WAS.

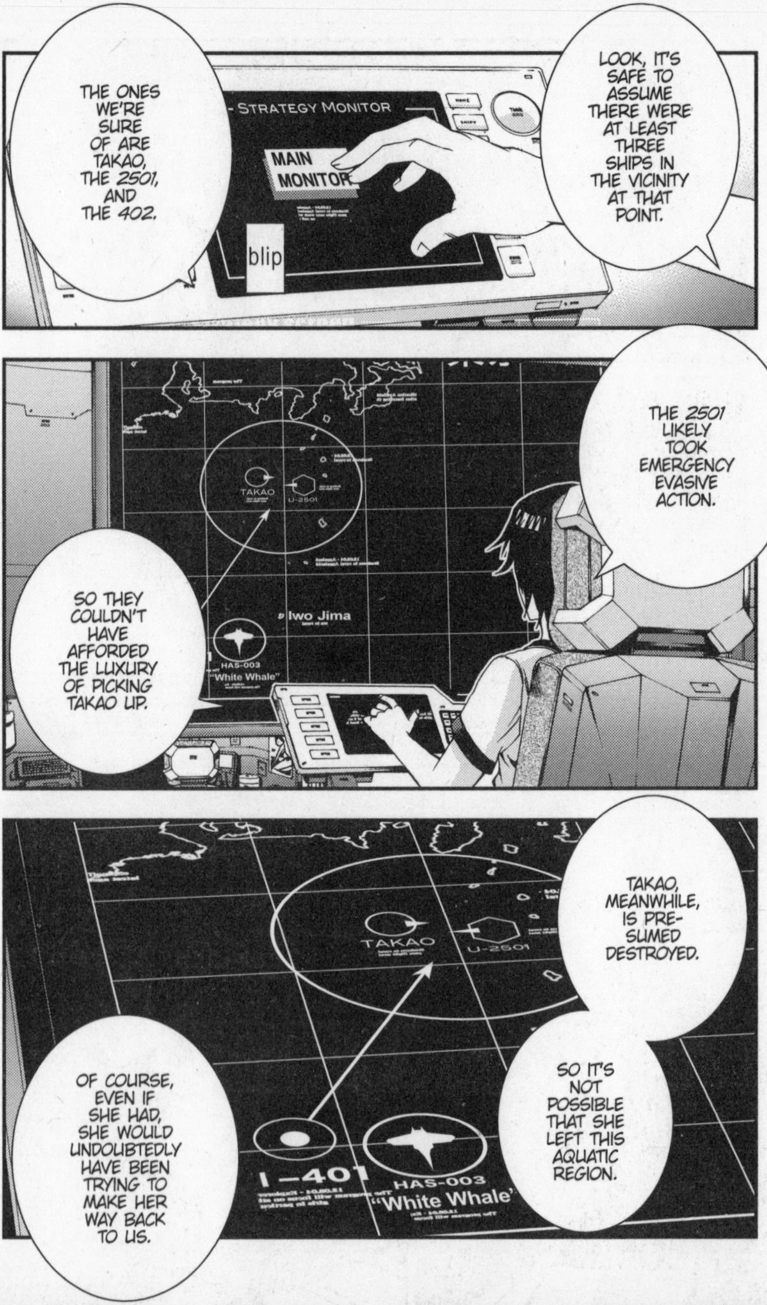
STRATEGY MONITOR
MAIN MONITOR
LOOK, IT'S SAFE TO ASSUME THERE WERE AT LEAST THREE SHIPS IN THE VICINITY AT THAT POINT.
THE ONES WE'RE SURE OF ARE TAKAO, THE 2501, AND THE 402.
blip
THE 2501 LIKELY TOOK EMERGENCY EVASIVE ACTION.
TAKAO
U-2501
Iwo Jima
HAS-003
"White Whale"
SO THEY COULDN'T HAVE AFFORDED THE LUXURY OF PICKING TAKAO UP.
TAKAO, MEANWHILE, IS PRE-SUMED DESTROYED.
SO IT'S NOT POSSIBLE THAT SHE LEFT THIS AQUATIC REGION.
TAKAO
U-2501
I-401
HAS-003
"White Whale"
OF COURSE, EVEN IF SHE HAD, SHE WOULD UNDOUBTEDLY HAVE BEEN TRYING TO MAKE HER WAY BACK TO US.

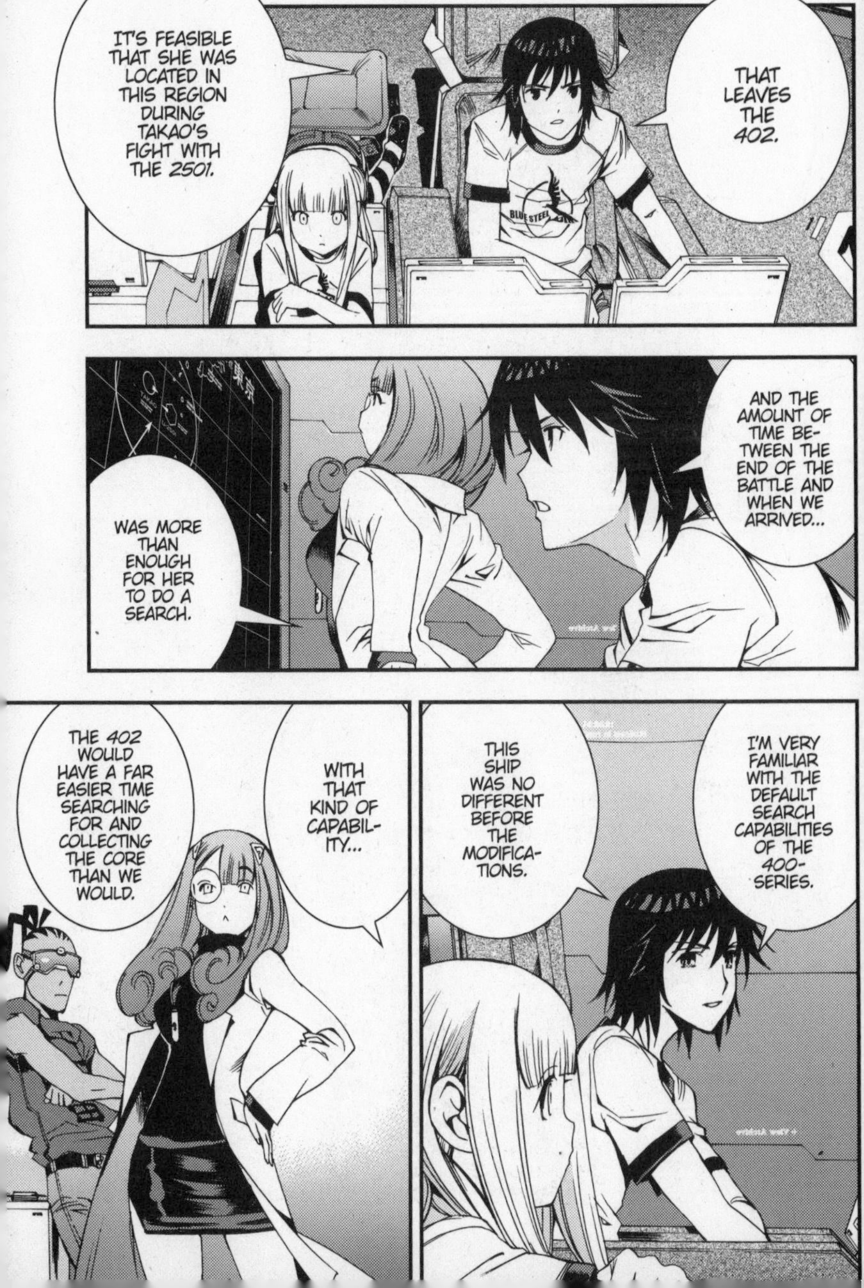
THAT LEAVES THE 402.
IT'S FEASIBLE THAT SHE WAS LOCATED IN THIS REGION DURING TAKAO'S FIGHT WITH THE 2501.
AND THE AMOUNT OF TIME BE-TWEEN THE END OF THE BATTLE AND WHEN WE ARRIVED...
WAS MORE THAN ENOUGH FOR HER TO DO A SEARCH.
I'M VERY FAMILIAR WITH THE DEFAULT SEARCH CAPABILITIES OF THE 400-SERIES.
THIS SHIP WAS NO DIFFERENT BEFORE THE MODIFICA-TIONS.
WITH THAT KIND OF CAPABIL-ITY...
THE 402 WOULD HAVE A FAR EASIER TIME SEARCHING FOR AND COLLECTING THE CORE THAN WE WOULD.

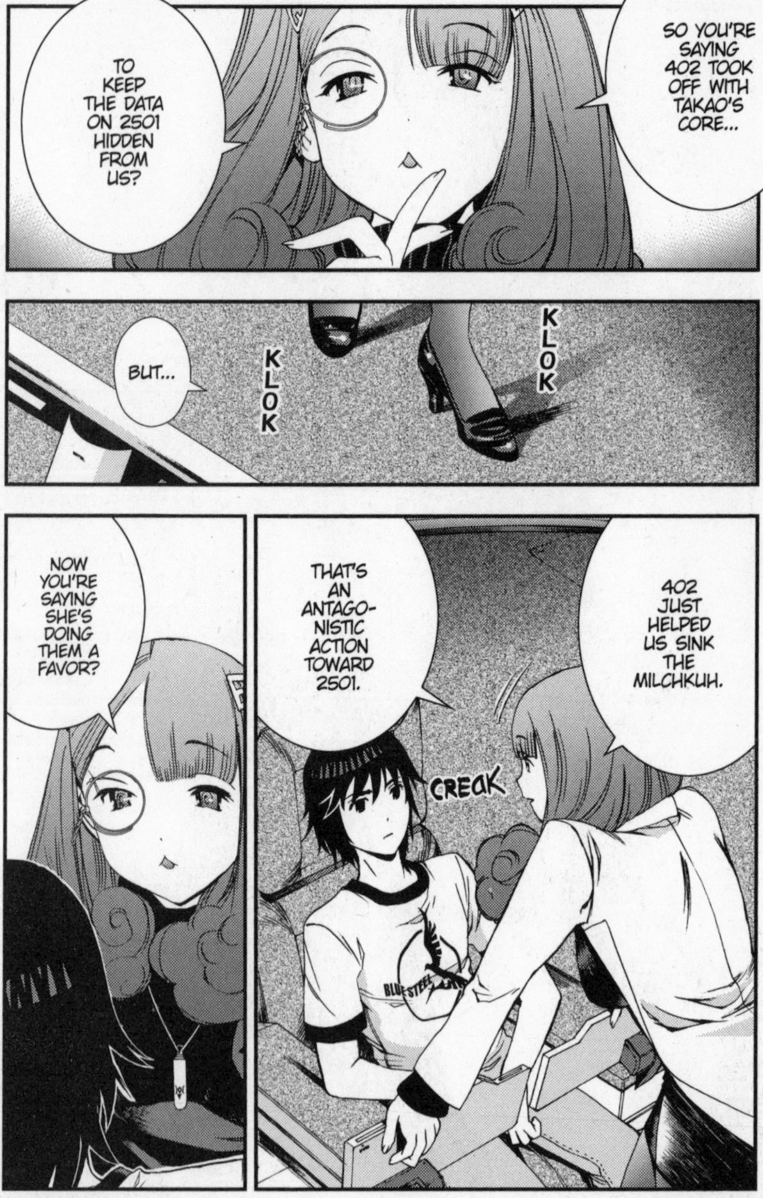
SO YOU'RE SAYING 402 TOOK OFF WITH TAKAO'S CORE...
TO KEEP THE DATA ON 2501 HIDDEN FROM US?
KLOK
KLOK
BUT...
402 JUST HELPED US SINK THE MILCHKUH.
CREAK
THAT'S AN ANTAGO-NISTIC ACTION TOWARD 2501.
BLUE STEEL
NOW YOU'RE SAYING SHE'S DOING THEM A FAVOR?

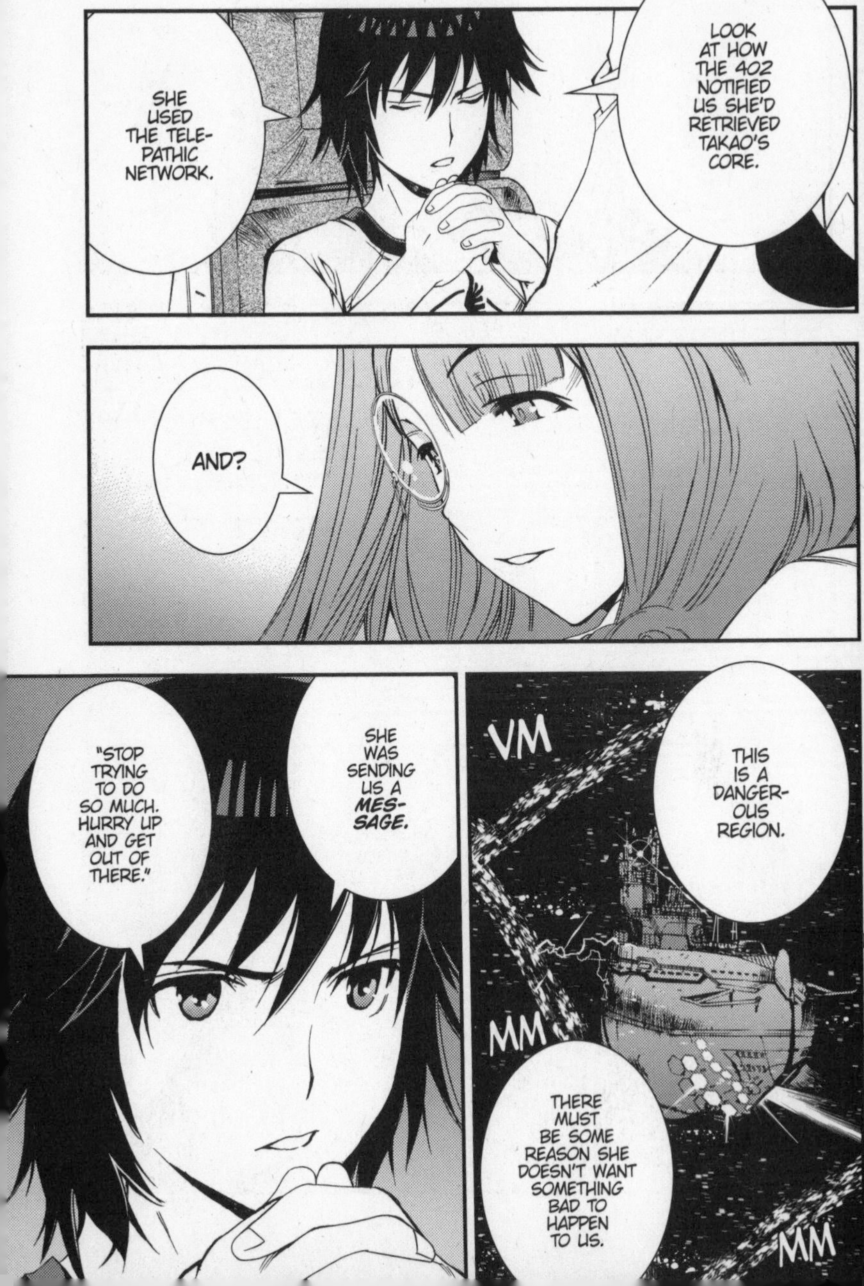
LOOK AT HOW THE 402 NOTIFIED US SHE'D RETRIEVED TAKAO'S CORE.
SHE USED THE TELE-PATHIC NETWORK.
AND?
VM
THIS IS A DANGER-OUS REGION.
MM
THERE MUST BE SOME REASON SHE DOESN'T WANT SOMETHING BAD TO HAPPEN TO US.
MM
SHE WAS SENDING US A *MES-SAGE.*
"STOP TRYING TO DO SO MUCH. HURRY UP AND GET OUT OF THERE."

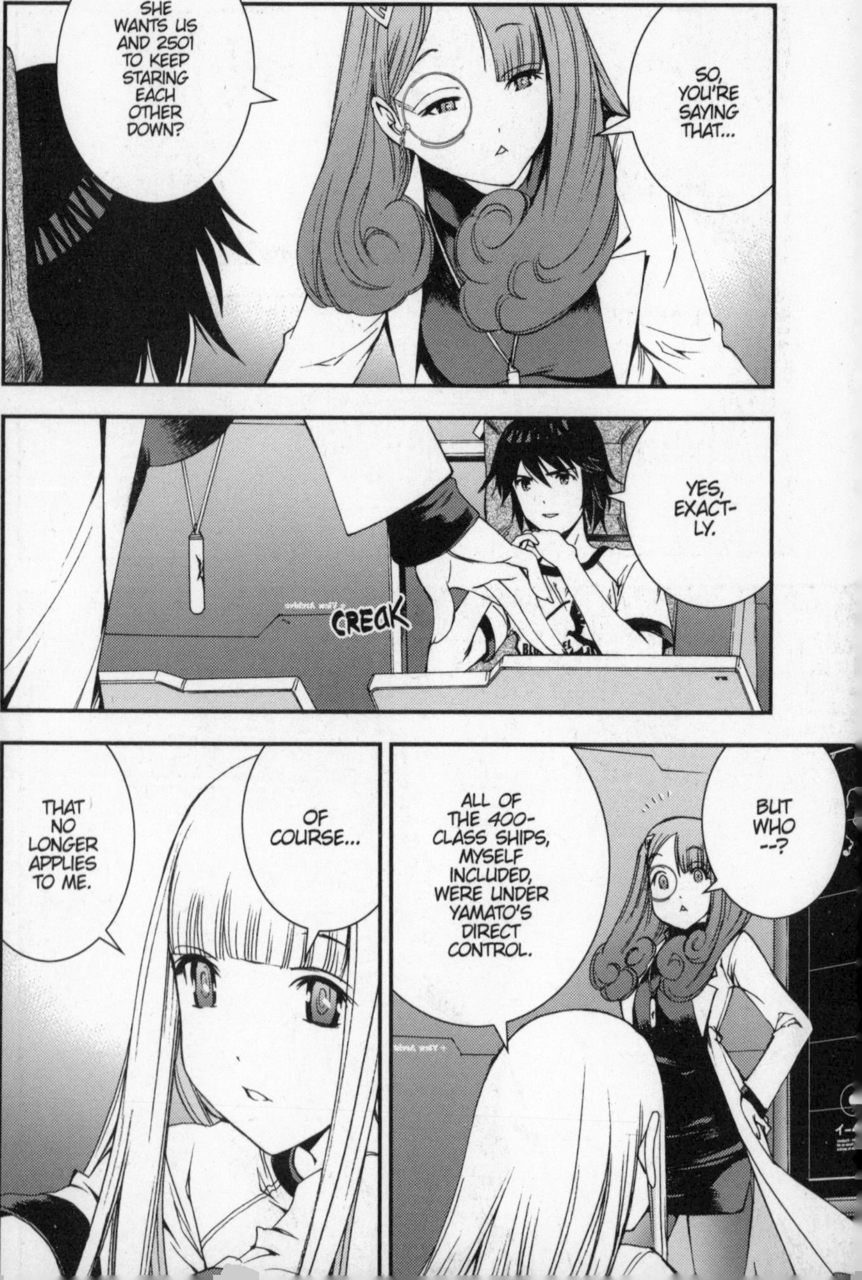
SO, YOU'RE SAYING THAT...
SHE WANTS US AND 2501 TO KEEP STARING EACH OTHER DOWN?
YES, EXACTLY.
CREAK
BUT WHO--?
ALL OF THE 400-CLASS SHIPS, MYSELF INCLUDED, WERE UNDER YAMATO'S DIRECT CONTROL.
OF COURSE...
THAT NO LONGER APPLIES TO ME.

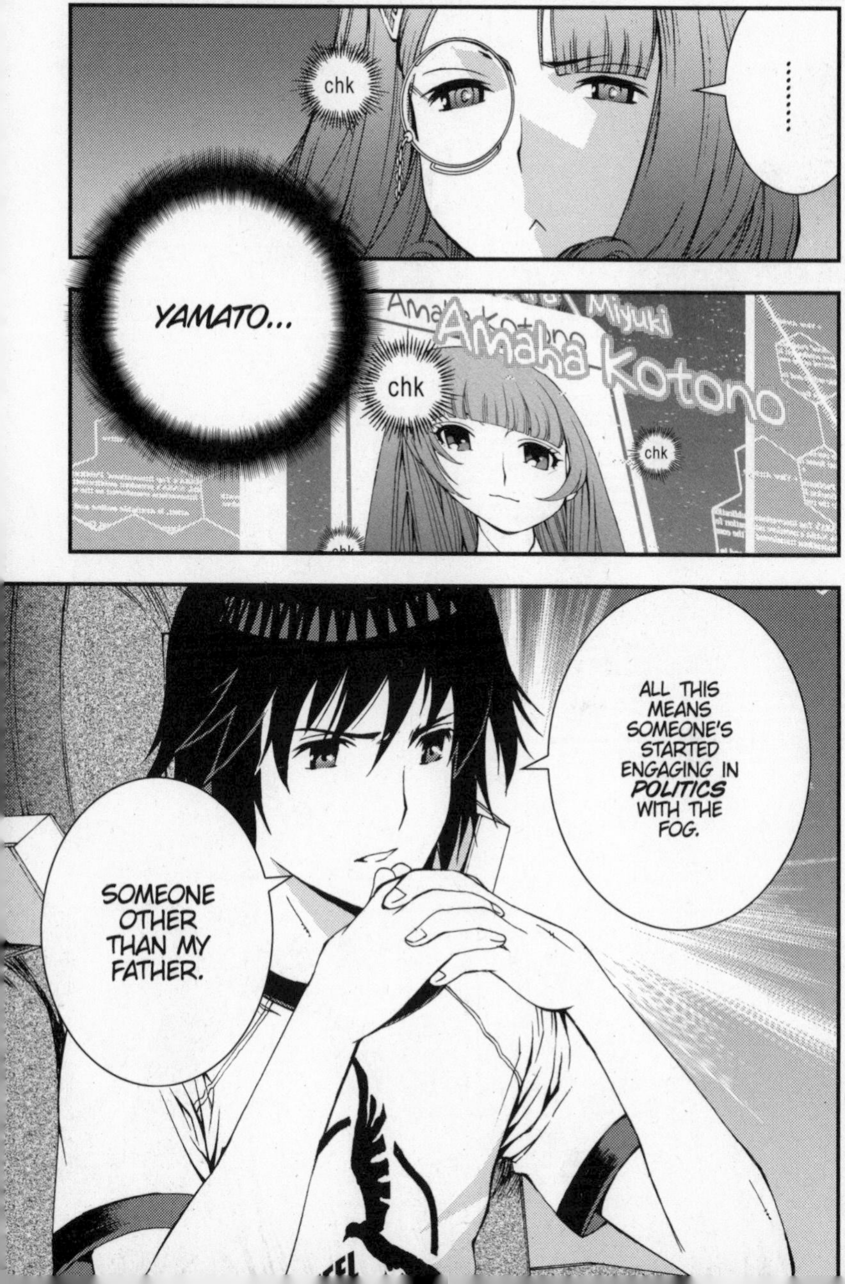
......
chk
YAMATO...
Miyuki
Amaha Kotono
chk
chk
ALL THIS MEANS SOMEONE'S STARTED ENGAGING IN *POLITICS* WITH THE FOG.
SOMEONE OTHER THAN MY FATHER.

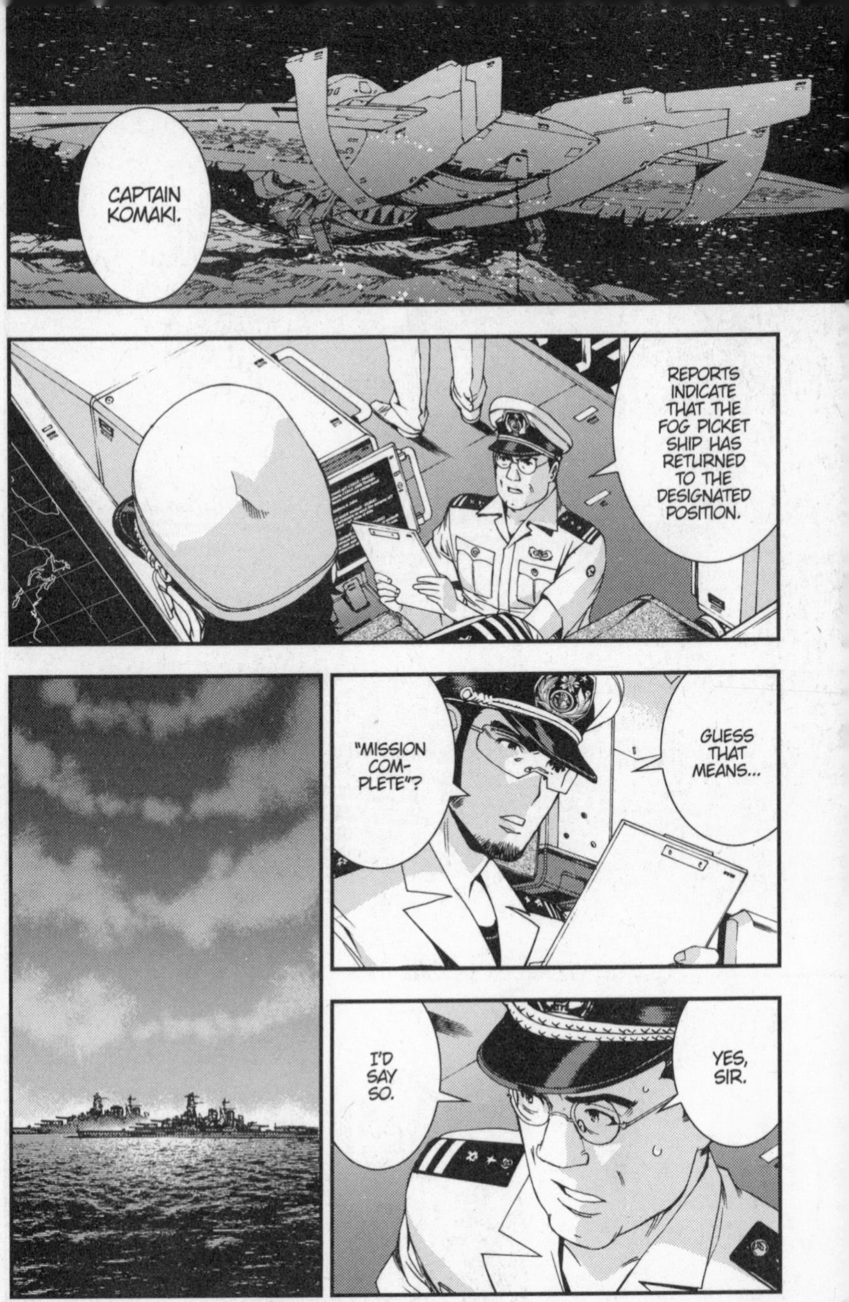
CAPTAIN KOMAKI.
REPORTS INDICATE THAT THE FOG PICKET SHIP HAS RETURNED TO THE DESIGNATED POSITION.
GUESS THAT MEANS...
"MISSION COM-PLETE"?
YES, SIR.
I'D SAY SO.

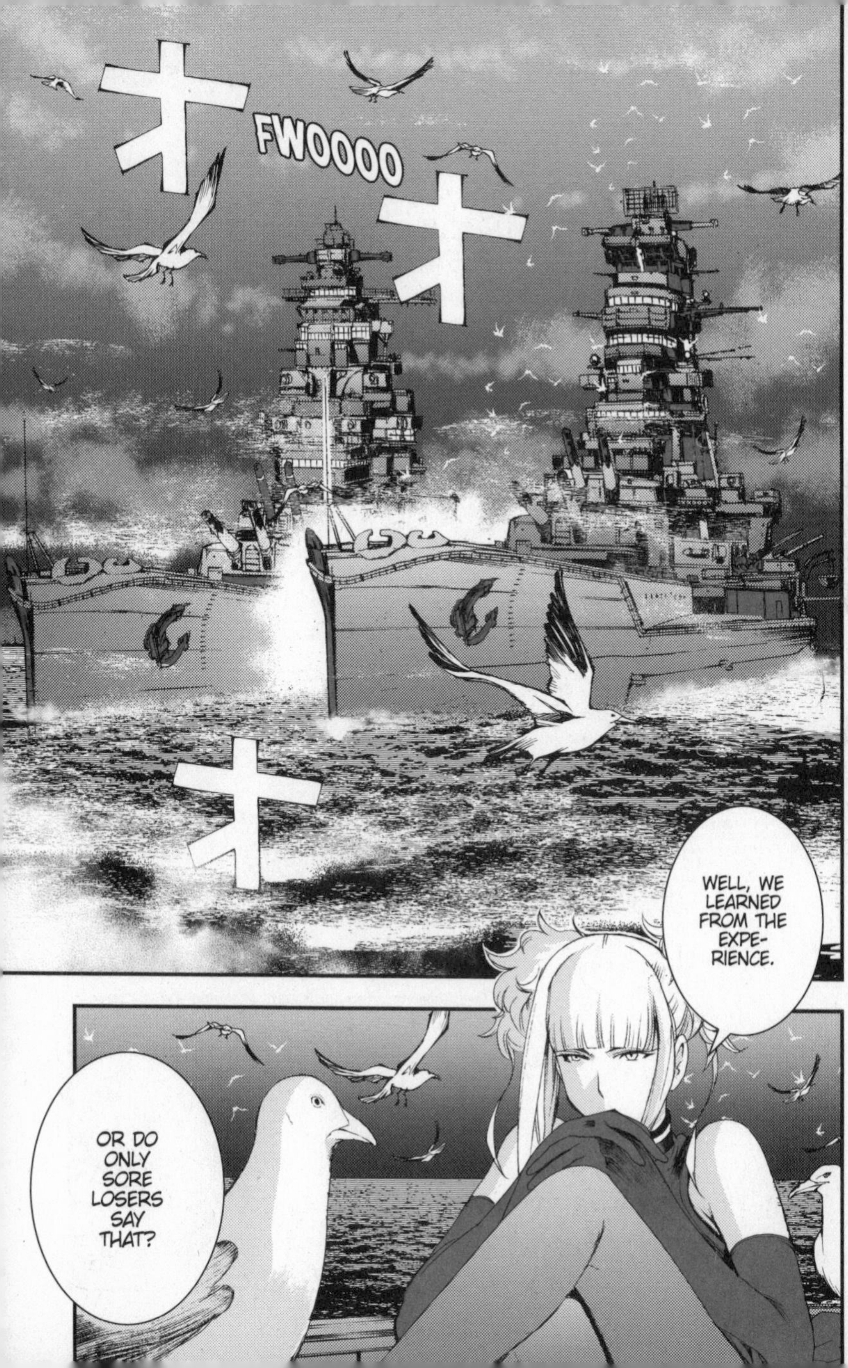
オオオ
FWOOOO
WELL, WE LEARNED FROM THE EXPE-RIENCE.
OR DO ONLY SORE LOSERS SAY THAT?

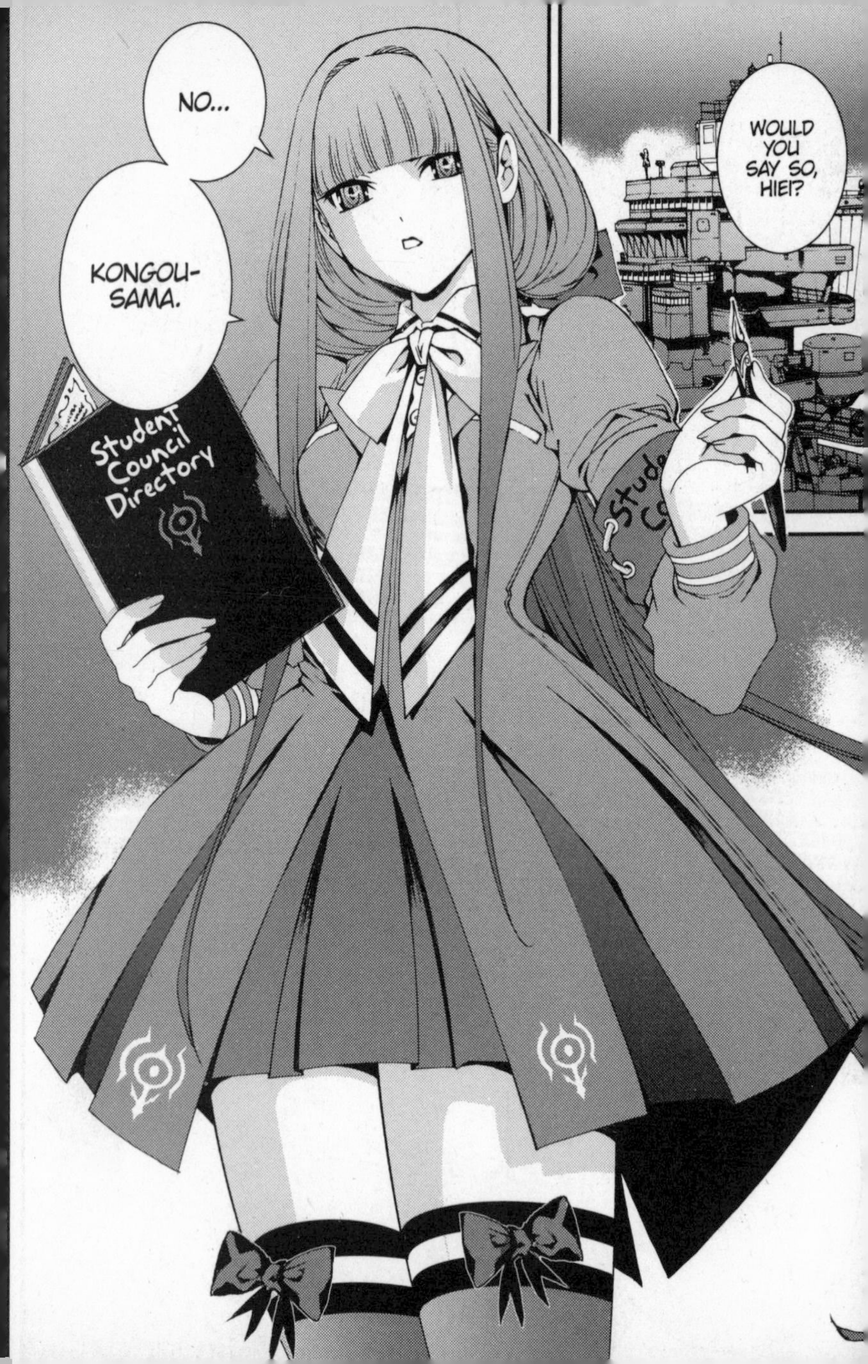
WOULD YOU SAY SO, HIEI?
NO...
KONGOU-SAMA.
Student Council Directory

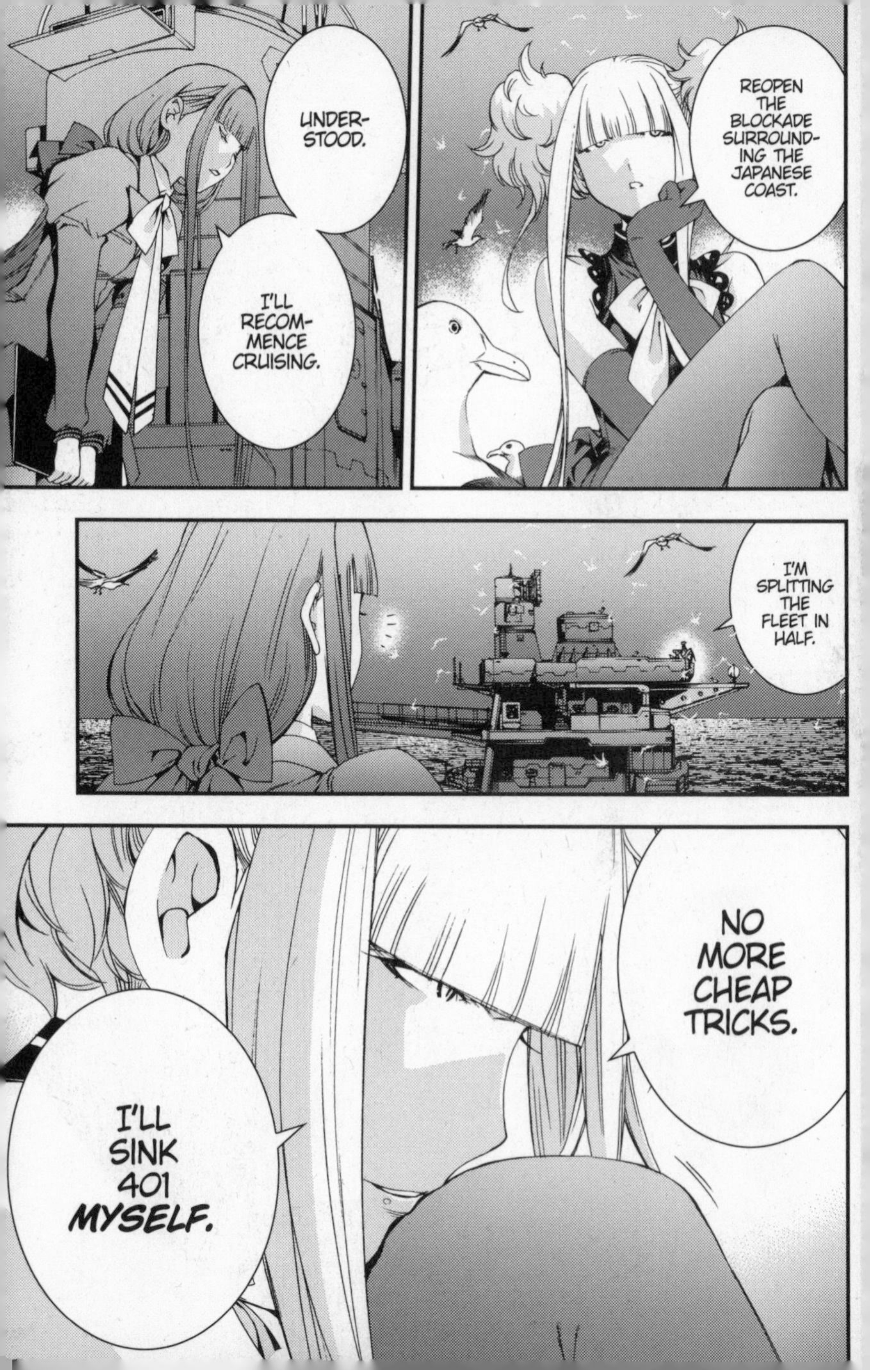
REOPEN THE BLOCKADE SURROUND-ING THE JAPANESE COAST.
UNDER-STOOD.
I'LL RECOM-MENCE CRUISING.
I'M SPLITTING THE FLEET IN HALF.
NO MORE CHEAP TRICKS.
I'LL SINK 401 *MYSELF.*

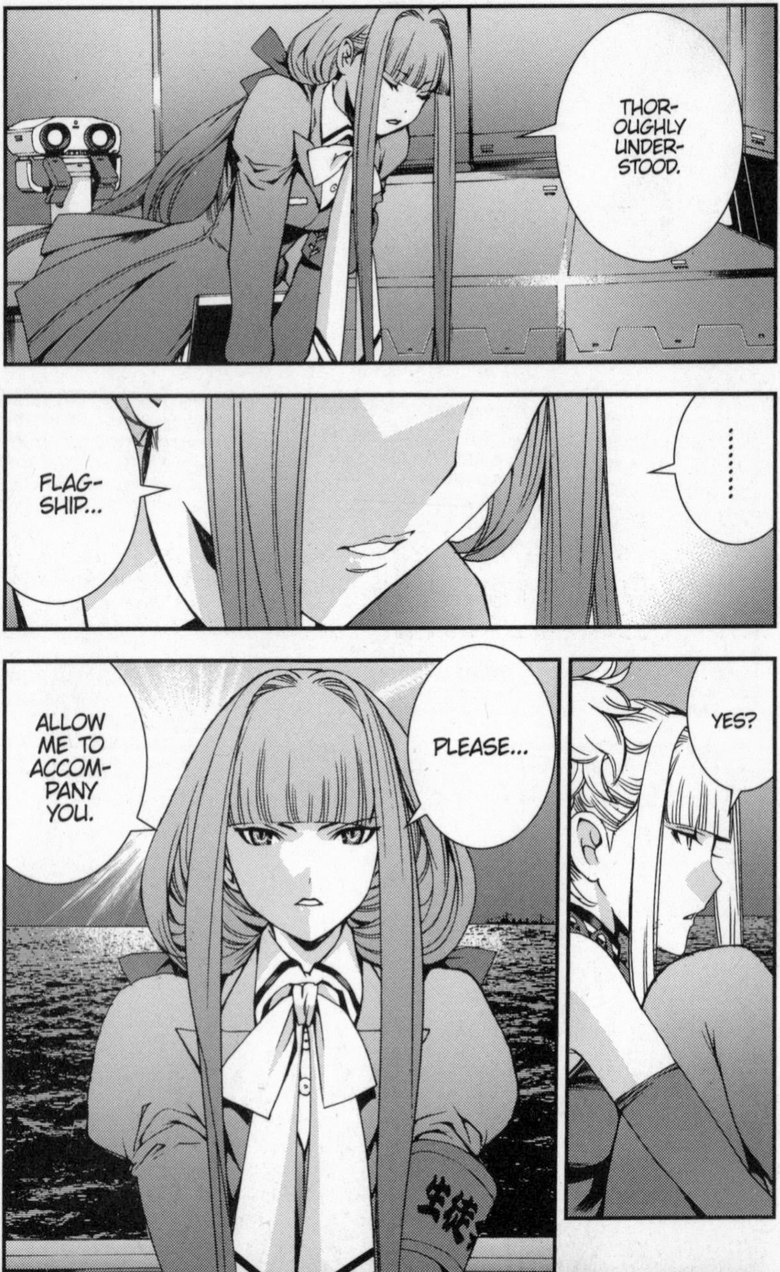
THOR-OUGHLY UNDER-STOOD.
......
FLAG-SHIP...
YES?
PLEASE...
ALLOW ME TO ACCOM-PANY YOU.

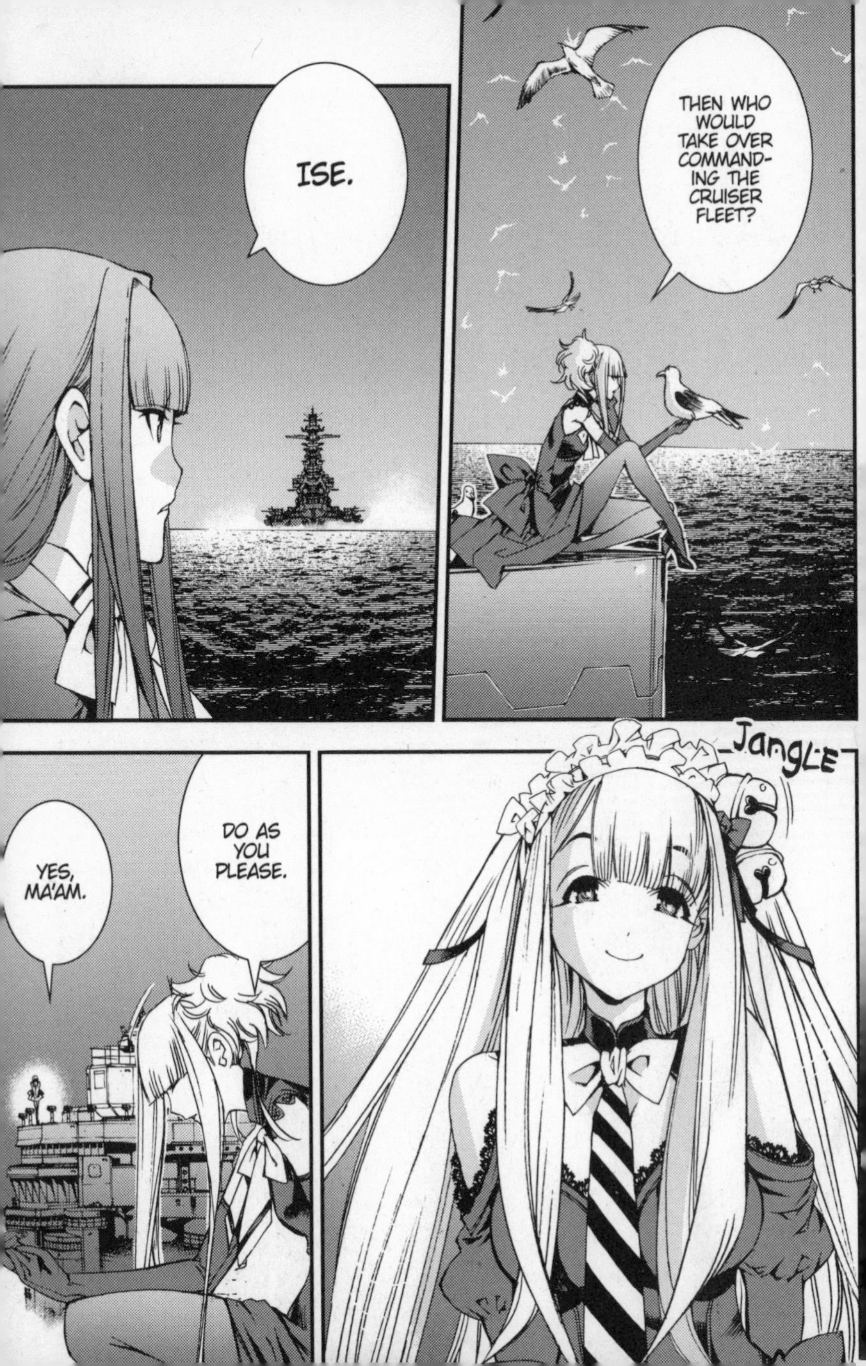
THEN WHO WOULD TAKE OVER COMMAND-ING THE CRUISER FLEET?
ISE.
Jangle
DO AS YOU PLEASE.
YES, MA'AM.

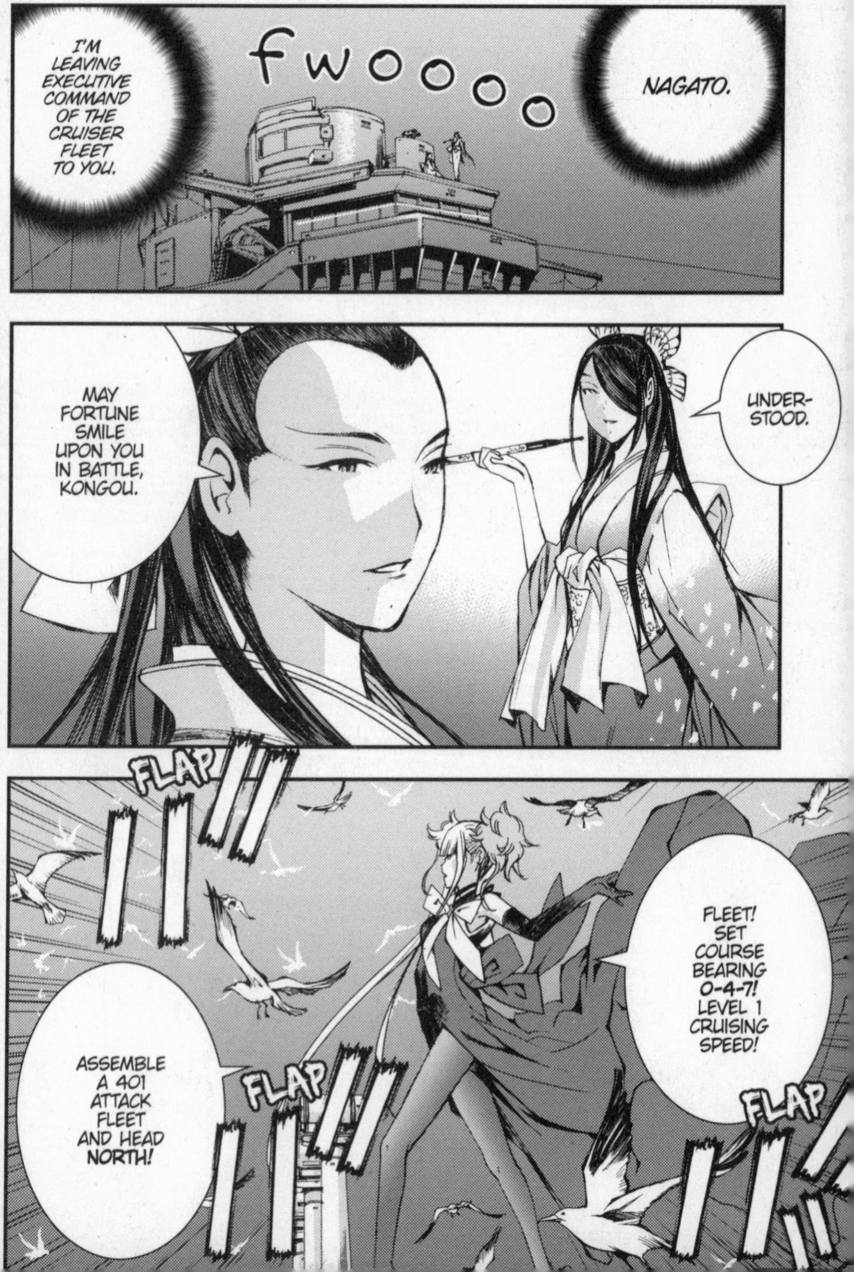
NAGATO.
fwoooo
I'M LEAVING EXECUTIVE COMMAND OF THE CRUISER FLEET TO YOU.
UNDER-STOOD.
MAY FORTUNE SMILE UPON YOU IN BATTLE, KONGOU.
FLAP
FLEET! SET COURSE BEARING 0-4-7! LEVEL 1 CRUISING SPEED!
FLAP
ASSEMBLE A 401 ATTACK FLEET AND HEAD NORTH!
FLAP

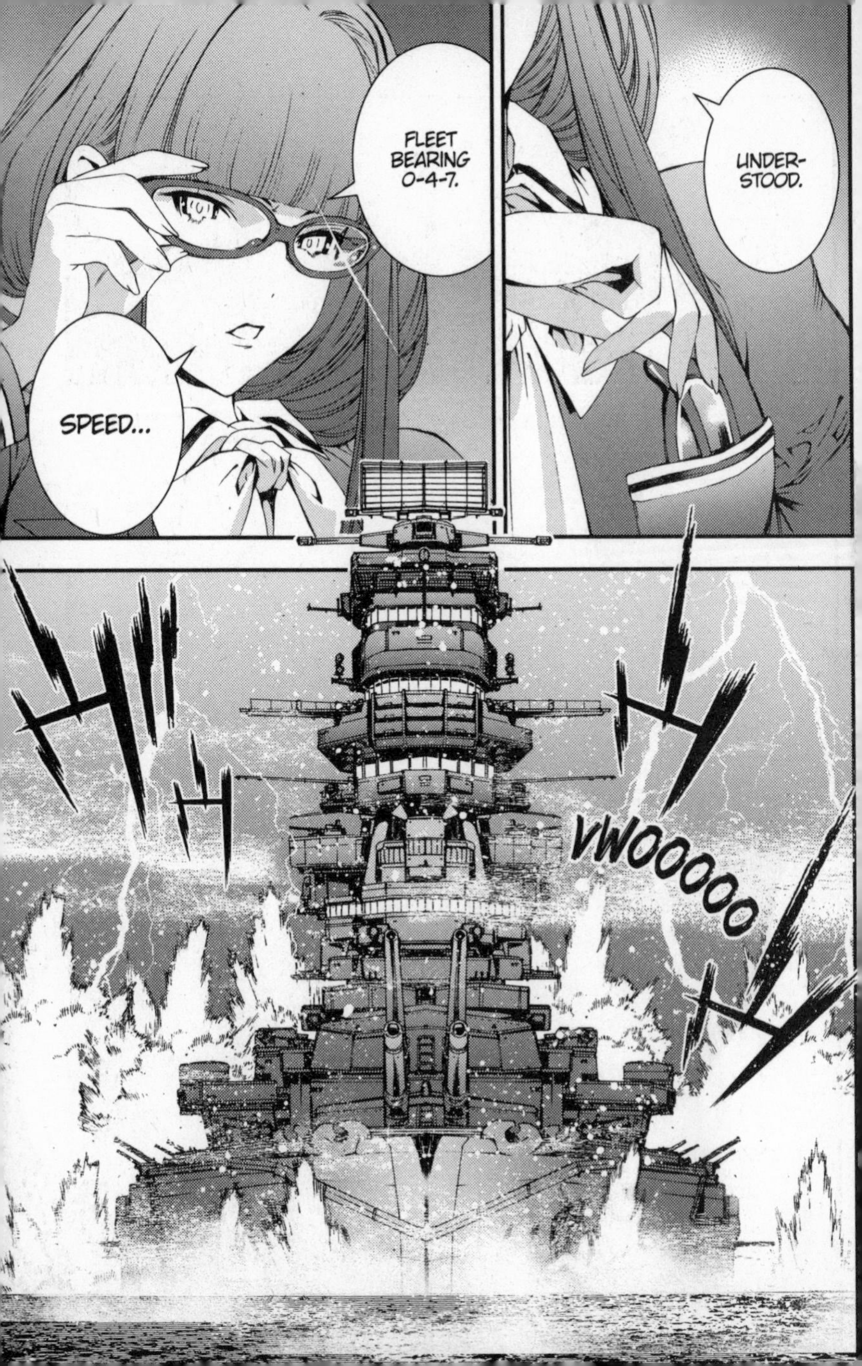
UNDER-
STOOD.
FLEET BEARING 0-4-7.
SPEED...
VWOOOOOO

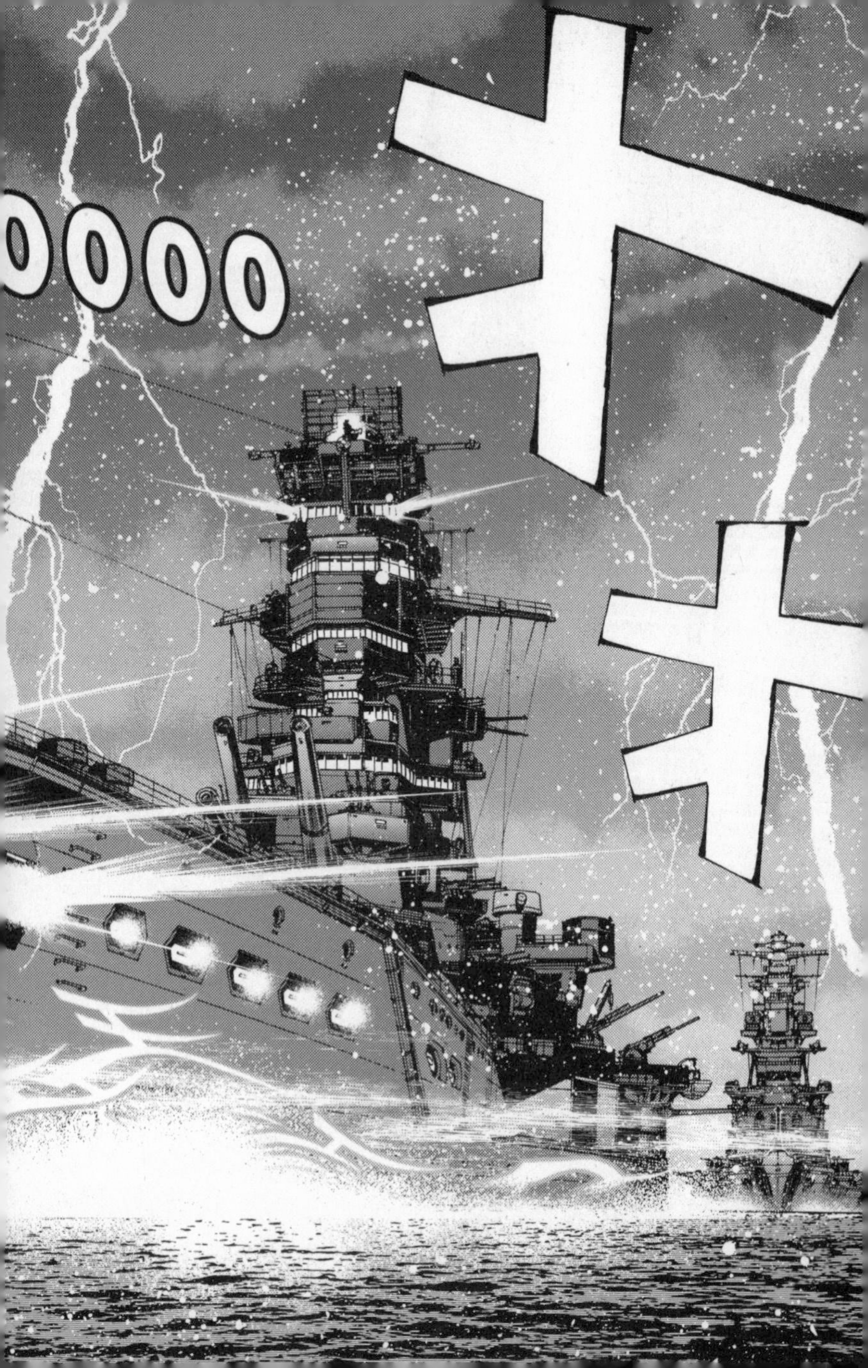
オオ
OOOO

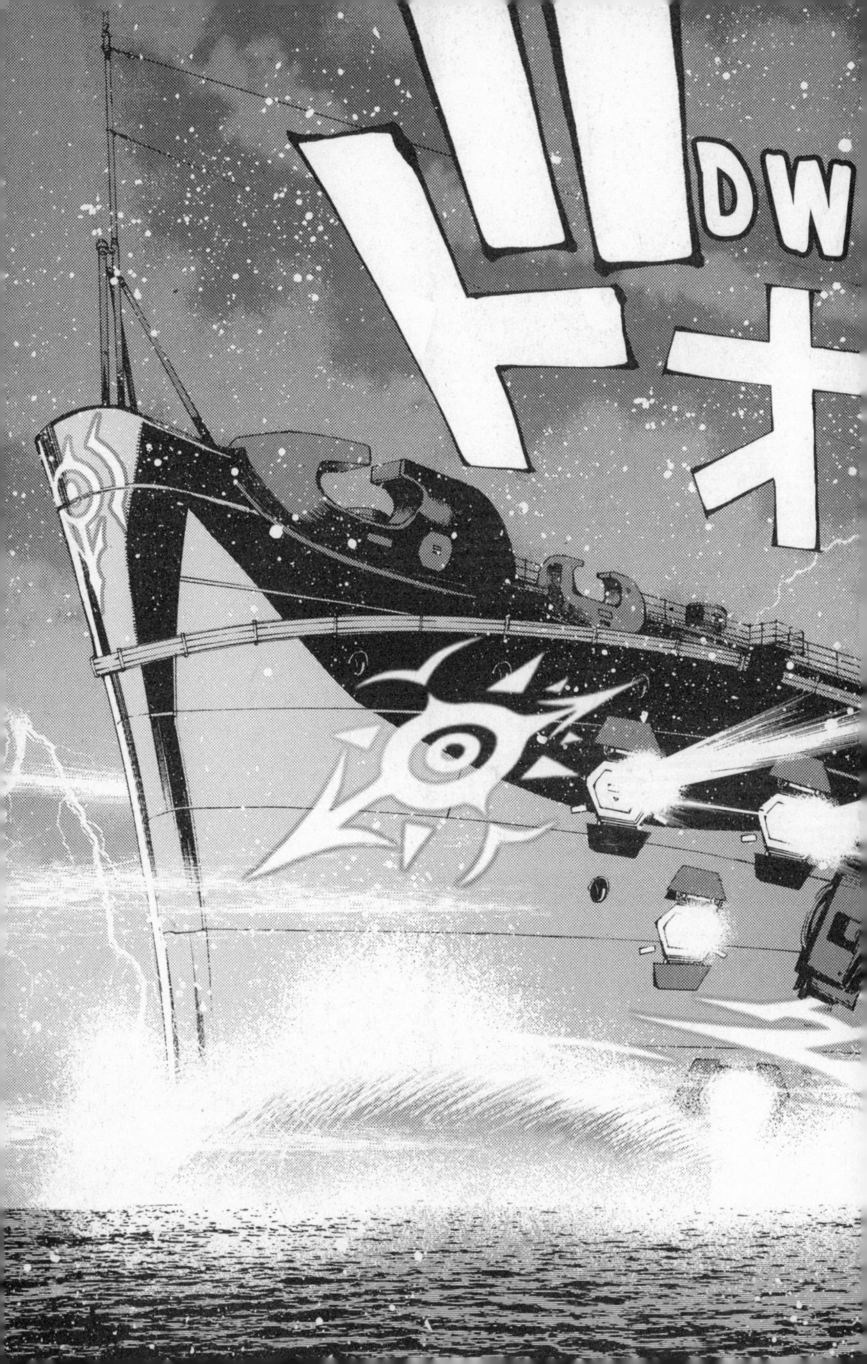
ドオ
DW

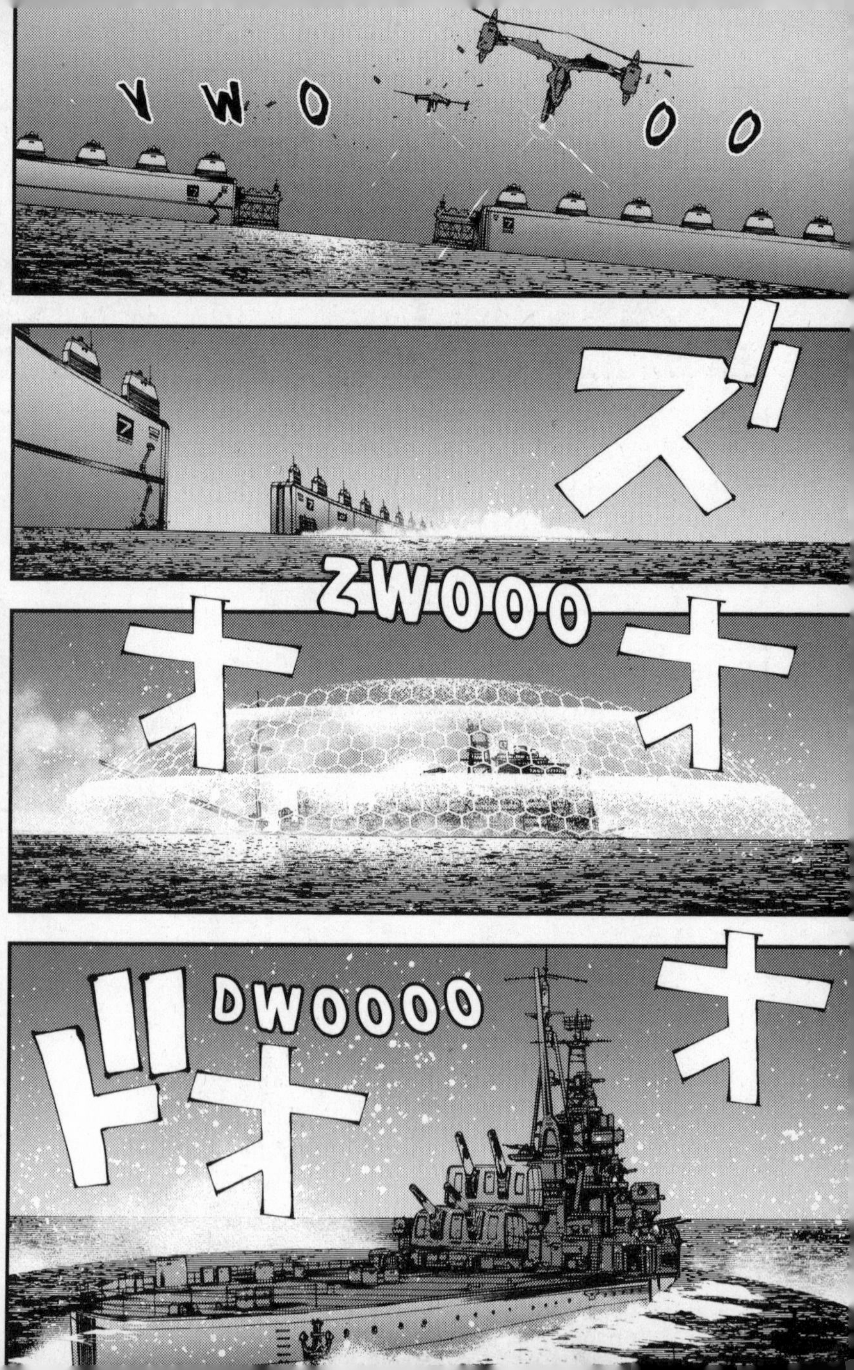
YWOOO
ズ
ZWOOO
オオ
オ
DWOOOO
ドオ

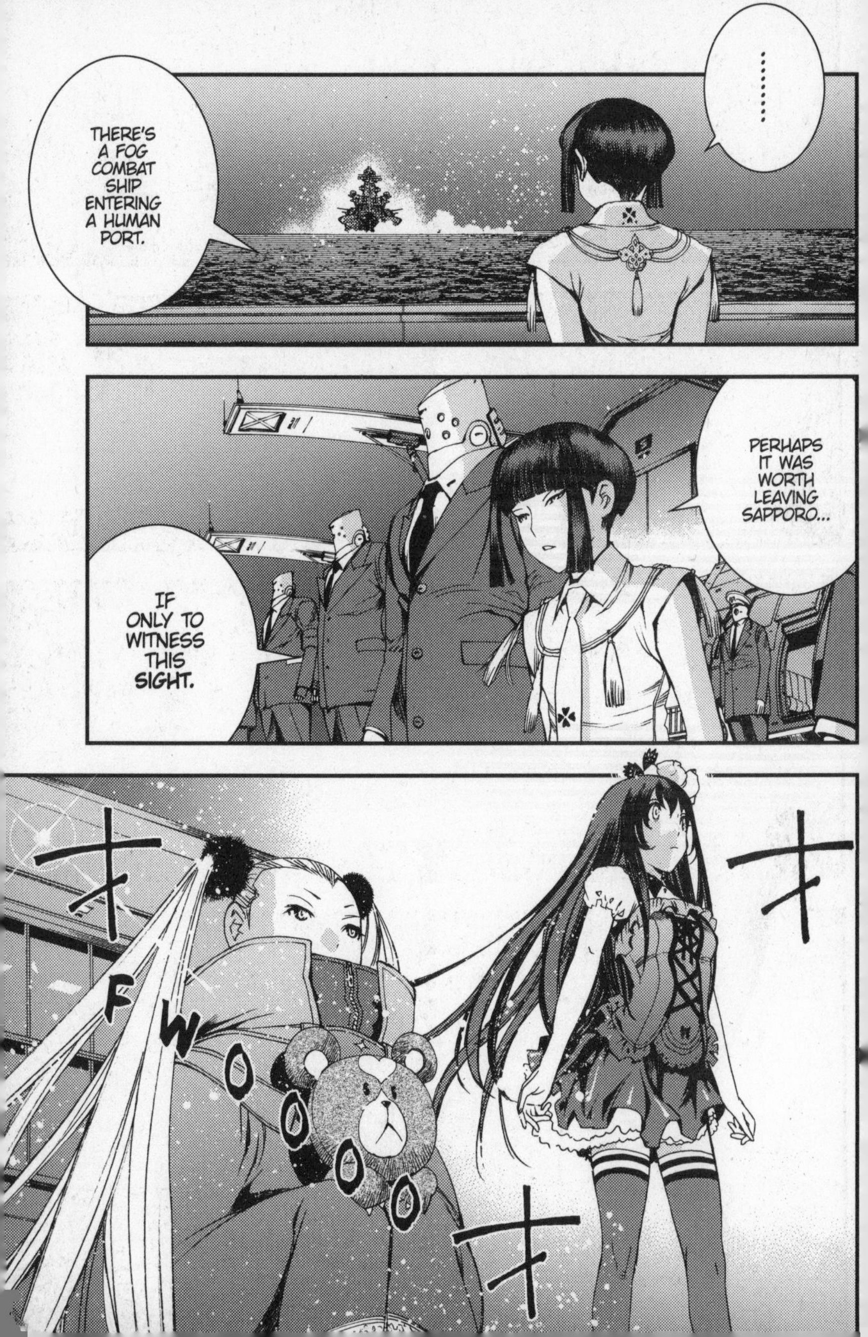
......
THERE'S A FOG COMBAT SHIP ENTERING A HUMAN PORT.
PERHAPS IT WAS WORTH LEAVING SAPPORO...
IF ONLY TO WITNESS THIS SIGHT.
FWOOOO

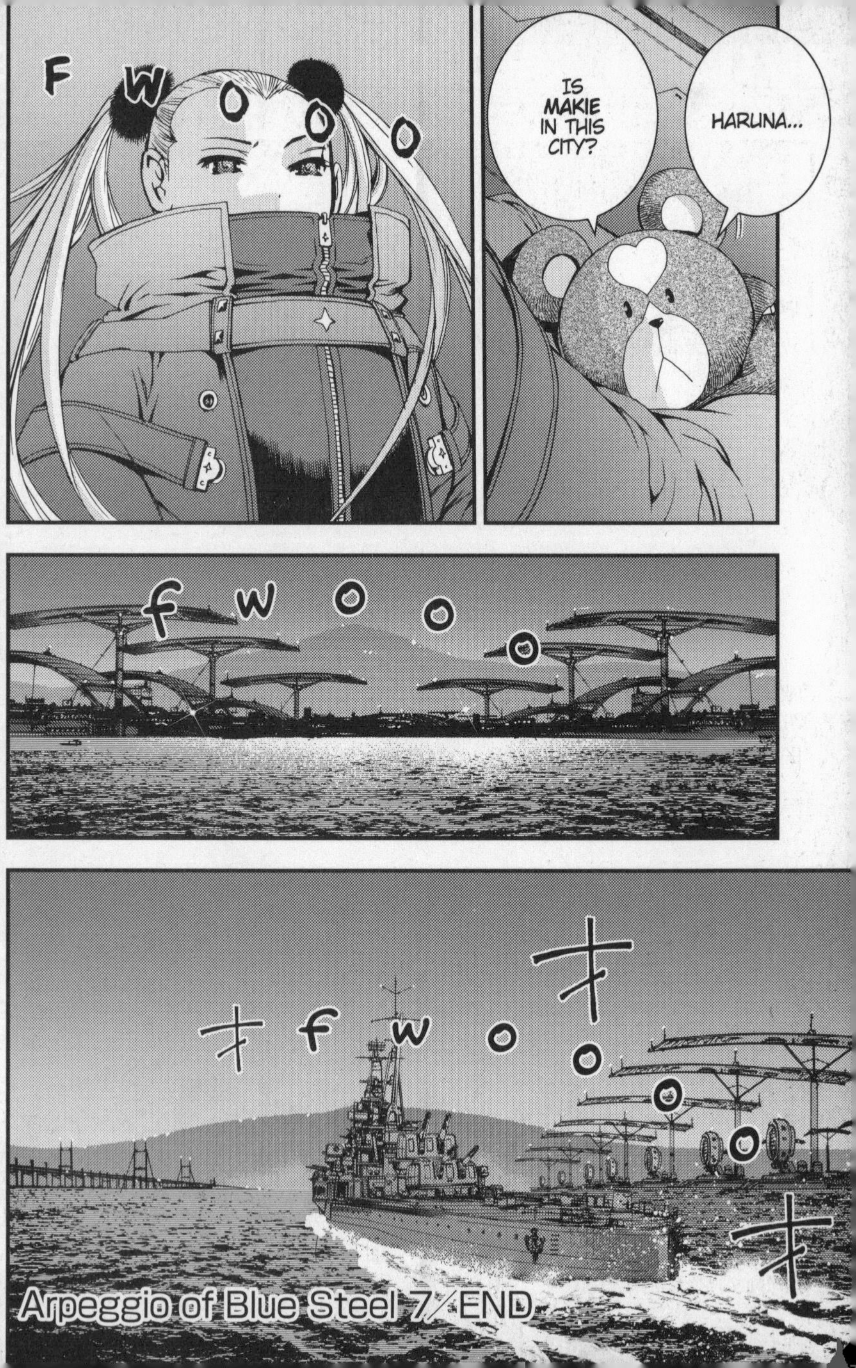
HARUNA...
IS MAKIE IN THIS CITY?
FWOOO
fwooo
オ
オ fwoooo
オ
Arpeggio of Blue Steel 7/END

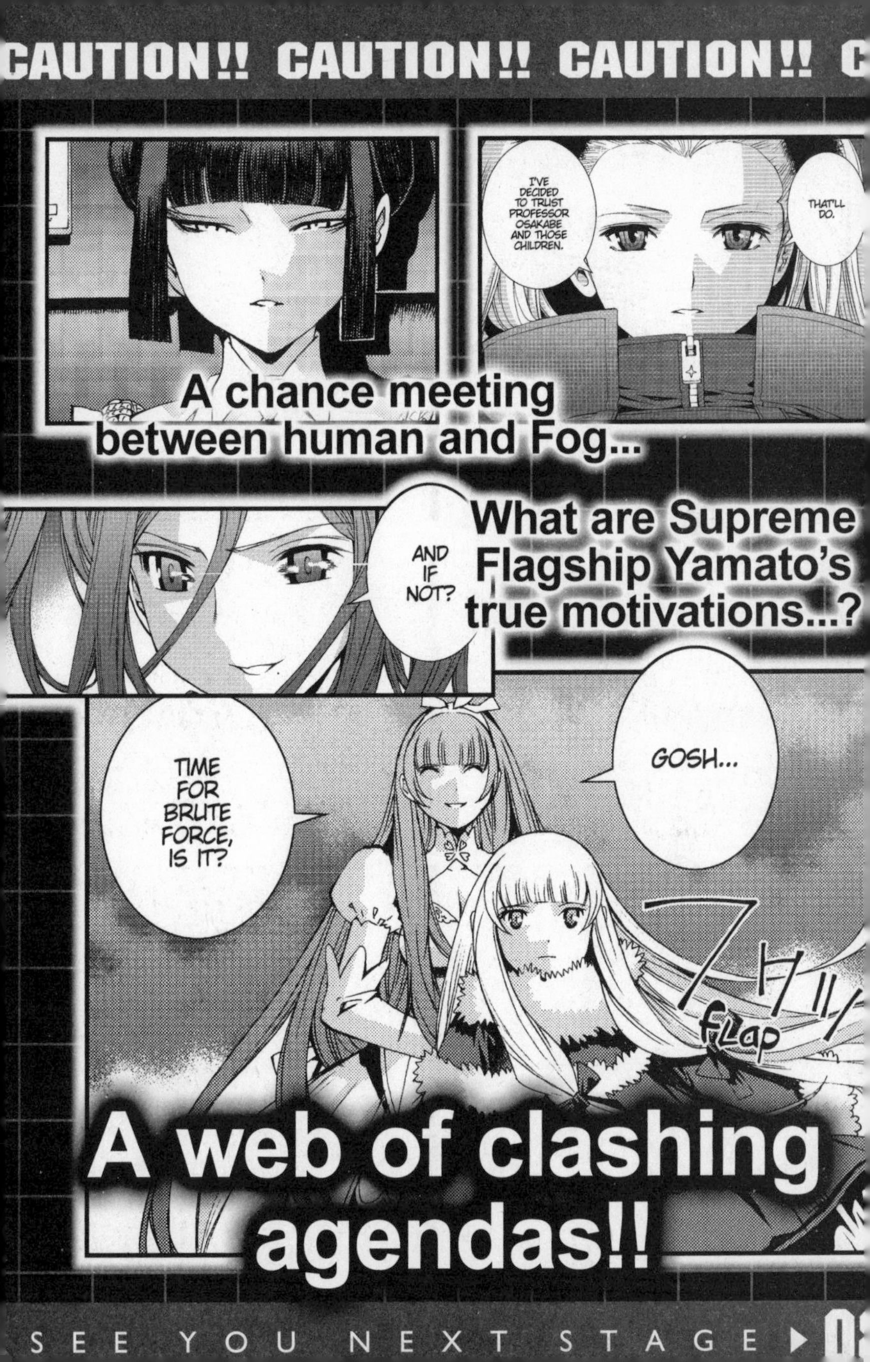
CAUTION!! CAUTION!! CAUTION!!
I'VE DECIDED TO TRUST PROFESSOR OSAKABE AND THOSE CHILDREN.
THAT'LL DO.
A chance meeting between human and Fog...
What are Supreme Flagship Yamato's true motivations...?
AND IF NOT?
GOSH...
TIME FOR BRUTE FORCE, IS IT?
FLAP
A web of clashing agendas!!
SEE YOU NEXT STAGE ▶

POWER DIAGRAM

Arpeggio's Guide

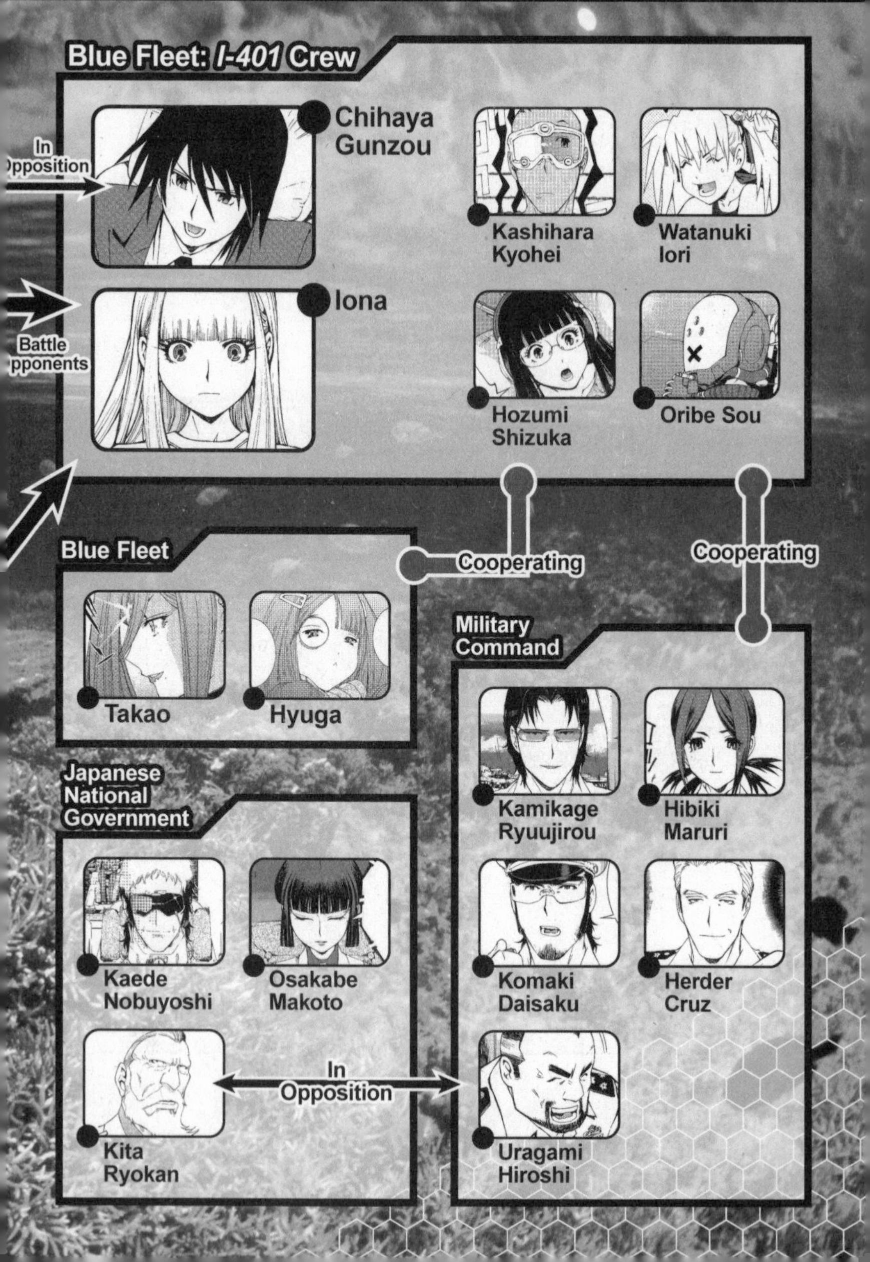

Blue Fleet: *I-401* Crew
Chihaya Gunzou
Iona
Kashihara Kyohei
Watanuki Iori
Hozumi Shizuka
Oribe Sou
In Opposition
Battle Opponents
Cooperating
Cooperating
Blue Fleet
Takao
Hyuga
Military Command
Kamikage Ryuujirou
Hibiki Maruri
Komaki Daisaku
Herder Cruz
Uragami Hiroshi
Japanese National Government
Kaede Nobuyoshi
Osakabe Makoto
Kita Ryokan
In Opposition

ARPEGGIO OF BLUE STEEL POWER DIAGRAM

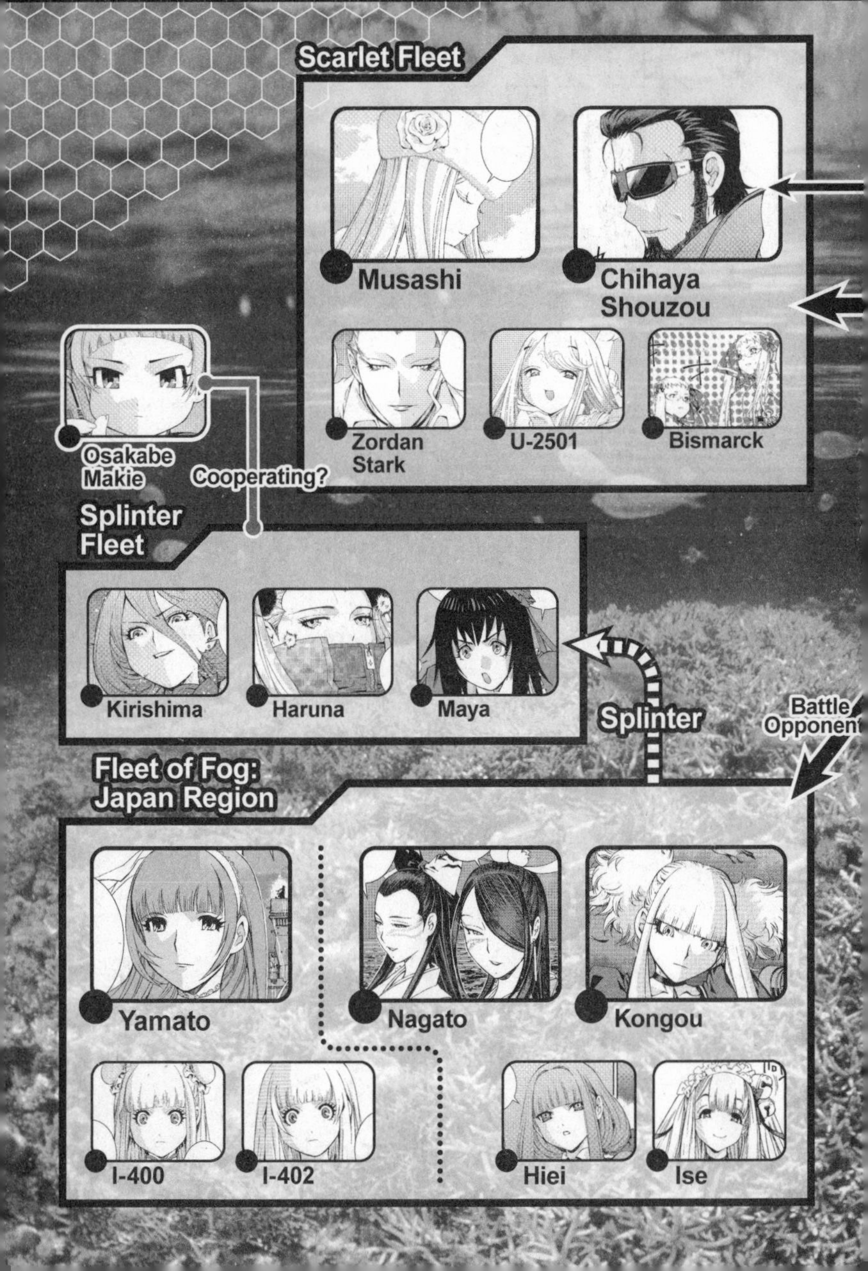
Scarlet Fleet
Musashi
Chihaya Shouzou
Zordan Stark
U-2501
Bismarck
Osakabe Makie
Cooperating?
Splinter Fleet
Kirishima
Haruna
Maya
Splinter
Battle Opponent
Fleet of Fog: Japan Region
Yamato
Nagato
Kongou
I-400
I-402
Hiei
Ise

SEVEN SEAS ENTERTAINMENT PRESENTS

ARPEGGIO
OF BLUE STEEL
story and art by ARK PERFORMANCE   VOLUME 7

TRANSLATION
Greg Moore

ADAPTATION
Ysabet Reinhardt MacFarlane

LETTERING AND LAYOUT
Paweł Szczęszek

LOGO DESIGN
Courtney Williams

COVER DESIGN
Nicky Lim

PROOFREADER
Lee Otter

PRODUCTION MANAGER
Lissa Pattillo

EDITOR-IN-CHIEF
Adam Arnold

PUBLISHER
Jason DeAngelis

AOKI HAGANENO ARPEGGIO VOLUME 7
© Ark Performance 2013
Originally published in Japan in 2013 by SHONENGAHOSHA Co., Ltd., Tokyo.
English translation rights arranged through TOHAN CORPORATION, Tokyo.

No portion of this book may be reproduced or transmitted in any form without
written permission from the copyright holders. This is a work of fiction. Names,
characters, places, and incidents are the products of the author's imagination
or are used fictitiously. Any resemblance to actual events, locals, or persons,
living or dead, is entirely coincidental.

Seven Seas books may be purchased in bulk for educational, business, or
promotional use. For information on bulk purchases, please contact Macmillan
Corporate & Premium Sales Department at 1-800-221-7945 (ext 5442)
or write specialmarkets@macmillan.com.

Seven Seas and the Seven Seas logo are trademarks of
Seven Seas Entertainment, LLC. All rights reserved.

ISBN: 978-1-626922-66-2

Printed in Canada

First Printing: May 2016

10 9 8 7 6 5 4 3 2 1

FOLLOW US ONLINE: *www.gomanga.com*

READING DIRECTIONS

This book reads from *right to left*, Japanese style.
If this is your first time reading manga, you start
reading from the top right panel on each page and
take it from there. If you get lost, just follow the
numbered diagram here. It may seem backwards at
first, but you'll get the hang of it! Have fun!!

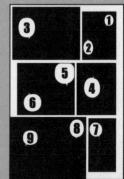